The Acts of the Reappearing Pheasant

Casa Italiana Zerilli-Marimò
New York University

THE RE-APPEARING PHEASANT

NEW YORK>2022
November>11>12>13

AN ENCOUNTER OF AMERICAN AND ITALIAN POETS AND CRITICS

"Poetry is a pheasant disappearing in the brush" (Wallace Stevens)

PROGRAM

Convened by Luigi Ballerini

CASA ITALIANA ZERILLI-MARIMÒ
NEW YORK UNIVERSITY
Dir. Stefano Albertini

In cooperation with
THE ITALIAN CULTURAL INSTITUTE OF NEW YORK
Dir. Fabio Finotti

Italian Coordinating Institution
ASSOCIAZIONE DI POESIA, Milano
Dir. Giovanni Bonoldi

Steering Committee
Chiara Basso (NYU)
Nick Benson (Zero Prophet, Washington, Ct)
Beppe Cavatorta (U. Arizona, Tucson)
Sandro Angelo De Thomasis (Juilliard School, New York)
Kostja Kostic (NYU)
Iuri Moscardi (The Graduate Center, CUNY)
Federica Parodi (Yale U.)
Gianluca Rizzo (Colby College, Waterville, Me)
Julian Sachs (NYU)
Federica Santini (Kennesaw U., Atlanta)

Participating Institutions
Agincourt Press (New York)
Biblioteca Comunale (Milano)
Biblioteca Elio Pagliarani (Roma)
Edizioni del Verri (Milano)
IACE (New York)
MUDIMA (Milano)
Netseven (Pisa)
PennSound (U. Penn, Philadelphia)
Poetry Center of the University of Arizona (Tucson, Az)
Radio Popolare (Milano)
Radioitineraria (Cologno Monzese, Mi)
RAI 3 (Roma)
School of Visual Arts (New York)
Sistema Bibliotecario della Svizzera italiana
(Bellinzona, Lugano, Mendrisio)
St. Mark Poetry Project (New York)
Teatro Florian Metateatro (Pescara)
The Brooklyn Rail (New York)
Università degli Studi Gabriele D'Annunzio (Chieti-Pescara)
Università degli Studi Suor Orsola Benincasa (Napoli)

FRIDAY - NOVEMBER 11
CASA ITALIANA ZERILLI-MARIMÒ – NEW YORK UNIVERSITY

11:00 – Stefano Albertini (NYU) – Luigi Ballerini (UCLA, Emeritus)
WELCOMING REMARKS
11:30 – Marjorie Perloff (U. Stanford, Emerita)
ON ITALIAN POETRY IN TODAY'S AMERICA
12:00 – 13:00 – BREAK
13:00 – 13:30 – Andrea Cortellessa (U. Roma 3)
THE LEGACY OF THE NEO-AVANT-GARDE/1
13:30 – 15:30 – POETRY READING
Charles Bernstein (Brooklyn, New York), Antonella Anedda (Roma),
Peter Gizzi (U. Mass., Amherst), Marco Giovenale (Roma),
Tommaso Ottonieri (U. Roma, La Sapienza)
15:30 – 16:00 – BREAK
16:00 – 16:30 – Chris Mustazza (U. Penn, Philadelphia)
THE EXPERIENCE OF PENNSOUND
16:30 – 17:00 – Fabrizio Bondi (Suor Orsola Benincasa, Napoli)
THE INTERACTIVE WUNDERKAMMER OF CONTEMPORARY ITALIAN POETRY
17:00 – 19:00 – ROUND TABLE – THE LOGICS OF POETRY
Paul Bové (U. Pittsburgh), Franca D'Agostini (U. Milano), Tom Huhn (SVA. New York),
Achille Varzi (Columbia U.). Chair: Luigi Ballerini

SATURDAY - NOVEMBER 12
ITALIAN CULTURAL INSTITUTE – NEW YORK

10:15 – Fabio Finotti (IIC) - WELCOMING REMARKS
10:30 – 11:00 – Cecilia Bello (U. Roma, La Sapienza)
THE LEGACY OF THE NEO-AVANT-GARDE/2
11:00 – 13:00 – ROUND TABLE – TRANSLATION AS COMPOSITION
Kenneth Goldsmith (U. Penn, Philadelphia), Gianluca Rizzo (Colby College, Waterville, Me),
Charles Bernstein (Brooklyn, New York), Luigi Bonaffini (Brooklyn College, CUNY).
Chair: Tom Peterson.
13:00 – 13:30 – BREAK
13:30 – 15:30 – POETRY READING
Mary Jo Bang (U. Washington, St. Louis), Maria Grazia Calandrone (Roma), Vincenzo
Frungillo (Napoli), Rosmarie Waldrop (Providence, R.I.), Laura Liberale (Venezia)
15:30 – 17:30 – ROUND TABLE – RESEARCH POETRY? A POEM BY ANY OTHER NAME
Fabrizio Bondi (Suor Orsola Benincasa, Napoli), Marco Giovenale (Roma),
Luigi Severi (Roma), Francesco Muzzioli (U. Roma, La Sapienza),
Daniele Poletti (Viareggio). Chair: Federica Santini.

SUNDAY - NOVEMBER 13
CASA ITALIANA ZERILLI-MARIMÒ – NEW YORK UNIVERSITY

13:30 – 14:00 – Giorgio Patrizi (U. Molise)
FOUND BY THE AVANT-GARDE AT THE END OF THE MILLENNIUM:
EXPERIMENTS OLD AND NEW
14:00 – 14:30 – Ugo Perolino (U. Pescara):
NEO-EXPERIMENTALISM AND *RAPPEL À L'ORDRE*:
A FEW OBSERVATIONS ABOUT "QUARTA GENERAZIONE"
14:30 – 16:30 – POETRY READING
Mariano Baino (Roma), Anselm Berrigan (New York),
John Latta (U. Michigan Ann Arbor), Susan Briante (U. Arizona, Tucson),
Ivan Schiavone (Monza)
16:30 – 17:00 – Massimo Bacigalupo (U. Genova)
ON AMERICAN POETRY IN TODAY'S ITALY
17:00 – 17:30 – BREAK AND TRANSFER TO ST. MARK'S CHURCH IN THE BOWERY

17:30 – 18:30 – Diego Minciacchi (Firenze), CONCERT – XANTABLACKZ
A Verbiage and Sounding Event for Current Communication
(Lauren Cauley, violin; Caitlin Cawley, percussion; Nate Wooley, Trumpet;
Luigi Ballerini, voice; Cecilia Bello, voice)

Invited critics and correspondents
Barbara Anceschi (Edizioni *Il Verri*, Milano)
Alessandro Giammei (Yale U.)
Phong Bui (*The Brooklyn Rail*, New York)

The Acts of the Reappearing Pheasant

The Return of Experimental
Italian and American Poets and Critics
(NYU, Casa Italiana Zerilli-Marimò, November 10-12, 2022)

Edited by Iuri Moscardi & Sandro-Angelo de Thomasis

Agincourt Press
New York, 2025

Opuntia is an imprint of Agincourt Press
Luigi Ballerini and Gianluca Rizzo, Editors
Agincourt Press is a non-profit organization chaired by Berardo Paradiso

This volume is published under the aegis
and with the financial assistance of Casa Italiana Zerilli Marimò.

© 2025 by Agincourt Press

All manuscripts are subject to peer review.

All rights reserved.

ISBN: 978-1-946328-50-2

AGINCOURT PRESS
P.O. Box 1039
Cooper Station
New York, NY 10003
www.agincourtbooks.com

Table of Contents

ix   Editorial Preface: The Vow of the Pheasant by Iuri Moscardi and Sandro-Angelo de Thomasis
xxiv Acknowledgements
xxv Foreword: A Conversation with Luigi Ballerini by Nicholas Benson

Day 1 – Friday, November 11, 2022

1   The Reappearing Pheasant: Opening Address by Marjorie Perloff
15   The Nightmare of the Novissimi by Andrea Cortellessa (Translated by Thomas E. Peterson)
31   Poetry
31   Charles Bernstein
39   Antonella Anedda
50   Peter Gizzi
73   Marco Giovenale
90   Tommaso Ottonieri
103 PennSound and the Italian Audiotext: Archives, Producers, Platforms by Chris Mustazza
113 Research Poetry between Utopias, Metaphors, and the State of Things. Part I. A Conversation with Fabrizio Bondi
117 Critical Poetic Grace by Paul A. Bové
131 What Poetry Can Teach Logic (Preliminary Ideas) by Franca d'Agostini
139 The Reappearance of "On Lyric Poetry and Society" by Tom Huhn
147 On the Logic of Poetry by Achille C. Varzi

Day 2 – Saturday, November 12, 2022

- 161 The Legacy of the Neo-Avant-Garde II. Structures of the Return in Italian Poetry from the Late Twentieth Century to the Present Day by Cecilia Bello Minciacchi
- 175 A Violent Inclusion: Translation as Composition (or What Cannibalism Has to Do with Poetry) by Gianluca Rizzo
- 191 An Intervention and a Brief Foreword by Charles Bernstein
- 195 Playing Cricket without a Paddle by Charles Bernstein
- 201 Translating Dialect Literature by Luigi Bonaffini
- 215 The Imperfect and the Ideal: On Poetic Translation by Thomas E. Peterson
- 235 Poetry
  - 235 Mary Jo Bang
  - 243 Maria Grazia Calandrone
  - 256 Vincenzo Frungillo
  - 273 Rosmarie Waldrop
  - 282 Laura Liberale
- 297 Writing Poetry is a Political Action by Maria Grazia Calandrone
- 299 Poetry between the End of History and the Determinism of Nature by Vincenzo Frungillo
- 309 Research Poetry between Utopias, Metaphors, and the State of Things. Part II. A Conversation with Fabrizio Bondi
- 313 An Effects Machine. Some Spare Parts for Descriptions and Theories of Contemporary Writing by Marco Giovenale (Translated by Nicholas Benson)
- 319 Breaking Fences and Putting Up Barricades. "Scrittura Complessa" as Overcoming and Resistance. Between Formlessness and The Continuous Word by Daniele Poletti (Translated by Sandro-Angelo de Thomasis)

Day 3 – Sunday, November 13, 2022

- 333 "And the Avant-Garde Found Something, Right?" by Giorgio Patrizi (Translated by Sandro-Angelo de Thomasis)
- 343 For The Reappearing Pheasant by Ugo Perolino (Translated by Nicholas Benson)

355	Poetry
355	Mariano Bàino
366	Anselm Berrigan
373	John Latta
386	Susan Briante
398	Ivan Schiavone
409	Four Little Objects to Befit a Request for a Note on Poetics, Drawing Upon the Present of the Past by Mariano Bàino (Translated by Sandro-Angelo de Thomasis)
415	Poet-re-mix by Ivan Schiavone (Translated by Sandro-Angelo de Thomasis)
423	intermezzo by Tommaso Ottonieri (Translated by Sandro-Angelo de Thomasis)
425	"The Body's Beauty Lives": U.S. Poetry in Italy Today by Massimo Bacigalupo
435	CONCERT – XANTABLACKZ
459	Afterword: Notes on The Reappearing Pheasant by Nicholas Benson
483	*Biographies*
501	*Works Cited*

Charles Bernstein: *As If the Trees by Their Very Roots Had Hold of Us*; *Contradiction Turns to Rivalry*; *Gertrude and Ludwig's Bogus Adventure*; *Catullus 5*; *Covidity*; *Rivulets of the Dead Jew* by permission of the author.

Peter Gizzi: *Findspot Unknown*; *Revisionary*; *Roxy Music*; *Speech Acts for A Dying World*; *The Present is Constant Elegy*; *Archeophonics*; *When Orbital Proximity Feels Creepy*; *This World is Not Conclusion*; *Now It's Dark*; *From This End of Sadness*; *A Telescope Protects Its View*; *A Note on The Text* by permission of the author.

Mary Jo Bang: *This Supposed Alchemy*; *The Year Chases Its Tail*; *In the Book of All That's Befallen*; *The Downstream Extremity of The Isle of Swans*; *When Meeting Beauty*; *The Constant Bride*; *A Case of Asymmetry*; *The Mouth in* Clarity; *On* This Late Stage; *The What Within* by permission of the author.

Rosmarie Waldrop: *Object Relations*; *We Will Always Ask, What Happened?*; *Isomorphic Fields*; *Intentionalities*; *Enhanced Density*; *Photo*; *Time Ravel*; *The One Who Counts, Who Paints, Who Buys and Sells. ZERO, THE CORROSIVE NUMBER* by permission of the author.

Anselm Berrigan: *Not all there*; *The cultural revolution*; To *what end is what we've got...*; *Advice to a young philosopher*; *Ode to election day*; *Looking up my balance*; *Fortune's Drift*; *Security* by permission of the author.

John Latta: *Morgenmusik*; *Elogio di Frank O'Hara*; *Blank, with Blandishments*; *Dirty Weather*; *Parisian Miniatures*; *Rue Taitbout*; *Reading Cicero's* De Oratore; *The Wag of the Inconsequent*; *Explication de texte* by permission of the author.

Susan Briante: *Love in the Time of NAFTA*; *Eventual Darling (Galang Island)*; *Eventual Darling (Kinshasa)*; *The Cartographer's Son*; *The Groom Stripped Bare*; *7th Day of the Rainy Season*; *15th Day of the Rainy Season*; *Towards a Poetics of the Dow*; *Meditation*; *The Market is a Parasite That Looks Like a Nest*; *The Lesson of the Nest* by permission of the author.

Iuri Moscardi and Sandro-Angelo de Thomasis

Editorial Preface: The Vow of the Pheasant

> Poetry is a pheasant disappearing in the brush.
> — Wallace Stevens, "Adagia." *Opus Posthumous*. 1957, 173.

> La puissance des signes est alors dans leur apparition
> et leur disparition, c'est ainsi qu'ils effacent le monde.
> — Jean Baudrillard, *De la séduction*. 1979, 129.[1]

Le Voeu du Faisan by Édouard Riou (1833–1900).
Engraving with pastel overlay. Musée de l'Hospice Comtesse, Lille, France.

---

[1] "The power of signs is thus in their appearance and disappearance, it's how they erase the world" (authors' translation).

On February 17th, 1454, several Greek exiles gathered in Lille at the Hôtel de la Salle for a special feast. That evening, Philippe le Bon (1396–1467), Duke of Burgundy, a patron of the arts and ardent supporter of Crusades, who is perhaps most famous for his capture of Joan of Arc more than two decades earlier, held a "Banquet du Faisan" in his luxurious court. This "Feast of the Pheasant" is perhaps one of the most famous parties in world history, setting the trend for all subsequent courtly extravagances. It also gave place to a "Voeu du Faisan," that is, a "Vow of the Pheasant," to launch a crusade against the Ottomans to recapture the recently fallen Byzantine capital, staging Philippe as the military leader of European Christendom. The main protagonist of this Feast is Philippe: he is 56, accomplished, and at the apex of his rule as one of Europe's most prominent Christian princes. As the chroniclers remind us before narrating the Feast, he had just successfully quelled a protracted rebellion in Ghent (1449–1453) with his victory at the Battle of Gavere in July 1453. As such, this Feast is also a military triumph. Evidently, this crusade never materialized. However, two chroniclers, Olivier de La Marche and Mathieu d'Escouchy, documented the event (Caron 269).[2]

The description de La Marche et Co. left brings us into Philippe's palace. For the occasion, the duke organized an extremely opulent setting that aimed to copy the trendy aesthetics of what Westerners believed to be the Greek Orient.[3] Tapestries depicting the Labors of Hercules covered the walls, while two columns stood at the room's center. On one, a fountain statue of a naked woman covered by a veil with Greek letters symbolized the captivity of the Greek church, while on the other, a real lion was fastened with a banner above it stating: "Ne touchez pas à ma dame!" ["Do not touch my lady!"] (Caron 275–276). Along the walls were three tables, on which a succession of *entremets* stood, i.e., illusion foods and edible scenic arrangements integrated within some form of musical entertainment. There was a commercial ship with its cargo and crew, Saint Andrew standing in front of a cross, an orchard with animals, twenty-eight musicians with their instruments on a single pâté, and,

---

[2] See Caron, Marie-Thérèse. "17 février 1454: le Banquet du Vœu du Faisan, fête de cour et stratégies de pouvoir." *Revue du Nord,* tome 78, n. 315, Avril-Juin 1996, pp. 269–288.

[3] "For Westerners, the Greek émigrés represented a world to copy. They were the prototype of people from whom one takes their values: active, rich, with technical knowledge, brilliant and cultured, taken by health and beauty. In fact, the *have-not* stayed in the East. Greek culture was effectively copied" (Waelkens 418, authors' translation).

at the end of the last table, four cantors, various organs, and a ringing bell, within a church (Caron 276). Those who did not partake in the Feast per se but were fortunate enough to be present watched in standing rows from four or five tribunes. The chroniclers have little to say about the meals. They simply insist on the abundance of meat present and the intensity of the culinary labor, enumerating the chariots required to transport the food.

They have much more to say about the entertainment, a *spectacle* alternating sacred and profane music, with scenes both mimed and spoken and the appearance of mechanical devices and dancers.[4] Among the automata present was a horse walking backward with trumpeters in silks on its back wearing masks, a half-man, half-griffon monster with a juggler standing upside down on its shoulders, a deer ridden by a child who sings, with the deer providing the bass voice, a dragon flying across the room, a heron chased by two falcons, who then kill it (Caron 277). Each act was introduced by gentlemen in livery, declaiming the program of the Feast. There were talking and singing animals, jesters, dwarves, jugglers, polymorph beings doing balancing acts; in sum, "Artifice rearranged the universe into a world of derision, carnival, a type of liberation of the imagination, a rupture from daily reality, from rationality" (Caron 278, authors' translation).[5] Across the room, facing the table of honor, was a theatre with curtains where the Greek myth of Jason and the Argonauts and the Golden Fleece was performed as a three-part pantomime—*un mystère en trois tableaux*.

All this was meant to communicate the duke's power via his patronage of the arts and sciences. This reference to the Greek myth of the Argonauts was not a mere happenstance. Since 1430, Philippe was head of the Order of the Golden Fleece, a Christian chivalric order dedicated to the defense of the faith, which consisted of promoting aid to the Byzantine Empire and combat-

---

[4] Walter Benjamin was particularly interested in such mechanical contraptions and automata, from his short stories, such as the floating mechanical ball in the Sultan's Court told by the famous juggler Rastelli, to his more essayistic works, such as his chess-playing Turkish puppet in his "Theses on the Philosophy of History." See "Rastelli's Story." *Walter Benjamin. Selected Writings*. Vol. 3, 1935–1938. Edited by Howard Eiland and Michael W. Jennings. Translated by Edmund Jephcott, Howard Eiland, et al. The Belknap Press of Harvard UP, 2006, pp. 96–98; and *Illuminations*. Edited and with an introduction by Hannah Arendt. Translated by Harry Zohn. Schocken Books, pp. 253–264.

[5] "L'artifice recomposait un univers qu'on peut voir comme un univers de dérision, de carnaval, une sorte de libération de l'imaginaire, une rupture avec le réel quotidien, avec la rationalité."

ting the Ottomans.⁶ Later on, a giant dressed as a Spanish Saracen rode in on a mechanical elephant, upon which stood a tower that held a grieving and veiled woman meant to represent the Greek Church—interpreted by the chronicler de la Marche himself, who then recited a long poem, beckoning Christian princes to come to their rescue. Finally, the knights of the Order of the Golden Fleece appeared, and the herald, carrying a pheasant and accompanied by two ladies and two knights, approached Philippe and reminded him of the tradition of swearing an oath either on a pheasant or a peacock.⁷ The chronicler d'Escouchy explains how the duke then handed the herald a note, which he, in turn, read aloud wherein Philippe swore to take on the voyage: "I vow to God, my Creator, to the Glorious Virgin Mary, to the ladies and *to this pheasant* that I will make and undertake what I vow by writing" (authors' translation, emphasis added).⁸ The Greek Church thanked him, and the giant and elephant left.

Allegedly, emotions ran so high that all those present wanted to immediately take the vow, to which the duke, overwhelmed by their response, asked them to do so in writing the next day (Caron 279). The Feast then ended, and the tables were lifted to make space for another group of musicians and entertainers about to perform the last entremets. A lady dressed in white, carrying the name "la Grâce-Dieu" on her shoulder, entered, followed by twelve knights and their respective ladies. She addressed the duke, to whom she promised victory, and then, a sequence of personified virtues—theological, cardinal, and noble—recited a poem (ibid.). Philippe eventually died never having completed his vow, but the mere mention of this strange Feast of the Pheasant cannot but evoke curiosity. It was, indeed, an epic party. So, what are we to make of

---

⁶ It is important to note that after declining membership in the Order of the Garter in 1422, which would have been considered an act of treason against the French King, Philippe created his own Order of the Golden Fleece on January 10, 1430, upon his marriage with Isabella of Portugal. This Christian order is loosely based on the myth of Jason and the Argonauts, the fleece of Gideon (Judges 6:37), and the Knights of the Round Table, eventually becoming the preeminent chivalric order in Europe. Today, two branches of the order still exist. See Caron, 278–279; and Boulton, D'Arcy Jonathan Dacre. *The Knights of The Crown: The Monarchical Orders of Knighthood in Later Medieval Europe, 1325–1520*. 1987. Revised Edition, Boydell Press, 2000, pp. 360–361.

⁷ See, for example, the wildly successful medieval French chanson de geste "Les voeux du paon" (1312–1313) by Jacques de Longuyon—with its forty-three surviving manuscripts and numerous translations—that introduced the chivalric notion of the Nine Worthies, synthesizing pagan, Jewish, and Christian heroes.

⁸ "Je voue à Dieu, mon Créateur, à la glorieuse Vierge Marie, aux dames et *au phaisant*, que je feray et entretiendray ce que je baille par escript" (emphasis added).

this Feast, or even this foreword? *Parturient montes, nascetur ridiculus mus*? Perhaps. Much like Philippe's elusive vow, poetry, too, exists at the edge of fulfillment—a pursuit that continues across time and borders.

The pheasant is a noble creature, standing apart from its peers with the brilliance of its plumage. Perhaps this elusive nature of the pheasant mirrors that of poetry itself, as Wallace Stevens mused, "poetry is a pheasant disappearing in the brush," leaving poets with the impossible task of pursuit. In 1991, under the guidance of Luigi Ballerini, a gathering of Italian and American poets and scholars took up this vow, knowing full well that the pheasant rarely lingers in the open. Thirty years later, the hunt quietly resumed. After three days of debate, some claimed to have glimpsed its dazzling feathers, while others argued that the bird had long since taken flight. And so, the search continues.

Day One: Friday, November 11, 2022

At NYU Casa Italiana Zerilli-Marimò, **Professor Emerita Marjorie Perloff**'s opening address set the tone for the conference, drawing parallels between contemporary poetic practices and historical movements. She highlighted how the Internet age has brought American and Italian poetries closer together, fostering overlap and mutual influence. Perloff reflected on the evolution from the 1991 *Disappearing Pheasant* conference, noting the shift from Marxist theoretical frameworks to a more eclectic and fluid poetic landscape. She emphasized the importance of recognizing and celebrating these cross-cultural exchanges, underscoring the dynamic and evolving nature of poetic discourse.

Professor Andrea Cortellessa from Università Roma Tre delved into the legacy and influence of the Italian neo-avant-garde movement, specifically focusing on the group known as the Novissimi. He explored how the neo-avant-garde's impact on Italian literature continues to provoke strong reactions and debates. Cortellessa examined the historical context of the 1960s and 1970s, highlighting key figures and events that shaped the movement, including theatrical performances and literary gatherings. His essay emphasized the ongoing influence and controversial reception of the Novissimi, suggesting that both admiration and resistance mark their legacy. Through a detailed analysis of literary and cultural dynamics, Cortellessa illustrated the enduring significance of the Novissimi in contemporary Italian poetry.

Following Cortellessa, the audience had the opportunity to listen to the first of the three poetry readings of the conference, which mixed Italian and American poets: **Charles Bernstein** and **Peter Gizzi** represented the latter, whereas the former consisted of **Antonella Anedda**, **Marco Giovenale**, and **Tommaso Ottonieri**.

The poetry reading was then followed by contributions from two speakers who showcased how digital technology can be instrumental in preserving poetry and making it more accessible. The essay by **Professor Chris Mustazza** from the University of Pennsylvania, "PennSound and the Italian Audiotext: Archives, Producers, Platforms," highlighted PennSound, the world's largest poetry recording archive, and its role in preserving and publishing audio performances of modern and contemporary Italian poetry. Professor Mustazza emphasized PennSound Italian's mission to make experimental and marginalized Italian poets accessible globally through audio and video. He also discussed innovative analysis techniques like "machine-aided close listening" and distant listening methodologies, which use visualizations and machine learning to reveal new insights into poetic performance, treating audio recordings as primary texts.

Professor Fabrizio Bondi from Università Suor Orsola Benincasa (Naples) presented the preliminary stages of "The Interactive Wunderkammer of Contemporary Italian Poetry," a digital humanities project aiming to recreate a virtual space where Italian contemporary poems can be read in a new, less traditional context. For its realization, Professor Bondi relied on the mnemonic technique of "loci," which associates concepts and images to memorize them.

Day one concluded with a round table focusing on the logic of poetry. **Professor Emeritus Paul Bové** from the University of Pittsburgh, in "Critical Poetic Grace," discussed the unique relationship between the poet and the critic, emphasizing that while the critic is secondary to the poet, this position is not inferior. Bové explored concepts like obligation, grace, and overmastering, arguing that critics serve poetry by recognizing and explaining the poet's imaginative intellect. He highlighted the distinction between moralists fixated on content and poets who create alternatives to the real. Using examples from poets like Reznikoff and Stevens, Bové illustrated how poiesis (the act of creation) challenges and transforms reality. Critics, he asserted, must understand their role as facilitators of this transformation, attuned to the nuances of poetic grace and its alternatives to the real. The essay ultimately called for a deeper appreciation of the critic's grace-filled service to poiesis beyond mere conversation and consensus.

Professor Franca D'Agostini, from Università degli Studi di Milano La Statale, in "What Poetry Can Teach Logic," faced the apparently impossible challenge of discovering the "logic of poetry." D'Agostini argued that language holds power, influencing thought and belief, and discussed how poetry, while seemingly anarchic, is still subject to the dominion of language. She introduced the concept of "recapture," where the inherent meaning and truth of language persist despite attempts to overcome them. Using metaphors like Michael Dummett's "seas of language" and Camillo Sbarbaro's imagery of the sea and a ship's wake, she illustrated the dynamic interplay between possibilities and actualities in thought. Ultimately, the essay suggested that poetry provides valuable insights into the fluid and resistant nature of language and thought, enriching our understanding of logical and metaphysical concepts.

Professor Tom Huhn, from the School of Visual Arts, in "The Reappearance of 'On Lyric Poetry and Society,'" revisited Theodor Adorno's 1957 essay to explore this intricate relationship. Adorno viewed lyric poetry as a delicate form that expresses the historical individual's experiences, marked by society's pressures and antagonisms. Huhn emphasized that the lyric poem reflects social contradictions and the individual's response to them. Adorno's analysis suggested that while lyric poetry arises from social conditions, it also transcends them by giving voice to individual suffering and expressing dreams of a different world. Huhn underscored the importance of suffering and language in lyric poetry, arguing that true lyric poems convey suffering's irrational nature, offering a critique of society and a form of transcendence. He tied this to Nietzsche's notion that art, particularly lyric poetry, acts as an illusion that helps humanity cope with the inherent suffering of existence. This nuanced understanding aligned with Wallace Stevens's idea that poetry is an elusive, disappearing pheasant, illustrating how poetry makes visible the unseen and unaudible aspects of human experience.

Finally, **Professor Achille Varzi** from Columbia University, in "On the Logic of Poetry," analyzed the two seemingly antithetical concepts of logic and poetry, proposing that they share common ground in exploring possibilities. Varzi argued that logic is not merely about rigid laws but the breadth of possibilities it considers, much like poetry. He challenged the conventional view that poetry thrives only in the absence of rules, highlighting that both poetry and logic can flourish within or beyond constraints. The critical difference lies in their focus: logic operates on propositions, seeking universal truths, while poetry engages with sentences, valuing the unique, nuanced, and idiosyncratic choices that shape each poem. Thus, the "logic" of poetry is not about applying logical laws but about understanding the specific, often personal rationales guiding poetic creation.

Day Two: Saturday, November 12, 2022

For the second day, the participants convened at the Italian Cultural Institute. The conference opened with a talk by **Professor Cecilia Bello Minciacchi** from La Sapienza Università di Roma. Like Professor Cortellessa on the first day, Professor Bello Minciacchi was requested to deal with the legacy of the neo-avant-garde, and her paper "The Legacy of the Neo-Avant-Garde II: Structures of the Return in Italian Poetry from the Late Twentieth Century to the Present Day," explores the complex and often overlooked influence of the Italian neo-avant-garde on contemporary poetry. Through a critical examination of the works produced by the Novissimi poets after the dissolution of the Gruppo 63, Minciacchi highlights the historiographical oversight that has marginalized their post-1970s contributions. She asserts that while much of Italian academia focuses on canonical figures like Montale and Sereni, the intellectual and formal advancements of the neo-avant-garde continue to shape contemporary poetic practices. These poets' continued engagement with form—especially their critical use of metrical structures—demonstrates a profound awareness of poetry's role as both a cultural and ideological intervention. Despite the apparent erasure of the neo-avant-garde from mainstream poetic genealogies, Minciacchi reveals its subtle yet persistent legacy, not as a nostalgic return but as a dialectical engagement with tradition. Through this lens, she connects the innovations of earlier poets like Sanguineti, Pagliarani, and Balestrini to newer voices, underscoring the enduring relevance of the avant-garde's challenge to normative modes of expression.

The round table "Translation as Composition" followed Professor Bello Minciacchi's analysis. Translation has been a critical concept since the first *Pheasant* conference: it is the only way to allow valuable exchanges between poems written in different languages. **Professor Gianluca Rizzo's** paper, *A Violent Inclusion: Translation as Composition (or What Cannibalism Has to Do with Poetry)*, examines translation through the radical lens of cultural and linguistic cannibalism, drawing on Oswald de Andrade's *Cannibalist Manifesto*. Rizzo contends that the act of translation, especially when approached as "transcreation," mirrors a process of devouring—absorbing, transforming, and reinterpreting foreign texts and ideas in ways that challenge the hegemony of Western cultural dominance. He advocates for this transgressive form of translation as a communal and politically charged practice, dismantling conventional notions of authorship, authenticity, and ownership. Rizzo's concept of a "we" in poetry emerges from this transcreation, a collective voice built not on passive reception but active, almost violent engagement with texts. This cannibalistic approach, he argues, serves as an antidote to the atomization fostered by late capitalism, pushing poetry beyond its confinement in lyricism and toward a broader, more inclusive social dialogue, one that also embraces technological transformations, artificial intelligence, and the need to reconfigure community in the face of ecological and technological crises.

After him, poet and **Professor Emeritus Charles Bernstein** (University of Pennsylvania) offered two short interventions ("An Intervention and a Brief Foreword" and "Playing Cricket without a Paddle"). In the first, Bernstein drew parallels between Rizzo's ideas and influential figures such as Gertrude Stein and Ezra Pound, emphasizing the transformative power of translation. He discussed the critical role of translation in shaping cultural narratives, highlighting how Haroldo de Campos's concept of cannibalism prevents works from becoming mere "local color" for export. Bernstein underscored the non-neutrality of translation and the importance of preserving the unique identity of a text. He concluded by reflecting on his bilingual book *Eco/Echo* (2022), which embodies the dialogue between Italian and American poetry, emphasizing translation's collaborative and dynamic nature. Following this, Bernstein reflected on the complexity and scope of the two-tome *Those Who from Afar Look Like Flies*, highlighting its immense set of poems and conversations among poets, critics, and translators. He emphasized the significance of "searching" in poetry and the influence of key figures like Luigi Ballerini in fostering Italian American poetic exchanges. Bernstein recounted his encounters with contemporary Italian poets, underscoring the lasting impact of these interactions. He concluded by celebrating the diverse and dynamic frequencies within the anthology, asserting that poetry thrives in contradictions and urging its continuation.

Then, **Professor Emeritus Luigi Bonaffini** from Brooklyn College, CUNY, in "Translating Dialect Literature," explored the complexities and challenges of translating Italian dialect literature, which has often been marginalized as "minor" or "subaltern." Despite these prejudices, dialect poetry has gained recognition and credibility, competing with Italian poetry on a national and international level. This resurgence is part of a broader reaction against the alienation of post-war industrial society, with poets seeking to reclaim ethnic history and personal roots. Bonaffini highlighted the unique richness of dialects, their cultural significance, and their inherent difficulties in translation, emphasizing that each dialect is an autonomous linguistic system, not merely a deviation from the standard language. He discussed various translators' strategies, noting that translating dialects often involves balancing literal and literary elements to preserve the original's essence. The essay also underscored the importance of dialect for expressing individual creativity and cultural identity, challenging the dominance of standard languages and offering a unique linguistic perspective.

Professor Thomas E. Peterson from the University of Georgia, the chair of the round table, also contributed to the discussion with a text entitled "The Imperfect and the Ideal: On Poetic Translation," wherein he addressed the inherent challenges and philosophical considerations of poetic translation, drawing on the works and theories of Dante, Steiner, Tynianov, Ortega y Gasset, Benjamin, Terracini, Poggioli, and others. He argued that translation is not merely a technical task but a profound engagement with the text that involves adaptation, empathy, and an understanding of the original's cultural and historical context. Peterson highlighted the dynamic nature of language and the translator's role in navigating the delicate balance between fidelity and creative interpretation. He concluded by emphasizing the importance of maintaining the poetic essence and mystery of the original work while allowing for new and innovative translations that resonate with contemporary audiences.

The second poetry reading of the conference allowed the audience to listen to **Mary Jo Bang**, **Rosmarie Waldrop**, **Maria Grazia Calandrone**, **Vincenzo Frungillo**, and **Laura Liberale**. Calandrone and Frungillo provided some theoretical contributions to explain their poetics: "Writing Poetry is a Political Action" by the former and "Poetry between the End of History and the Determinism of Nature" by the latter. **Calandrone** asserted that poetry is inherently political because it operates outside the market economy and can become a collective human voice, fostering compassion, which is the foundation of social and political life. She contrasted American poetry's deconstruction of language and explicit political critique with contemporary Italian poetry. Noting influences like Edgar Lee Masters's *Spoon River Anthology* (1915) and the Beat Generation, she highlighted their blend of irony, sarcasm, and intimate confessional tones. Calandrone appreciated the unique insights from American poets and felt encouraged to explore more subversive poetry in her work. **Frungillo** addressed the theoretical concept of the "end of history" postulated by Francis Fukuyama, where the fall of the Soviet Union signaled a perceived end to historical dynamics, leading to a crisis in poetics and a sense of emotional stalemate in Western society. Frungillo argued that poetry can counter this by highlighting our temporal nature and the relationship between history and natural life. He cited Roberto Bolaño's work as an example of exploring historical themes through a literary lens, emphasizing the intersection of bios and history. Frungillo's poetic work, such as *Ogni cinque bracciate* (2009), reflected this approach by portraying historical and real characters who embody both the weight of ideological history and the resilience of the human spirit. His poems sought to capture the complex interplay between historical events and personal experiences, offering a nuanced perspective on contemporary issues.

After the poetry reading, the conference moved onto another round table: "Research Poetry? A Poem by Any Other Name." During this discussion, **Professor Fabrizio Bondi** connected his talk with the other speakers through a shared defense of complex, multifaceted poetry. He expressed concern about the challenges of engaging readers today due to time constraints and educational deficiencies. Bondi explained the historical context of "research poetry," which evolved from the "avant-garde" and now reflects the discourse of "complexity" in system theory. He emphasized the need to bridge the gap between poets across cultures and overcome nationalism, highlighting poetry's role in fostering dialogue and understanding. Bondi concluded that the conference successfully manifested poetry, driven by the enthusiasm of participants and the charisma of crucial figures like Professor Ballerini.

After him, two poets intervened. First, **Marco Giovenale**, in "An Effects Machine. Some Spare Parts for Descriptions and Theories of Contemporary Writing," explored the concept of "an effects machine" in contemporary writing and criticism. He argued against traditional views of canonical poetry, advocating for a more dynamic, multifaceted approach that considers the diverse effects texts can have. Giovenale emphasized the importance of acknowledging the fragmented, varied nature of contemporary writing, which includes elements like phonosemantic qualities, visual components, and temporal flexibility. He highlighted examples from various authors and poets who challenge conventional structures and notions of narrative, rhythm, and coherence. Giovenale called for moving away from rigid stylistic analyses and recognizing modern literary works' innovative, often non-linear, and experimental nature.

Then, **Daniele Poletti** in "Breaking Fences and Putting Up Barricades. 'Scrittura Complessa' as Overcoming and Resistance. Between Formlessness and The Continuous Word," introduced the concept of "scrittura complessa" (complex writing) as a necessary response to the contemporary degradation of language and communication. He argued against creating rigid categories and instead advocated for a dynamic approach that considers writing a social and intellectual necessity, free from established labels. Poletti emphasized the importance of resisting the simplification and commodification of language, proposing that complex writing serves as an antidote to these trends. He outlined three key aspects of complex writing: the disjunctive function of language, formlessness, and the continuous word. These elements collectively promote a form of writing that challenges immediate consumption, encourages deeper reflection, and maintains a fluid, evolving relationship with language and meaning. Poletti concluded by stressing the importance of memory and discovery in literature, advocating for a continuous, transformative approach to writing.

Day Three: Sunday, November 13, 2022

The third and last day at NYU Casa Italiana Zerilli-Marimò began on Sunday afternoon with a brief presentation by **Professor Giorgio Patrizi** (Università del Molise), who delved into the legacy of the Italian neo-avant-garde initiated by Gruppo 63 in the 1960s. He reflected on Andrea Zanzotto's provocative question about the avant-garde's contributions and underscored the movement's critical stance against traditional literary norms and neo-capitalist society. Patrizi traced the trajectory of poetic experimentation through the 70s and 80s, highlighting influential groups like Quaderni di Critica and the Neapolitan collective K.B. He emphasized the significance of the anthology *Poesia italiana della contraddizione* (1989) and the emergence of journals such as *Baldus* and *Altri termini*, which continued to challenge conventional poetics. Recognizing the essential contributions of women poets, Patrizi argued for the ongoing relevance of experimental poetry in resisting market and media homogenization. Concluding with a call to maintain a critical, questioning approach to poetry, he aligned with Adorno's advocacy for an ethical commitment to obscurity, urging poets to explore new expressive forms and preserve the transformative potential of poetic language.

Professor Ugo Perolino (Università di Chieti-Pescara) then examined the latent movements of revision and subversion in the language and institutions of poetry during the 1950s. Highlighting early experiments by the Novissimi, he underscored the decade's linguistic and theoretical shifts that expanded poetic expression and secularized its techniques. Perolino traced the critical reception of post-war poetry, noting the term "epigonism" used to describe the perceived lack of innovation. He emphasized the broader linguistic restlessness among younger poets, exemplified by various anthologies, which revealed a divergence from traditional Hermeticism and post-war realism. Highlighting the significance of the "San Babila" Prize and subsequent anthologies, Perolino illustrated how these collections showcased a mix of established and emerging voices, documenting a transformative period in Italian poetry. The essay also examined the ideological divides and critical responses of the time, particularly the contrasting approaches of different anthologists. It concluded by reflecting on the enduring impact of these experimental efforts on contemporary poetry.

These two interventions then gave way to poetry readings of **Mariano Bàino, Anselm Berrigan, John Latta, Susan Briante**, and **Ivan Schiavone**. The two Italian poets who bookended the reading, Bàino and Schiavone, also kindly contributed their theoretical thoughts and musings to this volume. **Bàino** shared with readers "Four Little Objects to Befit a Request for a Note on Poetics, Drawing Upon the Present of the Past"; first, a letter to Francesco Muzzioli about his book *Fax giallo* (1993); second, an excerpt from an interview about his dialect poetry; third, some annotations on the form of the sonnet; and, lastly, a letter to Andrea Cortelessa that found its way in the latter's anthology *Terra della prosa* (2014). **Schiavone** also chose a fragmentary contribution, a remix of various considerations on poetry and poetics that straddles the lines between poetry and essayistic prose, ranging from landscapes, the figural, and mannerism and complexity, to the status of Italian as a language and ending with what is to be done in literature in apocalyptic times. Another Italian poet, **Tommaso Ottonieri**, also provided a personal intermezzo, a brief text exploring the evolution of his writing process that blurs the lines between the personal essay and prose poetry.

Professor Massimo Bacigalupo's (Università di Genova) contribution explored the significant influence of American poetry on the Italian literary landscape, particularly post-World War II. He traced the introduction and popularization of American poets like the Beats through Fernanda Pivano's seminal anthology *Poesia degli ultimi americani* (1964) and subsequent translations and friendships fostered by Italian poets and scholars with their American counterparts. While American poets such as Lowell, Berryman, and Ferlinghetti became mainstays in Italian literature, the reciprocal visibility of Italian poets in the US remained minimal, often limited to academic circles. Bacigalupo reflected on the unique phenomenon of American poetry's appeal in Italy, citing the Corriere della Sera's selection of American poets for its 2004 series and the enduring fascination with figures like Whitman, Dickinson, and Pound. He examined the peculiar cases of Pound and Masters, whose works resonated deeply due to their distinctive appeals—Pound for his political notoriety and Masters for his cultural critique. The essay also delved into the profound impact of T.S. Eliot and Ezra Pound on Italian poets, emphasizing their formative influence on the modernist generation, including Montale, Luzi, and Sanguineti. Bacigalupo highlighted the contemporary reception of American poets such as Stevens, whose introspective and abstract style has found a receptive audience among Italy's younger poets, signaling an ongoing transatlantic dialogue in poetry.

Fittingly, Diego Minciacchi directed a spectacle for those in attendance: *Xantablackz. A Verbiage and Sounding Event for Current Communization*. Readers can view the performance by scanning the QR provided and following the texts and lyrics supplied in the pages of this volume.

Lastly, **Nicholas Benson**'s contribution reflects on the conference from the privileged perspective of retrospection and encapsulates the spirit of collaboration and mutual respect that defined the three-day event. Reflecting on the original 2020 postponement, he highlighted the relief and camaraderie shared by participants, who were grateful to Luigi Ballerini for fostering an inclusive environment where poets and critics from Italy and the US could exchange ideas freely. Benson noted the absence of conflict despite differing poetic approaches, attributing past divisions to misunderstandings. The conference echoed the ecumenical but biased inclusivity of Ballerini and Beppe Cavatorta's anthology, *Those Who from Afar Look Like Flies*, featuring diverse critical and poetic perspectives. Benson emphasized the vital connections between Italian and American literature, facilitated by figures like Ballerini,

Charles Bernstein, Massimo Bacigalupo, and Marjorie Perloff. He observed that the perceived belatedness of contemporary poets/critics, who often engage more in self-critique than direct sociopolitical action, contrasts with the dynamic, if sometimes contentious, alliances of historical avant-gardes. Francesco Muzzioli's critique of contemporary inaction, Marco Giovenale's ironic reflections, and Franca D'Agostini's assertion of poetry's role in preserving truth at the abyss's edge encapsulate the conference's thematic breadth. The afterword concludes with Susan Briante's metaphor likening poets to "trash trees," symbolizing resilience and adaptability in the face of ongoing cultural and political challenges.

The Reappearing Pheasant conference aimed to renew and invigorate the poetic discourse between Italy and the U.S. It highlighted the power of cultural gatherings to inspire, challenge, and unite individuals in a shared pursuit of artistic and intellectual excellence. Most importantly, the participants all contributed to the most important task they were required to fulfill: catching a glimpse of the elusive and fleeting Pheasant embodying poetry. This was achieved by putting American and Italian poets in contact, analyzing the relevance of avant-garde poetic movements, defining the peculiar elements characterizing contemporary poetry, either in the 1950s–60s and in the first two decades of the 21st century. Wallace Stevens was right in saying that "poetry is a pheasant disappearing in the brush." This means that poetry has not entirely disappeared, but, on the contrary, it is both momentarily hiding from and appearing to our view. As we chase this pheasant across centuries, from the banquet halls of Philippe to the modern stages of poetic inquiry, we are reminded that neither vow nor verse or prose can truly hold it. What we are offering readers in the acts of this conference are the traces of its presence.

Acknowledgements

The editors and publishers gratefully acknowledge the contribution of Professor Stefano Albertini, director of NYU Casa Italiana Zerilli-Marimò, whose generous support has proven fundamental in making the conference and the publication of its proceedings possible. He opened the doors of Casa Italiana, honoring the legacy of Luigi Ballerini under whose aegis, in 1991, American and Italian poets and scholars first convened.

A word of gratitude is also due to Julian Sachs, program coordinator, who helped with all the technical support, the online promotion of the conference, and the translation of many of the poems read during the conference. He also coordinated the live broadcast of the three days of the conference on YouTube.

Thanks are also extended to Kostja Kostic, administrator of Casa Italiana, who provided all the invited speakers with the necessary assistance in the practical aspects of their traveling and accommodation.

Last but not least, the sentiments of our thankfulness go to Dr. Berardo Paradiso, the president of the Italian American Committee on Education, and Chairman of the Board of Agincourt Press, whose personal support for Italian culture in North America knows no equal.

We would also like to thank the Italian Cultural Institute - the location for the second day of the conference - and the St. Mark's Church in-the-Bowery for welcoming all of us to the final event of the conference, the concert "Xantablackz. A Verbiage and Sounding Event for Current Communization" authored and directed by Diego Minciacchi.

New York, September 2024.

Nicholas Benson

Foreword: A Conversation with Luigi Ballerini

This conversation, held on March 24th, 2023, in New York with Luigi Ballerini, explores the prehistory of The Reappearing Pheasant. *The gathering held in November 2022 was the fourth of Italian and American poets and critics over four decades of bringing together critical and creative voices from the two shores. The first gathering,* The Favorite Malice, *occurred in New York in 1979, followed by* The Disappearing Pheasant *in New York in 1991 and its Los Angeles edition in 1994. The most recent gathering revealed an evolution in the relationship between poets and critics. Diverse and diverging poetics within and between the two countries certainly remain, but mainly because of Luigi's work forging connections between Italy and the U.S.A., contacts have been made, relationships established, and avenues of dialogue opened—all in the interest, as he said half-seriously, of making "one poetry language out of two." Yet the relationship between the two literatures has always been somewhat imbalanced, and reciprocity is always in the making. Although many poets in Italy have demonstrated that they are aware of the modern American tradition, as Massimo Bacigalupo's talk at the most recent conference illustrated, it's not as evident that the reverse is true. This conversation is offered to give the reader greater purchase in the proceedings and provoke further interest in the* percorso *of Italian poetry and its relationship with poetry in the U.S.*[1]

---

[1] Editorial Note (EN): For ease of reading, in transforming this spoken interview into text, it has been altered to minimize fillers and similar cues of spoken language, and discourse markers have been transcribed using punctuation. Hereinafter, EN stands for "Editorial Note" whereas AN is for "Author's note."

The Favorite Malice, 1979.

NB: Let's discuss the circumstances around the first gathering of poets and critics in 1979.

LB: The conference we had at NYU was called "Ontology and Reference in Contemporary Italian Poetry"—an insane title—and its proceedings were later published as *The Favorite Malice*. The idea was to gather poets and philosophers. We had specially invited Gianni Vattimo because he was *the* Heidegger man in Italy, then. But you know, we had no clue who Heidegger really had been, the fact that he stood by Hitler, that he was anti-Semitic, and so forth. We were interested in the fact that he had proposed a reading of poetry that was beneficial and productive. For example, there's one essay by him, a lecture, in which he quotes a poem by Trakl.[2] And he reads the line that says, "Where names are not available, nothing can be said." Or something like that... instead of reading "nothing can be said," he says, well, no—the *nothing* can be said. Gianni Vattimo was the first person in Italy to bring Heidegger to us in this respect, and that's just one example. As I said, it was a limited knowledge of Heidegger, but poets reacted very favorably to this notion. Where words drop off and stop functioning as referential signs, you can say things that might offer an unexpected opportunity "to signify."

NB: The conference in 1979 brought together people who otherwise might have only heard about each other.

LB: At the time, I consulted with friends like Nanni Cagnone, and decided that we would have beside Gianni Vattimo, Reiner Schürmann, of NYU, who would be perfect to interact with Gianni. We had poets such as Alfredo Giuliani, Nanni Cagnone, Angelo Lumelli, and Antonio Porta. At that point, Porta and Giuliani were not exactly seeing eye to eye, because Giuliani pursued a line of experimental and research poetry. In contrast, Porta, at one point, quote-unquote, betrayed. Of course, he was one of the *Novissimi* but in the early seventies he switched to *communication*. Poets had to reach the audience. Messages should be clearly understood. Transcriptions of personal experience would be welcomed. Language would return to its status as a vehicle of inten-

---

[2] EN: See Martin Heidegger's essays "Die Sprache" and "Die Sprache im Gedicht" in *Unterwegs zur Sprache*. Guinther Neske, 1959; and, in English, "A Dialogue on Language" and "Language in the Poem. A Discussion on Georg Trakl's Poetic Work." *On the Way to Language*. Translated by Peter D. Hertz. Harper & Row, 1971.

tions, etc.[3] In one of Porta's collections, there is a poem, dedicated to me, in which he alludes to this new persuasion of his and gently measures the distance that separated him from his former colleagues.[4] Alongside, I invited Fredi Chiappelli, from U.C.L.A: a philologist, and a great textual reader, he could bring to life all sorts of writings. You gave him the most sublime poem or the trashiest, and he would dissect it with the tools of stylistic criticism and historical semantics, in the tradition of Leo Spitzer. He was always coming up with something interesting. He hit it off exceptionally well with Nanni Cagnone. The two of them really bonded to the point that when Nanni started a little publishing venue called Coliseum, one of the books that he published—against my better judgment—contained a review of Manzoni's *Betrothed* allegedly written by Edgar Allan Poe.[5] It had appeared in Edgar Allan Poe's magazine, but Edgar Allan Poe did not author it. And I told Nanni that, but Chiappelli insisted that it was Poe. I was very close to Kenneth Silverman, a Poe scholar respected worldwide, and he said, "No, he never wrote that." So, in Italy, there's a book of Manzoni related reviews—including one by Goethe, who *did* write a review of Manzoni—and one by Edgar Allan Poe, who did *not*. At any rate, I'm certainly not the only one who has made contemporary Italian poetry available to an English readership. There are many. But you know, it's one thing to say I love this poem or poet, and I'm going to focus on that person; that's fine, but there needs to be a perspective—that is to say, a precise offering. Then you can debate it, tear it apart, even. But you have a handle. Otherwise, there are just individual predilections. And that's good, too. But there is a difference.

NB: Yes, and especially thinking of pre-internet times, unless you get the people together, you don't have a real chance for dialogue; instead, you can get a lot of misapprehensions.

LB: Exactly. And some interesting connections were actually established … like, recently, Marco Giovenale and Charles Bernstein, and in the 90s, Milli Graffi and Barbara Guest.

---

[3] EN: See Porta, Antonio. "Il grado zero della poesia." *Marcatré*, 2, January 1964, pp. 41–42.

[4] EN: See Porta's "Balene delfini bambini." *Invasioni: 1980–1983*. Mondadori, 1984; also found in *Tutte le poesie (1956–1989)*. Edited by Niva Lorenzini. Garzanti, 2009, which was translated into English as *Piercing the Page: Selected Poems 1958–1989*. Edited by Gian Maria Annovi. Translated by Anthony Baldry, Rosemary Liedl, Paolo Martini, Anthony Molino, Lawrence R. Smith, Paul Vangelisti, and Pasquale Verdicchio. Otis Books, Seismicity Editions, 2012.

[5] EN: See Poe, Edgar Allan. "Review of *The Betrothed Lovers*." *The Southern Literary Messenger*, vol. 1, no. 9, May 1835.

NB: The anthologies—*The Favorite Malice, Shearsmen of Sorts, The Promised Land*—contain a condensed prehistory of last year's *The Reappearing Pheasant*—which means they cover an amazing arc of conferences, from 1979 in NY to 1991 again in NY, when the pheasant disappeared, to Los Angeles in 1994.[6] And the compendious *Those Who from Afar Look like Flies*, Tomes 1 and 2, bring us a survey of Italian poetry of the last seventy years—since 1956—though through a selective lens.

LB: Well, you know if your pain doesn't bend the language, you're not in the anthology. Bernstein quoted that I don't know how many times, and even ended his lecture at the MLA in San Francisco, quoting me. "As Luigi said…" [laughing]

NB: You also remarked that the method of choosing what to include in the anthologies was "ecumenical, but biased," another memorable phrase. There is a sort of early theoretical elaboration of this in Tom Harrison's introductory essay to *The Favorite Malice*: "If there is to be a radically different language, one which might escape the referential captivity of the signifier-signified distinction, it must transform the very procedures of linguistic sense."

LB: Yes. The difficulty all along has been making things if not palatable then at least approachable to a readership that didn't know much about what we would term "research poetry," a type of writing that tends to, let's say, delve into language, structured or unstructured, searching for the meaning it might yield. There are many ways to do the searching, and that's the ecumenical aspect, but the will to empower language as an active source of sense and meaning, in and of itself, must be present in each poet, and that's the bias. I also felt that to make things more inviting we needed operate under an aegis both philosophical (hence the pivotal role of Gianni Vattimo and Reiner Schürmann) and linguistic (hence the presence of Fredi Chiappelli, but also of Angus Fletcher and Samuel R. Levin). We were not totally deprived of contacts with American poets operating in a vein that could be regarded as analogous: the language poets. Charles Bernstein was already among the attendees of *The Favorite Malice*. It is in fact rewarding for me how the American poets and critics have moved gradually from audience to active participants and advi-

---

[6] EN: See *The Favorite Malice. Ontology and Reference in Contemporary Italian Poetry*. Edited by Thomas J. Harrison. Out of London Press, 1983; *Shearsmen of Sorts. Italian Poetry 1975–1993*. Edited by Luigi Ballerini. Forum Italicum, 1992; and *The Promised Land. Italian Poetry After 1975: A Bilingual Edition*. Edited by Luigi Ballerini. Sun & Moon Press, 1999.

sors. The latest re-appearance of the Pheasant was conceived with the advice of Marjorie Perloff and Charles Bernstein. But at that initial stage, at the time of *The Favorite Malice*, we ourselves were groping, if not in the dark then certainly in some obscurity. In general, we felt a strong tie with the *Novissimi*, and the experimental poets of the 60s. Remember that the so-called neo-experimental and neo-avant-garde began in the late 50s with Sanguineti, Balestrini, Porta, Giuliani and Pagliarani. The mastermind, or at least the "general coach" of all this, was Luciano Anceschi, who in the pages of his journal, *Il Verri*, was showcasing and supporting with phenomenological arguments the type of poetry people would, at first sight, deem illegible. And you can rest assured that to seek the social validity of utterances that spelled out a truth that could neither be proven nor denied was not an easy task. Anyhow, in the mid-fifties that type of poetry to which we felt strongly affiliated was already under attack by many; probably the majority of the poets writing at that time thought the radical poetry we were proposing was an aberration.

NB: It's 1979. Was there already a palpable sense that things had changed? There's this general idea that 1975 was when the atmosphere somehow changed.

LB: Yes, and there's a sort of a misalignment between my perspective and desiderata and what was happening in Italy. In a sense, I was purposefully *in ritardo*. When the conference occurred, I wanted to hang on to the legacy of the to the 60's (plus the Heideggerian fascination). There is the notion that the 70s were a desert, or a time when all experimental poetry had been rejected in Italy, that poets were ashamed of it. It's simply not true. *Some* people felt like that. But the paradox is, for instance, that Balestrini, who basically endorsed the notion that poetry should cede before actual revolutionary action, kept on writing *a lot* of poetry, while Giuliani, who was always campaigning for the autonomy of the poetic act, didn't write any, or very little, in the 70s. One of the crucial moments is the demise of journal *Quindici*. You will find references to this in the introduction to the second volume of the *Flies*. There are several pages in which we debate what the 70s meant. Because the prevailing idea is that 1975 was the annus mirabilis, when poets went back to writing poetry after a hiatus of doubts, hesitations and, in some case, total retraction. Italy was indeed in turmoil, throughout the seventies, but radical, language-first poetry writing never stopped. These were the years of the Red Brigades, of terrorism, the years of lead, as we called them. However, while all these tragedies were occurring, the Italian society was undergoing an irrevocably positive change. Imagine: abortion became legal; divorce became legal; asylums for the so-called insane were closed. You could create your own radio station. Unfortunately, all of that also enabled the rise of the Berlusconis. But in any case... Think of the *diritto di famiglia*—women no longer had to assume their husbands' names. The contract that said women were supposed to follow their husbands wherever they chose was eliminated. *Both* were responsible for the raising of the children. It was a gigantic leap forward. And where do you position poetry in all this? Some people revamped the Adornian refusal. In reality, hardly anybody stopped. And worse, some people began to write about themselves, confusing lyricism with confessionalism. We ourselves were confused about the very notion of *lyricism*. We thought lyricism was bad, period. A wonderful essay by Adorno would have taught us differently, if we had only read it at the time.[7] In poetry, in fact, it is impossible *not* to be lyrical, even if you're writing about Genghis Khan. Lyricism is that swerve, that twist, that improbable connection between qualifiers and substantives. You are yanked away from expectations, and that's what makes you a human being rather than a being molded into a pattern established by dictionaries. Now, at that time, all this was not so clear. We were just fascinated by the input of Heidegger, and behind Heidegger, his take on the ancient Greeks. We wanted to become oracular, like the Delphian prophet who neither spoke nor remained silent, but signified,[8] happy in the experience of saying (somewhere, Heidegger says the word 'experience' comes from the Latin *ex per ire—coming from* and *as you go*). And what do you do with that? You build on it in unpredictable ways. And that's what we wanted to do ... that's why, in 1975, I published Nanni Cagnone's *What's Hecuba to Him or He to Hecuba*. It is perfectly representa-

---

[7] EN: See Adorno, Theodor W. "On Lyric Poetry and Society." *Notes to Literature*, vol. 1. Edited by Rolf Tiedemann and translated by Shierry Weber Nicholsen. Columbia UP, 1991, pp. 37–54. Adorno's essay was originally given as a talk for Berlin radio in 1957, and subsequently revised. In 1974, it was published in English in *Telos: Critical Theory of the Contemporary*, vol. 20, pp. 56–71.

[8] EN: See Heraclitus's Fragment XCIII: "ὁ ἄναξ οὗ τὸ μαντεῖόν ἐστι τὸ ἐν Δελφοῖς οὔτε λέγει οὔτε κρύπτει ἀλλὰ σημαίνει" ("The lord whose is the oracle at Delphi neither utters nor hides his meaning but shows it by a sign") (DK B93). George Steiner explains how "[c]ontrary to Adamic nomination, Heraclitus does not label or define substance but infers its contradictory essence. Semantic ambiguities, a second order of difficulty, both relate the internal to the external and signal their dissociation. In what may again derive from archaic precedents, riddles are crucial (they are the crux)" (*The Poetry of Thought* 33).

tive of those years.[9] When my mother died, I inherited, I don't know exactly, the equivalent of $3, perhaps 4.000. I invested the whole amount in Nanni Cagnone's book [laughing] because I thought he would eventually win the Nobel Prize. I published 3,000 copies of it—2,900 of them remained for a long while under my bed—but I still believe *What's Hecuba* to be a major book, and, I repeat, it was 1975. All this is spelled out in the introduction to *The Flies*, Volume Two— proving that, as far as advanced, radical, innovative poetry-writing is concerned, there was no continuity between the waning of the officially recognized neo-avantgarde and 1975. Viviani's *L'Ostrabismo cara was published* in 1973;[10] my own *eccetera. E* in 1972.[11] Even Pasolini, despite all his venomous invectives, fell under the spell of the new and in 1971 issued *Trasumanar e organizzar*: If you did not know any better, you would think him a turncoat.[12] We were confused. *He* wasn't confused, but he didn't know what he was talking about. If, as he is reported to have said, anyone who "dealt with the avant-garde" ought to be ashamed of having done so, he should be the first to blush, for the poetry he published in 1971 was suspiciously infected by the same venom he had detected in the vessels of his enemies.

NB: I like what Peter Gizzi said in an interview about being called a lyric poet. He said what he's doing is "simply an ongoing narration of my bewilderment as a citizen in the world." It's as though the lyricism of his poems, which is very much there, happens along the way due to that pressure.

LB: Since the time of *The Favorite Malice*, my notion of poetry hasn't changed much. I think I would have the backing of some linguistic structuralists; for example, Jakobson, in his essay on grammar and poetry, emphasizes the reader's role in the conative function of language.[13] If you tell someone: *eat*, there isn't much the addressee can do but eat. That is the zero degree of independence. Now, poetry is precisely the opposite; it uses the conative to its maximum, to create interaction with the message being sent.

---

[9] EN: See Nanni Cagnone. *What's Hecuba to Him, or He to Hecuba*. Translated by David Verzoni. Out of London Press, 1975.

[10] EN: See Viviani Cesare. *L'ostrabismo cara*. Feltrinelli, 1973.

[11] EN: See Luigi Ballerini. *Eccetera. E*. Guanda Editore, 1972.

[12] EN: See Pier Paolo Pasolini. *Trasumanar e organizzar*. Garzanti, 1971.

[13] EN: See Jakobson, Roman. "Poetry of Grammar and Grammar of Poetry." *Lingua*, 21, 1968, pp. 597–609.

NB: Here's a Nanni Cagnone quotation that, as I read, Charles Bernstein likes a lot: "Poetry is the action of going beyond what one can think."[14]

LB: Yes—an admirable way of putting it. Nanni has always had a real talent for piercing aphorisms.

NB: Here's something else from *The Favorite Malice*. At one point in his poem "Felicità obbligata,"[15] Angelo Lumelli says, "non c'è tempo per la cronaca" ["there's no time for the news"], which is a great piece of reverse psychology because it can't help but make you interested in whatever is in the news. But you understand what he means. His characters, the personages implied by the poem, live with a constant barrage of news. And we have no choice but to be aware of it. So, then, we have a sense that we have no time. But we live in time. You're forced to think about this problem, which is a nice paradox.

LB: "Non c'è tempo per la cronaca" in poetry. Indeed a paradox to be savored in its full etymological implications: that which runs contrary to prevailing opinion. The word was used to indicate that the Earth was orbiting around the sun and not viceversa. A paradoxical discovery in so far as it contradicted what the prevailing (indeed written in stone) opinion held as an inviolable truth. There's a poem by John Donne in which he mentions this...[16] Why not revamp the original acceptation of the word? What Lumelli affirms is a perfect example of a reversed opinion. And he's right; there *should* be no room in poetry for *cronaca*. [...]

The Disappearing Pheasant, 1991.

NB: Let's leap ahead to *The Disappearing Pheasant* conference of 1991.

LB: Yes, this time we cast a wider net and involved the Poetry Project at Saint Mark's, the newly established Casa Italiana of NYU, the Italian Cultural Institute. I don't remember how I pulled it off, financially, but I am certain that my friend Furio Colombo, a former member of the neo-avantgarde and, at that time, director of the Italian Cultural Institute, came to the rescue. Some of the

---

[14] EN: "Poesia è agire inoltre, oltre quel che si riesce a pensare," "Exordium." Æschylus-Agamemnon. Translated and edited by Nanni Cagnone. Edizione Galleria Mazzoli, 2020, pp. xiii–xiv. See also *Agamemnon*. Translated by Nanni Cagnone. Editore La Finestra, 2010.

[15] EN: See "Happiness Compelled." *The Favorite Malice*. Translated by Thomas J. Harrison. Out of London Press, 1984, pp. 184–191.

[16] EN: Perhaps "Love's Growth," which describes a heliocentric universe.

most significant Italian Poets of the secondo Novecento came to witness the virtual disappearance of the pheasant: Elio Pagliarani, Paolo Volponi, Alfredo Giuliani, Giancarlo Majorino, Amelia Rosselli. Twelve years after the first conference. Most of the poems read and essays written for the event found asylum in *Shearsmen of Sorts*—it's not a perfect documentation of the proceedings, but much of what transpired is there. And more. I do not think that philosophy of language and logic can ultimately explain "poetry" but not all philosophers are poetry-haters, and here I want to acknowledge the great contribution made by Remo Bodei, who knew how to handle both poiesis and dialectics.

NB: I appreciated very much Marjorie Perloff's address at The Reappearing Pheasant for her clarity and because she does an excellent job referencing the conference of 1991. She recounts, in fact, the episode when Bruce Andrews, founder of L=A=N=G=U=A=G=E along with Charles Bernstein, turned to the Italian contingent and told them: "We don't have anything to learn from you."[17]

LB: Well, then the next day, Tom Harrison, who grew up bicultural and bilingual and was speaking on behalf of the Italians, so to say, addressed what Marjorie Perloff humorously referred to as "the U.S. team," and he said, "We knew all about Marxism before you people started writing poetry," which is factually the case.

NB: She said at this comment, a hush fell over the audience that was never quite resolved.

LB: True.

NB: And she said, "The situation now is much more eclectic and fluid. The two poetries, Italian and American, have come closer together. They even overlap. They are very symbiotic."

LB: Bruce was speaking as someone who feared colonization. I don't think Charles [Bernstein] would say anything like that, at any rate the poets who took part in the first disappearance of the pheasant had not come to NY to teach; they had come to say 'this is what we have been doing.' Maybe there are commonalities we can share. One of the people who came over, a cultural impresario by the name of Gianni Sassi, who co-sponsored the event, had for ten years convened a festival called Milano Poesia to which he had brought dozens of Americans to Milan. For the last three editions of Milano Poesia, he

---

[17] EN: See Andrews, Bruce and Charles Bernstein, editors. *The L=A=N=G=U=A=G=E Book*. Southern Illinois UP, 1984.

engaged me as some sort of scout of the American poetic territory. I "chaperoned" to Milan John Ashbery, Amiri Baraka, Jerome Rothenberg, Charles Bernstein, Rosemarie Waldrop, and Michael Davidson, Paul Vangelisti, and others. Gianni Sassi, by the way, was very close to John Cage who had spent time in Milano studying the work of futurist musicians. Cage not only performed at Milano Poesia, Gianni also recorded his music for Cramps Records, a label he had founded. Milano Poesia wasn't devoted to verbal poetry exclusively; there was also visual poetry, music, performance, dance, and so on. It was a festival of the arts. Several people from Fluxus also came to Milano Poesia: Emmett Williams, Dick Higgins, Allison Knowles, and may others. And each year Gianni published a catalog of all that happened during the week-long gatherings.
NB: At that time, far fewer people spoke both languages or knew the scene in both countries.

The Reappearing Pheasant, 2022.

NB: That's a critical difference. At *The Reappearing Pheasant*, most of the Italians spoke in English. We had both languages and even, humorously, something in between. I'm thinking of Cortellessa joking that his presentation was in "pidgin."
LB: Yes, impediments can be turned into opportunities.
NB: One talk given in English by an Italian speaker that I found especially notable was by Cecilia Bello Minciacchi's. Also, Andrea Cortellessa's on "L'incubo della neoavanguardia." Both touched on an extremely crucial and sensitive subject.
LB: Right. For many years, the partisans of the neo-avant-garde, those who acknowledged to be working in the wake of its legacy maintained that the radical change in the making of poetry it had brought about simply could not be ignored. Cecilia [Bello Minciacchi] wrote a beautiful introduction to a second edition of my very first book, *eccetera, E.* in which she points out how my book, written in 1972, could be appreciated as a stepping stone between the neo-avant-garde and what happened later. There are other books, of course, like that. Others would look at it differently and maintain that the neo-avant-garde was something to be put in parentheses and called for a return to the poetry of Vittorio Sereni, Linea Lombarda, Lirici nuovi, etc. There were two encampments at that time, in the 70s. Now, the situation is blurred. But the

confrontation was meaningful. And Enrico Testa, in his anthology *Dopo la lirica*, speaks of the neo-avant-garde in very negative terms.[18] Andrea Cortellessa, on the other hand, is saying the exact opposite. In fact the neo-avant-garde was so successful that even those who deplored it were employing modalities borrowed from it.

NB: Then Cecilia Bello Minciacchi said that the current practice is to ignore the whole thing altogether. There's a kind of omission.

LB: There's a forgetting of the controversy. Today, you have writers who have matured beyond this type of confrontation. But certainly, the two main tenets of the neo-avant-garde, that is to say, the diminution or the degradation of the *ego* and the schizomorphic vision (see my introduction to the *Novissimi*, Agincourt Press, New York, 2017) are, in my mind, points of no return.

NB: Cecilia Bello Minciacchi did conclude by saying, about the *neoavanguardia*, "the shocks of method now seem ordinary."

LB: Yes, it's no longer a surprise. But don't forget that the 70s and 80s, and even our present time would not be so manageable without the neo-avant-garde. Today everybody seems to have assimilated the notion that there is no I without the other. In his essay of Lacan's *The Mirror Stage*, the child recognizes himself as an individual, and the first thing he does is to turn around and point to some *other*, whoever is holding him to assert his/her self.[19] Without this other, he wouldn't be capable of saying, "I am I." And so, on all this, everyone agrees. But not everyone *practices* the otherness in the I.

NB: It seems like the poetry scene now, in both countries, is more diverse…

---

[18] EN: See Enrico Testa's "Introduzione," in *Dopo la lirica. Poeti italiani 1960–2000*. Einaudi, 2005, pp. v–xxx: "È difficile trasmettere a chi ha avuto la sorte di non sperimentarlo, il senso di cupezza che caratterizzò gli anni Settanta. [...] Le ricostruzioni della poesia del periodo tendono ad isolare, con ricorsività quasi ossessiva, alcuni fenomeni ritenuti essenziali: l'isterilirsi della sperimentazione neoavanguardistica, troppo spesso collage di slogan o combinatorio spartito virtuosistico" ["It is difficult to convey to someone who has not had the fortune of experiencing it, the sense of glumness that characterized the 70s. [...] The reconstructions of poetry in that period tend to isolate, with an almost obsessive recursiveness, a few phenomenon held as essential: the sterilization of neo-avant-garde experimentalism, too often a collage of slogans or virtuoso combinatorial sheet music [...]"] (xiii). He later compares this to a "literary bankruptcy" ("bancarotta letteraria"), quoting Siciliano (xiv).

[19] EN: For an English translation by Jean Roussel of Jacques Lacan's notion of the mirror stage, see "The Mirror Phase as Formative of the Function of I." *New Left Review*, 51, Sept./Oct. 1968, pp. 63–77.

LB: Yes, it's almost impossible to create a map of contemporary Italian poetry, but, in the Anthologies of the Flies,[20] Beppe Cavatorta and I venture to sketch some portolan charts, some incipient maps. We don't know what the continent is, but we have charted a section of its coast. Whatever goes on inland, is beyond our grasp. For instance, we sighted a group of people who chose to confront media language and turn it around. The language deployed by the media is practically meaningless, but poets like Marco Giovenale, Alessandro Broggi, Michele Zaffarano, Gherardo Bortolotti have proceeded to decontextualize it and re-assemble syntagms borrowed from diverse, unrelated, but always recognizable specimens of journalist prose

NB: Marjorie Perloff summed this up by saying we are at "an exciting threshold moment." One interesting parallel she drew was between John Ashbery's and Mariano Bàino's poetry. There seems to be more back and forth between the U.S. and Italy now, more shared experience than there used to be. I like a term Bernstein uses in what will be an introductory text for *The Flies*, volume 2—he says, "What's striking, in reading the poetics and poems gathered here, is the way these frequencies merge, clash, and morph" (*Echo* 145). I think "frequencies" is a good term because people may not even know that others are on that same frequency. He also suggests "searching" as a less laboratory-like term than "research poetry."

LB: Yes, the term *poesia di ricerca* is only one of the labels. Daniele Poletti objects to the term and suggests *writing of complexity*. I myself am partial to *poesia alla ricerca* – akin to Bernstein's *re-searching poetry*. There's a very lively "nominalistic" debate going on around this issue.

NB: Here's another quote that I really like, which seems to describe research poetry or the poetry of complexity. This is from Alfredo Giuliani in 1965. He said: "Whatever his political and sociological interests, the poet must above all study the influences, the signs, the wounds that this language wields over him," which reminds me of what you were saying about knowing your own history.[21] Here, he's talking about the fact that language is acting on us, too—again, as

---

[20] *Those Who from Afar Look Like Flies: An Anthology of Italian Poetry from Pasolini to the Present*, University of Toronto Press, Vol. 1 2017, vol. 2 forthcoming.

[21] EN: See Giuliani, Alfredo. "Introduction to the Second Edition of I Novissimi" (1965). *I Novissimi. Poetry for the Sixties*. Translated by David Jacobson, Sun and Moon Press, 1995, pp. 41–57.

Jack Spicer said, "My vocabulary did this to me."[22] But to return to the connections between the two literatures: you were drawn to American poetry long ago. Which American poets have been really important to you?

LB: Well, the two most important poets of my life have been Ezra Pound and Wallace Stevens, for two completely different reasons. I don't think I would exist as a poet without them. I wish I had the subtlety of Stevens, which I don't. He's so far superior to anybody I know. And sometimes it's very simple. He moves some spatial observations to temporal ones, and he is always so very agile, light, and *always* bewildering. "Poetry is a finikin thing of air / That lives uncertainly and not for long, / Yet radiantly beyond much lustier blurs."[23] You have the notion that poetry is a blurring of lust, aimed at surpassing it . Don't ask me to be specific. But I know it makes sense, sense out made out of sensation. Now, that is number one to me, that kind of language. The second is that I believe that poetry ought to be rooted in history, and that's where Pound comes in. I mean, Pound's neo-epic poetry. I've always dreamed of combining these two great poets. Even though I started with Charles Olson. Thanks to Olson, I also got into the neo-avant-garde. Because Pagliarani translated *The Distances* by Olson into Italian, and his English was not up to it. So, I volunteered and said, I'll do the rough translations for you. And he turned it into beautiful poetry. [...] And then I met Alfredo Giuliani, a very subtle creator of pseudo-signifiers. In the beginning I was overwhelmed by their presence, but then we became friends and my tongue loosened. The fact is that prior to my meeting up with them I was a devoted reader of realistic novels. In poetry I did not venture far from Montale. It took me a while to realize that the greatest Italian poet of the forties was Emilio Villa, whose books were published by perhaps the smallest presses, and were very had to find. But *geduld überwindet alles*. Of course. So, it was a major change for me, at age twenty-three or twenty-four. Actually, in the beginning, I resisted it. I thought these poets were if not crazy, cvertainly beyond the pale. It took me a long time. Now, I've written ten essays on Pagliarani. And I think I'm beginning to understand [laughs],

---

[22] EN: See Jack Spicer's *My Vocabulary Did This to Me. The Collected Poetry of Jack Spicer.* Edited by Peter Gizzi and Kevin Killian. Wesleyan UP, 2010.

[23] EN: See Stevens, Wallace. "Like Decorations in a Nigger Cemetery," *Poetry. A Magazine of Verse*, 45, 5, February 1935, p. 235. For obvious reasons, this is a conspicuously under-studied poem. Several contemporary African American poets have read and wrote back to, and around, Stevens's poetry: among them Rickey Laurentiis, whose "Of the Leaves That Have Fallen" directly confronts "Like Decorations," and Terrance Hayes in his "Snow for Wallace Stevens."

but I no longer confuse meaning with signified referentiality. But to go back to your question [...] Stevens and Pound and some Williams ... that's been my pasture more so than Italian poetry—except for medieval Italian poetry which has always been phenomenally important to me: Cavalcanti and Dante, but above all Cavalcanti, on whom I've also written several essays. But then, you know, there we go again—Cavalcanti comes to me through Pound. [...]

NB: Here's a quote that allows us to see the parallels between American poetry, specifically L=A=N=G=U=A=G=E poets like Charles Bernstein, and Italian research poetry. This is what Michael Davidson says in the commentary on language poetry in *Poems for the Millennium*:

> By thwarting traditional reading and interpretive habits, the poet encourages the reader to regard language not simply as a vehicle for preexisting meanings, but as a system with its own rules and operations. However, since that system exists in service to ideological interests of the dominant culture, any deformation forces attention onto the material basis of meaning production within that culture. If such a goal seems utopian, it has a precedent in earlier avant-garde movements, from symbolism to futurism and Surrealism. Rather than seeking a language beyond rationality by purifying the words of the tribe or by discovering new languages of irrationality, language poetry has made its horizon the material form rationality takes. (vol. 2, 663)

So, rather than an essentialist or utopian project, its work is much more like research poetry.

LB: Exactly. The idea of purifying language is so arrogant. There's a beautiful poem by Wallace Stevens, "The creations of sound," in which he says we have to make silence dirtier still!

New York, March 24th, 2023.

Day 1 – Friday, November 11, 2022

Marjorie Perloff

The Reappearing Pheasant: Opening Address

I begin with a text by Marco Giovenale called *"they were in danger"*:

> Nearly everyone by now goes through a nose job. Nearly everyone speaks when the argument is hot. Nearly everyone takes up residence abroad. Nearly everyone becomes poor again. Nearly all the rich are at rock bottom. Nearly all the poor wage war among the poor. Nearly all the sick are dying but nearly all the nearly dead sometimes come back to life. Nearly all the poised assholes fall miserably or fall not miserably. Nearly all the common denominators divide in the thick of it. Nearly everyone knows it. Nearly everyone has some knowledge of it. A wisdom of sorts. Nearly all the dividends had vanished from the balance sheet way before then. Nearly everyone in principle. Nearly everything had happened way before then. Nearly everything was already finished when you arrived. Nearly everything in principle. Nearly everyone notices one thing. Nearly everyone challenges it even before opening it up for discussion. At this point Nearly everyone shows a preference for Africa. Nearly everyone has their luggage ready at hand. Nearly everyone prefers to ship it. Nearly everyone nourishes some mistrust. Nearly everyone is depressed and Nearly everyone knows it. Nearly everyone will be in a matter of minutes. Nearly everyone is an enemy of Nearly everyone else. Nearly everyone has an enemy at home. You know Nearly all of them. Nearly everyone was here when you arrived. Nearly everyone emphasizes difference. Nearly everyone finds it hard to obtain a mortgage. Nearly everyone gets it. Nearly everyone is a criminal. Nearly everyone is a war criminal. Nearly everyone has decided. Nearly everyone has reached a decisive decision. Nearly everyone keeps their word. Nearly everyone no but Nearly everyone can sense it. Nearly everyone is distracted. Nearly everyone does not see the difference. Nearly everyone on the contrary sees it. Nearly everyone is like this. Nearly everyone is at random. Nearly everyone is caught up in sociology. Nearly everyone has their schedule. Nearly everyone salutes with their right hand. Nearly everyone thinks of pulling it off. Nearly everyone needs to have some words repeated to them. Not everyone, nearly everyone.[1]

---

[1] EN: Excerpt translated by V. Joshua Adams, and taken from "erano in pericolo," in *Quasi tutti*. Miraggi Edizioni, 2018.

Nearly everyone: it is the discourse whispered in our ears every day by the social media, the absurd level of generalization that the Tik Tok crowd recognizes and believes in. Hearing that authoritative "Nearly everyone. . ." we are terrified of being out of step. If nearly everyone salutes with his right hand, I'm safe, aren't I? Nothing different about me!! And in any case, "Nearly everyone is a criminal," so why worry? We all recognize the absurdity—but also the familiarity—of these Gertrude Steinian repetitions and variations, perhaps produced by the Google Grinder, as Giovenale calls it. Algorithms and statistics rule our day, never mind how they have been manufactured or arrived at. And in that wonderful punchline at the end, the speaker protects himself with the disclaimer, "Not everyone." What a great way of covering our tracks, of making sure we cannot be accused of anything. And, in a special irony, "Nearly everyone emphasizes difference," which is to say they (we) are in fact exactly alike, doing the same thing, and terrified that they will somehow be excluded from the pack! Yes, as the title tells us, "They were in danger."

If Giovenale's "Fast Track Living"[2] brings to mind a comparable American poem, it might well be one of Charles Bernstein's poems: for example, "Errata" in *Topsy-Turvy*:

> For "red" read "I should not have done it, should have left it alone. I don't know what came over me or why I could not, try as I might, overcome it. For "oceanic" read "leeward, as when the ball dribbles its way to the center of the earth and the heart barely hears its own beat but never fails to heed yours." For "lard" read "a studied casualness that disguises genuine casualness." For "incandescent" read "drowned in love's apposite fortunes, leering at gushes in the gust of a fragrance." [...] For "crustacean" read "crustacean." For "you be my gracious refuge now, song" read "why do you rouse my soul and stir up the past? Be merciful desist, desist, let the embers of my joy be." For "daemonic dispossession" read "season of mist and mellow fruitfulness." (21)

At the back of both these poems (as of Tommaso Ottonieri's and Alessandro Broggi's), we can always hear the winged chariot of social media, where input is likely to produce the most bizarre output, as I discovered the other day when I found in a Facebook post the imperative, "Stand tall!" and realized from the context that the transcription was meant to refer to a famous novelist, namely Stendhal.

---

[2] EN: See the corresponding poem in the poetry section for Day One.

Giovenale and Bernstein: in the age of Internet, I think our symposium will show that our two poetries, Italian and American have come closer together; they even overlap. It was not always thus. In 1991, some thirty years ago, when Luigi Ballerini organized *The Disappearing Pheasant*, the two poetries were in a very different place. In Italy, the personal lyric still predominated although there were poets like Biagio Cepollaro and Milli Graffi who were experimenting with street slang, dialect, and especially the vernacular. In the U.S., it was the moment of language poetry, at least in the case of the poets invited: Bruce Andrews, Charles Bernstein, Lyn Hejinian, and, from the earlier generation, Barbara Guest, Jackson MacLow, and Jerome Rothenberg.

Among the Americans and their students in the audience, Marxist theory, central to the first phase of language poetry, was very much in evidence. And because Marxism was one of the differentiae between language poetry and its enemy, official verse culture (made up, so it was felt, of countless trivial lyric epiphanies), the American contingent was, perhaps subconsciously, a bit condescending to the Italians, implying that the latter weren't quite hip enough or theoretical enough to know that the love sonnet or meditative nature poem was passé.

But then something remarkable happened. The second morning, Thomas Harrison, then at Penn, now at U.C.L.A., stood up and gave a stinging rebuke to the U.S. team. "Don't lecture us about Marxism," I recall Tom telling the group, "we knew all about Marxism long before you people even started writing poetry." And of course, it was true: in the decades after World War II, in the days of Eurocommunism, strong in Italy, the Left set the literary tone. To be an intellectual or artist was ipso facto to be on the Left. Poets may not have cited Derrida or Althusser, but they read Gramsci and, more important, Marx himself. So, when Tom—himself the son of an American father and Italian mother and brought up in Rome before he came to study at Sarah Lawrence and CUNY—made his little speech, a hush fell over the audience that was never quite resolved. The accused poets felt alternately guilty and angry at being called naïve. And accordingly, there wasn't very much exchange between the two parties.

In 2022, the situation is very different. In the U.S., the current stress on racial as well as gender identity has displaced the strong case made by the L=A=N=G=U=A=G=E writers for a poetry in which, to quote Charles Bernstein, "there is no natural look or sound to a poem. Every element is intended, chosen."³ The situation is now much more eclectic and fluid. Subject matter has come to dominate in ways we haven't known since the 1930s, when much poetry, now largely forgotten, was versified political statement and manifesto. And the calling into question of universal truth and the transcendental ego that characterized the age of theory, has been replaced by often vitriolic discourse about discrimination and oppression, as if to say, yes, we do have the answers, we do know THE TRUTH or at least we should.

When "poetry" qua poetry is defended, it is often at a kind of greeting card level: poetry, generically speaking, is good for you rather like therapy or yoga; indeed, poetry, in a formulation already put forward in the Victorian age by Matthew Arnold, is what has replaced religion. Recently, a book came across my desk published by our most distinguished presses, Farrar, Straus and Giroux, called *The Wonder Paradox: Embracing the Weirdness of Existence and the Poetry of our Lives* by Jennifer Michael Hecht. Hecht writes that

Poetry may well be the best art to organize our hearts in the absence of religion because of its shared traits with prayer and meditation. It slots right into established habits. It's the right kiss for awakening our sleeping beauty because poetry is

– Language, so it can relate a message or story.
– Free, to break rules and not make clear sense.
– Short, so we can have a moment's encounter with it, over and over.
– Metrical, a trance-inducing percussion instrument.
– Deep, made with creative intensity, expected to reward rereading.
– Intimate, a whispered secret
– Common at celebrations.
– Memorable, due to rhyme, meter, and form.
– Sublime. We call any work of art "a poem" to say it is perfect, balanced, true.⁴

The anti-intellectualism of these absurd formulations is disheartening. Fortunately, in the latest volume of Luigi Ballerini and Giuseppe Cavartorta's *Those Who from Afar Look Like Flies*, the choice of poets and scholarly

---

³ EN: See Andrews, Bruce and Charles Bernstein, editors. *The L=A=N=G=U=A=G=E Book.* Southern Illinois UP, 1984: "There is no natural look or sound to a poem. Every element is intended, chosen. That is what makes a thing a poem. Modes cannot be escaped, but they can be taken for granted. They can also be meant" (44–45).

⁴ EN: See section headed "Your Book of Poetry."

apparatus make it possible to understand what the most interesting Italian poets are doing today. As in the case of our own poets, we are now witnessing a revival of traditional forms—but traditional forms with a notable difference.

Take Mariano Bàino's "Scraps" ("Vrènzole"), cleverly translated by Luigi Bonaffini, which opens with the stanza:

usàbbele, 'nguacchiàte, grigge
juórne: velìnia pe' jì sotto, fàuzo
lettore mio, suóccio a me, frate mio
:velìnia ca fa filòscio
d'ogni portabbannèra.[5]

usable, greasy, gray
days: eggwhite in which to drown, my hypocrite
reader, my brother
:eggwhite that scrambles
every standard bearer.

The playfulness of Bàino's "Scraps" with its witty allusions and appropriations reminds me of our New York School, especially such Frank O'Hara poems as "Naphtha" ("I am ashamed of my century / but I have to smile") or "Song (Is it dirty)."[6] The "usable, greasy, gray /days" in which this scene occurs (the English nicely conveys the alliteration and assonance of the original *usàbbele, 'nguacchiàte, grigge / juórne*), set the stage for the poet's perception that he is drowning in eggwhite—a wonderfully absurd idea since raw eggwhite is a sticky substance that allows no easy passage through its whitish jelly. The address to "my hypocrite / reader, my brother" comes from Baudelaire's *Fleurs du Mal* (*hypocrite lecteur, mon semblable, mon frère*), but Bàino doesn't dwell on that apostrophe's bitterly ironic intent, moving on instead, to the notion of the eggwhite scrambling so as to destroy "every standardbearer"—the guardian of the flag or keeper of the flame. And further, the reference to drowning recalls another poet who cites Baudelaire's famous "hypocrite lecteur" line—

---

[5] EN: Excerpt taken from *Ônne 'e terra*. Pironti, 1994; Zona, 2003. Here is the Italian translation: "usabili, unti, grigi / giorni: albume per annegare, ipocrita / lettore, mio simile, mio fratello /: albume che fa frittata / di ogni alfiere."

[6] EN: Written in 1959, "Naphtha" appeared in the journal *Big Table* in 1960, and later with "Song (Is it dirty)" in *Lunch Poems*. 1964. The Pocket Poets Series: Number 19. Expanded 50th Anniversary Edition, City Lights Books, 2014, pp. 20, 25.

namely the T. S. Eliot of *The Waste Land*. Then, too, the phrase "eggwhite in which to drown" recalls another Eliot poem, "The Love Song of J. Alfred Prufrock," whose famous last line is "Till human voices wake us and we drown."

Indeed, "Scraps" delineates a kind of Waste Land, though a comic one, its allusive, carefully constructed surface full of references to such things as being "jaundiced like other parrots." But the most intriguing device in the quoted stanza above is the colon that precedes "eggwhite" ("velìnia"). In standard prose, colons follow clauses or phrases: they throw the meaning forward to the next section. But here the colon is oddly used at the beginning of a new phrase, where it serves to announce the making of the omelette that complicates the relation of "my brother" to the "eggwhite that scrambles." Indeed, the language throughout Bàino's poem is one of self-deprecating humor and studied colloquialism. As O'Hara put it in his pseudo-manifesto "Personism": "You just go on your nerve"—a prescription that sounds easy to follow but isn't.[7]

For a poet like Bàino, the "I" is no longer subject but an object, along with other objects—something to be dissected from an external perspective as the ego dissolves. Much of our own recent poetry is built on the same premise. The Romantic lyric, openly opposed in the U.S. by poets from John Ashbery to the L=A=N=G=U=A=G=E and Conceptual poets, has made a surprising come-back—but a comeback with a difference. Craig Dworkin put that difference very well in his essay "The Fate of Echo":

> Despite the genuinely contrarian and oppositional stance of contemporary uncreative writing in its open rejection of some of the fundamental characteristics of poetry, the resulting texts frequently evince far more conservative and traditional poetic values than most of what passes for mainstream poetry: the formalist artifice of measure and rhyme (if not in the form of received metrics and patterned end rhymes); classical rhetorical tropes of anaphora, apostrophe, and irony [...]; the evidentiary disclosure of the writer's most private activities (if not in the melodramatic style of the psychological confession); and more than a few passages of unexpectedly, heartbreakingly raw emotion, undiluted by even a trace of sentiment. In addition, if these poems are not referential in the sense of any conventionally realistic diegesis, they point more directly to the archival

---

[7] EN: See "Personism. A Manifesto." *The Collected Poems of Frank O'Hara*. 1971. University of California Press, 1995, pp. 498–499. Originally written on September 3, 1959, for Donald Allen's *New American Poetry* but turned down for its frivolity, the manifesto later appeared in *Yugen*, no. 7, 1961.

record of popular culture and colloquial speech than any avant-pop potboiler or Wordsworthian ballad ever dreamed. (xlv)[8]

Consider, in this regard, the use of anaphora and appropriation in the lyric of Peter Gizzi. The remarkable poem "Revival," for example, opens with the lines:

> It's good to be dead in America
> with the movies, curtains and drift,
> the muzak in the theater.
> It's good to be in a theater waiting
> for The Best Years of Our Lives to begin.[9]

"Revival" was conceived as an elegy for Gregory Corso, the famed Beat poet who died of cancer in 2001. In its original small-press version, the poem has an epigraph from Corso's own elegy ("Elegiac Feelings American") for Jack Kerouac: "What happened to you O friend, happened to America."[10] For the volume *Some Values of Landscape and Weather*, Gizzi removed the line, no doubt because it seems a shade sentimental, histrionic. His own lyric quickly leaves Corso aside, indeed quickly leaves elegy, as we know it, aside in order to take up the cultural phenomena that both shape and mirror the poet's inner (but hidden) self. His first line, repeated throughout as refrain, inverts the expected cheery "It's good to be alive in America," defining the poet's consciousness at a time when, as the poem puts it, "All the codes have been compromised."

And indeed, the poet's inner life is presented, not according to the Wordsworthian formula of "the spontaneous overflow of powerful feelings" or even "emotion recollected in tranquillity,"[11] but as a documentary catalogue of the films, poems, music, and artworks that the poet takes as central to his being. The cited titles are themselves ironic: the first, "The Best Years of our Lives," is one of the finest postwar films about return to civilian life after World War II, the three principals having given "the best years" of their lives to the years

---

[8] EN: See the second introduction to *Against Expression: An Anthology of Conceptual Writing*. Northwestern UP, 2011, pp. xxiii–liv.

[9] EN: See Gizzi's *Some Values of Landscape and Weather*. Wesleyan UP, 2003, pp. 47–52.

[10] EN: See Corso's eponymous *Elegiac Feelings American*. New Directions Publishing, 1970, pp. 3–12.

[11] EN: See Wordsworth's 1802 essay "Preface to the Lyrical Ballads," the de facto manifesto of Romanticism.

of conflict, and now struggling to survive. Or are the "best years" in the end the ones we witness in the film itself? How, in any case, can it be good to be "lost among pillars of grass"—an allusion not only to Whitman but to the line "To be lost among thirteen hundred pillars of grass," in John Ashbery's "They Dream Only of America"?[12]

Memory, in this new lyric, refers not to past incidents, events, or emotions—the poet tells us nothing about his own private life—but is made up of echoes of one's film viewing and reading. "How come," the poet asks, "all the best thoughts / are images? How come all the best images / are uncanny?" How, this pseudo-elegy asks, does the poet now express his deepest feelings? And the answer, as Gizzi puts it, echoing Wallace Stevens, whose "The Man on the Dump" he has quoted earlier in the poem, is "to collect rubble at the perimeter, hoping to build a house, "part snow, part victory." "The wise man," Stevens had put it in the last line of the long "Like Decorations in a [Country] Cemetery," "avenges by building his city in snow." Just so, Gizzi's speaker finds himself "stitching frames / to improvise a document: / all this American life." The poet IS what he has seen and read, and "since all the codes are compromised," confusion, chaos, and contingency reign. At the same time, the recitation of names and phrases gives the poet the strength to go on, to construct his own cities in snow. It is an equivocal "victory."

Gizzi's "cities of snow" find their counterpart in poems like Antonella Anedda's long and elegiac "Winter Residences," in which prose sections alterate with stark, hallucinatory images of war, bodily damage, and pain.[13] In her *Paris Review* interview with Susan Stewart, Anedda comments on the role her native Sardinia has played in her poetry:

> Geology has made me aware of the insignificance of human presence, of the absence of an intelligent design. The landscape of La Maddalena and Sardinia is harsh and barren and windswept. The vegetation is sparse, but also, often enough, scarred by arson, for humans have wounded the landscape as well. Since the early eighteenth century, when Sardinia was ruled by the House of Savoy, systematic deforestation was the policy. At the same time, I fully understand what Andrea Zanzotto means when he writes, "No, you never betrayed me, [landscape]"—his work registers an invocation that becomes painful when the landscape is wounded by greed and speculation. The strikethrough suggests how landscape has been scarred. [...] I'm not talking about arcadia or the world

---

[12] EN: See Ashbery's *The Tennis Court Oath*. Wesleyan UP, 1962.

[13] EN: See Anedda's *Residenze invernali*. Stamperia Bulla, 1989; Crocetti, 1992.

of idylls, but instead about the landscape that surrounds us and reminds us that we are not the masters of the natural world. It is an ethical condition. What is happening to the landscape in Sardinia and elsewhere is deeply worrying. Landscape has a relation, a spatial relation, to rhythm in poetry.[14]

Here the reference to Zanzotto's strikethrough of "landscape" is especially interesting: like Zanzotto, Anedda is ambivalent about the landscape, the natural world. "By putting aside my 'I,'" she remarks, "observing not myself but the world around me, I have learned to believe precisely in living." And so, her "1991," whose title refers to the dissolution of the U.S.S.R. after 1989 and the future of the Baltic Republics—a subject eerily apropos today—, the fear of the future is always that of a "we," not an "I."

> In nessun tempo c'è bisogno di noi
> le notte verticali
> e il viale del tigli, la lepre
> transparente nel cespuglio
> la schiena-ombra di chi allora sostava
>
> At no time is there need for us
> the vertical nights
> and the linden tree lined walkway, the hare
> transparent in the bush
> the back-shadow of those who were waiting then.[15]

Here the English translation nicely mirrors the effect of Anedda's intricate sound structuring "verticali," "viale del tigli," "lepre," "cespuglio" rendered as "vertical," "linden," lined," "walkway"—focusing on the way geographical locale defines emotion. Language, in this scheme of things, is kept at a distance:

> Ogni tanto uso una lingua mia
> la invento impastandola al passato
> non la consegno se non in traduzione.[16]
>
> Once in a while I use a language of mine
> I invent it, kneading it with the past
> I don't hand it over except in translation.

---

[14] EN: See "Antonella Anedda. The Art of Poetry. No. 109." *Paris Review*, no. 234, Fall 2020.

[15] EN: Translated by Eleonora Buonocore.

[16] EN: See Anedda's "Limbas." *Historiae*. Einaudi, 2018, p. 5.

Ezra Pound called his *Cantos* "a poem containing history." Anedda might call her sequences poems containing geography, or ecology. Their language, in any case, is always "impastandola al passato," never directly transparent. In a related vein, Luigi Ballerini, whose *Cefalonia,* incidentally, is an important "poem containing history," has also derived inspiration from a seemingly "other" activity—namely, sports. His sequence "Track Cycling and Road Cycling" has ten sections that use intricate sound structures to capture the feel of racing—whether bike or motor car racing or, for that matter, running.[17] Here is section VI, which is an unrhymed sonnet:

>Corse in pista e su strada
>chilometro lanciato, da lanciare, che, lancia
>in resta, lanceremo, che lanceranno in cielo
>in terra in mare, che slanceranno, questa
>parola in disordine, imbeccata, e che sarà
>bramosa e sugosa e brulicante, un rigoglio
>di adeguate sussistenze, coi cani al guinzaglio
>con vene terse, una pioggia d'estate, barocca,
>un'amnistia che viene di traverso, che aprirà,
>col violino, la prigione dei fuochi produttivi,
>degli amori incalliti, contagiosi, una sabbia
>prudente, difettiva, ma in vena di scherzi,
>di origini, di defezioni omologhe, o quatto
>quatto e sganciato, che sgancia e presta, che
>sganceranno, sopra li quattro maltirati stracci

>Track Cycling and Road Cycling
>kilometer to launch, for launching, with
>lance in rest we will launch and be launched
>in air land and sea, we will launch out this
>spoon-fed, disordered word that will also be
>yearnful, juicy and teeming, a lushness of
>adequate victuals, a dog on a leash with sour
>and fiendish veins, a baroque summer rain,
>an amnesty gone down the wrong way, opening
>with violins, a jailhouse of productive fires,
>hardened, contagious loves, a disruptive,
>cautious but playful sand in the mood for
>dancing, for defections, hushed and unhooked,

---

[17] EN: See *Il terzo gode*. Marsilio Editore, 1994.

unhooking and landing and twirling to be unhooked
from spinning upon some four ill-timed rags[18]

The translators have done wonders in rendering Ballerini's sound play and punning: "launch," "launching" give way to "lance"—in Italian the words *lancia* (noun) and lancia (third-person singular verb) are the same—and then to more cognates of "launch" so as to make the actual speed of motion concrete. There follows a sequence of metaphors for the *feel* of making one's way in the race of bikes around the track, "a dog on a leash with sour / and fiendish veins, a baroque summer rain," and so on, until the "defections, hushed and unhooked / unhooking and landing and twirling to be unhooked" takes place. The reader participates in the onomatopoeic soundscape (*quatto e sganciato, che sgancia e presta, che/ sganceranno*), racing along with the poet. Ballerini's poem is an interestingly public lyric, identity defined vis-à-vis physical sensation and action, rather like in Boccioni's Futurist compositions of racing cars and trains. It is a bravura exercise in sounding the self.

One of the most interesting poems from the New Millennium section of the second volume of *Those Who from Afar Look Like Flies* is Alba Donati's elegy for the children killed in the Beslan school siege, which began on September 1, 2004, and lasted three days, involving the imprisonment of over one-thousand people, two-thirds of them children, as hostages, many of whom were killed. The siege in question began when a group of armed Chechen separatists occupied School Number One in the town of Beslan, North Ossetia (an autonomous republic in the Caucasus). On the third day of the standoff, Russian security forces stormed the building with tanks and rockets and ended the attempted coup. Needless to say, Donati's poem anticipates what is now going on in Ukraine.

In a note at the end of her poem, Donati tells us that she conceived her Beslan poem as a "reworking of an anonymous Russian text, an epic story of the invasion of the Mongol Golden Horde, heirs of Genghis Khan, that destroyed Ryazan in 1237." But she also thanks Giampaolo Visetti, correspondent for *La Repubblica*, whose reports from Beslan impressed her with their absence of rhetoric, their straightforward reportage. "These two pre-texts," she

---

[18] EN: Translated by Thomas Harrison and Jeremy Parzen.

notes, "have given me support, helping me to write what is already written, without the annoying and culpable risk of inventing and poeticizing."[19]

Donati's words recall Craig Dworkin's "Fate of Echo," but we might stop to consider what a curious view of the poetic function this really is. Aren't poets by definition creators? Don't we want our poets to invent, to poeticize? In the Digital Age, perhaps not. Conceptual poets like Dworkin and Kenneth Goldsmith have argued that *invention* is no longer the goal, given the glut of information available to all of us with a single click or two on the computer. In Donati's case, the aim is not to invent lyric language, but to reframe existing language from the newspapers or other sources like photographs so as to create a new way of looking at familiar data. Context, in this instance, is all.

Donati takes the reader step by step through a series of numbered sections, detailing the particular slaughter of the innocents that is her subject. "Pianto sulla distruzione di Beslan" ("Grief on the Destruction of Beslan") is a catalogue poem, a seemingly neutral listing of what happened:

> 2. Quello tornato. Quella scelta.
> Quello con i fiori tra le braccia nella foto in rete. Quello andato. Questa che canta
> [prima di entrare.
> Questa festa per tutto il paese. Quello dentro.
> Quello uscito con i vestiti del padre morto.
> Quello che li spingeva. Quella che salta in aria
> con i bambini per mano. Inaudita. Fatta.
>
> 2. He who returned. That choice.
> That boy holding flowers in the online photo. He who's gone. She who sings
> [before going in.
> This celebration for the whole town. He inside.
> He who left with his dead father's clothes.
> He who pushed them. She who blows herself up
> with children in her arms. Unheard of. Done.[20]

Here the sequence of simple declarative sentences or phrases recall film stills where we see X and then Y and then Z. But she intersperses in her reportage such lines as the following quotation, found on a prison wall: "'I'd learn Rus-

---

[19] EN: Translated by Richard Dixon, see *Those Who from Afar Look Like Flies*, Tome II. For the original, see Alba Donati, "Pianto sulla distruzione di Beslan." *Idillio con cagnolino*. Fazi, 2013.

[20] EN: Translated by Richard Dixon.

sian if only just because it was the language of Lenin' / Vladimir Mayakovski" (Part 6), reminding us of the original hopes of Russia's great avant-garde poet for the future of the Revolution—hopes long since ground to dust. The forty-two short sections of the elegy work to produce a sense of the cyclical: it happened in the days of Genghis Khan, it happened in 2004, no doubt it will happen again. All we can do is celebrate and mourn the dead. "Who will not despair," we read, "for so many dead"?

Donati has produced a striking elegy. But, in conclusion, I can't help feeling a bit uneasy about this new "poetry" made largely from the already existing language of news reports by those who are, after all, experiencing the events in question at second hand. Can't documentary film, to take a different art form, record such disasters more fully and convincingly? Think of a film like *The Battle of Algiers* or, to take a fictional example, the French TV series about D.G.S.E. intelligence operations, *Le Bureau?* Or the remarkable Israeli video series *Fauda*, which presents us with horrifying—but often absurdly funny—images of the Israeli Defense Force at work. In this climate, what can *poetry* as the language art do better than video or film? And what will future poetic movements look like? Will others follow Marco Giovenale, who is now composing primarily asemic poetry as is the Polish-Danish poet Grzegorz Wroblewski? The pheasant, in any case, is reappearing, providing us with answers to these questions and raising new ones. It is an exciting threshold moment for both our poetries and we Americans have much to learn from our Italian counterparts.

Andrea Cortellessa (Translated by Thomas E. Peterson)

The Nightmare of the Novissimi

To the working title of the organizers, "The Legacy of the Neo-Avant-Garde," I have given a hopefully not-too-tendentious twist: "The Nightmare of the Novissimi." I am not the first to use it, as this was the title of a *performance* given in the spring of 1977 by Gregorio Scalise, a Calabrian poet in the Bolognese *milieu*, during a revue of theatricalized readings curated by Franco Cordelli at Beat 72, a historic *cave* of the Roman theatrical avant-garde during the previous fifteen years. In the early 1960s, for example, the talent of Carmelo Bene was all the rage. As the readings proceeded, some of the most frightening clashes of that violent season were taking place "upstairs" on the city streets. Thus, poetry chose to sink into an "aside" of history in a way perhaps not that different from how, in the aftermath of 1968, Corrado Costa, Giulia Niccolai, and Adriano Spatola had done at Mulino di Bazzano: they had not wanted to follow Nanni Balestrini (with whom they had shared the experience of "Quindici") in his more militant political trajectory. The "Plan for a *Maison Poétique*," physically located below ground, elaborated by Spatola some years earlier together with the very young Claudio Parmiggiani, also demonstrates how a fantasy of "elocutionary disappearance of the subject"[1] pre-existed that split and was instead the secret partner, so to speak, of the ever more pronounced political *engagement* professed by the poetic neo-avant-garde in the course of the 1960s.

In the late 1970s, however, the season of performances at least appeared to mean the exact opposite of the "disappearance" predicated in his day by Mallarmé. The presence and bodily posture of the poet were openly "textualized." The theatrical direction seemed the most appropriate after a decade, the

---

[1] EN: See Mallarmé's "Crise de vers" (1897): "L'œuvre pure implique la disparition élocutoire de poète, qui cède l'initiative aux mots, par le heurt de leur inégalité mobilisés" (246).

1960s, rightly or wrongly considered "all intellect." Even though not everyone agreed with this, which Porta called the "choice of voice." Among the protagonists of that season, Andrea Zanzotto, for example, took a contrary position.[2] It is not by chance that, in the aftermath of his tragic end, Pier Paolo Pasolini was unanimously chosen as the patron saint and martyr of this attitude. But the performances of Beat 72, with the avant-garde tradition connoted by that location, were very *sui generis*. The theatrical was not simply a metaphor but a genuine *mise-en-scène* of the poet as "object" (almost an *objet trouvé*, in fact, by the sadistic Cordelli). The photos of Agnese De Donato and Giorgio Piredda documented Scalise's *performance* and were included the following year in the unique book "fuoriformato" (not an essay, not a novel, not a *reportage* but a bit of all these together) that Cordelli culled from the experience, giving it an emblematic title, *Il poeta postumo* (*The Posthumous Poet*).[3] Others are also documented, including Dario Bellezza, Maurizio Cucchi, Gino Scartaghiande, Cesare Viviani, and Valentino Zeichen, many of whom had been included two years earlier in the anthology edited by Cordelli with Alfonso Berardinelli: *Il pubblico della poesia*.[4] Those catacumbal readings of 1977 surprisingly served as a dialectical premise to the no less sociologically eloquent season of the maximum *jouissance* and not-to-be repeated mass success of Italian poetry. In June 1979, this culminated with three incredible evening swims—on the final night, they counted 30,000 spectators, mostly nude—on the Lazio beach of Castelporziano. Cordelli also drew from this "international festival of poets" a book, edited by him together with Ulisse Benedetti and the late Simone Carella, as paradoxical as *Il poeta postumo* but, unlike that explosive and euphoric book, bitter and turned in on itself: starting with the title stolen from Nabokov, *Proprietà perduta* (*Lost Property*).[5]

---

[2] EN: See Andrea Zanzotto's *Vissuto poetico e corpo* (1980) and *Poesia e televisione* (1989) found in *Le Poesie e Prose scelte*. Edited by Stefano Dal Bianco and Gian Mario Villalta. Mondadori, 1999, pp. 1249–1251, 1320–1331.

[3] EN: See Cordelli, Franco. *Il poeta postumo. Manie, pettegolezzi, rancori*. Lerici, 1978. Le Lettere, 2008.

[4] EN: See *Il pubblico della poesia*. Edited by Franco Cordelli and Alfonso Berardinelli. Lerici, 1975.

[5] EN: See Cordelli, Franco. *Proprietà perduta*. Guanda Editore, 1983. The title is a reference to Nabokov's first English novel, *The Real Life of Sebastian Knight*, published in 1941, where the protagonist V. discusses a fictitious book titled *Lost Property* by his half-brother Sebastian Knight.

Scalise's *performance*, held on May 7, 1977, is recalled by its director as a "triumph: an epiphany, a surprise explosion." In *Il poeta postumo*, Cordelli remembers the event, above all, for its theatrical proxemics, modeled on that of the Last Supper, which "was also the Last Scene." Was it then the transmission of an apostolate? Or the staging of a betrayal? If so, would that betrayal also be remembered, *a posteriori*, as the necessary premise for survival, a transfiguration?

Cordelli, as on other evenings and then again at Castelporziano, cast himself as a waiter—or, wishing to mythologize as was his custom, a cupbearer—pouring wine for those at the tables. Thus, he writes, "Who was Judas, Scalise or Cordelli?" (*Il poeta postumo* 97). One can also ask who was Christ. Was he perhaps the *lògos*, embodied by the book covers with the unmistakable graphics of Feltrinelli's "Materiali" series scattered over the table of that Last Supper?

The fact is that, as Cordelli continues,

> The wine, as always, went to the head. The audience took over. Scalise gave his guests some verses from collections of 'very new poets.' Among those reading were Prestigiacomo, Bellezza, Perlini, Serrao, women poets, feminists, elderly actors, young aspirants, and Rossella Or. First, everyone read in turn, some naturalistically, some parodically. Then, a guest, Ferroni, got up from the table and began to walk and recite, like an old professor, an old trombone. Finally, the word was taken from his mouth; Bellezza snatched it from Ferroni, as Prestigiacomo did from Bellezza, Rossella from Prestigiacomo, and the actor from the

actress. It was a Babel of languages, chance, the loss of semanticity, as would have been said fifteen years ago. This time, perhaps, and completely by chance, the contents of the happening mirrored faithfully its thematic contents. Wasn't the 'linguistic Babel' a theoretical presupposition of the Novissimi? Nothing had been foreseen, and everything was so faithful, so extraordinarily, insolently homogeneous. The pure repetition, on diverse planes, of the same structural mechanism... (97)

The situation, which gets out of control by subverting the canonical separation between the reader and the listener, anticipates with singular exactness the chaos, which in its aftermath will be seen as far less amusing, of two years later on the beach of Castelporziano. But above all, it denies, in the eyes of those like ourselves for whom this scene is ulteriorly *posthumous*, the implicit assumption, *in votis*, of the *performance*: that is, that of overturning the sense of the genitive in the title *The Nightmare of the Novissimi*: "From being the subject, the Novissimi become 'victims,' a pure grammatical object," Cordelli wrote, so that "the nightmare was first 'them,' then it became 'us'" (94–95). Thus, with semi parodical "officialness," Cordelli intended to authorize what he had decreed to be the "experience of liberation from the 1960s that our generation had by then brought to its completion" (94–95). Eloquent, for example, was the situation of Giulio Ferroni, who, in those years, had accompanied his studies of 16th-century mannerism with pioneering essays—never taken up again—on the poetry of Alfredo Giuliani and the prose of Giorgio Manganelli.[6]

Seen today, instead, these images tell us precisely the opposite: by dramatizing not the hoped-for *liberation* but the most complete illustration of a theoretical principle that, formulated a few years earlier, is not cited by Cordelli but whose spirit circulates in his books, as seen in the respective titles, *Il poeta postumo* and *Proprietà perduta*. I am talking about *The Anxiety of Influence*, theorized in 1973 by Harold Bloom.[7]

---

[6] EN: See Ferroni, Giulio. "La poesia di Alfredo Giuliani o l'impossibilità dell'avanguardia." *La Rassegna della letteratura italiana*, 1, 1970, pp. 90–111; "Giorgio Manganelli." *Novecento. I contemporanei*. Edited by Gianni Grana. vol. X, Marzorati, 1979, pp. 10057–10081; and *Giuliani, Alfredo. L'escrescenza del significante, l'algebra semantica degli oggetti: dall'astrazione fenomenologica al collage, alla manipolazione libido-fecale della lingua tautofonica*. Edited by Gianni Granna. Marzorati, 1983.

[7] EN: See Bloom, Harold. *The Anxiety of Influence. A Theory of Poetry*. Oxford UP, 1973.

In the decade before *The Anxiety of Influence*, the Novissimi had exercised their influence above all, as is evident, on the poets, narrators, and critics of the next generation, as was the case of Scalise (b. 1939) and Cordelli (b. 1943). It is precisely in light of the adverse reactions—such as the one just described, even taking account of its "theatrical" ambiguity—that the "institutional" importance of the Novissimi event in our literary culture is measured. It never ceases to surprise me how all those eager to bash them, even today, sixty years after their publication, do not understand such an elementary mechanism, thus unwillingly making a decisive contribution to their continuing relevance.

When I use this term, *institutional*, I never adopt one of the most cowardly criticisms aimed at the neo-avant-garde, that of having joined together to achieve literary and cultural "power." As Umberto Eco was accustomed to saying, the "dissident friends" of 1961–1963 were already in the institutions: universities, publishers, newspapers, etc.[8] Instead, I adopt a concept of Luciano Anceschi, who, obviously in a phenomenological and not a juridical sense, defined as *institutions of poetry* those "novelties" that, not only in a formal and specifically linguistic sense, establish a *before* and an *after* in the literary world.[9] Or, as Alfredo Giuliani will translate with an emphasis justified by the circumstances in the Preface to the 1965 edition of *I Novissimi*, the "[creation of] an *epoch-making* literary language it will now be impossible to turn back from."[10]

Reasoning with just a touch of dialectical malice, in short, it is precisely the "restoration" that followed it that marked the character of a decisive watershed that, however one wants to judge it, represented the Novissimi "revolution." Paraphrasing a famous, cynical joke by Giulio Andreotti, cultural hegemony "wears down those who don't have it." It is taught once again today by

---

[8] EN: The reference to "amici dissidenti" is to a volume edited by Eugenio Battisti titled "Gli amici dissidenti: Il Gruppo 63 a Reggio Emilia." *Marcatré*, 11–12–13, 1965, pp. 36–52. For Umberto Eco's take on Gruppo 63, see his *Sugli specchi e altri saggi*. Bompiani, 1985: "[Il Gruppo 63] non era una massoneria in cui, con buone raccomandazioni, ci si potesse iscrivere. [...] Era piuttosto come una festa di paese, in cui fa parte chi è presente e partecipa dello spirito generale e del genius loci" (94) ["not a Masonry that you could secretly join if you were recommended by the right people, [...] but rather a village feast, where you join in if you happen to be there and take part of the general atmosphere" (my translation)].

[9] EN: See Anceschi, Luciano. *Le istituzioni della poesia*. Bompiani, 1968.

[10] EN: See Giuliani, Alfredo. "Introduction to the Second Edition of I Novissimi (1965)," *I Novissimi. Poetry for the Sixties*. Translated by David Jacobson. Sun & Moon Press, 1995, p. 50.

the right-wing government that has remained the last in Italy to remember the long-dead leftist hegemony. So, it happened for the neo-avant-garde hegemony over our literary culture. Therefore, one cannot be surprised at the violence of the reaction that, in the following two or three decades, has attempted to restore postures and movements of poetry from a time *well before* the "revolution." In other Western literatures that did not know that revolution, no one would even dream of re-admitting it into their texts. This is not the case for Scalise, whose production, though quite neglected, is among the most interesting ones of his time.[11] It is enough to think of the neo-Dannunzian poses of Giuseppe Conte[12]—a disheveled follower from the start, or, rather, a self-defined "thug" who opposed Anceschi's *Verri*—to get an idea of the reverse backlash, in every sense, that the *Novissimi big bang* produced and, alas, continues to produce to a large degree.

This is also true in another sense. The influence of the Novissimi on what Gilda Policastro called the *last poetry* (with a slippery pun used previously by her mentor Giulio Ferroni) is vast and profound; in certain minor cases, still today, it is all too widespread.[13] Cecilia Bello Minciacchi will talk about that here. But beyond its "negative" impact, as in those who wished to contrast themselves with the Novissimi in an improbable poetic Vendée, on the "positive" side, the post-Novissimi neo-neo-avant-garde, which in the second half of the 1980s gave itself the eloquent name of Gruppo '93, saw the indubitable energy of many of its exponents constrained by the very comparison to the Totem of '63, seen by them as obligatory, and the—in some cases suffocating— embrace of those ex-Novissimi most prominent on the cultural scene of the time. These discussions are also perhaps amusing with respect to the symmetrical reversals of 1963, as the "expiration date" instead of the founding date, or the apostrophe to re-admit before the date from which it takes its title, to point the finger at a conceptual subalternity that is difficult to deny. It is likely that, in a context very different from the mediatic one to which Gruppo '93 aspired and to a certain extent achieved, the so-called "research poetry," of those who

---

[11] EN: See Scalise, Gregorio. *Opera-opera. Poesie scelte 1968–2017*. Sossella, 2007.

[12] EN: See Cortellesa, Andrea. "Giuseppe Conte, l'uomo che volle farsi Re" (2005). *La fisica del senso. Saggi e interventi su poeti italiani dal 1940 a oggi*. Fazi, 2006, pp. 382–285, 592.

[13] EN: See Policastro, Gilda. *L'ultima poesia. Scritture anomale e mutazioni di genere dal secondo Novecento a oggi*. Mimesis, 2021; and Ferroni, Giulio. *Gli ultimi poeti. Giovanni Giudici e Andrea Zanzotto*. Il Saggiatore, 2013.

arrived on the scene later and are today fully active, has greater room for maneuvering by virtue of the limitations imposed on their publishing possibilities and general visibility by the editorial establishment, which they should safeguard, in my opinion, instead of ceaselessly complaining about it. In addition, the Novissimi were indeed not unanimous in encouraging their disciples; for Antonio Porta, whose phenomenological pen-name was an omen, or for Nanni Balestrini with his tireless political activism, or for Elio Pagliarani whose "pedagogical muse"[14] was applied in genuine "laboratories" of poetic writing, I distinctly remember the death sentence pronounced by Edoardo Sanguineti, in Bologna, in 2003: "After us the deluge."

No less paradoxically, however, the "anxiety of influence" exerted by the Novissimi was also *retroactive*. This is the theme on which I would especially like to concentrate in this setting. As in the famous paradox formulated by Borges about Kafka, the Novissimi "invented," or in this case concretely influenced, even their "predecessors."[15] Apart from great old early-20th-century masters like Ungaretti and Palazzeschi, who were no less than venerated by the Novissimi and who, by that semi-posthumous enthusiasm, in their respective final works of the 1960s and 1970s, felt entitled to a happy "return to disorder" (as predicated by Sanguineti),[16] emblematic among all is the case of Montale: the influence of whose "poetics of objects" on the phenomenological framework "in re" of some Novissimi, had been in its day challenging to circumvent. His "scatological" as well as "eschatological" attitude, although divined in him by Andrea Zanzotto[17] already in 1953, is manifest only with *Satura*, a book of 1971 written entirely in the preceding decade: it is here that one finds exasperated once again that vision of the desolate or "devastated"

---

[14] EN: See Raboni, Giovanni. "La musa pedagogica di Pagliarani" (1963). *Poesia degli anni Sessanta*. Editori Riuniti, 1976, pp. 79–81.

[15] EN: See Borges, Jorge Luis. "Kafka and his predecessors" (1951). *Other Inquisitions. 1937–1952*. Translated by Ruth L.C. Simms. University of Texas Press, 1975, pp. 106–108.

[16] EN: A recurrent formula in the critical lexicon of Sanguineti. See, for example, his "Introduzione" to "Parnaso italiano" in *Poesia italiana del Novecento*. Edited by Edoardo Sanguineti. Einaudi, 1969: "Siamo già al momento del proclamato ritorno al disordine che è, per ora almeno, la conclusione di tanta vicenda" ["We already are at the moment of the proclaimed return to disorder, which is, at least for now, the conclusion of so many vicissitudes" (my translation)] (lx).

[17] EN: See Zanzotto's interpretation in "L'inno nel fango" (1953) and "Sviluppo di una situazione montaliana (Escatologia–Scatologia)" (1966). *Fantasie di avvicinamento. Le letture di un poeta*. Mondadori, 1991.

reality, in whose exploration the Sanguineti of the *Palus putredinis* (*Marsh of Decay*) had been a pioneer.

More generally, as Enrico Testa instructs in *Dopo la lirica* (*After the Lyric*),[18] in the 1960s, virtually all the major authors of the generation before the Novissimi see their own language radically modified, and even before that, the ever more masked management of the "best person of the screen" (as Sanguineti, diverting Dante, will define the lyric I).[19] Mario Luzi's "magmatic" turn, coeval with Vittorio Sereni's phenomenological one, Roberto Roversi's "concrete" *Registrazione di eventi* (*Recording of Events*) or even the thingish more than objectual turn of a still neglected master like Bartolo Cattafi (more oblique, but not imperceptible, the reactions of authors such as Caproni, Giudici, Fortini and even Bertolucci).[20] Also, Emilio Villa, whose trajectory precedes albeit slightly the first Novissimi flashes, knows in those years a maximum—not necessarily shareable—of material abstraction and multilingual extremism. Perhaps only Amelia Rosselli, who, for biographical reasons, made contact with the "originals" of the historic avant-gardes before them, carried on apart from her Novissimi peers. Between the multilingual texts of her beginnings and the extraordinary *Variazioni Belliche* (*War Variations*), published in 1964 under the aegis of one who professed to be an archenemy of the Novissimi like Pasolini, her greater extremeness had been formed independently from the "institution" of the neo-avant-garde.[21]

The case of Andrea Zanzotto, the major author of the immediate pre-Novissimi generation, is paradigmatic while also wholly idiosyncratic. This is thanks to the recent archival excavations, partially published in *Il Verri*, of Chiara Portesine, who has dedicated an excellent recent monograph to Sanguineti's inclination to ekphrasis.[22] She documented the samplings at the limit of creative plagiarism—made virtually explicit by the perpetrator—from Sanguineti's *Laborintus* and writings just after, in the elaboration of the "lunar" long poem *Gli Sguardi i Fatti e Senhal* (1969), and more, in general, the "turn" represented by *La Beltà* (*Beauty*) in 1968, "like a first attempt to respond ef-

---

[18] EN: See *Dopo la lirica. Poeti italiani 1960–2000*. Einaudi, 2005.

[19] EN: See Sanguineti's "Codicillo 22" (December 1983). *Il gatto lupesco. Poesie (1982-2001)*. Feltrinelli, 2002, p. 32.

[20] EN: For Roversi, see *Registrazione di eventi*. Rizzoli, 1964.

[21] EN: See Rosselli, Amelia. *Variazioni belliche*. Garzanti, 1964.

[22] EN: See Portesine, Chiara. *"Una specie di Biennale allargata." Il giuoco dell'ecfrasi nel secondo romanzo di Edoardo Sanguineti*. Fabrizio Serra Editore, 2021.

fectively to the neo-avant-garde provocation, passing from words (essays) to facts (of versification)" (106).[23]

Thus, Portesine alludes to the reaction, much less "composed" with respect to the texts of later years, that the release of *I Novissimi*, in the Spring of 1961, had roused in Zanzotto: the public and famous "lambasting" released a bit coldly the following year in *Comunità*,[24] but especially the private one in the letters written by him to his friend, writer and editor Carlo Della Corte and to Anceschi himself, the main sponsor of the anthology and with whom his relations, before and after, will always be marked by the maximum cordiality, and then to the poet and translator Cesare Vivaldi, who was close to the Novissimi.[25] Letters "too full of references to private matters or almost," as Zanzotto says in closing to Anceschi, "which disallow him"—as the director of *Il Verri* would have liked—to send to the magazine "three pages on the Novissimi,"[26] which one can suppose coincide more with the "letter to Anceschi" than to the text of *Comunità*, which will also deviate from that letter by excising some but not all of the "private questions."

The actual critical abreaction provoked in Zanzotto by *I Novissimi* derives especially—I am trying to synthesize in a linear form its twisting, brilliant, and more than usual endophasic almanacking—from the "convivial joke" that escaped from his mouth during a certain cursed dinner in Rome, and, "badly reported by the 'totally deaf,'" but also capricious, Francesco Leonetti in an issue of *Officina* of 1957: Zanzotto's joke about the "nervous exhaustion" that could have been the only possible excuse for Sanguineti's excesses in *Laborintus* (published a year earlier). Sanguineti, already angry with *Officina* and its leader Pasolini, whom he could easily suspect of that polemic, was offended.

---

[23] EN: See Portesine, Chiara. "'Una febbriciattola di lieve paranoia.' Varianti 'novissime' nella *Beltà*." *E l'avanguardia ha trovato, ha trovato? Andrea Zanzotto*. *Il Verri*, no. 77, October 2021, pp. 105–117.

[24] EN: See Zanzotto, Andrea. "I 'Novissimi.'" *Comunità*, no. 99, May 1962, pp. 89–91, later included in *Aure e disincanti nel Novecento letterario*. Mondadori, 1994, pp. 24–29; and now in *Andrea Zanzotto. Scritti sulla letteratura*. Vol II. Edited by Gian Mario Villalta. Mondadori, 2001, pp. 24–29.

[25] EN: See Zanzotto's letters to Anceschi (11 April, 1961) and Cesare Vivaldi (1 July, 1962), transcribed with commentary by Francesco Carbognin and Chiara Portesine in *E l'avanguardia ha trovato, ha trovato? Andrea Zanzotto*. *Il Verri*, no. 77, October 2021, pp. 30–32, 88–89.

[26] EN: See Zanzotto's letter to Luciano Anceschi (23 July, 1961), p. 35.

In a rather "private aside" to one of his notes on *I Novissimi*, he had replied that it was a question instead of "historical exhaustion" (170).[27]

But neither Sanguineti nor even less Leonetti, and not Anceschi—who knew him even better than they did—could imagine that the misunderstanding generated by that joke had touched the most hidden, but as is seen hyper-reactive, nerves of a Zanzotto who had always been a great neurotic, and repeatedly visited by the risk (and phobia) of psychosis. It is no coincidence that Zanzotto evokes the anti-model of Henri Michaux, who, like him, implicitly nourishes for *nervous breakdown* "a 'respect' that is perhaps still anxiety, but is also for trauma experts circumscription-circumspection," insofar as the Novissimi, in general, and the author of *Laborintus,* in particular, seem to him to "believe that everything is still alright" (*Scritti sulla letteratura* 26). The canon of "schizomorphism" introduced by Giuliani in the introduction to the anthology made Zanzotto ethically indignant, if the term is sufficient, for "believing they could mimic the decay by remaining outside of it, in so many words, or be outside of the contagion of words" (27); and, in fact, the real sin of Sanguineti, according to Zanzotto, is the "lack of respect not so much of the healed and exorcised (still unreal), but of the not fully infected" (26).

The *anxiety of the influence* of the Novissimi, and, in this case, specifically of Sanguineti, since, with regard to Pagliarani, and later Porta, Zanzotto's feelings will be in contrast marked by great respect and attention, derives therefore precisely—outside of Bloom's metaphor—from the problem of *anxiety*. And such a short-circuit can easily be assumed to have the value of a moral. It is certain that the remarkable course of Zanzotto's poetry in the following years, between *La Beltà* (Mondadori, 1968) and *Pasque* (Mondadori, 1973), fully demonstrates, precisely, Bloom's assumption, according to which a "strong poet" is one who does not escape the Agon, who doesn't "sneak away"—to use an expression of one the most extremist poems of *Beltà*, "Oltranza oltraggio"—, rather, a strong poet overcomes his own highly anxious antagonists by descending onto their *field*.

This is what Pier Paolo Pasolini tries to do in the last glimpse of his tragically amputated trajectory, he who openly had always battled the Novissimi on the *field*, lambasting them in several essays in the 1960s, collected in 1972 in *Empirismo eretico*.

---

[27] EN: See Sanguineti, Edoardo. "Poesia informale?" *I Novissimi. Poesie per gli anni 60.* 1965. Einaudi, 2003, pp. 169–173.

Apart from the deliberate recourse to "informal" ways in his penultimate poetic collection, *Trasumanar e organizzar*,[28] it is in his final, unfinished, and rather extraordinary narrative, or rather meta-narrative, season that the connotations of the Agon with the Neo-avant-garde whom he always opposed come to light. However, in less suspect times, it was even somewhat encouraged in the already referenced *Piccola antologia neo-sperimentale* hosted in *Officina* in 1957.[29]

Finally publishing one of the unfinished documents that Pasolini cared most for, the rewriting of Dante's *Inferno* to which he had given the Auerbachian title *La Divina Mimesis*, begun precisely around 1963 but soon abandoned and resumed only on the eve of its sudden publication, at the end of November of 1975,[30] he proposes a short presentation note in which he polemicizes with those he calls his "enemies" for once in subtly ironic tones instead of, as was customary, in coarse and angry ones:

> *The Divine Mimesis*: I publish these pages today as a "document," but also to spite my "enemies": in fact, offering them another reason to despise me, I offer them another reason to go to Hell.
> *Faded Iconography*: these pages want to have the logic, better than of an illustration, of a (rather, very *legible*) "visual poetry." (Preface 2)[31]

In the "pseudo-philological" congeries in which the text is organized, one of the notes—where it is precisely the imaginary "philologist" who gathers together the papers left by the author (in an updating, then again adopted in *Petrolio*, of the traditional artifice of the "discovered manuscript")— gives the news of the author's death, specifying that he was "killed by blows from a club, in Palermo, last year" (93). The note is dated "1966 or '67" and, by men-

---

[28] AN: Published in the same 1971 as *Satura*, *Trasumanar e organizzar*, with exception taken for a number of isolated episodes, is an eloquent example of how the last Pasolini, as stated by his greatest interpreter, Walter Siti, tended to "a poetry that wants to be ugly" and succeeded in this intent even beyond his own intentions.

[29] EN: The *Piccola antologia neo-sperimentale*, edited by Pasolini in the numbers 9 and 10 of June 1957 in *Officina*, included texts by Alberto Arbasino, Elio Pagliarani, Mario Diacono, Massimo Ferretti, Brunello Rondi, Edoardo Sanguineti, and Michele L. Straniero.

[30] AN: Therefore, it is his first book to come out posthumously, but Pasolini had corrected it in every detail and sent it to the publisher.

[31] EN: Pasolini, Pier Paolo. *La Divina Mimesis*. Einaudi, 1975. See the English translation by Thomas E. Peterson, *The Divine Mimesis*. Contra Mundum Press, 2014.

tioning the location of the crime, clearly alludes to the "enemies" of the Group 63, whose inaugural meeting was held precisely in Palermo in October 1963, and who returned to the same city to meet in September of 1965 for a conference on the Experimental Novel, during which there was no lack of "blows from a club"—that is, critically liquidating references—directed at Pasolini. In his "visual poetry," that is, the series of photographs added by him *in extremis* to the page proofs that allow him to send it off finally, Pasolini singles out his "enemies" for public ridicule, portraying "Some of the "Gruppo 63" (we recognize Balestrini, Sanguineti, and Giuliani) and "Early 60s: fascists." The two images are not "mounted" facing each other: that of the "enemies" of the Neo-avant-garde is placed opposite the "Frontispiece" of *Poesia in forma di rosa*, the poetic collection published by Pasolini in April 1964, while opposite the "fascists" is another group photo, taken "At the Nympheum in Villa Giulia," the traditional seat of the Strega Prize.

In a venomous note of 1966, later added in *Empirismo eretico*, Pasolini evoked as follows the conference on the novel held in Palermo the year before:

> There may still be some conferences in which some ignorant and petulant youths talk about the anti-novel as if they were talking about Parma ham. Then the end: and those who have some qualities, even those of an abbot, can continue, while on the others a well-deserved silence falls, as on the faded groups of photographs of hermetic poets at the café, or of fascist squads: that's exactly how it is. (vol. I, 1418)[32]

The parallel between the "fascist squads" and the young "anti-novelists" clearly anticipates the succession of *faded* images in *La Divina Mimesis*. In this text, Pasolini's guerrilla war against the hated "thugs" of the avant-garde—as he defines them in *Empirismo eretico* and elsewhere—is quite bitter. One cannot help but be struck by the circumstance in which Pasolini openly borrowed a typical *modus operandi* of his opponents and even the definition they used to define it. The *Faded Iconography* truly is "visual poetry," a term used at the time of the drafting of those "cantos" by the members of the Florentine Gruppo 70, Lamberto Pignotti and Eugenio Miccini, to define their poetry (Pasolini deliberately insults Pignotti and Miccini by comparing them to cumbersome fellow Florentines, *hermetic poets at the café*) who were separated from those of Gruppo '63 by a resentful rivalry, but with whom their exchanges were continuous. In the same year of 1963, when Gruppo '63 was founded, as was the rival Gruppo 70 a few weeks earlier, the first organic collection by Balestrini—who participated regularly in the Florentine meetings—was published, *Come si agisce* (Feltrinelli). This book ends with a series of verbal *collages* that Balestrini called *Chronograms*. This, too, was "Visual poetry," although very different from the one that twelve years later, proudly claiming their "legibility," Pasolini will lay out on the page. The polemic over "legibility" and "illegibility" was waged in bitter tones in 1967 between Giorgio Manganelli on the pages of *Quindici* and Alberto Moravia on those of *Nuovi argomenti*.

But even more resounding is the circumstance for which Pasolini certainly does not speak of "anti-novel," as he does not speak of "Parma ham,"

---

[32] EN: Pasolini, Pier Paolo. *Empirismo eretico*. Garzanti, 1972; later included in *Saggi sulla letteratura e sull'arte*. Vols I–II. Edited by Walter Siti and Silvia De Laude. Mondadori, 1999.

but he writes one, *La Divina Mimesis*, and he plans another even more macroscopic one as its sequel: *Petrolio*. It was interrupted by his death and released posthumously only in 1992, and shares the pseudo-philological structure of the earlier text and especially the idea—unrealized, for reasons of legal rights, also by the new edition edited this year with Maria Careri by Walter Siti, who has however described in detail its presumed order—to include a "figural integration": precisely an ulterior "visual poetry," how legible it cannot be known. In his last years or months of convulsive activity, in short, Pasolini fully adhered to the practice of an "expanded poetry," as I like to define it, borrowing an expression used for the cinema of those years by Gene Youngblood, which his "enemies" had codified in time.

Though earlier against the avant-garde—or, more accurately, against the *ideology* of the avant-garde—in many cases, Pasolini had an attitude that is difficult to define other than "avantgardist": not hesitating to adopt, in battling his "enemies," communicative methods and concrete textual solutions very similar to theirs, if not in some cases, as seen, precisely the same ones. It is enough to consider the collection *Poesia in forma di rosa* (1964), whose naked and defenseless frontispiece, in the "faded iconography" of *La Divina Mimesis*, is to contrast with the "fascist squads" of the Novissimi. Not only does the collection take its title from the poems, then excerpted by the author, of the section *Il libro delle croci*—even if later, with a symptomatic change of mind, Pasolini expunges these compositions from the second edition of the book, published two months after the first edition in June 1964—that are again "visual poems" although in the more traditional form of the "calligram" of Alexandrine, baroque, and Apollinairean tradition. However, comparing the *découpage* of the poem-masterpiece *Una disperata vitalità*—explicitly modeled on the vortical one of Jean-Luc Godard's *À bout de souffle*—to the sumptuous but heavy panoramas in pseudo-hendecasyllables and the long exhortative harangues of *Le ceneri di Gramsci* seven years earlier, it seems one is reading two different poets. Different or, perhaps, "enemies" among themselves.

There is no need to make explicit what appeared on the scene in that stretch of time. Still, once again, in *La Divina Mimesis*, Pasolini exposes his own *anxiety of influence*, hiding it for all to see. As a mirror of his culminating collection, like a parallel text, his "enemies" are transfigured into images. That is precisely what those "enemies" had encouraged him to experiment with.

I certainly do not want to suggest with this talk that the Novissimi and their adversaries were peers, even less that they were the same thing. Readers of poetry will continue to be divided, with complete satisfaction, between those who prefer the "originals" of the Neo-avant-garde and those who appreciate more the compromise formations of their "enemies." But I think the time has come to recognize how the genuine schism produced sixty years ago in the *field* of Italian poetry, starting a feud that incredibly still drags on today, was even at that time, above all, a colossal misunderstanding: a bit like the one that arose between Zanzotto and Sanguineti with the help of the deafness, literal or not, of a malicious intermediary. Today, it is up to us to sharpen our ears and eyes and thus to recognize, on either side, those who can accompany us in this new century. We have already wasted over a fifth of it, so it is critical not to delay any longer.

Poetry

Charles Bernstein

As If the Trees by Their Very Roots Had Hold of Us

Strange to remember a visit, really not so
Long ago, which now seems, finally, past. Always, it's a
Kind of obvious thing I guess, amazed by that
Cycle: that first you anticipate a thing & it seems
Far off, the distance has a weight you can feel
Hanging on you, & then it's there – that
Point – whatever – which, now, while
It's happening seems to be constantly slipping away,
"Like the sand through your fingers in an old movie," until
You can only look back on it, & yet *you're* still there, staring
At your thoughts in the window of the fire you find yourself before.
We've gone over this a thousand times: & here again, combing that
Same section of beach or inseam for that – I'm no
Longer sure when or exactly where – "& yet" the peering,
Unrewarding as it is, *in terms of* tangible results,
Seems so necessary.

Hope, which is, after all, no more than a splint of thought
Projected outwards, "looking to catch" some*where* –
What can I say here? – that the ease or
Difficulty of such memories doesn't preclude
"That harsher necessity" of going on always in
A new place, under different circumstances:
& yet *we* don't seem to have changed, it's

As if these years that have gone by are
All a matter of record, "but if the real
Facts were known" we were still reeling from
What seems to have just happened, but which,
"By the accountant's keeping" occurred years
Ago. *Years ago.* It hardly seems possible,
So little, really, has happened.

We shore ourselves hour by hour
In anticipation that soon there will be
Nothing to do. "Pack a sandwich
& let's eat later." And of course,
The anticipation is quite appropriate, accounting,
For the most part, for whatever activity
We do manage. Eternally buzzing over the time,
Unable to live in it. ...
"Maybe if we go upaways we can get a better
View." But, of course, in that sense, views don't
Improve. "In the present moment" (if we could only see
It, which is to say, to begin with, stop looking with
Such anticipation) what is enfolding before us puts to
Rest any necessity for "progression".

So, more of these tracings, as if by some magic
Of the phonetic properties of these squiggles... Or
Does that only mystify the "power" of "presence" which
Is, as well, a sort of postponement.

Contradiction Turns to Rivalry

Comradery turns to rivalry when 12 medical students learn that only seven of them will be admitted to the hospital.

A CIA agent is ordered to feign a breakdown to trap a spy at a mental hospital.

A field study of Zululand's mosquitoes and velvet monkeys reveals them to be carriers of viral diseases that cause high fever and bonewracking pain.

Defeat comes to the Nazi conqueror: Film footage highlights the February bombing of Dresden; the advance over the Rhine, through the Ruhr and into the heart of Germany; and, from the east, the Russian encirclement of Berlin.

A brilliant doctor's erratic behavior causes concern at the hospital.

On-the-street subjects render fragmented versions; a two-way mirror provides some unexpected "reflections"; a pair of outdoor phone booths and two muddled conversations befuddle a man.

A backstage view is interwoven with a tragic story.

A detective is captured by a mobster who plans to hook him on heroin and then deny him a fix until he reveals the whereabouts of the jealous hood's former girlfriend.

A retarded young man witnesses a murder but is not articulate enough to tell his story to the police.

A husband is betrayed in medieval Japan where adultery is punishable by death.

Julie grows attached to an abandoned baby.

A grim smuggling operation and a dead hippie lead to intrigue in Malta.

Boxed candy includes frog-filled chocolates.

A girl finds herself between the worlds of the living and the dead.

Henrietta Hippo believes she can predict the future by reading the letters in her alphabet soup.

A man withers away after being exposed to a strange mist.

Conspiracy of silence hampers look into fatal beating of teenage thug.

Bachelors are all agape over a new girl in town.

Rob sees red when Laura goes blond.

"Genocide." Graphic film footage depicts Hitler's persecution and extermination of the Jewish population in Germany and in the occupied countries.

A mental patient returns home to a cold mother and a domineering husband.

A freewheeling narcotics agent works with a junkie's vengeful widow to track down a shadowy syndicate boss.

Everyone chips in to help Henrietta Hippo bake enough pies for the country fair.

It's the dog pound for Roger when Jeannie turns him into a poodle.

Nellie has the most lines in the school play, but the player to get the most out of the project is a girl who uses the play to bring her reclusive widowed mother back into society.

A hot-shot flier thinks he can wage a one-man war in Korea.

A woman tries to keep her individuality after marriage.

Bilko feverishly schemes for a way to escape the summer's heat.

Lucy makes an impression on her first day at her new job when she breaks the water cooler and floods the office.

Midget creatures emerge from the center of the earth.

An emotionally unstable woman unconsciously blots out all memory of seeing her date murdered by her closest friend.

The corrosiveness of envy and jealousy is demonstrated.

A blind girl is terrorized by persons unknown at a country estate.

Strange signals from a nearby island.

A young woman's horror of leprosy plagues her.

Gertrude and Ludwig's Bogus Adventure

for Gabriele Mintz

As Billy goes higher all the balloons
Get marooned on the other side of the
Lunar landscape. The module's broke –
It seems like for an eternity, but who's
Counting – and Sally's joined the Moonies
So we don't see so much of her anyhow.
Notorious novelty – I'd settle for a good
Cup of Chase & Sand-borne – tough when
The strings are broken on the guitar
You can always use it as a coffee table.
Vienna was cold at that time of year.
The sachertorte tasted sweet but the memory
burned in the colon. Get a grip, get a grip, before
The Grippe gets you. Glad to see the picture
Of ink – the pitcher that pours before
Throwing the Ball, with never a catcher in sight.
Never a catcher but sometimes a catch, or
A clinch or a clutch or a spoon – never a
Catcher but plenty o'flack, 'til we meet
On this side of the tune.

Catullus 5

Let's live and love, my Lesbia,
forget those tired rumbles of the old –
who could care less?
Day's light rises and falls
till it sets once and for all
on our never-ending sleep.
Give me a thousand kisses, then hundreds –
one thousand and a hundred more
forever add thousands to hundreds
and when we get beyond count,

we'll lose track of numbers, forget them all,
so that no one who'd harm us
will ever know how many times we kissed.

Covidity

The covid gonna get me
If not now, it will
The covid gonna kill me
Find me where I live

Buried under covers
Sheltered in the hall
Trading goodbyes to all my friends
Through goddamn 15-foot walls

The covid'll get me
Get me bad
My lungs are weak
And I am much misunderstood

I practice social distance
Even got an oversize mask
Feel like the Lone Ranger
Just before he got the clap

The covid going to find me
If not today, in time
The covid after me,
Find exactly where I am

Call it social distance
I call it pain in the soul
You say I can handle it
But it's too heavy a load

The covid 'round the corner
'll trash me till I blue
But that's not my worry
Terrified for you

You've always been distant
But not from me
Now I feel you drifting
Like you're far out at sea

The covid gonna get me
If not now any day
The covid got my number
Knows just where I stay

You say I'll manage social distance
That I can make it work
But if I'm distant from you
I'm sunk before I swum

The covid gonna get me
If not now, soon
The covid has me up all night
Fighting 'gainst all this gloom

Too much death surrounding
I darn near given up
Keep calling on the telephone
But you're hung up on Skype

The covid coming
Sure to get us good
Our lungs are weak
And we are much misunderstood

Rivulets of the Dead Jew

Fill my plate with *boudin noir*
Boudin noir, boudin noir
Fill my plate with a hi-heh-ho
& rumble I will go

Don't dance with me
'til I cut my tie
Cut my tie, cut my tie
Don't fancy me 'til
The rivers run dry
& a heh & a hi & a ho

I've got a date with a
Bumble bee, bumble bee
I've got a date with a
wee bonnie wee
& ahurtling we will go

Antonella Anedda

Translated by Eleonora Buonocore

Now Everything Calms Down, Everything Reaches the Darkness

I was not talking if not to the lain coat,
to the basket with only one apple
to the meek objects bound
to an abandonment outside of us
yet with us, inside the night,
unheard.

from *Altars* of Rest

I

Welcome, removing the bone that blocks your heart, this corner of stone. Here bitterness matures, the weak encampment of the angels, the shadows of the conic tunics, cold on the sand, the bodies vertical and hard. Devastated by images of figureheads, redoubled in birds we are as they are, faceless and bloodless. As they do, we compose our geometries fleetingly, in the fastness of the collapse, in the cries along the roofs, in the fists of winged hands.

II

It was this. The sand raised in dunes
the rocks without flowers
the earth that has no season, the grass
transferred into thin tubs
on the line of the walls

and the warm room as though inhabited
flame of branch and candle
minimal-light, wax-light
in front of the stone of the dead

Wild air. Bone
sharpened, you without enchantment.
To you
        (in evenings of fires and lighthouses, in the glass
flung by the wind onto the piers)
I owe certainties:
neither return nor union, not any comfort
resentment for your grey beauty of a drowned one.
Yet it is a collapse
thick with nuts, footsteps
in which the wreckage is already the root
the breath of couples in the compartments of ferries.
Not courtyards of the sea but galleries
iron tools that negate the quiet.
From them I learn.
Not to stash objects,
but to open wide baskets
until the body is made into another space.
Calmly
now that among the clods
I am a light trace of an animal
        (lower than the night
in which darkness is labor)
with water I close the cracks, the great vases.

from Winter Residences

IV

With a heart full of cold
with the cautiousness of a mole that scurries on the wintry pavement
forlorn, despite the relief of being on your feet.

We went down to the hospital chapel: tightly clad in night robes, without shoes, feet rolled up like soldiers in retreat. We were grazing the beds without looking at the sick, the eyes fixed in the glimmering of the windows and in all those objects that bear the mark of a faraway home.
Beyond the door of the kitchens a plate fell in the water. In the smoke and in the steam, in the fire that surrounded the pots, in the blue of the light against the walls: in everything there was earthly peace, enchantment of a grotto. But we were walking with the pace of survivors, stone after stone, under the vault of the stairs until the nightly sky of the dome. We hugged a lamb sewn in a hospital ward, its muzzle made of wadding, two buttons for eyes, the body the cloth of our pajamas.

And the nurse thrusted open the glass window,
just as Spanish cities thrust open churches.
Filled with nocturnal wind the cathedrals of Madrid
tremor
of fires among the stone
wind of snow
on the tips of the candles
on the feet of the statues
on the curve of the gratings.
The lamb shielded the church candles
its large body obscured the altar.
We raised our chin
lamps wood and emptiness
legs numbed by the beds
misery
not white musk
not light of water through the bushes. Wall
blocked by the raised elbow of the Angel
and time slipping from fever.
From the kitchens descended the smell of broth
someone in the distance was cutting down a hedge.
The air was still amid the naves
and warm from radiators amid the beds
time again without beginning or end.
Which glory

in the merry sound of a bell against the rock of a tower
which peace in the olive branches
under the wood of the crucifixes.
Early Easter in March.
Surrounded by young pines the hill of the policlinic
enclosed by shadows as the walls of Gezer
tomb-green among pointy palaces.

The centurion raised his lance
and it began to rain on the naked skin of the bodies.
The water was striking the vases' rim
in the courtyards mud and leaves were blending
lightning was beating on high
without thunder
without time to clear the rooms.
The night, not darker than any other night, was passing by.
Only, they saw at dawn the emptiness
of a cave without a body
the glimmering of a sheet
shadow and not flesh
steps without footprints
hollow air and morning.
The light falls on the stone table, on the bread
on the wine that trickles down the chin of men.
Bewildered they were calling each other with sad unknown words
in the misery of solitude
until the silent pitter-patter of a dove on the hay of the roof
until the flight of a mantle.

As ghosts we will come back to this hospital garden
where now wander the relatives of the dead
and the embarrassment joins other embarrassments.
The grass grows in front of the sepulcher
but we know only the heavy sleep of the soldier.

Who will want to bend down to reclaim the body?
Let the heart cool down as skin on a kitchen's marble.
Let the bones open up.

V

Stunned by nostalgia, confused by dreams, with beach towels full of wind, with the speedy incomplete vision of a house in the morning. Down there in the air the buzz of the vacuum cleaner on the carpets and the thuds of the carpets against the walls. In the long hours of an April storm before they came to move us to the side and thrust open the glass doors for visits. Then lights and sounds change: the wall whitened by the water, the high ceiling above the heads, the cautious steps in the corridors remain.

Not defense, not quiet
not the voice of human beings
but the plant moved in front of the balcony
and the windows open to the rain.
Beyond the tree and the roof
high bolted houses and lamps next to tables
(now round, now square)
small tables
on which are scattered papers.
The water was running, not the hale;
no fury in the rumble of the thunder
the tree bent white
the dark roof and perfect
axis
of an embodied geometry
the city divided by the air

The disorder was elsewhere
in the glasses knocked over on the nightstand
in the crumbs scattered on the bed.

As loveless presence
crammed around our supine bodies
as the needles with which we knit sweaters
with the same remote clinking
creak the steps
in the spring afternoon.

Rest your back on the pillow and remember
the pitcher on the marble, the earth
and the fog the dull blue
of their dust,
iron of a shovel among the clumps of dirt
and low hills
with bushes, fast in the Sienese wind.

The rain is dry on the windows and motionless
the window becomes dark in the sky.
It is arriving, I fear
the summer
and a very hard sky
without a cloud for a shield.

from Voices for Allies

for the death of M.A.

I

As you safeguard, as
        for a long time your womb encloses the earth.
Now
journey would be the cry of the birds
that ignore the spheres
the tense route of the flight.
Theirs the world of nests, the warmth of the mud
not this oblique passing with the lanterns.

II

Not voice but number
that which was carving
that distant tongue
fulcrum
around which to turn
the white heat of the lights.

Without a landscape
the mind had unleashed
the rivers
rendered distance the bone.

from Floodgate of Wind

The house watches over the pictures of the dead
each wall tightly close
to their vertical smiles.

I

Think the household tools
the hammer in the shadow of the shed
the nails scattered on the rag, the saw
the frozen fretwork of the basket.
They put out fire and lampposts
they closed the wooden shutters
each room knows only
a line of winter's moon.
Veiled sofas and chairs
knocked over a bottle and a glass
the halls dissolved
in the haze of the sheets and of the darkness.

With care the winter prepares its misfortune
with sorrowful obsession piles up light on snow
one by one it trains the birds
in the cold of threads and branches, in beds made only of slats
in the wave of the mattresses
left to fray with the wind.
Nothing obscures the chaste beauty of this misery
the ember burns in a distant fireplace
the water gathers elsewhere
in vessels of domestic quietness, in luminous houses
from the driveway to the front door.
The winter arranges his time

like bread it lays it down on stony windowsills
calmly it gathers my gaze
your neck the geranium pierced by the sparrow
the paper that got wet in the rain.

The key dangles in the nocturnal gesture
Count the steps, count the flakes from the beams between the shoes.
We will go for long now
body next to body
in the short space that has been assigned to us.
Still able to cast a shadow on a wall,
still mortal.

VI

They have gathered the lamps, they have covered the objects. One match would suffice and this house with its woody light and its crossed beams would become brushwood and log, a country fire.

Home is that from which one is removed.
   Training
the wait on the edge of the bricks
the pavement so small:
   divided rock and threads
of unhinged earth
the abandonment, the light
   tied to the railing.

The children do not have a home
they lower a shelf on the carpet
it's enough the imprint
   of a large pot
and from down there, from the wool and the crock
   from the uncertainty of the forms
that transform into winter games
comes the sorrow that will be preserved in the years.

There is the vacant space of the deeper room
still the pain comes from the light
from the day in which something
the wing of a bird or the edge
of a curtain
have dug a shadow along the wall
and the light has withdrawn into the night.
It is not the wind that announces the earthquake
but the objects by having edges
    too narrow too short pauses
between the space and the hands
they are the thuds, the elevator's gratings
    that beat an unknown rhythm
they are the pulse of the dead
that mime Chinese shadows
darkness after darkness accompanying us
until the last oblique crossing.

    Winter's field, peace
    that follows the battle.

The home can be closed again
upon our lain heads.
    His keys are
    tibias
    among broken
    rabbit tails.

from 1991

for F.

No need for us, nowhere,
in a month the year
will have a Baltic cipher, white
nineteen ninety-one
where the nineteen moves backwards
to the centuries-steppes

and the one, hollow
jingles.

No one has called us
they were orchard voices, whistles
to shoo away the birds
the little rain that trickles down
from the pipes of the house
deserted
like paper.
There is only the breathing
and the fogged-over washbowl
and the nuts that say
autumn multiplied on the tables
stones on empty places.

At no time is there need for us
the vertical nights
and the linden tree lined walkway, the hare
transparent in the bush
the back-shadow of those who were waiting then
now tired, are blowing
on the forehead of the century.
There is food in the evening, flashes
on the abrupt photos
and we drink among the dark forks
and the faces clinging to the glasses
for the slow fear that carves itself
on the elbow that raises a garland.

No time has need of us
no one says
the number of blows
the exact amount of grass
nor how the air
lashing against us
will toughen our skin,
squirrels.

The sliding of leaves
the distance of the constellations.

I do not have deep words
not deep enough.
The pine tree sinks into the night
with difficulty I decipher the memory.

On the side there was something like a fence
and there things were lasting.

from Three Stations

I

Throw your bread on the surface of the water, you will find it in days: we will not find the food, nor the reward – not the lightness but the heavy axe of the benediction.

Those who loses have free backs to carry the world. No luggage to better drag along the iron and the wood of a wagon, to let the air and the rain pile up on its rear, the multiplicity, the disorder of things. It is not the earthly resignation but the meek strength of Christ who in Gethsemane responds to the soldiers: "yes, it is me;" the poverty of the rock, of the funereal cloth empty for the weight of human sins.
(...)

III

(...)
The useless artfulness of making them eat us last. The illusion of every coward act. Power does not need the just but the outcast, it will kill the outcast last and it will have the justification for his hatred. Bedazzled, even before any threat, the outcast went towards hate and surrendered to it generously, quickly.
(...)

Peter Gizzi

Findspot Unknown

Thus far we have spoken
only the codes,
a litany of survival.
Thus spoke the silvered asphodel
next to the factory ruin.
Sound carries on water.
My subject is the wind.
To take umbrage at what a tree can do,
watching one single birch
become lightning stunning the sky.
Landscape is a made thing,
to see the mind seeing itself.
To see thought, a wing
in night, the long brooding.
Take it, listen, the night is orchestral
when the power's on.
Everything disporting.
A furred wand upon nothingness.

I get it, it was good to leave the world,
to find myself in thou.
There's a lot to be said
for seeing in the dark
and more to the light
when there's nothing to see.
If I write about the moon
it's because it's there.

I am landlocked, surrounded
by rivers and lakes, pills and leaves.
I saw a better life, it was far off,
sun on moss next to a friend,
the softening air, the dandelion fluff.
It was kinda real, and kinda not.
Can't see it today.

And out of nothing, breath.
A beast-like shadow in the glass.
If I brought back every feeling I had
where would I put them,
what could they mean
to this world on the floor.
It was best to let the moon unravel
and focus the truth of the music.
It was best to let the music
unravel and focus the truth of night.
Like when I found you
in the back of my mind.
I am talking about people
and the night.
People inside the night.
The night and what we are made of.
The things and the people.
The signal and its noise.

Revisionary

I've decided to let my inner weather out.
Even in the nerves flashing, some things
        are only shadow.
What's up with that?
My muse bruises me.
Some days I sit hours to be relieved
        by a word.
Today's word is invisible.

I'm putting trouble into place, turning
        toward what is.
Listening to stone translate into silence.
Here is an old rock covered with lichen
        in the mossy forest inside the self.
I like it here when it's green.
This is me evolving.
I'm hanging on. A whisper.
Certain prayers are tied to this ribbon.

How in hell can nature throw clay into art
        into a speaking being into air.
I saw a world that was an afternoon.
This cloud in my hand.
Sky pouring into sky reflecting the absolute
        of the lake.
The flock and its tangle of shadow.

Nearing the end, I could hear a lark.
Its trill fixing itself to my brain.
It seemed a thing becoming a wave.
A thing dissolving into the world
        as I found it.
Illegible. Agrammatical.
To parse the velocity of trusses and stars
        flowering here at the edge.
Calling me home.

Roxy Music

The old language reminds us of tradition; of nights, of tapers billowing by the window; of balmy and aromatic breezes; recalls historically, our girl asks for a poem; each week or so says, where is my poem, you don't write no more, sluggard; I say, I don't care, when I see you and we buckle and your shirt is on the chair and the room is blowsy, poetry don't matter; after when I saw you in the mirror, I wrote: poetry died today.

But the Heart in a Sense Is Far From Me Floating Out There

Hold onto the afterlife of the beloved, it's the only thing
        that's yours

Hold on to whatever magic in the backyard where we bury
        our thoughts, things of the world

Things of the world like an afterlife of the world to bury
        our setting outness

It's right to extract bone from the afterlife, dust collecting shoes,
        relics of the afterlife

Cut a hole in the poem to play peekaboo with the afterlife

Rebuild my house out of sky, blur my memoria into song

Make my headdress the right size to salute the emptiness
        alive in the beloved

The humanness of the beloved, the beloved and the night sky

Shapes floating out there becoming the beloved, the abstract,
        the total

Speech Acts for A Dying World

A field sparrow
is at my window,
tapping at its reflection,
a tired
antique god
trying to communicate

it's getting to me

as I set out to sing
the nimbus of flora
under a partly mottled sky

as I look at the end
and sing so what,
sing live now,
thinking why not

I'm listening and
receiving now
and it feeds me,
I'm always hungry

when the beautiful
is too much to carry
inside my winter

when my library is full of loss
full of wonder

as the polis is breaking
and casts a shadow
over all of me,
thinking of it

when the shadows fall
in ripples, when
the medium I work in
is deathless and

I'm living inside
one great example
of stubbornness

as my head is stove-in
by a glance, as the day's

silver-tipped buds sway in union,
waving to the corporate sky

when I said work
and meant lyric

when I thought I was done
with the poem as a vehicle
to understand violence

I thought I was done
with the high-toned
shitty world

done with the voice and
its constituent pap

call down the inherited
phenomenal world
when it's raining in the book,
lost to the world
in an abundance of world

like listening to a violin
when the figure isn't native
but the emotion is

when everything is snow
and what lies ahead
is a mesmer's twirling locket

I thought I was done
with the marvel
of ephemeral shadow play,
the great design and all that

I thought I was done

with time, its theatricality,
glamour, and stuff

gusting cloud, I see you,
I become you
in my solitary thinging,
here in partial light

when I said voice,
I meant the whole unholy grain of it,
it felt like paradise

meaning rises and sets,
now a hunter overhead
now a bear at the pole
and the sound of names

the parade of names

That I Saw the Light on Nonotuck Avenue

That every musical note is a flame, native in its own tongue.

That between bread and ash, there is fire.

That the day swells and crests.

That I found myself born into it with sirens and trucks going by out here in a poem.

That there are other things that go into poems like the pigeon, cobalt, dirty windows, sun.

That I have seen skin in marble, eye in stone.

That the information I carry is mostly bacterial.

That I am a host.

That the ghost of the text is unknown.

That I live near an Air Force base and the sound in the sky is death.

That sound like old poetry can kill us.

That there are small things in the poem: paper clips, gauze, tater tots, knives.

That there can also be emptiness fanning out into breakfast rolls, macadam, stars.

That I am hungry.

That I seek knowledge of the ancient sycamore that also lives in the valley where I live.

That I call to it.

That there are airships overhead.

That I live alone in my head out here in a poem near a magical tree.

That I saw the light on Nonotuck Avenue and heard the cry of a dove recede into a rustle.

That its cry was quiet light falling into a coffin.

That it altered me.

That today the river is a camera obscura, bending trees.

That I sing this of metallic shimmer, sing the sky, the song, all of it and wonder if I am dying would you come back for me?

The Present is Constant Elegy

Those years when I was alive, I lived the era of the fast car.

There were silhouettes in gold and royal blue, a half-light in tire marks across a field — Times when the hollyhocks spoke.

There were weeds in a hopescape as in a painted backdrop there is also a face.

And then I found myself when the poem wanted me in pain writing this.

The sky was always there but useless — And what of the blue phlox, onstage and morphing.

Chance blossoms so quickly, it's a wonder we recognize anything, wanting one love to walk out of the ground.

Passion comes from a difficult world — I'm sick of twilight, when the light is crushed, time unravels its string.

Along the way I discovered a voice, a sun-stroked path choked with old light, a ray already blown.

Look at the world, its veil.

Archeophonics

I'm just visiting this voice
I'm just visiting the molecular structures
        that say what I am saying
I am just visiting the world at this moment
        and it's on fire
It's always been on fire

I'm saying this and it's saying me
That's how it works, seesaw like

The archive in the mouth and the archive is on fire
That's the story
The sun and the body and the body in the sun

It was like this just like this
The world that's coming toward me
And the world around me
Around me are words saying this
        saying fire
Saying something or all of it

When Orbital Proximity Feels Creepy

Right now there are teenage microwaves
screaming through your body
while you are having text with me.
This is the moment I'll need you to sing
        with me.
I am making my way in some dark room
looking for other structures to love.
From the left something speaking
        I can't identify.
The floor goes unfixed and moving
and this doesn't happen only at night
but during the day when I don't want
        to think on it.
That I saw a blood-orange ball caught
        out my window.
That I'm listening to light and it said time.
I'm listening to time, it says, ha.
You need to be howling at bloody torn space.
Need to be spooked out of your hidey-hole
        and its glowing mess.
But I love this ball I'm riding on.
The strange hunk of metal and rock whizzing
        around my loves and my loving.

The fact I spin and it spins and everything
        is spinning close up.
From far away it's so cool.
I guess they call this physics or they call it laws.
If they're so well-made, why do we suffer?
I thought the day was opening
but now I see it's already gone.
Outside the cruel dove has a broken window.
The day isn't friendly.
Who are you to me?
A way to understand the floor?
The floor that holds me up and leaves me
        standing.
I don't know where to go.
Me, Tuesday at 5pm.
What does it mean to be in a room,
        any room.
The wind banging against the clapboard.
I know enough to see the cracked pane
isn't going to be fixed anytime soon.
Who has time for such things in the song?
Breaking. Blooming.
The wobble of light on wood-grain late
        in the day.
In the loneliness of orange.
In the loveliness of orange.

Release the Darkness to New Lichen

But I found a way to say no
to the wood in my house

it kept creaking
wouldn't stop talking

I found a way to say no

I need to be standing

in the warmth of the wood
that the sun made

I need to find myself dissolving

otherwise it is all otherwise
I'm lost, did I say that

I saw the frill of light today
walking on the path

could you hear the stirring
in the wood, pine needles
and the branches

was it wind or a creature
am I here or is it over

this was the first day
the nothing day
in the nothing year

it gave me courage

it gave hints of blue,
clouds, electrical
and dancing

it gave me rays
I've never seen

shooting down
touching things

this was the first day

This World is Not Conclusion

for Emily Dickinson

When I look out your window I see another window
I see a wedding in my brain, a stylus and a groove
a voice waving there

When I look out your window I see another window
these trees are not real they grow out of air
they fell like dust they fell

So singing is seeing and vision is music
I saw diadems and crowns, daisies and bees, ribbons, robins, and disks of snow
sprung effects in pencil-light

When I look out your window I see another window
I see a fire and a girl, crimson hair and hazel eyes
a public in the sky

When the world comes back it will be recorded sound
that cooing shrub will be known as dickinson
the syllabic, fricative, percussive, and phatic will tear open

Out your window I see another window
I see a funeral in the air I see alabaster space
I read circumference there

Now It's Dark

Not the easiest day I'm having, clouds banking
and I dropped my signal.
I was trying to find my shoes and thought
I am overpowered by the gigantism
of commercial governing.
As I looked for my shoes this morning
the thought was where am I going?

There isn't a place I can walk out from
under this chemical sky.
So I thought I would write a poem.
I thought I would try and make art.
But the chemicals seep into everything.
Reader, if I could I would bring back for you
a sun made in crayon.
A sun unformed in the paper sky.
I wonder the paper that made me.
Being human I know that paper makes my mind.
Strange pulp reminding me I am far away.
When my brother could no longer speak
I said Tommy I got this
even if I don't want this, I'll sing for you.
When my brother had no voice there was only the couch
and a wooden floor
the ceiling and the TV with nothing blaring.
When my brother lost his voice I lost my childhood
lost the sun over sand in some place I can't remember
in Rhode Island summer.
So far from myself in a body I can't remember.
To no longer remember my body as a child.
To no longer remember today all that was.
Van Gogh was tormented by the sun and why not.
A constant blade-searing light that kills and cures.
I am not comforted by the cold stability
of universal laws
though one day I'll die and think, that's ok.
At least I'm writing and it makes a party in the dark.
A zombie feature that connects me to the undying.
I read every moment is an opportunity for grace
and think every moment is a possibility of art.
I tie my shoes and now I am standing alone
in some inky light.
Yesterday I passed a Budget Motel next to
the Peoples Bank.
If there's some connection it's lost on me.

My heart lost on me.
Weather like thought dissolves into static,
a wiggy keepsake like nesting dolls of my
spiritual blank.
Sky opening into blank.
I thought grief is a form of grace.
Then someone said the thing about money
is that it's money.
I live on the edge of an expanding circumference
alone in some inky light.
Now rain turns the world to constant applause.
The day is uncoupled.
All there is is thunder as the house decays
into a sound like me.
Freezing rain with silver seems to be speaking
and isn't asking me anything.
Just doing its thing in the gray morning.
I was down with materialism but
wanted mystery.
I've asked myself a lot of questions like
why the days cascade
swiping left for life, right for lost.
All of it a dumb show.
All of me invested in poetry and the
arrogance of this.
Wanting to transpose loneliness.
Why not take on the next life
with its silence.
On my desk there are small plastic creatures.
The light on them is unrealistic.
It uncouples me.
Or the sight of serious windows opening out
onto serious lawns.
This must be a government building.
This must be the anodyne room of
a hospital beeping.
Every pronouncement on the feed, alien.

I'm in this corridor wandering a mind.
But the day is past caring.
The rhythmus is blooming at the beginning
of the way back when.
I am sick with tradition and its weak signaling.
Sparkling eclogues drift and contribute
little to the cause.
I am an incident trapped in big data.
Just google it.
Dust jacket shows some rubbing,
near fine in cloth.

From This End of Sadness

A particular blur
attended my mind
from end to end.

These feelings
of futurelessness.

To free fall into it.

It feels like winter,
the light overcast
and the day lit up
from within.

To find a line in it.

I found a world
torched into renewal,
blackened stalks
pointing skyward.

I took fortification
from goneness.

At this end
the notation is green.

No stopping music
entering air
and tearing air,
the songs
were old songs.

They came
with the wren
and the robin.
Also the crow
so dear to reality
and elegy
and traffic,
its essential din.

The synesthesia
of the din.

From this end
of sadness
I identified
the voice as dead,
it was companionable.
I identified sky
turning topaz.

I did not
understand shadows,
did not understand
luminosity.

I did not understand
the code that held
me to the world.

From this end
glistening leaves,
cool air.

Wandering out into it,
wondering through it,
the day crumbles to dust
inside a blue dahlia.

I am that dust and dahlia.

I am coeval
with the rotting trunk
and the pine needles
regenerating soil.

I am happiest
with the forest floor,
branches listing
under a porcelain sky.

I'm into that medieval
light glancing
through leaves.
The tree's arches
are a great
kingdom now.

From this end
of sadness
there's nothing
out there I want
and wonder
if there's anything
in here I need?

I'm into the way

the technology of an I
is filled with the dead.

I'm heavy with light
when the old sun
is speaking,
when I'm not sure
the day is real.

When it's hard
to be in and of it,
to be here with it
and under it.

From this end of sadness
shapes come,
all the boldest shadows.

From this end animals,
the oldest eyes,
the cri de Coeur,
afternoons hung
with seeping light.

Poor sun,
waiting to die.
Poor sun
solo in space,
fueling
our heads,
a tiny sun
in the mind.

Right now,
a particle
decays
on the lawn.

From this end
gravity decays
in the mind.

To never forget
the corners
and dust bunnies
of the laughing sun.

But if the song
weren't a bright star
hanging in
the firmament
then what
can be said
for burning embers
in the fire.

I see you turning
and bending there
in the cold dream
of the past
braiding
with the now
of blur.

Blur with me
when I am sick
of dying,
fearful of failing
the song I love.

Be with me
whenever I sit
wasting days.

Comfort the hours.

A Telescope Protects Its View

I like to read the dead.

Part of a whole lost era campaign.

The bridge is up.

A portrait of you from what you aren't saying.

On my sleeve. The verb to be.

I'm plucky but thankful.

Death and the imagination equals life itself.

Letters from an old bottle,
junk in space.

A book or a boat?

The black ribbons of a spring day
might sound mawkish

but I like to read under a pale blue sky
animated and deepening.

I like to read the dead.

There's so and so going by
everyone, outside

everyone

the words scroll onto air.

Synecdoche: act of receiving from another.

Metonymy: change of name.

Who hasn't found themselves
praying in an awkward room.

She said but what of their sad work
by the river's edge

sad way of working the moth paper light

trellis of dented garbage cans
and debris at dawn.

A Note on The Text

The good poets defy things
with their heart

This is how a fragment
enters the people

Don't say beauty say the beautiful
say the people

Say it is through chants that writing
entered the people

Their imagery and love of nature,
englutted flowers

This place of fleshlessness
Here is my song

the only recourse of sun
Even its smallest syllables

can be sown into the mouth
It is on the tongue the sun abides

Two syllables fastened
to each end

To stretch the vocal pattern
Its linenlike thread

Marco Giovenale

Translated by V. Joshua Adams

from Excesses (on a little flight)

(...)
they are showing a b-movie in which a bearded gangster carrying a table leg like a club roams a subterranean forest protecting two children who have the keys to the secret garden. a robot threatens them and there are several fires. They end up talking politics.

*

seeing as how food laden carts block the access to the mine, humanity is saved and the vice-manager of the spanish phone company fills out a form to be allowed back in the hotel. she is very relaxed, when she sits down her tights become completely exposed. there is a convention of taxi drivers at the end of which a garage gets divvied up into a bunch of churches. some taxi drivers take the religious vows without exiting their cars.

*

a group of japanese scientists invents a photograph from which it is possible to escape, another group invents more powerful fixers. they fight it out.

*

three japanese scientists disguised as four chinese scientists move from a cloud of dust to a foggy passage. they sink and Roger Moore appears behind little white tablets. since gravity is down to zero playing cards are floating and the other players cannot be trusted. The headsets they wear inside the helicopter that carries them to safety are so large that they cannot move. they would destroy the cockpit. they land. only after the landing they take off the headsets. much pain. their ears bleed and are even bigger than the headsets. they are imprisoned and some shout, others give up.

*

a thunderous sound is heard inside the dinner. it comes from bowls of anti-matter on the other side.

from they were in danger

Nearly everyone by now goes through a nose job. Nearly everyone speaks when the argument is hot. Nearly everyone takes up residence abroad. Nearly everyone becomes poor again. Nearly all the rich are at rock bottom. Nearly all the poor wage war among the poor. Nearly all the sick are dying but nearly all the nearly dead sometimes come back to life. Nearly all the poised assholes fall miserably or fall not miserably. Nearly all the common denominators divide in the thick of it. Nearly everyone knows it. Nearly everyone has some knowledge of it. A wisdom of sorts. Nearly all the dividends had vanished from the balance sheet way before then. Nearly everyone in principle. Nearly everything had happened way before then. Nearly everything was already finished when you arrived. Nearly everything in principle. Nearly everyone notices one thing. Nearly everyone challenges it even before opening it up for discussion. At this point Nearly everyone shows a preference for Africa. Nearly everyone has their luggage ready at hand. Nearly everyone prefers to ship it. Nearly everyone nourishes some mistrust. Nearly everyone is depressed and Nearly everyone knows it. Nearly everyone will be in a matter of minutes. Nearly everyone is an enemy of Nearly everyone else. Nearly everyone has an enemy at home. You know Nearly all of them. Nearly everyone was here when you arrived. Nearly everyone emphasizes difference. Nearly everyone finds it hard to obtain a mortgage. Nearly everyone gets it. Nearly everyone is a criminal. Nearly everyone is a war criminal. Nearly everyone has decided. Nearly everyone has reached a decisive decision. Nearly everyone keeps their word. Nearly everyone no but Nearly everyone can sense it. Nearly everyone is distracted. Nearly everyone does not see the difference. Nearly everyone on the contrary sees it. Nearly everyone is like this. Nearly everyone is at random. Nearly everyone is caught up in sociology. Nearly everyone has their schedule. Nearly everyone salutes with their right hand. Nearly everyone thinks of pulling it off. Nearly everyone needs to have some words repeated to them. Not everyone, Nearly everyone.

informal for life

consoling, fortifying, teaching us everything and reminding us everything we were told by that schmuck of an explorer just before he passed away.

he describes to us the path rock by rock, the transformation of the character, how and why the protagonist of a great narrative changes.

with much satisfaction an additional growth has been reported, for the year 3 A.D., and with this we can call it quits.

now: social implication of the story:

everyone was on foot, except a few knights and squires on the wings. he casually told us :

try shooting the crossbow.

many years later we understood. it had been also very useful for breastfeeding as well, and for the palm dates

we all had tears in our eyes and other parts of our bodies.

Ø and the cocktail enthusiasts

at times it happens that it rains on the day of the party, and then with much regret the apostle to the gentiles rings the bell, he reaches the outlet where they sell the acid. can't you see it is terephthalic, goes back to Sardinia, in boxes of sushi, searching for the origins of the bel calcio, on loan from sophia loren, funky (orange, acid green, navy blue, ruby red), he takes the reins of the empire, he takes malta, historically in the minority, he falsifies the health certificate, of the chief of police, engulfed with a hot case, it is in fact everyone's common dream, it is the voice of the bag lady, it zigzags slowly, dangerously close, it's getting dark and something thereabouts frightens him, ocean related mysteries, let's talk about it seriously, let's talk about it with the audience

aficionado of boiled rice manages to grasp the awareness of nothing

the three principal elements for winning over a woman: limping on the field during the last match, it is the period of blood sucking even in peak summer, if you want to catch up with the peasants in a hurry, and it could have been more shining than the pleiades if they had not hidden the herds of the republic inside the inside. check.

he eyed her disorientedly and said to her: environmentalists are pointing the finger at the bureaucracy. but: "and I will tell you who you are by the company you keep" doesn't work. after all, the poor guy is too wretched and miserable. and even the more daring adventurer dies wherever he happens to be, it's the hard law of acupuncture.

but above all what matters is the will to underline the importance of the malarial polong, in the vatican: not only the mechanisms of state centralization, but also 90 percent of the harvesting lost in culture and fashion: thus nine are the government employees interested in digital pornography

admin

you go to the service center and they take care of administrative files. indeed administration enters into the things that matter in life, which are endowed with a very special sweetness and therefore must be processed in order to be brought back to regularized fecal material.

regularized fecal material carries out third level jobs, like actuarial calculus, foil match, dwarfism. even for these matters it issues certificates, or requests them, on the basis of symmetry.

it handles the register of companies, the cancellation of protests, and visits the central registry or the real estate registry. everyone can go to the real estate registry to have a property registered in his name.

for example if you want to be the owner of an aristocratic palazzo in the historic center, all you have to do is go to the real estate registry and ask first for an inspection report and then for a transfer of title, in this way you can take possession of the palazzo.

obviously this has no legal validity, and you can't enter the palazzo, but you have accomplished an action of great beauty and sweetness, that afterwards will be subject to management.

from Endoglosses

II.

He waits for the informer to do his job. In the meantime he polishes certain garlands of sand in mourning with a tiny branch, sitting down, facing the sea that from time to time tickles his fingers.

Then he wonders whether ultimately he should not have first "committed" a crime, escape, and so on. It is when it comes to misdeeds, more generally, that the informants and others flourish and then fail. Thus, it does not make any sense to wait for him, to think that he will come. He is innocent, all things considered. (*There's plenty of innocence*, etc.)

Luckily he also thinks (immediately) that the world, older than he who is anyway rather old, speaks his same rhetoric, uses the same rags, wipes the hematic comb over cheaply with the same light. Patience, patience.

(Turns) the head sideways, slightly. Already he gets the drift upside down. *Fills in the background.*

You put in on cold. They call him.

IV.

He is the internal librarian of the internal library in the intestine of a mouse, rather, a rat. He interprets: the guts. He conducts enterological research, he examines the constituting elements of fecal matter.

He archives reality directly. No holidays. It is a prestigious position, people consult with him: they wish to know.

Luckily, there's hunger for knowledge.

V.

1.
It's in the semidarkness or so they say. The walls, in as much as you can imagine them, must be somewhere, but you can't see any of them from here. The same goes for the ceiling. The ground is there, instead, this is a fact, given that he kneels down on it. It is dark. He does not rise, he remains perpetually down, if he tries it is just to stop: he has a continuous kneeling, he stops.

The noose is soft at the neck, the rope rises slowly but so loose that the hanging never occurs, he is not even threatened with it. His hands are free and this is why he does not remove the rope from his neck.

2.
The woman is lying down. Her ceiling makes her remain on her back, it touches her stomach, it holds her down on her back always everywhere pressed to the ground. But here too there are no walls. She can crawl freely toward any cardinal point.

X.

Found by chance at the mouth of the Tiber, or at Sentinella Pass or at Fiumara Grande, the sea by contrast did not hesitate to drop on the square shaped rocks — that form a bastion — copper cables, anagrams perfected with glass, plastic.

They won't end up on some piece of furniture, turning themselves into local cheerful household gods.

The fishing winches of the shacks are rusting sticks ruling over an empty room-church, the cross is black anodized objects it is indeed anodyne, two straight edges of dirt on green signal the spot where the cars to be disassembled must stop.

XI.

After the insomnia at night comes the insomnia of the day.

He tries in any case to sleep, or stay awake like this: he clamps the shutters running the risk of ruining the curtains, they overflow — he forces himself to bed, he searches for some comfort, understandably. Every noise records something. Every thing has something to do with another, it's impossible. (He rebels.)

He would like to say to himself — exaggerating a traklian slant — an exposed/exposable film, written though from the other side of light, from the range of blacks, and then he finds the negative of a film of a fixed sequence that narrates a small, much detailed blaze. The perseverance the miniation of an anxiety of subtraction, of blackening. Exactly — one says. Rather: *more* than exactly.

XVII

If he needs to imagine the mother of a father he thinks of a woman with blue eyes — who plays the whole *Kreisleriana* from memory fixing her absurd gaze high on the perfectly out of tune upright piano and all around a neat white hairdo. Plump down syndromed triplets with catalogs in their hand give orders to the security of the deliveryman one two three despoiling of the walls, packaging of mirrors, *arabesque arabesque,* books in boxes, *bourrée?*, no, inlayings paintings, *Schnell und spielend*, and and the furnishings, a stuffed hobbyhorse, four X, five upsilon, the basin. They take off the hat au revoir madame, they do not even wait she has done playing when they leave. The music muffles in the crowning note, she turns around maybe as happy as she could be. She goes to the window the only thing left besides the still life on the easel that she was painting in brown, tepid and kind hues, with one two unwarranted apples she looks outside the sundial in a corner with the apples – done – it's evening, she moves a whole pale blue, less sharp than her eyes – it doesn't matter – outside the coldest ditch the ditches the hard sketched out branches the cliff at the edge of the fortress, wind, the room, inside, eats shadows like an empty puppet where they slowly stuff grey rags until it is completely full.

She turns, looks around — the room. Has been emptied. She says oh; goes to the kitchen for something to eat. (If there's something).

The others are all dead. She too is dead, it doesn't matter; before the corridor ends before the kitchen before the cat she will be glad transparent disappeared nothing. Air

where are (from GFFDG (defexperiment manual)

Fact is there are different people. It's an extortion. He decants as long as possible then he decides. I must do some things so at least I have something else. I make him take it, they are those that I can stand the least, those strains of music. After all, I can't do more than get by. Eventually you get used to it, and start talking on the phone. It is Saturday if you want.
*

Better with pockets. The right hand. The first with tags, it is professional, it is Buñuel. He is 35. I do not have any broadcasts. As in Italy for the same week. Lungaretta street, then you take a guided tour, he's an American translator and a teacher already. The first will have a cup of coffee. Cough. Vatican. Mexico. Week. Caesar Gum.

I return to Buenos Aires. But I cannot follow you. With all that coughing he bothers the clients. Movida yes, moviola, but there's no work. Even if I speak Spanish. Totally ridiculous. They attempt to accost her. She must go back to Cagliari. *Me scribio.*

from tchotchkes

Facilitation

To prevent people from killing themselves they put up temporary fences, they erect barriers, some sort of barriers, their purpose is for people not to jump, they will have to think about it, not easy to climb over them, to climb over the walls, they also build walls, low walls, for chickens, for the movement of small animals but

they are deterrents — as they say — for whoever wants to throw himself over, for people, in the event they want to kill themselves, and then again someone might succeed anyway, and so they install some nets, strong nets, like those of a rabbit hutch, then for larger animals, a gibbon, two gibbons, they install whatever they have, tall ones, they lift, they lift the nets, and make them as high as possible, they make an effort, so that there might also be a distance from where one falls, a space, like in a set game, a loose one, the kind of ditch that they are digging, or may not dig, maybe it was already there and they took advantage of it, then

they go way back and align the deterring spears, or else barbed or electrified wires, or both barbed and electrified, so that people cannot kill themselves, that if they want to jump they get electroshocked, electrocuted, they explode, fried there and burnt, they do not jump cannot do it, they are pushed back, they stick, like chicken skin to the pan, they station a soldier:

they station a soldier every seven to ten meters, with bayonet, rifle, sub-machine-gun, beretta, he patrols back and forth, to stand watch, so he may shoot if they try, if they try to get closer, the guard shoots them, they shoot him so that they do not kill themselves, so that they don't do it, these those and the others, so that someone doesn't jump, doesn't even think about it, to make people quit, quit thinking about these things you would need to enter their heads, to spare all the walls, railings, gratings, cordons, cables, soldiers, it would be easier, perhaps it is easier.

Fast Track Living

After the traffic light it's all countryside. After the traffic light it's all encyclopedia. From here on it's all countryside, from here on it's all encyclopedia. From now on all has changed, all changed in the last thirty years. From now on it's all encyclopedia, it has been all encyclopedia for thirty years. Past the encyclopedia there's nothing but countryside: the countryside with its direct and heterodirect encyclopedic knowledge, the vegetation, the birds, the insects. It is all countryside. Then after thirty years there is no more countryside. From here on it is only encyclopedia. Names, from here onward the names begin, the insects, the vegetation, the thefts begin, the "I'll show you" begins, the city councilors, from here onward it's all city councilors, thirty years, all city councilors, thirty years ago not even here was here. First it was all countryside. City with spots of countryside. In prehistory, before, the word itself says it. Before, forget about it. Before the word, wouldn't you know, forget about it. Now in the courtyard there are hens, six or seven of them scratching about. They are fat and brown. Only now. From here onward it's all cenozoic, crossbred animals, bits and pieces of plants, detached and mixed, a spore there a frond here, a coral in the beak, an impracticable unrealizable scan, some pieces, pieces that remain bewildered on the table, the anatomical table, on the unpleasant anatomical table. Among the pieces they breathe, a labored breath, in the cenozoic, one could hardly breathe, the hens dance, they boil, in the countryside, victuals are passed, one passes, two, it's all encyclopedia, there's little food, one gets tired, three. You see as if all around. As if it were around, they maybe six or seven, maybe four. You see as if around a disc everything has become encyclopedia. In less than thirty years perhaps. You can see a disc as well as around it.

text for a special occasion

The university is a place that also contains people. ||| The university, both as a building and as an institution, includes a number of them. ||| It includes people, who most of the time go to it of their own will. ||| It may also happen at times that some people, other people, not the same people, get locked in it against their will. ||| In this case the people inside the university tend to get out but impediments unrelated to them keep them from doing so. ||| Other people who would tend to enter of their own will sit (pensive) on the doorstep of the university, understood both as an edifice and an institution. ||| The latter who would tend to enter the university of their own will and sit (pensive) reach at times the end of the day without anything happening to them. ||| Other days follow that either look or do not look like the previous ones. ||| The number of people inside the university and the number of people outside the university can diverge and, normally, does. ||| All that is contained in the university, understood both as an architectural site and an institution, includes other things besides people. ||| The number of nameable things within the university but not coincident with people is different from the number of the people contained therein, logically. ||| It is also different, often, but not as a rule, from the number of people not contained within the university. ||| The people contained in the university move freely within the university, following trajectories that are either obligatory or free. ||| The people contained in the university also do not move at their pleasure, following the same variety of trajectories. ||| The people not contained inside the university, though allowed to walk through the university understood both as an architectural site and as an institution, may decide not to walk through it in either direction ||| The people contained within the university related to one another in various ways, just as they do without. ||| The people not contained within the university related to one another in various ways, just as they do within ||| It is well-known to people inside and outside the university that the university has both an interior and an exterior. ||| The same people are not less aware that other things also have an interior and an exterior. ||| Not all the people outside the university have spent a portion of their life during which they found themselves inside the university ||| Similarly, not all the people inside the university have spent a portion of their life during which they found themselves inside of the university. ||| The number of children born inside the university, who grew up there, grew old there, died there, came to be buried there, and who have never left the university is low or equal to zero.

On getting distracted at the movie theater

Some zen disturbance, as if in a sequence. Too many distractions during the projection, but it doesn't matter. Some kind of indifference. As if people were losing interest. I am not interested. As if distracted, distracted by the noise, by the zen racket of montage, by the film clacking the film, floating (*gloating*), flickering, it competes with the soundtrack. Loses interest, in the film. Becomes interested in the flickering, in the clacking of the disturbed film, it is untouched. It matters not to him. He looks up in the air, and listens.

All that matters to him is to see the film, the film in itself does not matter much to him, he is distracted, he wants to be distracted. There is the film. Things happen in it.

I don't know, they weep on the screen. They remember an episode from a long time ago (but not so long ago). They remember it n times. They grieve $n+x$ times. If you divide n by x the resulting number is different. At times a number with a lot of decimals or a few decimals. Decimals don't count. Custom dictates that when talking to the citizenry only integers be considered. Only the numbers before the decimal point.

They are less distracted. They are integral, integer numbers. The law, by contrast, to encompass everything, in abstract, includes decimals in its recordings. This way it establishes a precedent, and makes a film as well. Indeed, if you think about it (though by law you are not obliged to do it), the whole film is not simply measurable in meters, but always in meters plus another unpredictable something after the decimal point. The ace law has up its sleeve is to predicate also the second something, unknown to most. To predicate the unpredictable. With a zen quiet, making a loud noise that does not get distracted by the film playing, which has its own meters to unroll, in the given time, and cannot keep track of everything.

The fitters raise the partitions, pierce the drywall, pull out the nails without thinking much of the noise they make when falling, breaks included. It's all in the bill. Analogously, he is completely uninterested in this kind of performance. When I say "completely" I mean not only that his mind and gaze are distracted, but also his left and right heel, and his femurs, his tender parts, the four humors, the pituitary gland and the bile, his hair and his eyebrows, spread out and not arched, his elbow, his fingers. Everything or nearly everything in him (let's not exaggerate) is distracted, luckily he is distracted following some sort of concentration, not chaotically; if so you'd end up with a chaotically distracted body, with calves pointing to the east and feet to the east, disrupting every possible interpretation, even a Jungian one. Everything a radial swarm of molecules, a white dwarf, so impatient, imagined, Egyptian silhouetted, that you could use a fire extinguisher to break the little attic window and escape from it, from the haunted house.

His, however, is a concerted (concentrated) distraction, he is very attentive (certainly in an inattentive, distracted way) to the total coherence of his distraction, no leftovers, particles, residuals, no decimals left behind.

Gone / Returned (series of the intellectuals)

Vimeo is very clean.
Vimeo is much cleaner.
Even if spasms and intermittence.
But these are bodily things, nothing to do with it.
You must bet on what's right and on the right technique.

One trick is to look at the silhouette.
It's better if they do not flit.
Heidegger went to Greece, he would sit down properly.
He would eat a sandwich, it gave him confidence.
*

It gets cloudy, they cover the tv camera with plastic
Otherwise they would risk getting wet
Not a good idea
They will air the report anyway
It's live
It was announced for a long time
It rains
The report is already likely to win a Pulitzer
The title of the report
It rains
*

Ah when Pasolini was around
So many regrets
Pasolini and the intellectuals
The intellectuals, Pasolini
They hang on, the intellectuals
They watch or make films on Pasolini
Some sort of solution
One solution leads to another
To the age-old problem that comes back each season
Timely
*

Let's have a cup of coffee
They say
Let's have a cup of coffee
With more passion
Let's go to the café they have
An orange soda, two slices of cake, lemon soda
Let's go right away
So we go
For big surprises
*

Let's have a cup of coffee in the Sixties
Moravia is there Pasolini too
We take part in the heated discussion
We use adjectives
Ending at times with "istic"
We go into
That lasts longer
Television
To criticize it from within.

*

And for certain he's an intellectual
Piazza di Spagna, Piazza del Popolo
They come and go as you can see
Let's imagine that one afternoon
As if reserving
Like in flakes
One' home was at number 20 or right across at 19
Moravia can count on a little revenue
In the biographies Pasolini makes the film
Luckily the Seventies
Even now one remains
And what can I tell you
One pays attention to understand as well as he can
That a road then all
And nearly everyone threads on it
Hard to understand

*

The situation got complicated
After the tragic disappearance of the intellectuals
Before they were there then all of the sudden
So the first thing that everyone thought
Was
They must have stepped out for a moment but they will return
They were not returning
People were very worried
They were complicated, there were issues
Without any interpretations some were wondering

What are we going to do what are we going to do
The elevator had stopped at the floor
They must have gone to buy milk, matches
As if they were sold out at the tobacco shop (let's go somewhere else)
Now we'll see them again it's a matter of minutes
But it did not happen, not even when we called the carabinieri
They were laughing up their sleeve
Where on earth did they go it has been days months years
At this point nobody seems to mind their disappearance
But in the beginning it was difficult
Every morning going to work you were visited by anguish
What to say what to do
We did not know how to pull the bolt from the wheel
Open the ladder sell the codfish
Everything came to a halt an entire nation adrift
Practically civil war they were handing out fines
Fortunately in the morning Berlinguer
Spoke twice on tv for three five minutes
He said stay calm it is all under control
Everything will be fine.
*

At the end of the Seventies everyone joined
Then nobody joined
It was not forbidden but they did not join
The fault lies in part with the intellectuals
When the intellectuals realized it they all flock to it
Before nobody had much of a presence on tv
Two, three hosts maximum five
Then they realized that they could be there and they went
At first the tv cameras couldn't frame them
Suddenly they were in the frame
Suddenly they would not exit
*

Where are they where are they
Such despair
Look carefully
*

One day the intellectuals will return
It will be a totally different matter
They will no longer be venial with their writings like they say
There were unspeakable horrors it was disgusting
The human species
But they will return exiting from pockets
They will finally have/have again their role
Society qua society will breathe a sigh of relief
It smiles
Goes on an outing with miling/smiling motor vehicles
We'll go to the beach at Ostia at Fregene
All the moms out on balconies with babies laugh
Meanwhile springtime is here
they recover once and for all from their rhinitis
*
Otherwise later their schedule gets all screwed up
By then they push the wrong button
No field trip or
They would like to return to the spotlight
With a blank check
And refund themselves,
Or the sun smiles on them,
They wish to come back
And to have their revenge
For the injustices they suffered
And during all of that
Interpret the voice of the people even in its absence
Focus, focus, they cry,
You have to wait a moment for the technician to come back
Then it will happen
This documentary is really interesting
*
They watch a documentary on the Assyrians
It explains how they manufactured their manufacts
They were swift even on human rights
There was something superficial
They were dying like flies

External

We are in agreement, there are no reasons for disagreeing. They also produce a bag.

We will not argue about this, we will not protest.

We are in agreement, afterwards there will be some cookies bearing this name.

They are all courteous, professional, and thoughtful. They accompany us and we can't complain.

Outside they give us a bag, they gave it to us now after queueing. So many of us here, we are all waiting in line, we agree.

We have the bag.

On Game

It is all very clear. It's a matter of sentences. I make sentences. Often in literature there are not sentences but ideas, and the sentences are filled with ideas.

I don't have ideas.

Tommaso Ottonieri

Translated by Philip Balma

in apostrophe,

                        among the synapses an angel backs away.   like a drop
       pierces my contacts.   it filters among the footsteps, the moment
corrodes.   I'm this pulse

INSOMNIA, movie

    …..(you divert your gaze to the sails, that know how to   you stop
  at the edges of these layers   you wander   and if you return
       you don't know on what to   land, and inside
                                                                               where):

Lothian:

                                                    from 'Rime', *Part the Fourth*
……. at the end of the bright shade of the boat
drag sails were cutting the tails off the waves:
sinuous on the white, shiny wakes
they arched their backs, in an elfin light –

                                                            light

fallen into flakes, that melts with vapour:

I, inside the closed shade of the boat,
rotating at the spiral of the edges, –
black-velvet blue-greens sparkle, –

I was watching them twist in the suds:

                                                    and every wake

was a flash of incandescent gold,

scale that may founder straight to the iris:

Autour de la gare

…Night:steps:fog:dark –
(husky to be heard smooth my fear)

      …late – I deaf, how fate gets stretched out –
      with pants, squeaks, on San Gottardo Lane no. (…)
(train station area) I was dark, heavy (used to
a stingy star being in suspension – the sex

      seed pulsates sterile at her breasts)
      until the end of the darkness… a train sss-

hisses a return in the night (when I don't
know where to find oneself) (and myself: gasping) it

wasn't, no, it wasn't, same anxiety same
sky (at 4 in the morning) (go on

so philomela extends her arms to the darkness
advancing) veil of the self she weaved

on her own faraway simulacra of Hatred (a
chocolate panettone conceals

in its dough a lump that is solute?):
if the world that looks at its reflection in its tin cans

           hatching latrines and slumbers, now you fall back
           on hot ecstasies of caffelatte vortex.

Last Days of Disco

and then without fiber at the end of the leather
couch that the vigil is walking around
>> beyond the flashes shot out by the strobes
>> at the end of the flashes shot out and the strobes

which then in the dark dilates strangely
the retina the lounge the body the edge
>> of disco music the leather in which I was sinking
>> clings around me like Play-Doh

slowly spills outside the sound of the world
that absorbs my outline
>> when the shafts of light from one part to the next
>> spread over and through me, and you're alone

the bombastic mask you wear
you are not if not in the wave that moves you
>> the pumice the powder that engulfs
>> coarse ray among the shaken profiles

vapour that rises up that deodorizes
on the swarm of pins from the dead
>> skin that you sit on or the bodies headlights off
>> you're in a whirl the white light the headlights

shone in your face so you feel sick
everything moves to be felt coming undone
>> the spirit that fades from your cocktail
>> the wave that starts to burn to the fire of the TV ad.

Kitchen (in New Haven)

> *an and yet, and yet, and yet –*

you ruinous daily calm
sharp in the eyelid, the orbit throws open
the beating of eyelashes on the truncated
disaster of the expectations: and the hour widens, floods

from the suspended calm of the instant
       of this calm, shadow that you set aside
       with weary, long afternoon calm
       the house opens wide, the eyelid is a desert

of insomnias swallowed in one bite
of anxieties vomited in the warmth
of half a raw chicken to get out of it

pull out of it

       spaces, vertigos of spaces, eviscerate
       vertigos all ready to cook
       bake these hungers in the hard
       calm voracious door to your surrender

surrendering to the pulse of the television
beat heart in your mouth in one bite
surrendering space, hunger in the pallor

       heart (of creaminess!) in which the space
       absorbs you no its only memory
       the thirst no the algid sphere
       that assaults you, at night, if you're alone

… and you disarm –

the food: the
food, the space, the hunger, the food
of hunger the mouthful swallowed and spit-
ten away – I where here to undo myself
to unravel
        at my gulping down rich of images
embankments

                heart-of-creaminess hunger for the images
                and the soda; squirted; and then the clangor
                of pluto freddie mickey, splat, the
                night *le cauchemar* the shells squirts the cone
                the horn of the night erect on
                the edge this edge of ed
                ge of
                (slave, incubus) of an incubated
                night
                the night
                of soda
                we die
                alone
                from soda
                you die
                from television.

… darkness,
darkness tube on end, prostrate, bulb
flutters shadows from the darkness, from the tube
from the food from the silt from the bottom of the
tube, and from sleep, and from the eyes of sleep
and the exhausted mind that falls heavily
guts pouring out collapses
aeropaghial nightmares from the soda to the cone to
the tube hole bulb, fulvous
from which the sound pours, it crumbles to dust.

        …

the light

...

the mind
so
the bulb
I say
the hole:
the calm:

dark I say dark
tube I say tube
hole the mind from the bulb to the valves
to the hibernated
leaks, (I say), dark, juicy super-
tasty to
refrigerating hermi-
tages:

Lights on the Asphalt

(for Garbo)

     I who am walking in parallel
     acclimated imago to this glass
light the night already fused on the back
of my nervously going limp,
     while, in my eyes, headlights beat
     the mind consumes itself in becoming asphalt
of a wave struck levelled arc is the gaze
that reabsorbs me into my pose, radio,
     I, who leave my image as a stain
     or rather who ring out at the end of the combustion
of the most secret metallic abode
motor that assimilates me to its headlight,

               fire, I
               who was leaving the street straight
                 towards motels to cultivate insomnias
divided enough now this sound
to never distract me from the right course,
       now that light pierces through me thick
       from one side to another drilling through the glass
that is, it perforates me inside from my verse,
now that I am the fire of the light
       I burn of this light that I pour in myself
       so that now I weld myself to this light, I
           who crumbles of myself,
               who crumbles:

El Conquistador

(The Poe-m)

... There: it's the Gala night already
       Of the last looonely years!
Crowd of ornate angels / Brawl of soft wings –
       ...From the veils that are dripping with worries...
From the lowest Auditorium to Applaud
The "*pièce*" of Fear & *Desire* –
If Orchestra of its spasms exhales
       celestial Harmonic of Spheres –

       o One Thousand Lire Music! – Mimi:

Masks of the God: up High
Mumbling the squeaky low voice –
They flutter entropic mobile mass -
Nothing more than puppets, that come and go
Drifts of vast of the shapeless /

         deformed things
    they transmute the scene from one side and from the other
                (unconsoled: eroded)
Shaking their Condor wings they spread
      Invisible sorrows & hidden Worry

Pints, piled up, theatrical Poses!

Changeable *Mélo*! Nothing
    Will be forgotten for you
The Puppet ghost that the Crowd
    Chases after without really grabbing him –
In the middle of a circle that always returns to
    The same center of the Self -
            And the Madness
Which is a lot, and even more so is Sin -
    And Horror that animates/changes the fairy-tale!

    It's Horror that moves the mud That traces the
route That breaks away from the Circle That offsets the edges! Horror of
the adorned backdrops Horror of my dark days Of The Black Sun of
the Eternal Roll!

- *Check it out!* - In the midst of mimicked brawl
              (and lubricious)
    A form intrudes that's slithering!
                (and it acts a worm!)
Bloodsucker the Thing / That thrashes about & creeps in
On the Deserted Disconcertment of the Empty Stage!
It writhes! - and squirms! - of death the spasms
   - Made the mimes his meal -
And at the fangs beasts hiccup seraphs
Full of blood and lumps, globules in little nibbles-

> *It bottles it by the liter among Twisting Coils:*
> *It intrudes on the Scheme of already Dead Forms:*

The lights go out - the jaws light up
    And on the Shiver of each Form, the
Curtain falls – gloomy plot, & fatal - which tumbles - then –
    Down with the roar of a storm - that rumbles, that sinks
Which the pallid exhausted angels which the hoarse angels
    Rising up Exposing themselves to the Lost Sight,

        ANNOUNCE:

That "MAN" is the name of the Tragic Farce,
    AND WORM is its Hero, *the Worm,* yes, *the WORM* –

"It's the WORM that CONQUERS!!"

CNN the Storm: IX Arias for Combustion

… but it's late. feel the fire, *Scheherazade,*
up, down, it's raining from the Setting Stars –
it rains on you: and your sisters' Wings and Dances
dazzle the *Nights* in *Bagdad* ….

… it's late: the Words that dilate
Wind, Eyes, Seas, Mouths when they explode
from Lead to Bone Voices that pick off your flesh
in Event performing you faraway …

… no *I don't* know no *I don't know* how to dismember
this Pile of Refracted Images –
Spazzed-Out Tongues levitating attracted
into the Vortex of Occidental Word …

... Image of Voice isn't Voice
the Groove that you carve on the Syllable
the Red that clots the Pupil
Eager Advent of Surgery Peace ...

       ... the Alchemic Brawl of *our* End
       shadows distils from Techno-Ossuaries
       already you can hear the Fanfares rattle
       they sublimate the Alkaline Retinas ...

       ... and already planted to fecundate the Videos
alive we are not, Corpses to germinate
until the *show* can render the Luxuriance
of Raw Seed to renew its Rite ...

... Eyes on Eyes still Eyes still
Hordes and Mutes they grab on to the Killed
       the Voice that reanimates its own I Saw
Remote Death is returned to Video Gora ...

... *but the pyre is here*: late, in the star's
plunge for it to tilt to the west
       you can already smell the oil that slices through the air
       her theories of the spaces of the sphere ...

... you feel and you can no longer stave off
this scorching sunset that calls to you
in the plasma that inebriates us it's *Our* vain
       Quête for a Philosophical *Estèsi* ...

Playful March for Rudi

       Homage, to (from) Elio, for his 75 years

In the care of slumber
       The human body explodes

                        Gravity is this force
                                Taken by the last game
That doesn't open throwing
                        The anxiety of the masses
                                Scans his black body
                                        The rhythm that tears
It'd be like saying
                        For eight hours a day
                                In the time between two lighting-bolts
                                        Watching while remaining immobile
Without wings the spirit
                        At San Siro the Siemens company
                                Tries all the roadways and
                                        The horizontal world
Supine on the sand
                        There are no colours
                                The astral virgin
                                        Needs lead
To be placed as ballast
                        And gunpowder
                                More need of lead
                                        To hear the noises
 It'd be like saying
                        The science of the merchandise
                                Is diamond on the glass
                                        Of a booth by Motta
That a guy who ain't down,
                        Who's got nothing coming
                                When he leaves the Astor
                                        Takes all kinds of walks.
At the intersection of Via Meda,
                        Drugs weren't enough
                                The radioactive rain
                                        The Geiger counters
The H-bombs in the Pacific
                        The Geiger counters
                                The asynchronous rhythm man

                        The engorged sex and the heart
It'd be like saying
            Welding wires by the thousands
                        This is the reduction of the times
                                    For the things that pass.
The drop of sweat
            The negative energy
                        The homicidal instincts
                                    The apparent reason
It'd be like saying
            Pretending like nothing's nothing
                        Hearing the sounds
                                    Smiling from the stage
It detaches from orbit
            The horizontal world
                        The inertia that is the flesh
                                    The dismay that is the body
In the temples, the veins
            Welding wires by the thousands
                        Spring onions in little slices
                                    This is the reduction of the times
Umbilical chord
            Dragged without wings
                        In the future that passes
                                    The force that tears
Over the meek bodies
            The gunpowder
                        Creaks the diamond on the glass
                                    In the depth of slumber,

(the diamond the sweat this dust
the lead the inertia cord the horizontal
body the glass the dismay
merchandise supine facing wires that come unsoldered:

carve on the glass the body take notes

remove the contact the bellybutton is anxious
in the science of the lead, gravitating,
subtle reduction in the rhythm that
stagnates)

Chris Mustazza

PennSound and the Italian Audiotext: Archives, Producers, Platforms

The following is an adaptation of a talk I gave at The Reappearing Pheasant Conference at NYU's Casa Italiana on November 11, 2022, aimed to introduce PennSound, the world's largest archive of recordings of poets, as a seminal resource for studying modern and contemporary Italian poetry. As such, this piece is meant to be "heard" rather than read as an article; thus, I have endeavored to keep the language conversational and upbeat and eschew the form of a standard academic article.

1. Publishers and Producers

I want to thank Dr. Ballerini and all of the conference organizers for inviting me here today to speak about the PennSound archive and the affordances it offers for studying modern and contemporary Italian poetry performances. I should say more about the word "archive" here. PennSound is indeed an archive—the world's largest collection of recordings of poets performing their work. With recordings spanning from 1913 (recordings of Apollinaire made in a Parisian dialect lab) through the addition of a constant flow of recent recordings, PennSound is comprised of over 60,000 audio files and over 1,000 videos totaling around 7,000 hours of material. For its roughly one million listeners worldwide, it serves as an important repository and reference, an archive that tells the unwritten story of poetic performance in the twentieth and twenty-first centuries. Like all archives, it is curated and constructed with preservation in mind.

Beyond its archival function, I would like to offer two other ontologies of PennSound. The first is that of an open-access and free-of-cost publishing venue for curated audio materials. To discuss this aspect, we need to take a moment to tarry with common understandings of what a poetic performance is. Almost every time a poetic performance is advertised or referred to, it is called a "reading." Of course, such a term plainly gives primacy to the written version of the poem—the performance is figured to take the words on the page and convert them to sound to help us better understand the written version. Charles Bernstein opposes this understanding of poetry in the introduction to *Close Listening*, calling us "to overthrow the common presumption that the text of a poem—that is, the written document—is primary and that the recitation or performance of a poem by the poet is secondary and fundamentally inconsequential to the 'poem itself'" (8). So, following Bernstein's prompt to treat performances as entities in their own rights, audio and video of performances must have a venue for publication and dissemination, just as their written counterparts do.

Historically, there has been little to no space for publishing these performances in a stable, accessible manner. There have been institutional and individual attempts to curate archives of poetry recordings dating back to the advent of recorded sound. Also, media/broadcast companies, such as the BBC, have recorded and broadcast literary performances. Still, these are often either ephemeral—in that the recordings float in and out of an accessible state or are difficult to access—or interspersed with other chronologically ordered content, which is not itself a problem.

There is an argument for poetry to be more embedded in everyday life. In the nineteenth and early twentieth century, light and occasional verse was published in newspapers and magazines alongside other kinds of content. Bartholomew Brinkman delineates the history wherein poetry became enshrined in dedicated, yet segregated, publications like *Poetry* magazine. He describes the thick white margins in the magazine as functioning like an ornate frame in an art gallery, literally offering the work up as an *objet d'art*, rather than as embedded in everyday life:

> This framing signaled an effort to make poems into aesthetic objects for contemplation. Although prose texts frequently reinforced one another in topic or theme, poems were to be taken as self-contained texts intended more as respite from the other writing on the page than as something to be read alongside it and integrated into the magazine as a whole. (*Poetic Modernism in the Culture of Mass Print* 90)

But what is the analog of a publisher of poetry chapbooks or, on the audio side of things, of a record label for the poetic audiotext? Where can a listener who understands a poetic performance to be an event tantamount to a book publication go to find new editions, new—I will not say readings—*productions* (more on this term later)? And what of works for which there is no printed version—sound poetry or other words that strain lexical boundaries? Louis Zukofsky figured poetry as existing in a calculus integral, "Lower limit speech / Upper limit music" ("A–12" 38). In this model, then, these sound-based works inhabit the upper bounds of the integral, closer to musical intonation than to everyday speech. They need a publication venue much closer to a record label than something like a printing house. They require engineers, producers, and infrastructure altogether different than the works sometimes called "readings."

I am being abstract, and being abstract is like... OK, let us look at an example and connect it with our primary topic of Italian poetry. PennSound features a significant collection of Italian poetry, known as *PennSound Italiana*, edited by Jennifer Scappettone, who, in turn, writes that the collection is an endeavor

> to offer a broad sense of the field, filling in the substantive gaps in global access to Italian poetry (as both written and sonic text—even within Italian borders), and [to expand] awareness of its range of practitioners, with an emphasis on marginalized and experimental voices of the twentieth and twenty-first centuries. ("Introducing *PennSound Italiana*" n.p.)

Using a term with a rich history in experimental Italian writing—"liberate," cf. F.T. Marinetti's "parole in libertà"—she continues that *PennSound Italiana*

> is an effort—a unique one, in our reckoning—to 'liberate' the spectrum of Italian poetry for as broad a public as possible through audio and video recordings, given that the publishing industry and the translation market are endangered and/or blinkered enough to condemn a significant swath of both historical and contemporary innovation to oblivion. (n.p.)

She concludes, "[a]s such, this live archive extends the task of PennSound writ large." Scappettone's introduction to her collection raises the two topics we've been discussing: the question of the archive and the publishing platform. She refers to her edition of these recordings as a "live archive," an elegant way of referring to PennSound's function as an alternative publication venue for poetry as audio and video. And she also alludes to the deficiencies of the wider world of textual publishing—particularly its elisions of more experimental poets. As we have been discussing, another dimension of this deficiency that needs to be noted, perhaps implicit in her comment, is the lack of publication platforms for sound-based poetry. Of course, some small publishers have done a great job of including audio with their text-based works—I'm thinking here of the edition Kora Press created of Tracie Morris's *handholding: 5 kinds*. But on a larger scale, it is important to recognize sound collections dubbed "archives" as producers and publishers.

Within the *PennSound Italiana* collection, many works must be heard or seen to be fully apprehended, works that could be called "sound poetry" or at least be called "performance forward." While these works might have a printed component, they rely on the medium of spoken language to transmit their poetics, sometimes straining against or altogether rejecting lexical bounds. Take, for example, the great experimental poet Milli Graffi and her vocal composition *Salnitro*. Scappettone writes of the performance: "*Salnitro* (Saltpeter) is a historic 1976 sound poem produced in the studios of RAI by Milli Graffi, a member of the Tam Tam group and current editor-in-chief of the experimental literary journal *Il Verri*" (n.p.). Of this piece, Graffi writes,

> I understood what my sound poem could be when I listened to Schwitters' *Ursonate* recited by Giuliano Zosi: half an hour of uninterrupted pressurized vocalizations, strongly rhythmical and exemplary. For me, it was the path of the first avant-garde, and one had to depart from there. An absurd tercet of hendecasyllables came to my mind in a flash. I prepared a rigorous plan of fragmentation, defined on every page of the score with tempos and directions for vocal execution [...]. Invited to take part in the Audiobox broadcast directed by Pinotto Fava, I realized the eighteen minutes of *Saltpeter* in the RAI studios of Rome in three days of rehearsal with the technologies of that time. From that point, using the cassette RAI gave me, I composed *Saltpeter* by improvising with my live voice and redoubling the effect by overlaying it onto the voice recorded on cassette. With the lights out, I had an animated play of liquids that Giovanni Anceschi had given me, which made for a good "saltpeter" effect, projected onto a screen at my back. I dressed all in white to become an integral part of the imaginary grotto. (n.p.)

There are two aspects of Graffi's poetics that I want to highlight here as they relate to the sonic archive. The first is that she provides the aesthetic lineage of the piece, locating it in the Hanover Dada of Kurt Schwitters and his *Ursonate*. Of course, even a cursory listen to *Salnitro* would reveal this. We can hear the same pre-linguistic—tones that evoke a child's language acquisition—and post-linguistic—as in the sense of lexical breakdown and fragmentation—that animate the *Ursonate*. From this sonic-linguistic primordial ooze, word-sounds arise and conjure semantics before receding into the abstract sonic ether. What is so interesting, though, is that Graffi says that she heard the *Ursonate* performed by Giuliano Zosi rather than the recordings of Kurt Schwitters or Ernst Schwitters (available in PennSound). One is left to wonder if Zosi had heard recordings of Schwitters or if he had recomposed the *Ursonate* from Schwitters' printed score. The latter seems unlikely, given the twice-removed sonic echoes of the recording of Schwitters' *Ursonate* in Graffi's *Salnitro*. This is to say that one way or another, the sounds of Schwitters magnum opus found their way into *Salnitro* through the circulation and publication of sound poetry, scarce as it was at the time. Graffi's work exists because the sounds of prior sonic experimentation were preserved and made available, somehow surviving even though they existed in the interstitial space between music and speech, an area notoriously difficult for most mainstream media to understand—we must give RAI and Pinotto Fava credit for recognizing the poem's value.

The other point is how Graffi foregrounds mediation technologies in her composition. She does not *write* this poem; she *produces* it in the sense of musical producers of the time (such as Phil Spector, George Martin, or Brian Wilson), using the same kinds of audio manipulation used for commercial musical productions. Moving from her score, which, it is important to note, is not the poem itself; she records a performance but does not stop there. The metaphysical poem comes into being in the post-production she applies, specifically in the technique of multi-tracking vocals, which was coming into its own during this relatively early period of recording to magnetic tape. Previously, to achieve polyvocal effects, there needed to be multiple people recording in the studio simultaneously. With the advent of tape recording, the same voice could be doubled and redoubled, either to create the illusion of depth—as is standard practice in vocal recording—or to create otherworldly effects. At the cutting edge of linguistic and audio technologies, Graffi goes beyond Schwitters' inspiration by consciously foregrounding the poem's reproduction technologies. This was the apotheosis of sonic-poetic postmodernity at the time, allowing for the work's procedural composition to be audible in both the polish and glitch in the recording. Through it all, Graffi, the poet, is more than just an author; she is a producer. She needed the infrastructure and distribution afforded to her by RAI to realize her leap forward for poetry. Much like the New Wave artists who were beginning to change music then, Graffi understood with *Salnitro* that the studio was an instrument rather than a space to house instrumentation. Today, her work is available in *PennSound Italiana*, a publication venue that allows it to be heard by a global audience, perhaps inspiring further poetic advances.

2. Platforms

Some of the topics discussed to this point may have been familiar to those interested in archive theory and the sociology of literature. From here, I want to turn to another affordance of poetry audio that may be less familiar. In this era of so-called big data, machine learning, and artificial intelligence, one might ask what new kinds of analyses are possible with a vast quantity of audio data—Sorry, I'm temporarily going to call the poems data!—present in these archives. In other words, what new kinds of literary questions can be asked and possibly answered by using these audio files as data rather than for close listening applications? I want to briefly discuss just a couple of these possibilities, with an example drawn from one of the most notorious Italian poets. In all of the cases discussed here, the archive is treated as a platform in the computational sense of the word. It is an environment optimized for converting data to information and information to knowledge. The archive here becomes not a container but a tool itself.

Before getting to the technological hinterlands of machine learning, I would like to ask how we might augment our human hearing to perceive poetic sound differently. This is the topic I covered in detail in my essay "Machine-Aided Close Listening," where I propose using new visualizations of poets' voices to aid our close listening of poems. I will not rehash the arguments from that piece save to say that I am interested in whether we can hear a poem in a new way by seeing it in a new way. Seeing the material form of a poem is often correlated with identifying line breaks, spacing, and arrangement on the page. But what are the ways we might read sound itself? The aforementioned essay offers tools for visualizing the pitch contours of poets' voices, the tempos of their readings, and other dimensions more often connected to linguistics or musicology than literary studies. These tools reside within PennSound and operate as a platform for analyzing poems in a new way. The idea is to provide premade visualizations that anyone could use, regardless of whether they have a background in computer programming. Knowledge of prosodic analysis helps, but even without that, a reader could speculate about the meanings of tempos. What does it mean for Frost to read some lines faster than others? How can that extend what is happening in the poem?

In addition to *PennSound Italiana*, another significant corpus of Italian poetry recordings is Voices of Italian Poets (VIP), directed by Dr. Valentina Colonna. This site is unique in that it is the fullest realization of what I have termed *the archaeo-platform*, a curated collection of art objects optimized and enabled for computational analysis. The collection of over 1,000 recordings allows close listening to a wide range of Italian poets from varying regions and poetic traditions. But in addition to links to the recordings, VIP provides precompiled prosodic data about many of the recordings, which can be used for quantitative analyses of the poets' performances. As the site puts it:

> Voices of Italian Poets (VIP) è un progetto-pilota per lo studio fonetico della lettura poetica ed è il primo archivio digitale nazionale online delle voci dei poeti italiani. In modo analogo al rapporto tra composizione e interpretazione in musica, centrale in questo progetto è il delicato rapporto tra il testo poetico e la sua lettura ad alta voce, analizzato con gli strumenti della Fonetica sperimentale. (Colonna et al.)[1]

So, the site was constructed to be a platform for a different kind of augmented listening rather than as a traditional repository that assumes close listening. It allows users to download prosodic analyses and consider whether these might alter their understanding of the poems and poets in the archive.

VIP and PennSound's Machine-Aided Close Listening tools privilege a kind of "closeness"—albeit via the addition of data—with individual poems. In other words, they are hermeneutic tools meant to aid in interpreting a literary object. However, they point toward audio platforms that can operate at larger scales, which Tanya E. Clement has termed *distant listening*, building on Franco Moretti's concept of *distant reading* or using machine learning to parse large collections of literary works.[2] Clement's work in this space has included, for example, metrics on the amount of applause various poets received in recordings of their performances. Other projects have analyzed laughter in poetry recordings and whether the provenance of a recording can be determined from recording noise.

In my work, I have sought to use distant listening methodologies through artificial intelligence and machine learning to determine whether poetic performances are modeled on or include other sonic genres. Are there

---

[1] EN: "Voices of Italian Poets (VIP) is a pilot project for the phonetic study of poetic readings and is the first national online digital archive of the voices of Italian poets. In a manner analog to the relation between composition and performance in music, central to this project is the delicate relationship between poetic text and its reading aloud, analyzed with the instruments of experimental phonetics" (my translation).

[2] AN: See Mustazza 2018 for an extended discussion of Clement's coinage of "distant listening" and its relation to Franco Moretti's "distant reading."

places where a poet is performing in a voice evocative of a sermon/a political speech/a comedy monologue/etc? For example, I sought to use machine learning to define and locate instances of sermonic performances in PennSound. As these questions relate to Italian literature, I also sought to define the sonic characteristics of Futurism as heard through the performances of its founder, F.T. Marinetti. In particular, I was interested in the sonic relationship between the aggressive cadences employed by Marinetti in "Definizione di Futurismo" (a work loosely based on the famous Futurist Manifesto of 1909) and the Italian political speeches of the time. Marinetti's complicated relationship with Benito Mussolini was well known, especially since they both developed their aesthetics of public address through journalism. I was curious about whether the intense, bellicose deliveries of their speeches shared a sound and mode. And if so, what did it mean to deliver a poem as a speech meant to persuade and motivate action, especially action aimed at destruction and erasure? If it were possible to define these voicings empirically and train a machine to locate instances of them in a wider archive like PennSound or VIP, how would that change the way we hear poems and interpret them? For example, we might find individual lines or sections of poems modeled on certain kinds of political speeches and could then read this genre as a dimension of the poem's—the performed poem's—content. As you can see, I am not interested in a methodology of scale that elides the individual poems and collapses them into a dataset, but rather in a way to use "distance" (as it were) to provide a new closeness to a literary object.

A proper environment must be provided to pursue machine or machine-aided listening, including access to the data presented in reasonable formats, helpful metadata, etc. When these conditions are met, an archive becomes a platform, too, an archaeo-platform. It suggests ways to use the information within it, manufacture new information, and create knowledge rather than just striving to represent a historical moment. In being protean and generative, such a platform is the true "live archive" Scappettone refers to. Said differently, why should the formal experimentation found in these poems cease at the level of the archive? Just as Graffi pushed the materiality of her sonic medium to the visible fore, archivists can also extend this ethos by making the infrastructure of their archives legible as a platform.

So, there you have it: archive, publisher, producer, and platform. These dimensions will allow the poem as a sounded entity to persist, proliferate, and offer itself for varying modes of interpretation. Given the rich history of modern and contemporary Italian poetry that exists as sound, from Marinetti through Graffi, resources like PennSound and VIP are crucial for filling in the unwritten gaps in literary history. I hope this talk will inspire others to think about using audio in their work, not just as a way to explicate a written poem, but to encounter sound as sound, as a primary medium, and to ask questions that cannot be answered from written texts alone.

Research Poetry between Utopias, Metaphors, and the State of Things. Part I. A Conversation with Fabrizio Bondi.

During the three days of the conference, Professor Bondi delivered two different talks on two different topics. The first of them, during the first day of the conference at Casa Italiana Zerilli-Marimò, was centered upon "The Interactive Wunderkammer of Contemporary Italian Poetry," a digital project promoting a new approach to Contemporary Italian Poetry. Professor Bondi ad-libbed his speech; for this reason, I interviewed him via email. In this way, I could focus on some of the most relevant aspects of his speech and expand on topics and perspectives that he didn't have a chance to focus on during the conference (Iuri Moscardi).

IM: You were invited to give two talks during the conference. In the first one, you described the preliminary stages of "The Interactive Wunderkammer of Contemporary Italian Poetry": what is this project?
FB: The first idea for this project developed from an informal conversation between Professors Luigi Ballerini and Lina Bolzoni. Bolzoni suggested the possibility of digitalizing the anthology *Those Who from Afar Look Like Flies* (2017). In Bolzoni's view, the model to be followed was the Palace (or Theatre) of Memory, an ancient method of organizing, memorizing, and sometimes transforming knowledge. Prof. Bolzoni has described this method in some of her famous books, such as *Il teatro della memoria. Studi su Giulio Camillo* (1984). After Prof. Ballerini enthusiastically endorsed the project, the idea was submitted to the web graphics and developers of NetSeven, partners of the enterprise: they had already worked with Prof. Bolzoni and her team. They suggested another model, more suitable to the subject—contemporary research poetry—and to the Web: that of the Wunderkammer or the Cabinet of Curiosity.

IM: In the Wunderkammer, you associated texts and authors with specific places. Is this because you followed the method of *loci* or to give Contemporary Italian Poetry a more concrete foundation?

FB: The choice of places where we situated the different groups of poets with their ideologies and various characteristics was influenced—I don't know how much consciously—by the model of the memory palace, which was rejected in a second moment. Nonetheless, for the *trouvaille* of the "Bar of Novissimi," I was also inspired by a poem by Nanni Balestrini where he mentions a "Malcontento Bar" (Discontent Bar).[1] I thought this sign would be perfect to give an idea of the rebel spirit of the Novissimi and, at the same time, of their modernism. Of course, this image needed a modern bar full of contemporary art and design: what better bar than in Milan, the city that in the Sixties symbolized the ideas of progress, industrialization, and economic development? In other words, we have chosen a non-documentary approach: every place must evoke a mood, not necessarily a historical and real place where, for example, Sanguineti and Giuliani met to drink and talk. The same happened for the poets of Officina: the title of their journal was chosen because it refers to a proper workshop, and it fitted perfectly with the themes of the poetry of Roversi, Pasolini, and the other poets. Finally, the cut-up technique I experimented with from the beginning—like in the "Gunfight" between Pasolini and Sanguineti—is not a contemporary superimposition but a poetic method already employed by the Novissimi.

IM: In developing the Wunderkammer, you relied on Digital Humanities (DH), one of your research interests and one of the subjects you teach at university. How did the Digital Humanities help you in developing this project?

FB: In my opinion, what we call "Digital Humanities" remains an object that is challenging to define and in continuous transformation, not only because of the constant progress of technology, which is a big deal. The problem is the rapid transformation of the relationships between humans and machines. I would define myself more as a practical employer than a DH theorist or, at least, a "sorcerer apprentice." In developing the Wunderkammer, what helped me make the right—I hope—choices, such as accepting to switch from the memory palace to the Wunderkammer model, was the habit of listening to the

---

[1] EN: See Balestrini's *Come si agisce* (1963): "prima di posare sul sagrato si librali tese / negli specchi di luce bagnata, rotti da un piede verde; *Malcontento Bar* ferisce mortalmente uno sconosciuto / scambiandolo per il suo seduttore" (35, emphasis added).

suggestions from the technical crew. They are not merely executors of abstract ideas conceived by humanists but an active part of the creative process, especially when they halt the Pindaric flight of our phantasy with some technical problems (the hard reality of the hardware). But these phantasies are, for them, a challenge to imagine new solutions. What I learned, above all, in my years of "digital jail"—to quote a famous joke by Giuseppe Verdi—is the importance of the interplay: only when this virtuous circle works can the complex and mixed mission of the digital humanist reach its goals.

IM: During the conference, you described the preliminary stages of the Wunderkammer. Is it complete now, online, and working? What kind of audiences did you imagine for it?

FB: The Wunderkammer is not yet complete nor online, but it is in an advanced state of elaboration. What I discussed before is just one level of the Wunderkammer, the most "engaging" one. The audience we imagined for this level is composed mainly of high school or university students, but also people of any age and educational level who are eager to discover, or know better, this particular poetical world. For this reason, we have imagined and realized the "loci" and their inhabitants in a playful, ironic, and pop(-ish) style, with animations and other interactive elements. In every landscape or environment, users can "discover" the main characters of the "show" and their dialogues with a simple scrolling of the mouse. But they can also reach a deeper level, in which they can find, for instance, the complete text of a poem they particularly liked and the other poems of that author included in the *Flies* anthology. This level of the Wunderkammer also comprises the didactic parts of the anthology, aiming to reach advanced students of literature or scholars. Eventually, a timeline gathers the different levels together, showing simultaneously how the poetical and cultural events are intertwined with the facts of the "short twentieth century."

Paul A. Bové

Critical Poetic Grace

The critic is always in a secondary position to the poet, but this secondariness is not an inferior position. The proper critical service to poetry and poetics obligates the critic to a version of imaginative intellect different from but closely related to the graceful poiesis of the poet. The critic cannot be a Spinozist.[1] The critic serves without derogation the mixing of intellect and imagination in poetry. To overmaster the poet, poetry, and poiesis is a sinful betrayal that condemns the fallen critic to the hell of conversation.

I will say a little about three terms: "obligates," "graceful poiesis," and "overmaster." The first and third of these should help with "sinful betrayal" and "conversation." "Hell" asks for little attention. Altogether, we might catch a glimpse of imaginative intellect.

"Obligates" stands there asking for a theoretician or a philologist, even perhaps for a comedian's riff. Worse, it might lure them and so us into the law and theological, philosophical, or conventional morals. To escape, let us look at or listen to obligation:

> What's most radical about [Reznikoff's] *Testimony* is the kind of reading his method makes possible. . . .. *Testimony* is numbing, but this experience of being numbed is the place not where aesthetic experience ends but where it begins [...]; he does not turn away from aesthetics but rather shifts the aesthetic frame from the "content" to the reading experience itself. (*Pitch of Poetry* 38–39)

On the obligation not to turn away from content, moralists will insist on the content, not the practice or the art. But the poet/critic can read, think, and write; moralists are naïve instruments, products of the forces that appear as

---

[1] EN: See Morrison, James C. "Why Spinoza Had No Aesthetics." *The Journal of Aesthetics and Art Criticism*, vol. 47, no. 4, 1989, pp. 359–65. *JSTOR*, https://doi.org/10.2307/431135. Accessed 16 Jan. 2024.

content, which they think aesthetics can store in a sort of nicety. The content of *Testimony* is the elision of linguistic excess endlessly regenerated by the unstoppable machine of legal diagnosis and assignment—the bureaucratic record of criminal inscription. The persons caught, the society that catches, the language routinized in repetitive torrents of incarceration—all these, irredeemable, invite mourning and so cries or indifferent silence.

Redemption and aesthetic transformation are off the table. Commodification is the normal, well-paved path, the one versified by the same forces that create the irredeemable. Stories of redemption, which palliate guilt or amuse indifference and alert emotions otherwise inert before content without commodity—these are what we normally find. Wallace Stevens, under whose sign this conference convened, says that a poem is not a success until others accept the poet's imagination as an alternative to the real. "The Noble Rider" says that the poet's "function is to make his imagination theirs and [...] he fulfills himself only as he sees his imagination become the light in the minds of others" ("The Necessary Angel" 660–661). Poiesis does not confuse content with the real. For poetry, the real includes the forces that make the content and those forces' extensions as the normalities, the habituations, the cultures that keep them in place, visible in the frames that make them familiar and readable. To keep with Stevens, then, poetic obligation is to create alternatives to the real, to the forces that obscure both art and the real, that safely turn us to content so we can obligingly lie in the language of conversation. Bernstein says Reznikoff's conceptual use of found language forces a change in our reading or leaves us with history unreadable. Reznikoff is a name for poiesis that turns us toward a new knowledge of reality and the value of challenged language. If Reznikoff delivers Stevensian success, his art is an aversion to the pressures that create horror or indifference and induce silence or conversation.

The poet is obligate to the real as the source of alternatives to it. This is the way it must be. The poet is bound. Poiesis is not permissive, no matter how fertile the poet's various faculties. Poiesis does not enact. The poet's obligation is not legal, moral, or dependent. Poetry and poems are not transactional. They are not profitable, and we might debate if they are valuable. Poets persist within the biometrics of the real, and, as poets/critics, express the invention of their own technical achievements, especially vis-à-vis the barbaric real in their histories.

Reznikoff's *Testimony* works because its irredeemable content is within reach of the poet's technique, which in attempted repetition becomes a barrier to poiesis that must discard it. "*Holocaust*," Bernstein writes, "overwhelmed the techniques" (*Pitch of Poetry* 40). He cannot get an effective distance from the content in writing. He needs to change voice from "world-embracing" to anger, defiance, and comic glee, from writing to sound (40). Voiced contempt liberates. This is what it means to be obligate, inseparable from the real but particular in nature and function as its alternative.

Critics can explain the success and failure of technique, but they must expose art as the alternative to the real from which it cannot secede. The critic is not obligate like the poet. The critic is, rather, in the real to which the poet is obligate. Whatever the critic is, it is by inescapable attention to the situation poiesis occupies. Criticism is an after-effect—if you prefer, an echo—of poiesis, a secondary quality of making, a quality inevitably responsive not only to alternatives but the entire cosmos so created within and against the real; we might even say alert to how this process produces the reality that we know as history. If we can secularize the word, we can say the critic is an effect of grace.

St. Augustine prays to God: "Guard me with the power of Your grace here and in all places." He has a Stevensian image of grace: "Will is to grace as the horse is to the rider" (Augustine). Religion might make this moralism. Theology could debate free will and determinism. Note, however, that for Augustine grace responsibly holds in place the numbers of beauty.

For this moment, a simple equation will do. The critic is an after-effect of poiesis and grace. Scholars have said that art is a secularized form of religion. M.H. Abrams and Mario Praz made books of this idea. However, what if grace is a trope of poiesis, an appropriation of the human making of good works by the powers of religious thinking and institutional power? Along these lines of re-establishing priority, the poet is the location where grace lives, where poiesis does its essential work of creating the real and its alternatives. The critic's secondariness lies within the project of grace. I am trying to approach the fundamentals of force and will.

Just as Reznikoff changes the pitch in reading *Holocaust* so that, by the grace of sound, he creates contempt and liberates us from horrible silence, Bernstein separates grace from will, echoing Augustine. "We don't earn it [language]," Bernstein writes, "but it is forever there for us." The critic says it does not matter much; what the poet says is always there: grace, language, and sound. What matters is the poet's existence as the embodied agent of poiesis, as the place in the species where the imaginative intellect lives and works.

Tradition knows the echoing permanence of poetic grace. Consider the founding myth: Orpheus, shielded by the grace of gods to descend to hell, charming death, but, as always, failing at redemption—yet always left singing, a head—a brain—a voice—a mouth and song. According to the myth, others save the essential fragment of Orpheus, even when the Maenads tear him apart or Zeus blasts him. These others are critics.

Conversation and sinful betrayal are close friends. "Sound is grace," Bernstein wrote, imagining new works in new media. We can hear a saving grace in Bernstein here since we know full well that corporate and state power dominate the new media, but he knows voice will sing even adrift on the current of these forces. But ever the comedian—once again, we are in the shadow of Stevens—Bernstein says how the head came to sing alone, just as a body part on someone else's stream. Sound is grace and forever there, plentifully "as the social-material dimension of human language" (*Pitch of Poetry* 33). The Utopianism of such high-toned speech deserves the mock that comes with a change in the pitch, the sale, the tone, and the turn: "Its fleece was white as snow" (33). So, how innocent of us to believe in this plenitude's permanent presence—it's been said before—and we have the horrors. So, the mockery of white snow makes us realize our conversational assurances, with their comforting packaging of concept and category—the mock makes us feel the instability of the statement or belief that it's always there. Even in the most basic and long-standing forms, the poet is also always there to remind us that there are alternatives even to the assurances on offer, even as the mockeries that decry our desires for surety. "We don't earn it" (33). The grace is out there, doing all of this—the promise and mockery, which is itself the originality of music (the child) within the whole. Content is packaged, given, and taken away with the assurance that the poet sings and laughs bitterly but with original innocence. For just a moment, the poet-become-critic seems to have joined the conversation, but it was all the trick of art—call it comedy, the essay's theater turning the readers and the work back toward the world hopefully now resident in the mind.

To see what happens when the poet takes on conversation, see Bernstein's peacefully entitled "The Pataquerical Imagination," in which, among other things, in echo of Beckett's trilogy, a mountainous entanglement of conversations about poetry, language, politics, theory and so on run, not loose, but into victories and words that hold their space. So, in the spirit of this critic's ghost, let me cite one exemplary instance of victory over conversation:

> Dickinson's "meaning," says [Walter Benn] Michaels, is aligned with "grace rather than works"—which doesn't sound kosher to me. But then we have seen the problem these textual wild beasts have caused before. Michaels is nothing if not dogged in his distrust of midrashic antinomianism, and like an American Sancho Panza he makes a habit of charging at chimeras. This is the price of being an aesthetic: —"show me, I'm from Missouri"—nativist. (*Pitch of Poetry* 324–325)

This sounds like critique, but do not be misled. This is puppeteering at a high level of comic reduction. Pound could cite the Adams family when getting his Americanism on in *The Cantos*. Bernstein cannot do the Pound schtick because the world has changed. Michaels is what has become of the American aesthetic now as an enforcement mechanism, in the dark shade of American prejudice—there is a trivial difference—that has little use except as an example of how the American "leaders" do not even try to see the real—of which they are a symptom. The puppeteering is art, alongside the blind but noisy real.

For Stevens, the poet's pitch plants their imagination in the reader where the real held the ground. So, then, there can be new knowledge of reality. Poets sell their goods in unusual ways, and no matter how elegant or high they sound, their line is a spiel or a patter. The critic knows the differences matter and how to buy and resell some judged right or better. The critic's job is to buy and resell, assaying which promotion is the name and work of graceful poiesis pointing to itself. "The poetics of disfluency and disability is the horizon for a querical poetics of de-arrangement" (*Pitch of Poetry* 338). This sentence opens a movement that sounds the poet's imagination as a field of interests turned away from conversation—"narratives of social/cultural identities or disabilities"—toward the responsibility of poetry and poetics—new poems, new readers. Or, it finds a horizon that creates a field where the "*otherwise intelligible*," as it calls its task and creations, emerge and stand out as different from the unreliable "junk bonds" of normal conversation. Within the horizon, slanted or bent in a certain way, the otherwise intelligible is averse to conversation, to the community of forced converts turned together. And what does conversation demand now? The mellowing of the bent, tamed into pity-ful objectification. Ending work, process, emergence, and grace.

Can a critic make a mistake? If so, it would take the form of misreading and misrecognition. It would mean not seeing the poet naming the emerging alternative to the real, bound as it is to the real, the poet keeping open the field to where the alternative emerges, now seeing the poet at work. Borrowing from

R. P. Blackmur, we learn that the critic's job cannot take the form of a mistake.[2] Criticism is a function found active and distributed irregularly across the spectrum of obligation, where the real and its alternatives converge and avert.

If the critic is a quality, an emanation of poiesis, then Augustine and Stevens's idiom obliges the critic's will to serve grace or accept its guidance. To assert will against grace is an old story that, in this case, betrays poiesis. How is this sinful? Because it rushes to join the conversation, to convert, to become one of the conversos but from desire or conviction rather than coercion. In *The Rape of Lucrece*, Shakespeare makes evil, consensus, and limited sight—indeed, confidence in limited sight—the nature of sin:

> They think not but that every eye can see
> The same disgrace which they themselves behold;
> And therefore would they still in darkness be,
> To have their unseen sin remain untold. (Shakespeare 1427)

It does not matter which conversation the ersatz critic joins or adds to. The sin lies in thinking that all eyes see only the "same disgrace" they see and that, one way or the other, motivates their will to move along a well-versed path. Safe within the conversation, they trust their common sin will remain unseen. Consensus—not only to consent, and there is the act of will, but to feel at home in agreement. To remain in accord, to join a harmony, and not to hear the bend in their own pitch—that holds them close—or to want, or feel, the new pitch, the new slant when it comes. Indeed, it might then feel like robbery, taking away home and accord. Shakespeare's *Lucrece* is useful: "O comfort-killing Night, image of hell! / Dim register and notary of shame / [...] /Vast sin-concealing chaos!" (Shakespeare 1427).

The sinfuls see only the same as they believe all others see. Together, they produce the "Vast sin-concealing chaos," which is still home to most and invisible to more. All of this together is the "image of hell." It is the dark counterpart to poetic work obligate to the real.

---

[2] EN: See Bové, Paul A. "R.P. Blackmur and the Job of the Critic: Turning from the New Criticism." *Criticism*, vol. 25, no. 4, 1983, pp. 359–80. *JSTOR*, http://www.jstor.org/stable/23105101. Accessed 16 Jan. 2024.

"State Your Own Ideas as A Response to Others" (Graff)

As it happens, Gerald Graff and Cathy Birkenstein wrote that command. It could as easily have come from Richard Rorty, who got the neopragmatist movement going with his 1979 book *Philosophy and the Mirror of Nature*. An essential element of this movement is Rorty's idea that conversation is the device and convention by which—and where, if we change the metaphor from tool to site—truths emerge, at least for a time, from discussion, agreement, and concession, only and always to undergo revision, dismissal, or erasure. Conversation becomes the field of truth and its archive. It frees truth from metaphysics and grand projects or narratives motivated by will, desire, or tradition. Freedom brings with it the tragicomic acceptance of contingency, which itself will or should bring to the conversants their own freedom from the sometimes monstrous but inescapable failures of grand projects and grand illusions. Rorty writes, "[T]here are no constraints on inquiry save conversational ones—no wholesale constraints derived from the nature of the objects, or of the mind, or of language, but only those retail constraints, provided by the remarks of fellow inquirers" (165). Despite objections by scholars of traditional pragmatism (Webb 2012) or political thinkers dissatisfied by his assignment of virtue to dominant forms of liberalism in rich, specifically Anglo-Saxon countries (Tambornino 1997), intellectuals, especially academics, were open to the authority of Rorty's main street claims about truth and contingency. In turn, it established a view of conversation as a necessary, inescapable, versatile, and virtuous domain. This protean manifold can take form as collegial discourse, as a practice of institutional struggle for social justice (or injustice), but always appearing as a social condition essential to agreed and, therefore, contingent knowledge. These claims, precisely because of their institutional establishment, found resistance from less mainstream and more engaged thinkers. Cornel West, for example, forcefully rejected Rorty's framework on political, moral, and ethical grounds. His own prophetic pragmatism "shuns any linguistic, communicative, or conversational models and replaces them with a focus on the multileveled operations of power" (West 223). Nonetheless, conversation became and stays a valued meme and sometimes a practice of liberal belief and institutional and social practice.

Rorty says that conversation is the sole limit condition on truth-seeking and social agreement.[3] Historians of American pragmatism see Rorty's

---

[3] EN: See, for example, Rorty, Richard. "Pragmatism, Relativism, and Irrationalism." *Pro-*

insistence on this point as an original development of John Dewey's thinking about inquiry. They debate if Rorty's position enriches or impoverishes his predecessor's work. Because, however, the history of philosophy often traces lines within the archive called philosophy, it sometimes misses influences or contexts external to philosophy that belong to the genealogy of their studies. For example, there is a non-pragmatist element in the genealogy of Rorty's claims, one that enables it, gives it space to develop, and has already put in place a grammar of knowledge production that silently resides outside Rorty's own discussions. This element could lead to a new set of questions about Rorty, most outside this essay, whose thought sits within the rise of computing. Shortly before Rorty reworked Dewey's theory of inquiry, "Conversation Theory" assembled several advanced sciences to provide a cybernetic foundation for knowledge production. It prefigured and opened a space that facilitated Rorty's thinking about the primacy of retail conversation.

Conversation Theory "refers to concepts, memories and the like manifest in detailed transactions: either stretches of dialogue, or stretches of many faceted behaviour" (Pask 11). It extends beyond one-to-one exchanges "to conversation with many participants or many aim topics," in other words, to social institutions, communities, parties, and societies in toto (186). In any conversation of whatever size, Conversation Theory allows "for the existence of many *aims* at once" (202). Conversation Theory and neo-pragmatist views on knowledge production in conversational frames converge, agreeing that "verbal conversation" exteriorizes "cognition," making conversation about conversation possible. For Rorty, with his unironic embrace of contingency, infinite regression within relativism is no problem.

In contrast, since the goal of conversation theory is to study the cognitive processes revealed in conversation, conversation about conversation must yield to cybernetic method or "the information available to an external observer [...] will decrease very rapidly to the vanishing point" (Pask 1). Truth for a Rortyian is entirely contingent, argued, agreed, local, dissolving, reforming, and draining away. It always draws any observer inside conversation where freedom (most ironically) lies alone. Conversation is an ethical obligation despite its quality as a social accident, as contingent, or even as a regulated life practice such as listening. Truth appears in conversation—can it move out?

ceedings and Addresses of the American Philosophical Association, vol. 53, no. 6, 1980, pp. 717–38. *JSTOR*, https://doi.org/10.2307/3131427. Accessed 18 Jan. 2024.

Can it exist elsewhere?—because of "consensual practices and norms among those conversing," yet, as Rorty has it in a remarkable inversion of Socratic practice, "truth" only appears there because the truth work is and has always been forensic. As classical pragmatists point out debating Rorty's claims to derive his work from Dewey, "the natural world of which we are a deeply embedded part imposes constraints independently of the 'remarks of fellow inquirers.'" Events, which we might call history or poetry, have "the capacity [...] to produce a brute surprise contrary to any individual belief or group 'conversation'" (Webb 57). Rorty might have hoped to free our minds from the metaphysical or positivistic ambitions of institutionalized philosophy by bringing truth into the social world of human action and interest. Still, for those who are not philosophers, his project was less informed and more constrictive than Cornel West's strong critique suggests.

Rorty makes truth the dependent and prisoner of conversation, a mode of life with specific grammars, fashions, and entangled histories, all reified, to the exclusion of all other forms of life. Furthermore, as far as he finds truth-seeking and the condition of truth itself in conversation without reserve, it is an essential, necessary, and seemingly inescapable phenomenally natural part of being human, of species identity. (This is, in other words, ontology and anthropology.) Yet, Rorty is unsophisticated about the character of conversation. Consider, for example, names as a special instance of words. A conversant under the sign, Kardashian, presents pure consumer fetish identity in the semblance of proposed uniqueness. Whereas Arden or Brighton might present the utopian efforts in struggles of liberation, which are already marked by the necessity of their difference, as placed inevitably within the system of repression itself. What speaks, then, or transpires in conversation—when the names at play denominate ranges of determination, testify to the dialectic of inescapable control and determined resistance, and enact the perpetual churn of commoditization after the death of hope and revolution? Conversation becomes another unexamined utopia, competing with and underlying others as an imagined space of rich life and resolution. From this comes careers and prizes.

In 1588, Montaigne published the opening sentences of his essay, "De l'Art de Conferer." Authorized English translations of "*conferer*" are "discussion" (Frame 1958) or "conversation" (Screech 2003). Philologists, concerned with etymology and usage, insist that *conferer* or *conference*, without the acute accent, *conférence*, in usage denoted "a strictly polemical exchange" (Szabari

1003), a form common in the neoclassical Renaissance. As "debate," *conferer* is a literary alternative to scholastic disputation and, undoubtedly, a predecessor to literary criticism. But first, it is a capacity or form of the essay, and because it is essayistic, it can always be staged, performed, and set before our eyes and ears, doubled, allowing it to be fully displayed. *Le Littré, Dictionnaire de la langue française* has an entry for *conferer*, the usage of which it illustrates with quotations from Montaigne's essays. It describes the word's etymology and development in this way:

> [D]u latin *conferre*, par un changement de conjugaison ; de *cum*, et *ferre*, porter. La série des sens est « porter avec » , qui se dédouble en accorder et comparer, puis, neutralement, contribuer, qui se rapporte, à accorder, et raisonner ensemble, qui se rapporte à comparer. (Littré)[4]

If we believe *Littré* on the mobilization of *conferrer*, on the working out of transformations potential within *cum* + *ferre*, especially as a mode of *dédoublement*, we see, as we must, our obligation to the art of the word, which is to say, to its work, its play of textures and details in the essay's movement along the lines provoked by its potential. Yet, a reader can find a seeming authority to evade the obligation.

Montaigne famously said he would rather lose sight than hearing or speech because *conferer* is "the most fruitful and natural exercise of our mind." By contrast, the essay continues, "The study of books is a languishing and feeble activity that gives no heat, whereas discussion teaches and exercises us at the same time" (*The Complete Essays* 704). However, the author of those lines is nowhere more at home with himself or his thinking than in his library. In lines written after 1588, in an essay weighing "three kinds of association," Montaigne describes the architecture of his chateau's tower in Dordogne. On the highest of its three floors is a library, to which he twice famously withdrew from public and political life. "In my library," he says, "I spend most of the days of my life, and most of the hours of my day." Only a long walk within its walls would make his library a better fit for life and work. "Those who study

---

[4] EN: "From the Latin *conferre*, by a change in conjugation; from *cum* and *ferre*, 'to carry.' The sequence of meanings is 'carry with,' which doubles in 'to grant' and 'to compare,' and neutrally, 'to attribute,' which brings 'to grant' and 'to reason' together, which leads to 'to compare'" (editors' translation).

without a book are all in the same boat," he writes, "as those unable to walk and think." Montaigne's library, atop his tower, exercises him and keeps

> the crowd away. [...] There is my throne. I try to make my authority over it absolute, and to withdraw this one corner from all society, conjugal, filial, and civil. [...] Sorry the man, to my mind, who has not in his own home a place to be all by himself, to pay his court privately to himself, to hide! (629).

Montaigne, in the eighth essay of book three, sounds different from the writer of the third essay. What do we have? A writer of his own ideas and emotions, recording and testing contingently in the occasion? Fallen one day on the task of thinking about place and the need for privacy as a desire for life and, on another day, into the recognition that debate better stimulates his thought? If so, does it matter if he comes to the tower's reading and thinking as a settlement after realizing debate or conversation are time-wasting practices? Do they record the general "situatedness" of writing, speaking, and thinking? How foolish to imagine we read records of personal experience when we read these essays! Inquiring these ways assumes a relation between the essayist and the essays that lacks justification other than habit and an ideological commitment to a phenomenological realism within which lies a psychological personalism.

The 1950s are one marker in the gradual displacement of such inappropriate ideological responses, ways of positioning reading and words, in Montaigne. Yet, before Roland Barthes and Michel Foucault differently made authorship complicated and unstable, a contingent, functionally coded concept, Mallarmé, one of their influences, articulated a poetics that did away with the "person author" and established what we once called the impersonality of poetry, or to put it another way, escaped the categories of the personal that caged no matter how comfortably the poem in biography, context, or motive. In 1897, Mallarmé published his essay, "Crise de vers" ("The Crisis of Poetry"), dissolving the poet to free the poem: "L'œuvre pure implique la disparition élocutoire de poète, qui cède l'initiative aux mots, par le heurt de leur inégalité mobilisés" (246).

Some philologically trained readers see apparent contradictions in Montaigne as contingencies grasped in writing, whereby the constantly expanding contingency stabilizes in the aesthetic project, not of self-representation but the more profoundly realistic idea that the self exists only in and as the writing. This aesthetic aspires to the redemption of contingency (and circularly of the self), making it not transportable or permanent truth but, for the better, an infusion of value into the contingency of verbal production within speech or writing.

> It is rather that in writing, *and only in writing*, Montaigne claims to escape mere accidental being and to translate it into a 'substance': yet, it should be added that this is so only in the particular piece of writing that he calls *The Essays*, a text that is never weary of exposing this accidental, contingent character of its own production by additions. (Szabari 1003)

Something must be said of conversation and contingency—for conversation as a form of contingency, as immersed in the larger frame of contingency—that gives them value. Work must be done. For the philologist, the poet redeems contingency as the necessary, inescapable material condition of self-existence as formed by self-expression and self-presentation. This is just as it is for Rorty: freeing truth from masterful grand projects redeems conversation. The primary characteristic it acquires is as a concept device for saving contingency from meaningless, chaotic existence, as ruin in deformation. An act that also would save from the same ruination, as a disguised aesthesis, the human, obligated to conversation.

Mallarmé has it that the qualities of elocution must fade out for the mobilized inequalities of words to clash. Against this impersonal poet, the philological reader comes across an essay on the art of *conferrer* and, unable to tolerate or think contingency, repurposes the essay as an ontological redemption of human beings in self-writing, as the transfiguration of contingency into permanent value. This reader is obligate to the real and averse to jumping wild words. There is a Gnostic urge in the philological critic, as in the neopragmatist. Montaigne's essay tempts readers to use metaphors of motion and flow to describe the experience of reading, which, in turn, they assign as qualities to the art itself.

Take up instead a critical practice that creates a position obligate to the essay. Describe it as art: this essay compiles or assembles elements of *conferrer* as this intensely mobilized word breaks itself open in the essayist's mind. In a remark added after 1588, Montaigne says that when he reads, he looks for style, not subject. He says this is a way to know a famous mind (708). Style is not mind; it is not a possession—it is not the property of an author, or the author made *propre*, that is, his own, a self. Montaigne looks not for a person but for a mind adequate to language, those mobilized words so unequal in status and force. "Ineptitude," "stupidity," and "obstinacy"—these words name what he finds and cannot tolerate in the processes of carrying on with debate or proleptically conversation.

In the essay, the mind and imagination follow where led, carried along by the word with the concept. When this leads to comparing, to relation, to the effort to agree or reason, then comes what he cannot tolerate. In conversation, staged in the essay's imagination, the essayist and the obstinate are at each other's throats. There is no hope of agreement or education because the minds are different: "[F]rom a stump there is nothing worthwhile to be hoped or enjoyed" (708). Montaigne inscribes this fragment of *conferrer* firmly in place by superimposing it on another figural fragment in which the essayist reflects on encounters with obstinacy and stupidity to show the stupidity of anger and intolerance that comes with being "worked up and stung by the absurdities of the world" (709).

If it seems absurd to readers to consider Montaigne as lacking elocutionary qualities as Mallarmé insists the poet must be, consider that this essay on *conferrer* contains these sentences, which require such a reading and sense of Montaigne as the place where the art of carrying together creates the palimpsestic assemblage of what moderns would call conversation:

> I dare not only to speak of myself, but to speak of only myself. [...] I do not love myself so indiscriminately, nor am I so attached and wedded to myself, that I cannot distinguish and consider myself apart. [...] I who am king of the matter I treat [...] do not for all that believe myself in all I write. I often hazard sallies of my mind which I mistrust [...] but I let them run at venture (720–721).

We must recall that the images traced throughout this essay are set as debate. The essay traces the mobilized elements of *conferrer*, depositing them together in a palimpsest that leaves their conflicts there as a contribution to thought. Those who make conversation serve their Gnostic desires should take Montaigne's effort seriously. They should seek their own pre-emption. Or, we might say, they have taken that essay seriously and moved against it for their Gnostic purposes. They scratch out tracings to reduce the word to their own desire. This is how the critic flees the responsibility of secondariness. For the ideologue, the poet must be made secondary, beheaded. But the head sings.

In *Pitch of Poetry*, Bernstein says that the L=A=N=G=U=A=G=E poets rejected the Rortyian relativism that made "truth and meaning [...] fundamentally unknowable" (68) while also assuming the identity of pragmatism. To my point, however, of the poet's obligating function, Bernstein says the proper poetic logic is constructivist, which means that "[i]n the poetry, syllogistic logic and naturalistic plot gave way to intuitively felt, aesthetically designed, or programmatically arranged connections among elements of a work" (68). This sentence is a gloss on Mallarmé's hard-to-translate negative quality of the impersonal poet, one who is without elocutionary qualities or qualities that might be called elocutionary. Mallarmé's poetics has a place for the poet as a collocation of capacities, which neither depend upon a pre-existent poetic subject or psychological person nor create the same as a fashioned artifact or mainstream commodity. Design is a Renaissance term, the property of Michelangelo, that designates an intellectual capacity to do art with the media at hand—stone, sounds, paint, or graphemes—to design, connect, and feel.

Is this a species quality made by conversation or that converses or converts? Recall names in conversation and the wish-fulfillments of self-fashioning, which comes in place of anthropology, psychology, and ontology. Thinking about the art of poetry, Bernstein, setting all firmly outside conversation, writes this: "[O]ne isn't imprisoned by the identity that one is given, or that one is stigmatized with, or even that one chooses as one might a name" (198). Design is embodiment without reference and ideally without an author. Rather than shaping your words always in response to others, in anticipation of their response, of the vast echo chamber of repetition, the post-Mallarmé poet will, while creating, move as far from the hell of repetition not by simulation but by emptying expectation that enjoys simulacra, the age without aura. The local name for this would be Echopoetics, "a network of stopgaps." Accidents, damns, and organs—"Echopoetics is the nonlinear resonance of one motif bouncing off another within an aesthetics of constellation. Even more, it's the sensation of allusion in the absence of allusion. In other words, the echo I'm after is a blank: a shadow of an absent source" (x). "Bouncing off another" is also a translation of Mallarmé: "mots, par le heurt de leur inégalité mobilisés."[5] Or is it an echo? It cannot be a conversation, for that's where names stand averse to design.

---

[5] EN: Here is the full sentence: "L'œuvre pure implique la disparition élocutoire du poëte, qui cède l'initiative aux mots, *par le heurt de leur inégalité mobilisés.*"

Franca d'Agostini

What Poetry Can Teach Logic (Preliminary Ideas)

1. Introduction: Is There Any 'Logic' in Poetry?

In the text I wrote for the collection of Italian poems edited by Luigi Ballerini, I have tried to imagine what 'a logic of poetry' could be. Clearly, I did not imagine a logical system or a definite semantics. I rather reflected on what happens to the activity we call 'poetry' when we look at it through the lens of logic, from a logical perspective. I have advanced a simple argument, which I try to summarize now.

1) The primary evidence is that language has *power*. It helps us think in certain ways and not others; it makes us think certain things and not others. More specifically, it has *power to-* (disposition) and *power over-* (domination).

2) We can assume that the enterprise we call 'logic' is concerned with the latter, specifically with the *semantic constraint*, in the two senses of 'semantics': the constraint coming from *meaning* and the one coming from *truth*. They are two different, though deeply connected, sources of 'coercion.'

3) Indicatively, the enterprise we call 'poetry' is not directly or strictly concerned with truth; and, allegedly, it is less interested in- and less submitted to- the laws, rules, or constraining forces of meaning. So given, one could say poetry is anarchic, while logic is normative, coerced and coercive since it ratifies and supports the dominion of language (logos). But this is not exact; there is *freedom* in logic, especially in philosophical logic (see Sect. 2 below), and poets are submitted to the power-dominion of their material (language), as all artists are. So freedom and constriction are variously distributed in both of them.

4) Now the challenge is to discover the 'logic of poetry,' that is, the specific action that language, semantically intended (as conveyer of truth and meaning), exerts over the action of poets. The proposal is ambitious,

especially if we want to work at it in general, searching for the *universal rules* that poets—all poets—are forced to respect, whether they like it or not. Are there rules of this kind?

5) I think we may accept that poetry is especially submitted to the mechanism I call *recapture*. By this term, I mean the typical power of the two normative forces—meaning and truth—to distort, get over, exceed, and overcome any attempt to exceed, distort or overcome them. Michael Dummett typically ascribed this power to the *indefinite extensibility* of logical concepts (454). I have intended it by pointing to the *aboutness* of language—the simple fact that words are about the world—the world is the first semantic force. (In this sense, the *recapture* is also expressible as the 'thrown away key': when you find a word, you lose the thing, and when you try to regain the thing, canceling the word, you get another word, and the thing gets lost again.)

6) There are reasons to believe that poetry continually plays with this 'overcoming the overcoming,' or 'canceling the cancellation,' in various ways: sometimes by respecting and reviving the semantic (meaning-generative) forces of ordinary language, other times by distorting and destroying them. Sometimes, the poetical fighting against and within the recapture intends to have a political impact. Another time, the game is played by an apparent refusal of meaning and truth and/or, let's say, by trying to recover mere sound. But if all this is *still poetry*, then the recapture works: meaning and truth survive.

In this way, I have tried to isolate the recapture mechanism as a distinctive 'logic of poetry,' intending it, ultimately, as the indefinite resistance of meaning and truth even when—ideally, supposedly—there is no meaning, no truth.

Now, in this new text, I try to specify some possibly obscure points, by—very briefly and preliminarily— reflecting on what poetry can teach logic. What is the point in comparing or simply connecting two different and putatively incompatible enterprises, such as logic and poetry? My answer is simple: the aim is to attempt a new reflection about the power of language, possibly discovering something which is underrated in principle or not always considered by logicians.

I begin by recalling two 'metaphorical explanations' of logical concepts. The first is Michael Dummett's idea of 'the seas of language' (taken from Wittgenstein's rapid notation: "See how high the seas of language run here!" *Logical Investigations*, I.194), so as a wide, unstable, open, and disordered set of waves. The other is Camillo Sbarbaro's use of seawater as a poetical source of comparisons specifically endowed with logical and metaphysical impact.

2. Dummett's Sea

Michael Dummett was a distinguished analytical philosopher; he worked mainly in the sector of philosophical logic, whose basic concern is to reflect on truth, paradoxes, non-classical logics, relations of logic to metaphysics, epistemology, and philosophy of language. Such a reflection is normally undertaken by exploring natural language and, more specifically, what Kant and Hegel called *natural logic* (see Ficara 12–15, and Russell 34–35) intended as the appearance of forms (laws-regularities) in natural language. This idea is not far from what Frege meant when he wrote: "I assign to logic the task of discovering the laws of truth" (*Posthumous Writings* 290). We discover these 'laws' by looking at what happens in natural language; the nature of language gives us regularities, empty and repeatable structures (forms), and then laws. The metaphorical explanation expresses what is 'natural' in logic and what its subject matter is, so it tells us something about what I specified on point 1 of my argument (see also Sect. 4 below).

Is there any regularity or law in the 'seas of language'? In principle, there is not, so the logical enterprise is doomed from the beginning. Apparently, meaning and truth do not work as normative sources (see step 2) as they are—just like—ungraspable waves of living water. And yet, the sea has shores, isles, and territories, and the mutual overcoming of waves under the impact of winds. So in accepting Wittgenstein's image, Dummett intended to point out the specific, anarchic, but *resistant* nature of logical laws (laws of truth). He wanted to stress their intrinsic revisability and mutability, their being grounded on the wide, unstable, open, and disordered seas-waves of natural language and thought.

So ultimately, there are 'laws of truth' since the logical sea, like any sea, has power, specifically power over human thoughts (beliefs). Not by chance, it has the super-grounding regularity of the hydrostatic pressure: is the *recapture* of point 4 comparable to a similar super-grounding law? Maybe it is. We arrive at a critical point. Everything (logic, philosophy, poetry, rhetoric, democratic politics) begins with the power of language, whose discovery, for our culture, is ascribed to the sophists. But what does language exactly do, and why does it have poetic and logical power? This is the hypothesis: maybe the force of poetic images could provide a fairly clear answer. An answer, I suppose, in the line of the *aboutness* clarified on point 5.

3. Sbarbaro's Sea

The other largely metaphorical explanation I want to quote is given by a few lines of Camillo Sbarbaro's poem "La trama delle lucciole ricordi," from *Versi a Dina* (1931, in *Poesie e Prose*, 2022).

La trama delle lucciole ricordi	The texture of fireflies, do you remember,
sul mar di Nervi, mia dolcezza prima?	over Nervi's sea, my first sweetness?
(trasognato paese dove fui	(dreamy country where I was
ieri e che già non riconosce il cuore).	yesterday and already the heart fails to [recognize).
Forse. Ma il gesto che t'incise dentro,	Maybe. But the act that carved you within,
io non ricordo; e stillano in me dolci	I do not remember; and drip inside me
parole che non sai d'aver dette.	[sweet words you do not know you said.
Estrema delusione degli amanti!	Lovers' ultimate delusion!
invano mescolarono le vite	In vain mixed their lives
s'anche il ben superstite, i ricordi,	if even the surviving good, memories,
son mani che non giungono a toccarsi.	are hands that cannot touch one another.
Ognuno resta con la sua perduta	Everyone remains with one's lost
felicità, un po' stupito e solo,	happiness, vaguely surprised and alone,
pel mondo vuoto di significato.	in a world empty of meaning.
Miele segreto di che s'alimenta;	Concealed honey nourishes memory,
finché sino il ricordo ne consuma	up until remembering wears away
e tutto è come se non fosse stato.	and everything is as if it had never been.
O come poca cosa quel che fu	How such a poor thing divides
da quel che non fu divide!	what was from what was not!
Meno che la scia della nave acqua da acqua.	Less than the ship's wake water from [water.
Saranno state	There might have been
le lucciole di Nervi, le cicale	Nervi's fireflies, the crickets,
la casa sul mare di Loano,	the house by Loano's sea,

e tutta la mia poca gioia—e tu—	and all my little joy—and you—
fin che mi strazi questo ricordare.	until remembering will torture me.[1]

Sbarbaro was a subtle creator of poetic comparisons. In particular, he launches here, in passing, an image endowed with clear logical and metaphysical impact—namely in the line of what Dummett suggested: "How such a poor thing is what / that what was from what was not divides / less than the ship's wake water from water." Sbarbaro is talking about the frailty of memories, which rapidly disappear, more rapidly than what remains of the wake, after the ship's cutting water.

I propose something that may sound like diminishing the lyrical tension of these verses, which talk about memories of love and their failed survival over time—despite the gentle reminder of fireflies seen over the sea. I read these lines as a contribution to modal logic and the philosophical analysis of possibility, contingency, and necessity. Such a reading might not be ultimately reductive because here, we may find that poetry is inspiring for philosophical logic. Even more, I think it gives us a specific contribution to the foundations of logical choices.

Modal logic from Leibnitz onwards is based on the idea of worlds, which are—for our needs—sets of states of affairs expressed by sentences (thoughts, beliefs). 'Possible' is what occurs in *some* worlds, and 'necessary' occurs in *all* possible worlds. In saying or thinking, "Kennedy might not have been killed," we mean that, in some possible world(s), Kennedy was not killed but lived a long and very happy life with his wife and children. In the same way, in some possible world(s), circumstances were such that the poet could have loved Dina in a different way—maybe without any fatal resistance of time.

The nature and borders of worlds are not specified for contemporary logicians and metaphysicians. There is a wide and unsolved discussion. Now, we can say that the metaphorical explanation reveals the special, subtle, but irreparable difference between lost possibilities and actualities, what was and what was not. It reveals it expressly by appealing to what Dummett intended by pointing to the seas of language.

---

[1] EN: The English translation is the author's own, with some minor editorial assistance.

Between the actual world and all the worlds that are irreducibly elsewhere but are present simultaneously (as far as thought, here and now), there is an even frailer difference than the one that divides water from water. Our seen and dreamt worlds differ from the actual for a "poor thing," almost nothing is the frail edge of imagined or remembered possibilities within contingency, even for something that is "carved within."

4. Materiality

What this kind of poetry teaches logic—and metaphysics—is given by two images. The first is *water* as the material, the stuff by which logical possibilities (worlds) are made. The second is the *ship's wake*: the difference between worlds.

As to the first image, water, we may ask what the connection between Dummett's 'seas of language' and Nervi, the 'dreamy country' with fireflies glowing over the sea, could be. An important specification is needed. Both authors are talking about water as the material of 'language' but not in the late modern sense of the term, more specifically in the sense of language-thought. The material of poetry and logic is ultimately what the ancient Greeks called *logos*. Frege, namely, put it as the basis of logic (1956), and Dummett clearly meant it as the material within which and about which logic works. Both authors see in the living water of the sea the living nature of thought, just that 'thought' which is the conveyer of sense (meaning-truth), thanks to the mediative work of words.

By referring to the image, the two contexts capture some evident features of language-thought—of names, words, conceptuality, and its progression in the activity of thinking-speaking. They reveal its ungraspable nature, its intrinsic rebellion against any effort of regimentation by fixed unmodifiable forms, and also its soft ductility and docility face to human creative needs and human concerns. Just like the sea makes us travel, and helps us reach countries and new shores, in the same way the language-logos (so intended) makes us think, and its forms-laws guide us throughout the seas of meaning and truth.

5. The Ship's Wake

What is especially enlightening in Sbarbaro's poem is the idea of the ship's wake. It works, figurally, as the difference among possibilities and, specifically, between possible and actual facts.

The first aspect we have noted in the image is the extreme frailty of modal boundaries because, ultimately, what we do in thinking about possibility is to establish a difference within a vague material. Can you cut clouds? You can, but the cut-off soon disappears. Can you distinguish water from water, a drop of rain falling in the ocean? Our reasoning about possibilities and necessities is not far from this. Modal thinking is, ultimately, cutting thoughts—a desperate proposal, apparently. Searching for the borders of thoughts means searching for the borders of meaning, and borders are typically and systematically vague. The wake appears and then immediately melts away.

Sbarbaro's image seems to be more psychological than metaphysical. The figured sense is lost memory:

Forse. Ma il gesto che t'incise dentro,	Maybe. But the act that carved you within,
io non ricordo; e stillano in me dolci	I do not remember; and drip inside me sweet
parole che non sai d'aver dette.	words you do not know you said.

The historical fact of love is forgotten, but the 'first sweetness' *carved* something within the poet's mind or heart, and the unsaid sweet words drip inside. And there is a second and more subtle aspect of the image. Yes, the wake is merely an instantaneous appearance, and its memory does not survive the instant of its appearance. And yet, *while the ship passes*, the difference is clear, sharp, and irreparable.

The previous, discouraged verses confirm it. We read that even love, such a formidable fact of 'mixed lives,' has poor survivals. And we read that these survivals are, ultimately, "hands that cannot touch one another." In the empty world of lost happiness, there is still the concealed honey, but "everything is as it had never been":

Miele segreto di che s'alimenta;	Concealed honey nourishes memory,
finché sino il ricordo ne consuma	up until remembering wears away
e tutto è come se non fosse stato.	and everything is as if it had never been.

The last line prepares the following verse, the ship's wake: the ship passed, and it is as if nothing had changed the water's surface. We can generalize the image. These lines are about the frailty, but also inevitability, of any sort of difference, so while the living water of the sea tells something about the nature of possible worlds—the material they are made of—the ship's wake helps to understand the uncertain and at the same time temporally invincible action of the differences we impose onto the living water of thought. The ephemeral frailty of the wake is not only the psychological frailty of memories but also the logical uncertainty of the cut-off points that separate the extension and the anti-extension of properties, so distinguishing actuality and possibility, what was and what was not.

Tom Huhn

The Reappearance of "On Lyric Poetry and Society"

I would like to take up the opportunity of having assembled here the particular mix of poets and literary theorists to return to the 1957 essay by Theodor Adorno titled "On Lyric Poetry and Society" to see if we might together make something still more interesting from it. Though Adorno does quote two specific lyric poems for somewhat close analysis, Eduard Mörike's "*Auf einer Wanderung*" ["*On a Walking Tour*"] and one of the songs from Stefan George's *Seventh Ring*, he has far more to say about the aesthetic *form* of the lyric. What's particularly interesting to him in the form of lyric poetry is that he takes it to be—and this in good Hegelian fashion—the *historical expression* of the individual. Of course, the individual itself is a thoroughly historical product, and we might even hazard that the ontogeny of the individual, and even each individual, indeed the *form* of the individual, recapitulates the phylogeny of individualism having come into being. And yet we should also acknowledge that the project of individualism—according to what Schopenhauer and then Nietzsche called the principle of individuation—remains an incomplete achievement or perhaps an unfinished, ongoing disaster, depending on your point of view. (We'll set aside, for some future academic conference, the question of the success or failure of the form of the individual.)

Instead, we turn to Adorno's more particular concern with the meaning of how the form of the individual comes to specific historical expression in the aesthetic form of lyric poetry. At the very start of his essay, Adorno acknowledges the peculiar difficulty of even approaching lyric poetry, given that lyric poetry is "the most delicate, the most fragile thing that exists"(37) and that any attempt to analyze it, let alone to speak on its behalf, might succeed at best only in affixing a label of one sort or another to it but could in no way penetrate or inhabit it. This difficulty, or indeed prohibition, nonetheless offers an initial indication of how lyric poetry came to exist precisely in opposition to what Adorno calls the "bustle and commotion" of the modern world. The examination of lyric poetry threatens to turn it into its opposite, insofar as it came to be as a "sphere of expression whose very essence lies in either not acknowledging the power of socialization or overcoming it through the pathos of detachment" (37). Baudelaire is then named as a premier example of the lyric poet. One wants—following this—to envision the relation of society to the individual as akin to the operation of a stranglehold around the throat of the individual and that the peculiar voice of the lyric poet is not so much an expression *by* the individual but rather the sound of the grip *on* the individual. What we hear in the lyric poem is the increase in the vise of the social. What, then, might we say about the vaunted *autonomy* of the individual, an autonomy that we believe comes to some of its fullest expression in the lyric poem?

I would like to suggest a roundabout path toward an understanding of autonomy. Rather than weigh the possibility or measure the degree of the autonomy of the individual, I propose that we find our way toward it by measuring the extent of the autonomy of the *social,* of just that which stands opposed to the individual. I believe that at the point of the individual, at the place of individual experience, we regularly feel the totality of the social, even when, or perhaps especially when, the social totality appears disjointed, uncoordinated, fragmented, and confused. I believe it's a mistake to imagine that the whole of the social appears to us holistically. The totality of the social whole, if it even exists at all, remains opaque to us. And it is by dint of the opacity of the social totality that we arrive at the opacity of the lyric poem. The task then, in trying to discern what takes place in a particular poem, is to "discover how the entirety of a society, conceived as an internally contradictory unity, is manifested in the work of art, in what way the work of art remains subject to society and in what way it transcends it" (39). This quest is central to Adorno's overall aesthetic theorizing, the attempt to understand the relations between those artifacts that are, so to speak, merely mechanical repetitions of a society and those things, those works of art that—also by mimetically reproducing the social totality—somehow thereby transcend it. Those artworks do not begin as autonomous but achieve their autonomy in the same way that the social totality achieves its autonomy from the people who compose it. In this light, Adorno partially defines modernism as the making that no longer expects its products to be comprehensive or expects that its objects might best reproduce a that no longer congeals as such.

It's easy enough to find in Adorno seemingly straight-forward characterizations of the role of art in society; for example, when he writes, "The greatness of works of art, however, consists solely in the fact that they give voice to what ideology hides" (39). This sounds like a rather conventional, even traditional formulation to the effect that art unveils some hidden truth. However, this understanding is incomplete because it fails to include Adorno's insistence on the complexity and contradiction within ideology. For him, ideology is not simply false consciousness and untruth (even if sometimes it seems only to amount to that), but rather the concept of ideology is also "intended to unmask spirit that is specifically false and at the same time to grasp it in its necessity" (39). Or, to put necessity differently, to capture the truth of ideology.

A short digression here to illustrate this complex character of ideology using the current political situation in the U.S.A.: what has been properly labeled as white grievance and the MAGA phenomenon that is meant to ameliorate it are not simply delusions or misdirected nostalgia but rather contain within their ideology the truth (however unclear) that the social whole is more opaque than ever, and the increasing frustration with that opacity is what fuels the re-emergence of white supremacy. What would give legitimacy to these regressive tendencies is to acknowledge their necessity without recognizing the moment of untruth in their ideology. It perhaps helps to recall Marx's suggestion that religion, though it falsely projects an idealized human life, is one of the most thorough and truthful critiques of the ongoing inadequacy of the status quo to be properly human.

Returning to lyric poetry with this understanding of ideology and especially with the distinction between what we might call better and worse-directed critique, we note that Adorno indeed describes lyric poetry as a protest, one that is directed "against a social situation that every individual experiences as hostile, alien, cold, oppressive" (39), and that "In its protest the poem expresses the dream of a world in which things would be different" (40). We might well ask what makes the lyric poem's dream and projection more privileged than any other dream, fantasy, or projection.

In Adorno's essay, two answers present themselves: one has to do with suffering, the other with language. Concerning suffering, it's helpful to remind ourselves of just how central it figures in Adorno's aesthetic theory. For him, suffering is the only candidate worthy of expression in works of art. And here we need not imagine that it is the suffering of others, of victims, that is the substance of art, but rather it is the suffering not only of all the past pains of human beings but so too the suffering at the heart of human existence in an inhumane world. Every genuine work of art expresses suffering and, thereby, attempts to reconcile and do justice to it. Recalling the earlier distinction between artifacts that mimetically repeat the world's actuality and those that succeed in transcending it, we might imagine suffering as the experience that art expresses in its attempt to transcend it. (By the way, this is a good spot to appreciate Adorno's criticism of all so-called light entertainment, which proceeds not so much just by making light of things but rather by an ideological commitment to forgetting suffering. This is the injustice of kitsch and all the products of what Adorno and Horkheimer labeled the culture industry: it is an injustice toward the dead and the history of human suffering. There is no proper justice for suffering, especially not for unnecessary suffering. For Adorno, in expressing suffering, the work of art attempts to transcend it. Marx's comment comes to mind here when he suggests that a truly humane future would be one where all the unanswered hopes of previous human beings would be fulfilled. We could imagine that as indeed a fitting justice to past human suffering.

The natural condition of suffering is that it expresses itself; Adorno describes this as the cry of pain common to most animals. However, human society has somehow developed itself such that human suffering is no longer automatically accompanied by the expression that is its natural complement. This denial of suffering, that we have been developed to suffer our suffering, that we are alienated not only from ourselves but from our suffering too, is the condition that gives rise to the necessity of the work of art as the displaced locale where suffering comes to expression. For Adorno, this accounts for the thorough falseness of the artwork; the semblance character of all art arises not from its being an imitation but rather from its expression of suffering not being its own. Its semblance character is meant to announce this, and further, it accounts for why the expression of the work of art, especially that of the lyric poem, is opaque. It expresses the suffering of something other than itself.

One of the most perplexing features of suffering is our ambivalence toward it. We are often inclined to too readily rationalize it, to accord it a place in a well-ordered world where suffering can potentially be meaningful. Some even embrace it as salutary; I'm reminded of the resistance to the use of anesthesia by many surgeons in the 19th century as they had convinced themselves that the pain of surgery was a necessary component of the recovery from surgery (what peculiar homeopathy). Of course, Nietzsche saw Christianity as an abomination in its worshipping of the figure of sacrifice unto death. In this light, we might consider the work of art's relation to suffering as an attempt to de-rationalize it, return it to its irrational meaninglessness, and, in that way, to its natural condition as the complement to its expression. Here, we can appreciate Adorno's debt to Walter Benjamin's characterization of mimesis as a wholly automatic unfolding of the continuities inherent to nature. Expression, we might say, is the mimetic completion of suffering, and that completion, one hopes, somehow brings a kind of closure to the suffering. This helps explain why Adorno thought that all didactic art was destined for failure. It was not the failure of its message, regardless of how true or helpful, but rather that having a message interfered with the artwork's more genuine mission to express suffering.

Adorno's critique of didactic art provides a bridge from one answer to the next as to the question of what makes the dreamworld of lyric poetry more poignant than other forms of expression, that is, from the first key element of lyric poetry, suffering, to the second, language. To best approach language's shape and role in lyric poetry, it helps first to return briefly to the earlier characterization of the relation between lyric poetry's subjective fabrication and society's objective character. It seemed earlier as if Adorno had suggested that the lyric poem is a kind of reverse image of society or a kind of seismograph that writ small the upheavals and vacillations within the social. However, this image of the relation between subject and object would restrict the lyric poem to being but the trace or echo of the social.

Adorno introduces a further complication into this schema, which we might call its most robust dialectical moment when he writes: "I am not trying to deduce lyric poetry from society; its social substance is precisely what is spontaneous in it, what does not simply follow from the existing conditions at the time" (43). What strikes me as especially dialectical here is the reversal of how and where spontaneity occurs. It is not so much a feature of the individual, of the subject breaking with any and all determinations. It is, instead, curiously, an objective thing and, indeed, a central plank in society's foundation and ongoing existence. Spontaneity belongs exclusively neither to the social nor to the individual. Adorno has it as the product of how the individual and the social both determine and liberate themselves from one another.

Society spontaneously becomes something other than the sum of individuals, and likewise, the individual achieves spontaneity only through its interchange with the social. In the case of lyric poetry, language is taken up as how the individual encounters and engages with what is objective, with what is other than it and exceeds it, or perhaps we might instead say the individual engages with what eludes it. And with the thought of what is objective and what eludes the subject, we are not so far from Wallace Stevens' line that "Poetry is a pheasant disappearing in the brush" ("Adagia," *Opus Posthumous*, 173). The lyric poem aligns the language's objectivity with the individual's subjectivity, as both somehow momentarily overcome their mutual opacity. For me, here comes to mind the opening stanza of Stevens's "The Idea of Order at Key West" (1934):

> She sang beyond the genius of the sea.
> The water never formed to mind or voice,
> Like a body wholly body, fluttering
> Its empty sleeves; and yet its mimic motion
> Made constant cry, caused constantly a cry,
> That was not ours although we understood,
> Inhuman, of the veritable ocean.[1]

The lyric is the modern medium in which the subject becomes more than subject. Or, in the words of Adorno's explicit formulation of this dynamic: "My thesis is that the lyric work is always the subjective expression of a social antagonism. But since the objective world that produces the lyric is an inherently antagonistic world, the concept of the lyric is not simply that of the expression of a subjectivity to which language grants objectivity" (45). The thing that can't be eluded here is not the antagonism of the social but the character of the *inherency* of the antagonism, which, for Adorno, is the correlate within the lyric of its subjective universality or, we might say, of its truth. However, as Adorno noted at the beginning of his essay, we cannot really approach that truth, let alone speak it.

Instead, what we might approach, especially in the case of the lyric, is the nature of the opacity that it both confronts and makes, well, even if not explicit, at least more prominent. In this light, or perhaps it is better to say, in this twilight, we can find no better resource than Nietzsche's provocative celebration of the darkness reflected by the most probing works of art. In his justly renowned *The Birth of Tragedy, Out of the Spirit of Music* (1872), he reminds us of art's pointedly non-illuminating character. Nietzsche tells us that "the 'I' of the lyric poet sounds out from the deepest abyss of being; his 'subjectivity,' as this concept is used by modern aestheticians, is imaginary" (30).[2] Note that

---

[1] EN: See *Ideas of Order*. Alfred F. Knopf, 1936.
[2] EN: See Nietzsche, Friedrich Wilhelm. *The Birth of Tragedy and Other Writings*. 1872. Edited by Raymond Geuss and Ronald Speirs. Translated by Ronald Speirs. Cambridge UP, 1999.

sound rather than image arises from the innermost recesses of the lyric poet. Recall Nietzsche's schema in which tragedy comes into its historical being precisely as the imagistic relief from music's too-penetrating force. Images hover at a safe distance; music instead threatens to undo us; tragedy is birthed to mediate between the suffering of the world and how it resonates in us. We are granted the whole realm of aesthetic images as protection from experiences of music that would otherwise melt and disassemble us. But here, we ought not to put Nietzsche on the side of enlightenment too readily and thereby imagine that, for him, aesthetic images illuminate something or other about the world or ourselves. He instead offers a rather homeopathic figuration of the healing work of art. He explains that just as our eyes, after looking too directly at the light of the sun, produce dark spots—images—to heal themselves, so too then does opacity, the dark imagery of the aesthetic, arise homeopathically in response to our having looked too directly into the suffering and darkness of existence. In both cases, the dark spots in our vision are not the illumination or revelation of anything in the world but rather only illusion in service of restoring our health. And it is as illusion—Nietzsche calls it semblance, *Schein* in German—that it also shows itself to be *merely* illusion.

Here, I want to try to knit together the Nietzschean insight regarding the necessity—though not truth—of illusion with Adorno's specification of the necessary objectivity of the form of lyric poetry. With that, we can surmise how we might come to see but not hear the limits of language in lyric poetry. In other words, and returning to Stevens, through poetry, we might well be able to see the disappearance of the pheasant in the brush, but we cannot hear what disappears; poetry is the visualization of what we cannot hear.

Achille C. Varzi

On the Logic of Poetry

The title of our session, *The Logics of Poetry*, is judiciously vague. Not only are the two nouns, 'logics' and 'poetry,' open to multiple qualifications; there is also ample flexibility in understanding the preposition 'of,' hence the intended link between the realms of logic and poetry, when suitably qualified. These are substantial and complex questions, and I won't attempt to address them directly. However, I will try to offer some preliminary thoughts regarding their scope and significance. More specifically, I shall begin with three observations, if not about the logics *of* poetry, at least on the larger relationship between logic *and* poetry, broadly construed. I am going to say that:

(i) logic and poetry share an important common ground, much broader and deeper than commonly assumed;

(ii) a certain common way of distinguishing the methods and purposes of a discipline such as logic from those of poetry is ill-considered and misleading, if not outright mistaken;

(iii) and there exists, nevertheless, a crucial distinction between the two that warrants recognition.

Based on these premises, I will briefly suggest a perspective on approaching the idea that poetry may possess its own logic, perhaps even multiple logics. Hopefully, it will become evident that the central question is not whether this means that poetry is *governed* by a logic, i.e., by logical laws or principles of the sort we find at work in other domains. Instead, the core issue concerns the *reasons* guiding the practice of creating poetry. If there is a logic of poetry, it pertains to the nuanced choices and decisions that underlie each poetic composition, the rational determinations that result in it being what it is and not something else.

I

Let's begin with the first point: (i) do logic and poetry share any common ground? Obviously, this is exactly the sort of question that presupposes a clear demarcation of these two domains. Moreover, let me emphasize from the outset that I am not equally involved in both. I am primarily a logician. I have been teaching and writing about logic for my entire academic career. By contrast, poetry is simply a personal passion of mine—almost a clandestine one that I generally shy away from discussing, and I normally avoid theorizing about it. That being said, I have my views, and my unequivocal response to our question is affirmative. Indeed, no matter how you specify their respective boundaries, logic and poetry have much more in common than one might initially suppose.

There are several reasons why I say this, but the main one is easily stated: in both cases, we find ourselves operating within a similar vantage point, a similarly broad and all-encompassing horizon of perspectives. There is a line in the early pages of Robert Musil's *The Man without Qualities* that beautifully encapsulates what I have in mind: "If there is a sense of reality, there must also be a sense of possibility."[1] With regard to logic, it was precisely this line by Musil that brought me to its study in the first place. Where else can we find a theory that cares about the sense of possibility? What science do we have, if not logic, that concerns itself with how things are just as much as with the innumerable ways they could be or might have been? Physics, Chemistry, Biology, History, Sociology, Economics—they all focus primarily on this world of ours, the world as it happens to be, the *actual* world. Logic invites us to consider every other world as well. To say that a proposition *P* logically implies a proposition *Q* is to say there is no *possible* world where *P* is true and *Q* isn't. We may not know how our world is, hence whether *P* and *Q* are actually true— that is the business of the other sciences. But we may work with our imagination. We may imagine how things would be if *P* were true—and there are many possibilities compatible with this supposition—and check whether *Q* would be true in every case. This definition is at the core of logic; implication is *the* fundamental notion in logic, and clearly enough, its application requires that we literally consider all possibilities, no matter how far-fetched or improbable

---

[1] AN: See *Der Mann ohne Eigenschaften*. Erstes Buch, 1930, p. 16: "Wenn es Wirklichkeitssinn gibt, muß es auch Möglichkeitssinn geben." English translation by Sophie Wilkins and Burton Pike. *The Man without Qualities*. vol. 1. Knopf, 1995, p. 10. The line is actually the title of chapter 4.

they might seem to us. Thus, while it is true that logic is ultimately intended as a tool for rational deliberation and argumentation—an ὄργανον ["organon"], as Aristotle's followers called it—this tool is only adequate insofar as it rests on an adequate picture of all possible truth conditions. Essentially, logic is, first and foremost, a science of possibility.

And so is poetry. Perhaps poetry isn't a *science* of possibility but deals with possibility in crucial ways. In his *Sketch of the Poet's Knowledge*, Musil himself was explicit about this: "There is in the poet's territory from the start no end of unknowns, equations, and possible solutions. The task is to discover ever new solutions, connections, constellations, variables, to set up prototypes of an order of events, appealing models of how one *can* be human."[2] But one doesn't need Musil to appreciate the sense of possibility that fuels most poetic compositions.

Perhaps the best poetry is the one that "cares about the real," as Paul Bové noted in his contribution. Even so, even when it is *bound* by the real, the magic of poetry lies first and foremost in its ability to transcend. Like logic, poetry possesses a unique potential to transport us beyond the narrow horizons of the world as it is and as we tend to see it, beyond a certain narrow way of describing how things are and how we feel about them. Like logic, it can push our minds into new, unexplored directions. Like logic, it reveals scenarios we might otherwise overlook, paths that may have escaped our notice, and possibilities we may not have contemplated.

Of course, this is not to say that the sense of possibility is the same in both cases. On the contrary, I think logicians have much to gain from the poet's multifaceted ways of venturing into the vast land of what is not, just as poets may find value in the logician's more abstract, combinatorial way of mapping every corner of that territory. What *is* the same, I think, is the Musilian sentiment that the sense of reality isn't all: there is a sense of possibility that is equally, if not more, important. Everything depends on the range of possibilities we can discern, beginning with our hopes and projects.

---

[2] AN: "Skizze der Erkenntnis des Dichters." *Summa*, vol. 4 (1918), pp. 164–168, at p. 167. English translation by Burton Pike and David S. Luft, "Sketch of What the Writer Knows," in their edition of Musil's *Precision and Soul: Essays and Addresses*. The University of Chicago Press, 1990, pp. 61–65, at p. 64. (I am not sure why the translators rendered 'Dichter' with 'writer'; in the quotation, I have replaced the latter word with 'poet').

In fact, there is no reason to think that the relevant sense of possibility must be uniform even within each domain. Surely, not *everything* is possible short of triviality. Yet, logicians may disagree about where exactly to draw the line, just as different poetic schools, or even distinct individual poets, may draw the line differently. In logic, for example, classical theories used to assume everything is possible *except for contradictions*. Today, there are logical theories known as paraconsistent logics that are even open to the possibility of contradictions being true, not least because of the beneficial consequences that might arise. As Graham Priest once put it: "To be and not to be—that is the answer."[3]

It isn't difficult to imagine similar shifts in the realm of poetry, see Aristotle's famous remark in the *Poetics*: "A likely impossibility is always preferable to an unconvincing possibility."[4] But regardless of how one feels about contradictions, there is no question that the range of possibilities contemplated by different authors may vary. Surely, Carducci's range wouldn't align with Marinetti's, or Shakespeare's with those of Sylvia Plath. Such a variety of perspectives is undeniable in poetry and logic. Yet this is irrelevant to the main point. It's the nature of the perspective that matters and that is shared throughout and across the board.

II

That being said, the existence of common ground doesn't mean there are no important differences between the methods and purposes of logic and the endeavors of poetry. It would be absurd to say there aren't. So, let me now turn to this part of the story. There are differences, yet they might not be what we commonly assume. In particular—this is the second point (ii)—I am convinced that a certain natural way of distinguishing the two is seriously ill-considered and deeply misleading.

Consider that passage in the fourth part of de Sade's *Juliette*, where Chigi tells Olympia about the creative effects of passing over the laws: "It

---

[3] AN: See Priest, Graham. "To Be and Not to Be—That is the Answer. On Aristotle on the Law of Non-Contradiction." *History of Philosophy and Logical Analysis*, vol. 1, 1998, pp. 91–130.

[4] AN: See *Poetics*, XXIV, 1460a26: "προαιρεῖσθαί τε δεῖ ἀδύνατα εἰκότα μᾶλλον ἢ δυνατὰ ἀπίθανα"; English translation by Ingram Bywater, in *The Complete Works of Aristotle. The Revised Oxford Translation*. Edited by Jonathan Barnes, Princeton UP, 1984, vol. 2, p. 2337.

is only in that moment when the laws are silent that greatest actions burst forth."[5] Chigi was talking about anarchy in the political sense, contrasting it with all forms of government that rely on enforcing various kinds of laws. But the passage can be read and has often been read metaphorically: creativity, especially poetic creativity, flourishes most vividly in the absence of restrictive laws. Since logic, by definition, deals with laws—specifically, the laws of implication—logic would be the exact opposite. I see why one may be inclined to put it this way, especially considering contemporary poetry's diverse and wondrous array of expressive techniques. Nonetheless, I believe we should resist the temptation for two separate reasons.

In the first place, poetry does not *only* shine in the absence of laws. Sometimes, it precisely shines because it obeys several stringent laws. Think, for example, of the many formal laws that have governed poetic composition across the centuries: laws of meter, laws of rhyme, structural laws (as in a sonnet, an ode, a limerick, a Persian Ghazal, a Japanese Tanka), and so on—what Franca d'Agostini, in her remarks, called the "power-dominion of language." Or think of the many alternative forms of constrained writing that poets have been exploring, such as lipograms, written under the constraint of systematically omitting certain letters (the first lipogrammatic poems go back to Lasus of Hermione, none other than Pindar's teacher[6]), or anti-lipograms, written under the opposite constraint of using only certain letters—as in Ernst Jandl's univocalic poem *ottos mops*.[7] Giuseppe Varaldo went as far as writing univocalic sonnets, each constrained by the further requirement that its content should recap a literary classic.[8] Even the most radical forms of experimental poetry may involve strict laws: in the verse itself, in the way it is displayed on

---

[5] AN: See Donatien Alphonse François Sade (Marquis de). *Juliette, ou les Prospérités du vice*, in *La nouvelle Justine, ou les malheurs de la vertu, suivie de l'Histoire de Juliette, sa sœur*, Hollande, s.l., 1797, vol. VIII, p. 237: "Ce n'est que dans cet instant du silence des loix, qu'ont éclatées les plus grandes actions." My English rendering differs from the published translation by Austryn Wainhouse (Arrow Books, 1968), which strikes me as somewhat too prosaic: "Only at moments when the laws were held in contempt do stupendous actions occur" (731).

[6] AN: See Porter, James I. "Lasus of Hermione, Pindar and the Riddle of S." *The Classical Quarterly*, vol. 57, 2007, pp. 1–21. According to the Suda, Nestor of Laranda even rewrote the whole *Iliad* lipogrammatically, with no alphas in book 1, no betas in book 2, etc., and Triphiodorus did the same with the *Odyssey*; see Bekker, Immanuel, editor. *Suidae Lexicon*, Reimer, 1854, p. 739.

[7] AN: In his *Der künstliche Baum*. Luchterhand, 1970, p. 58.

[8] AN: *All'alba Shahrazad andrà ammazzata. Capolavori in sonetti monovocalici*. Vallardi, 1993.

the printed page (think of Apollinaire's *Calligrams*),[9] in how the poem is to be read or performed, in the pitch. Whether manneristic or "creative," as the Oulipians would have it,[10] rule-governed writing has been driving poetry from antiquity to our days, and we can certainly counter Chigi's words with those of Baudelaire: "Because the form is constricting, the idea bursts forth all the more intensely."[11] Conversely, I am aware that sometimes poetry shines insofar as it *disobeys* the laws. In the "Preface" to the first edition of *Leaves of Grass*, Walt Whitman wrote:

> The poetic quality is not marshalled in rhyme or uniformity [...]. The profit of rhyme is that it drops seeds of a sweeter and more luxuriant rhyme, and of uniformity that it conveys itself into its own roots in the ground out of sight. The rhyme and uniformity of perfect poems show the free growth of metrical laws and bud from them as unerringly and as loosely as lilacs or roses on a bush.[12]

Yes, sometimes poetry shines when it takes us beyond the constraints of rhyme or uniformity—beyond the routinized, the reassuring, and the predictable. But then, again, so does logic. It may not shine in a textbook syllogism, as when we infer humans are mortal from the premises that humans are animals and animals are mortal. Logic does not shine in an inference of this sort any more than poetry shines in cheesy routine verse. But there is much more to logic than that. And when it takes us beyond common sense, where its laws fall silent, the greatest inferences burst forth.

Logic shines at the *limits* of thought. Think of the beauty of a proof whose conclusion is the opposite of what we expected. Think of the discovery of the logical paradoxes that have shaken the very foundations of mathematics. Think of the awe we all experience when faced with ground-breaking results such as Gödel's incompleteness theorems,[13] whose brilliance doesn't

---

[9] AN: *Calligrammes. Poèmes de la paix et de la guerre*. Mercure de France, 1918.

[10] AN: See Oulipo. *La littérature potentielle (Créations Re-créations Récréations)*. Gallimard, 1973.

[11] AN: Letter to Armand Fraisse, February 18, 1860, in Baudelaire, Charles. *Correspondance*, Tome I. 1832–1860. Edited by Claude Pichois. Gallimard, 1973, p. 676: "Parce que la forme est contraignante, l'idée jaillit plus intense"; English translation by Rosemary Lloyd, in *The Conquest of Solitude: Selected Letters*. Weidenfeld & Nicolson, 1986, p. 148.

[12] AN: *Leaves of Grass*. Andrew and James Rome, 1855, p. v.

[13] AN: See Gödel, Kurt. "Über formal unentscheidbare Sätze der Principia Mathematica und verwandter Systeme I." *Monatshefte für Mathematik und Physik*, vol. 38, 1931, pp. 173–198.

lie exclusively in their unimagined import but also in the imaginative method employed in their proofs.

This is another way of recognizing that poetry and logic engage with our sense of possibility, stretching it to its outermost boundaries, and both shine brightest when they unveil possibilities not considered before. That one is strictly governed by formal rules while the other isn't—that is certainly not the case or definitely not where they differ.

III

Where do they differ, then? Well, there are many answers one could offer. However, in this context, I shall confine myself to highlighting the most subtle yet crucial difference. It can succinctly be put as follows: logic operates at the level of *propositions*; poetry, by contrast, is all about *sentences*. I will focus on sentences, but you will quickly recognize that the point applies to all forms of linguistic expression.

A sentence is a grammatically well-formed sequence of words—symbols—in a particular language. Every sentence, at least every declarative sentence, expresses a proposition, i.e., a content. But the relationship is not one-to-one. For one thing, different sentences in the same language may express the same proposition. For instance, the sentences *The show begins tomorrow* and *The show starts tomorrow* are distinct, yet they clearly express the same proposition since 'begins' and 'starts' are synonyms. Similarly, *Dante loves Beatrice* and *Beatrice is loved by Dante* express the same proposition, even if one is in the active voice and the other in the passive. We may also express the same proposition with sentences in different languages, as with *Dante loves Beatrice* and *Dante ama Beatrice*. It is not easy to specify the exact criteria whereby two sentences can be said to express the same proposition—this is a major question in the philosophy of language, going back to Frege[14]—but the intuitive idea is clear enough: in each of our examples, the two sentences express the same proposition insofar as they stand or fall together. The range of possibilities that would make one true is exactly the same as those that would make the other true.

---

[14] AN: See Frege, Gottlob. "Über Sinn und Bedeutung." *Zeitschrift für Philosophie und philosophische Kritik*, vol. 100, 1892, pp. 25–50.

Now, since logic is about the relation of implication, which, as we saw, is defined in terms of truth conditions, all such grammatical differences are logically irrelevant. From a logical perspective, all that matters is whether the truth of a certain proposition necessitates the truth of another, irrespective of the sentences used to express those propositions. After all, it shouldn't make any difference whether an implication claim—an argument—is stated in English, Italian, or some other language, as it should be immaterial whether we present our premises and conclusion in the active voice or the passive, using different words with the same meaning, etc. Not so with poetry. As Mallarmé once said: "You don't write verse with ideas... You use words."[15] Since poetry is not about what follows from what, the mere fact that two sentences express the same proposition doesn't mean they are equally good. One sentence may serve our purposes better than the other. It might rhyme more effectively, align with the meter more naturally, possess a more pleasing sound, evoke stronger emotions, etc. Content is important, but so is form. Assonance, alliteration, order, repetition, punctuation—all play a significant role. To help myself with another quotation, this time from David Jones: "In poetry everything matters, and the greater the poetry so much the more is this true."[16] It's true in the classical and modernist poetry Jones was writing about, and it remains true, *mutatis mutandis*, even in the most avant-garde forms of postmodern composition. No poet ever selects a word solely based on its meaning; no one focuses exclusively on the truth conditions of what they say, as if *how* they say it carried no weight.

For these reasons, translating poetry proves to be such a challenging endeavor. It is not sufficient to translate every original sentence into a sentence with the same meaning, a sentence expressing the same proposition in the target language. This may be fine when translating an academic article, a textbook, or an encyclopedia entry, but not if we are translating poetry. The translation of a poem—like its interpretation—must always respect the fact that the poet chose those specific sentences over others. It must do justice to

---

[15] AN: Cited in Valéry, Paul. *Poésie et Pensée abstraite. The Zaharoff Lecture*. Clarendon Press, 1939, p. 11: "Ce n'est point avec des idées, mon cher Degas, que l'on fait des vers. C'est avec des mots"; English translation by Charles Guenther, "Poetry and Abstract Thought." *The Kenyon Review*, vol. 16, 1954, pp. 208–233, at p. 217.

[16] AN: See Jones, David. *An Introduction to The Rime of the Ancient Mariner*. Clover Hill, 1972, p. 22.

the poet's *decision* to use those specific words in that specific order and to the *reasons* that guided that decision. For example, it must adhere to the same constraints as the original—a sonnet must be translated as a sonnet, a lipogram as a lipogram, etc.—and it must do so per the target language's grammatical, lexical, and phonetic rules.

Sometimes, it may even seem impossible to respect all the original constraints, as every English translator of Dante's *Commedia* or Goethe's *Faust* knows all too well, yet that is the ideal goal. Douglas Hofstadter's book, *Le Ton beau de Marot* (1997), contains no less than eighty-eight translations of Clément Marot's little poem, *Ma mignonne*,[17] some by Hofstadter himself, some by others, some by (old) computer programs; perhaps none can be said to fully meet the challenge of recreating the exquisite qualities of the original French, yet that was the aim in each case. Sometimes, a translator may even have to be so inventive as to *recreate* the constraints to retain their original significance. In August 2005, to commemorate what would have been Ernst Jandl's eightieth birthday, the online cultural magazine *signandsight.com* organized a poetry competition to translate *ottos mops* from univocalic German into other languages. The winning entry was an English translation by the British philologist Brian Murdoch, titled *fritz's bitch*. Barbara Köhler, the head of the jury, praised the translation as "truest to the original" even though, as the title reveals, its unique vowel was 'i' instead of 'o'.[18] More precisely, the vowel used in the translation was the *phonetic* / ɪ /: since Jandl's 'o' has (roughly) the same sound in all of its occurrences, using words with multiple sounds of 'i', such as /iː/ or /aɪ/, would have been inaccurate. (Even more interesting, perhaps, is that one of the first published translations of the poem, Elizabeth MacKiernan's *Lulu's Pooch*,[19] trades the original 'o' for the phonetic /uː/, excluding words with /ʌ /, /juː/, /ɛ/, etc. but allowing the 'oo' digraph.)

We could continue, but I am sure it isn't necessary. Everybody is familiar with the challenges of translating poetry. The point is that these challenges reflect the challenges inherent in the very practice of *composing* poetry since the art of composition is, at its core, the art of translating one's thoughts ef-

---

[17] AN: Written in 1537 and originally published under the title *A une Damoyselle malade* (in the 1542 edition of Marot's Œuvres, Lyon, Dolet, p. 158).

[18] AN: 'And the winner is…', online at signandsight.com/features/290.html, September 2005.

[19] AN: In Jandl, Ernst. *Reft and Light. Poems with Multiple Versions by American Poets*. Edited by Rosemarie Waldrop. Burning Deck Press, 2000, p. 33.

fectively into tangible words. Poetry is all about such nuances and intricacies; logic disregards them altogether. That, in my opinion, is the fundamental difference between the two.

IV

We thus come to the final point. Can we even speak of a logic *of* poetry? Isn't the title of our panel a mere oxymoron, given the difference we have just highlighted?

I believe it is not. Surely, poetry is not governed by the laws of logic in any conventional sense. It may not even care about such laws, whether classical, paraconsistent, or of any other kind. To quote Musil once more, the poet lives in "nonratioid territory": "If the ratioid is the area of the domination of the 'rule with exceptions,' the nonratioid area is that of the dominance of the exceptions over the rule."[20] However, that does not mean that poetry is a thoroughly irrational practice. I have heard this claim many times, but it sounds as bad as saying that poetry makes no sense. Indeed, it is the worst way of summarizing what we have been saying. The point is that in the land of poetry, every appeal to reason is highly specific and personal; we may even say idiosyncratic, hence hardly reducible to general rules.[21] No poet *follows* a logic when crafting a poem, not in the manner a mathematician uses logic to prove a theorem or an economist employs it to make market predictions. Yet every poet engages in choices and decisions that are anything but arbitrary. Every poem emerges from a series of specific deliberations, and each of these deliberations has its own underlying *rationale*, personal and unique as it may be.

So, is there is a logic of poetry? Indeed, there is. It's just that it is not logic applied to poetry, as with the logic of mathematics or economics. It is, instead, that complex array of specific decisional processes that lie behind each poetic composition. It encompasses the reasons that guide us when crafting individual poems, the justifications we might offer—even if not always, and not always with consistent clarity—to explain why a particular poem turned out to be the poem it is and not something else. If these justifications resist systematic

---

[20] AN: "Skizze der Erkenntnis des Dichters," cit., p. 166; English translation, cit., p. 63.

[21] AN: In his notebooks, Musil identifies the area of the nonratioid with that of "singular facts" (*Tagebücher*. Edited by Adolf Frisé. Rowohlt, 1983, p. 479; English translation by Philip Payne: *Diaries, 1899–1941*. Basic Books, 1998, p. 255).

regimentation and codification, if they privilege the exceptions over the rule, it is precisely because they are always, in every case, inherently specific. And they are inherently specific precisely insofar as they operate at the level of words and sentences, not propositions.

I realize this is all rather sketchy. It is also critically incomplete since we presumably won't get a full answer to our question unless we delve into its natural counterpart: is there any poetry in logic? That, in itself, is an interesting and difficult question, but I'll have to leave it to another occasion. For now, let me conclude with one last quotation. It is from the literary biography of an eminent poet, and it beautifully encapsulates the sketch I have tried to offer:

> At school I enjoyed the inestimable advantage of a very sensible, though at the same time, a very severe master. [...] I learnt from him, that Poetry, even that of the loftiest, and, seemingly, that of the wildest odes, had a logic of its own, as severe as that of science; and more difficult, because more subtle, more complex, and dependent on more, and more fugitive causes. In the truly great poets, he would say, there is a reason assignable, not only for every word, but for the position of every word; and I well remember, that availing himself of the synonyms to the Homer of Didymus, he made us attempt to show, with regard to each, why it would not have answered the same purpose; and wherein consisted the peculiar fitness of the word in the original text.

Day 2 – Saturday, November 12, 2022

Cecilia Bello Minciacchi

The Legacy of the Neo-Avant-Garde II. Structures of the Return in Italian Poetry from the Late Twentieth Century to the Present Day

> Il primo discorso che un'opera fa, lo fa attraverso il modo in cui è fatta.
> Il vero *contenuto* dell'opera diventa il suo *modo di vedere il mondo* e di giudicarlo, risolto *in modo di formare*.
> — Umberto Eco, *Opera aperta*, 269–270.[1]

For several years now, the Italian cultural scene has been experiencing a period of reaction and regression, which applies to the literary scene and largely to the poetry scene. The expansion of large publishing houses is crushing smaller ones, which are often more curious and virtuous but objectively less incisive—in terms of dissemination and market—or forced to work harder to disseminate the books they print. This does not refer to the enormous flowering of less media-conscious, more sentimental, instinctive, and trivially confessional poetry that invades the Web daily and amplifies the background noise by contributing to a chaotic parceling out. Without endorsing the rhetoric of victimhood, the poetry that seems to have the most to gain is forced to spread on the margins of a system that has firmly acquired means and power in the more than mature capitalism and globalization. Today, we can easily understand Mark Fisher's *Capitalist Realism: Is There No Alternative?* (2009) by reflecting on the ontological shift of Margaret Thatcher's infamous statement—or doctrine—that "there is no alternative." Back in 1989, the British Prime Minister meant that there was no alternative to neo-liberal capitalism because it is preferable to other systems. Today, capitalism—writes Fisher—is "not only the best possible system," as it then seemed to Thatcher, "but also the *only one*. The alternatives are confused, ghostly, barely conceivable" ("The Privatization of Stress" 124).

---

[1] EN: "The first discourse that a work does occurs in the way in which it is made. The true *content* of the work becomes its *way of seeing the world* and judging it, resolved *in its way of forming*" (Translated by de Thomasis).

However, it is not merely for market reasons that the more reader-friendly, emotional, and consolatory poetics are dominating. Beyond the complaint about the publishing market, a complaint that, while correct and sharable, is so often repeated as to appear empty, one must consider that those responsible for the reactionary trend are partly those who could—and should—have opposed it. In Italy, the neo-avant-garde is studied less than any other literary period. The academy seems to prefer pleasantly readable authors without destabilizing effects or having already entered the literary canon.

In several of our universities, courses and essays on poets with a well-recognized and validated profile, such as Montale, Sereni, Giudici, Caproni, Bertolucci, and Bassani, flourish. Courses devoted to the historical avant-garde and neo-avant-garde are scarce. While respecting aesthetic divergences, we cannot accept such a lack of historiographical perspective, nor can we accommodate the curious tendency to forget what the five Novissimi produced after 1969, the official end of the neo-avant-garde.

It is common for Italian scholars, albeit experts on the twentieth century, to scotomize the neo-avant-garde as if it had never existed, eliminating it from the contemporary poetic genealogy and denying its inheritance. Even some of them, when studying the 1970s, consider only those who began writing in that decade, such as Dario Bellezza or Milo De Angelis, removing (censoring) the production of the Novissimi after the end of the neo-avant-garde.

Some are not afraid to almost wholly overlook both the neo-avant-garde experience and the works of the Novissimi from the 1970s onwards. This is 'forgetfulness' and 'oblivion,' not negative critical study and interpretation based on careful textual analysis nor documented literary-historical profiles, which instead would have every right to validity.

Unfortunately, even some relatively young scholars have embraced this tendency toward removal, both of the Novissimi experience and of what, having disbanded the group 63, the Novissimi continued to produce from the 1970s to the end, sometimes yielding excellent poetic and narrative works grounded in aesthetic perspectives different from those of the unloved neo-avant-garde.

Instead, it would be historiographically and critically correct to recall with appropriate space for analysis that the ex-Novissimi continued to write even in the same decade in which Bellezza debuted with *Invettive e licenze* (1971) and De Angelis with *Somiglianze* (1976). The same decade that saw Pasolini's *Trasumanar e organizzar* (1971), Rosselli's *Documento* (1976), and Zanzotto's *Il galateo in bosco* (1978), to name only a few among those who were more or less distant from the poets of Group 63. Giuliani republished much of his earlier production in a fine volume of the "white" Einaudi series, *Chi l'avrebbe detto* (1973).[2] Sanguineti published *Catamerone: 1951–1971* (1974) and *Postkarten: Poesie 1972–1977* (1978). Balestrini initiated the extensive cycle of *Le ballate della Signorina Richmond* (1977). Pagliarani wrote the extraordinary *Rosso corpo corpo lingua oro pope-papa scienza. Doppio trittico di Nandi* (1977), an important nucleus of the later *La ballata di Rudi* (1995). The case of Antonio Porta is different: yes, he re-proposed his "novissima" production in *Quanto ho da dirvi. Poesie 1958–1975* (1977), but in the production of the 1970s he experienced a clear conversion to a more communicative poetic dictate: "I will choose the voice" is one of his new assumptions.[3] Except for Porta, who died prematurely, the other four Novissimi (Sanguineti, Balestrini, Pagliarani, and Giuliani) continued to write verse for several decades after the end of the Gruppo 63 experience (one of them, Nanni Balestrini, until 2019). Between the 1970s and the beginning of the 2000s, the dialogue between its members did not cease. Above all, their poetic voices did not remain silent.

These authors now had the neo-avant-garde behind them, and hypotheses of a return to the avant-garde's expressive, conceptual, and ideological modules appeared even to them fanciful and impracticable. It is also true that they continued to write along the lines of poetics far removed from those of the majority and those of the newcomers soon to rise to the mainstream. The differences have always remained stark: leveling (and depotentiating) critical readings that fail to consider the inseparable relationship between *ideology and language*, the famous binomial expounded by Sanguineti in the publication of the same name (*Ideologia e linguaggio*, 1965), are not convincing. The poetics of Zanzotto and Sanguineti, to choose a macroscopic opposition as an example—but one could also think of the poetics of Sanguineti and Pasolini—have always remained culturally, literarily, and politically irreconcilable, never even tangent with each other.

---

[2] EN: This collection of poetry is called "Bianca" (white) for the color chosen for its book covers, which are all completely white and contain the name of the author, title, and a few lines from one of the poems.

[3] EN: In this regard, see Terreni, Alessandro. *La scelta della voce. La svolta lirica di Antonio Porta*. Arcipelago Edizioni, 2015.

To ignore the neo-avant-garde and what the Novissimi produced in poetry after the 1960s makes their potential legacy scarcely comprehensible. A legacy that certainly touches poets like Giulia Niccolai, Corrado Costa, and Adriano Spatola, albeit with due differences, as well as Patrizia Vicinelli and Vittorio Reta, who mixed suggestions drawn from Sanguineti and Giuliani at the same time, or Luigi Ballerini who responded to the poetry of the Novissimi with his earliest book, *eccetera. E* (1972). This is a work that reemploys in strange and ironic ways some of the solutions of the neo-avant-garde, at times making fun of it, in any case showing its accomplished, critical, and necessary *crossing* and the possibility of a new departure concentrated in the period of the title, to which Spatola recognized *centrality*, and in the conjunction that opens to a new start. And all this to stay with well-known names.

The legacy of the neo-avant-garde, understood as the permanence or return of ideological-literary awareness and the material, concrete conception of language and its tensioning, reaches even the younger generations, including those active in our day. But it does so in dialectical terms, not as mere epigonic continuation. If one continued to remove the neo-avant-garde from contemporary poetry or ignore its effects, one would end up marginalizing or placing in the checkmate of leveling postmodernism (or oblivion) even a brief and debated experience in fertile friction with Gruppo 63, accomplished between 1989 and 1993 by the Gruppo '93, which was particularly active on the terrain of theoretical and aesthetic discussion. One cannot speak of direct inheritance from Gruppo 63 to Gruppo '93: the younger authors—as Lello Voce argued—are not the "grandchildren" of the Novissimi, and for many, including Marcello Frixione, the paths taken by the historical avant-garde and the neo-avant-garde were now impracticable because the techniques used historically, the collision, the shock, the disorienting intent, had become ordinary, almost quotidian:

> What of the avant-garde is no longer viable is the foundational project. As in mathematics, the search for foundations has led to paradoxes. The possibility that remains is that of an artistic practice that is always unstable, resting on stilts and requiring constant adjustments […]. And rebellious and provocative attitudes no longer make any sense in this perspective: it is no longer possible to scandalize anyone, there are no more doors to break through, and there is no more pattern that can be broken […]. Regardless of all this, the research of the avant-garde remains an indispensable heritage for any form of artistic work that places itself in a dimension of a, in the broadest sense, theoretical type; the avant-garde has made available to us an analysis of unprecedented lucidity of

the richness of the expressive tools, possibilities and mechanisms underlying artistic work, and at the same time has provided us with an opening to expressive possibilities that cannot be ignored, on pain of a return to forms that are to some extent naive and unconscious. ("Goedel, Blob e la merda d'artista" 88)[4]

Of course, critical perspectives that effectively consider the first and second avant-garde exist in Italy, but they are curiously more active abroad. For example, there is the monumental project devoted to Italian poetry from its origins to the present day, conceived for The Lorenzo da Ponte Italian Library, whose two-volume book on 20th-century poetry from 1956 to the present day has the evocative title *Those Who from Afar Look Like Flies*. A work that anthologizes poems and essays, proposing a genuine rethinking of the canon: being based on the innovativeness of the poetic language, it excludes from the most recent volume poets such as Attilio Bertolucci and Vittorio Sereni, who have their own space in the first volume instead. Alongside these volumes, edited by Luigi Ballerini and Giuseppe Cavatorta with Gianluca Rizzo and Dominic Siracusa, decisive translations such as Giuliani's *Novissimi. Poetry for the Sixties* by Luigi Ballerini and Federica Santini is worth mentioning, and the studies of critics such as Gabriele Belletti, Stefano Colangelo, Andrea Cortellessa, Alessandro Giammei, Francesco Muzzioli, Gian Luca Picconi, Gianluca Rizzo, Tommaso Pomilio, and Luigi Weber, all of them scholars attentive to writings that do not slavishly fit into the previously established canon.

Identifying and analyzing the legacy of the neo-avant-garde on more recent authors is a most challenging task and a work in progress. Among the traits that may allow a link to the lesson of the five Novissimi and their later production, the reduction of the "I" should be considered, implemented in poems that, in a different cultural landscape, do not propose the narcissistic exhibition of the ego and its lyricized and sublimated biography. The reduction of the "I" is naturally juxtaposed with the schizomorphic view of the real and proposals for a new "metric *texture* as separated from syllabic measure and founded on the intonation of groups or semantic nuclei (another measure, not free verse)" ("Preface to the 2003 Edition" 342).

Let's take one aspect as a particular example: the poem's relationship with its texture, with its metric texture. This is a fundamental relationship on

---

[4] EN: On the possibilities of the avant-garde in the late twentieth century, see Frixione's "Sull'eredità dell'avanguardia," p. 42.

which the specificity of the poetic text is played out, both when, on the formal structure, the poet makes a visible, exposed investment and when he or she undertakes to lower it with the aim of resetting it to zero. This component of the poetic text is chosen as a parameter of investigation for two main reasons: because it is the most controversial and risky knot and because it can be an excellent litmus test of the relationship that each author has, at the same time, with the past and the present. Therefore, some preliminary quotations are proposed, in the manner of a catalog of epigraphs that serves as a concise prologue, by points:

> There is no escape from metre; there is only mastery.
> — T.S. Eliot, *Reflections on Vers Libre*.

> I have said before that I believe in a social function of literature, a function which does not, of course, exhaust literature, but which is objectively verifiable regardless of any intentionality. The function is to keep language efficient for everyone. Said Pound: "It is as important for the purpose of thought to keep language efficient as it is in surgery to keep tetanus bacilli out of one's bandages." ["How to Read" 22]
> — Elio Pagliarani, "Per una definizione di avanguardia," 108.[5]

> Literature that, in addition to being realist (i.e., in addition to using language in all its semantic force) also aspires to an autonomy and to an objectivity as a specific use of language, requires the recovery and development of a rhetoric.
> — Marcello Frixione, "Il linguaggio è in ordine così come come è," 141–142.[6]

It is also worth noting that Frixione, in the same text, spoke of realist literature as "necessarily [...] cultured and complex" and of "recovery and development of a rhetoric" (142), thus not only recovery but also expansion and evolution. These three quotations can be usefully related to the possible legacy of the Novissimi. While it is true that Sanguineti, Pagliarani, Balestrini, Giuliani, and Porta had a non-peaceful relationship with the lexicon and forms of the canon, each of them was very clear about—and each was decisive about—the specificity of the text or literary object.

---

[5] AN: See Pagliarani's contribution to *Gruppo 63. Il romanzo sperimentale. Palermo 1965*. Edited by Nanni Balestrini. Feltrinelli, 1965, pp. 104–115. Translated by the author.

[6] AN: See *Gruppo '93. La recente avventura del dibattito teorico letterario in Italia*. Edited by Filippo Bettini and Francesco Muzzioli. Manni Editori, 1990, pp. 141–142. Translated by the author.

The second avant-garde, compared to the first, could no longer be naïve. Breaking with previous tradition did not entail abandoning rhetoric or metrical structures *tout court*; it implied their rupture, subversion, and renewal, the search for new paths and possibilities. In different ways from each other, they experimented with accents on the blank verse model, occasionally reducing the number from five to four—this is the case with Antonio Porta and Alfredo Giuliani. Or they obsessively interrupted the rhythm of the text by breaking it up into detached, anti-narrative frames through the repeated use of the comma—Porta again. Or they broke up the lines of verse by adopting a stepped arrangement, with accordion-like verses, perhaps alternating with blocks of hendecasyllables—this is the case with Elio Pagliarani. Or they constructed apocalyptic verb-soundscapes founded on cola sequences, according to an informal trend not only in the lexicon but also in the metrical substance, such as the *laborintico* Sanguineti (who with philology and medieval literature had initiated an authentic melee), or the "obvious atonalism" of verses that, strictly founded on the principle of montage, are mobile machines that invite one to "enter the *open order* of contexts (whose possible meanings move like the steel plates in a Calder mobile) and making the machine work" (thus Balestrini's texts) (*I Novissimi* 193). The immediately following production would confirm, with appropriate differences among the five Novissimi, the same innovative procedures in textual texture: texts are disharmoniously de-structured and simultaneously edify new architectures invested with meaning. This can be seen in the exaggerated use of paragraphemic signs initiated by Sanguineti from the end of *Laborintus* (1956) and confirmed with stubbornness in *Erotopaegnia* (1960, in *Opus metricum*), in *Purgatorio de l'Inferno* (1964, in *Triperuno*), and in a large part of the following texts, as much as in the dilation of the steps used by Pagliarani, accordions with an ever-increasing need for breath—think of *Lezione di fisica e Fecaloro* (1968)—as well as in Balestrini's textual machines whose montages are based on rigorous combinatorial and rhythmic systems (like in some of the texts in *Ma noi facciamone un'altra*, 1968).

In the following decades, some of the Novissimi would employ traditional metrical forms, from the sonnet and the octave to the ballad and the madrigal. Still, without any reactionary or regressive intent—this is the most remarkable thing—without nostalgia for a past to be recovered, instead with aspirations for a (metrical) future all to be built. That these structural outcroppings were not in the vein of recovering Canon and Poetry, with the temptation of the Sublime, is evident from the treatment of traditional forms: now subtle slippages or contraventions of the norm, now a violent, ironic twist, sometimes of vibrant comedy and outspoken virtuosity (such as Sanguineti's *Alfabeto apocalittico* (1984) and the coeval *Novissimum Testamentum* (1986)), now an estranged employment.

Their poetics relied upon a very clear concept, which was also a way of seeing the world, not only the literary one: no form of spontaneous and natural continuity with tradition was possible. Giuliani wrote this clearly in the 2003 Preface to the reissue of *I Novissimi*: "There is a crucial difference between those who feel the ruining of exhausted forms and are prodded by it and those who do not realize it and think they can continue using them with diversionary maneuvers" (342). Thus, it is one thing to have a "peaceful" neo-metricism, so to speak, deluded of serene recoveries with small maquillage variations, and quite another to have a (with or without the prefix neo-) critical metricism, to adopt a qualification that in the late 1980s gave birth to a formula of albeit difficult and discussed fate, that of "critical postmodernism." Here, critical (neo)metricism means a radically estranged use of traditional devices, a use that is countercultural and already in itself erosive, protesting, invested with meaning, and revelatory. This rests on an awareness of the specificity of the poetic text and the function of recursivity and variation, historically studied by Jurij Lotman,[7] but above all on the consciousness—already proper to the albeit "destructive" Novissimi—that their *poems for the Sixties* did not reset the metric but constructed a new one. Not otherwise would one explain the famous "metrical *texture*" clause.

All too obvious, but insufficiently considered by exegetes, is that atonal verse does not mean verse devoid of metrical structure or zero-metrical verse. The tonic accents exist anyway. The syllabic texture is not avoidable. Giuliani spoke for Balestrini's texts, among others, of "obvious atonalism of metrical structure," a structure that was thus not at all eliminated but permanent. Its rhythmic-phonic warp was renewed. It changed—this is the point—in the perception of the users, who no longer found the constituent props canonized and known to them, and therefore reassuring, but a texture no longer recognizable, unknown, and not immediately "pleasant."

---

[7] EN: See Lotman, Jurij M. *La semiosfera. L'asimmetria e il dialogo nelle strutture pensanti.* Translated by Simonetta Salvestroni. Marsilio, 1985. In English, see "On the semiosphere." Translated by Wilma Clark. *Sign Systems Studies*. 33, 1, 2005, pp. 205–229.

The theoretical paper included by Giuliani at the end of the *Novissimi* was titled *La forma del verso*, and it discussed some Eliotian and Poundian metrical reflections. It considered appropriate to adopt among the "tools" with which to write poetry, also the verse of the "American type," constructed as an atonal, open sequence, "in the measure of breath, and not for the eye but according to the ear," according to the proposal of Charles Olson's *Projective Verse* (1950).

To the "ruining of exhausted forms" mentioned by Giuliani in 2003, the five *Novissimi* poets did not respond with nostalgic regressions—after all, they were about to found a new avant-garde—nor, however, with the erasure, the zeroing of the metrical scaffolding, but by listening to the goad that flowed from that ruin, that is, by seeking new trends, new breaths for their "true contemporary poetry" ("Introduction to the First Edition (1961)" 29).[8]

A concept similar to the one formulated by Giuliani in 2003 was also expressed by Sanguineti, who, in an interview in the same year, said that the adoption of traditional metrical structures could take place either in a kind of false, impossible naïveté or in the awareness of their being historical wrappings, usable as citation and in a form that is not slavish but alienated and alienating:

> When metrical procedures are used, there are two ways to adopt them: one is to believe they are still natural to language and tradition as if nothing has happened in the world; the other is to use them in an estranged way. Just as in music, one can use tonal combinations as long as one understands them as one of the many ways in which one expresses a vision that is now atonal, so I can write a sonnet, but it must be clear that I am making use of a quotation: I am full of hendecasyllables, but these hendecasyllables are disguised as much as possible, mortified embedded with others. How not to use this treasure of experience? However, it is necessary to use it not as nature, but as history. ("A me della poesia m'importa pochissimo" 63)

And certainly not as nature, but as history—and, I will add, as history ironized and/or allegorized in its false flatteries and failures—the five Novissimi resorted to structures of the canon in their later, post-Novissimi experience. Between 1950 and 1975, poetry dispensed with closed forms. The resumption of closed forms is traditionally dated to 1978, when Zanzotto inserted his *Ipersonetto*

---

[8] EN: To use the Leopardian syntagma quoted by Giuliani in the incipit of his 1961 Introduction do the first edition (1961).

at the center of *Galateo in Bosco* and Sanguineti wrote *Sottosonetto*, a pseudo-sonnet later included in *Segnalibro*. The attitude toward the recovered metrical form is different, as is evident from the difference in language, always a revealing element, as Sanguineti made clear once and for all in his *Ideologia e linguaggio* (1965). An auroral recovery of the closed form had been made by Sanguineti in 1961, the year of the first edition of *I Novissimi*, in a poem dedicated to an exhibition of the Neapolitan painter Mario Persico at the Schwarz Gallery in Milan (July 1–14, 1961), a ballad "à la manière de Villon," recently studied by Gian Luca Picconi (2016). In the same year, Pasolini, curiously enough, also wrote a Villonian ballad, but again, the differences between the two poets, who seem to measure themselves against the same metrical form, sink deep, critically and materialistically, into the opposition between passion and language that famously distinguishes the one, author of *Passione e ideologia* (1960), from the other, author of *Ideologia e linguaggio* (1965). Since the mid-1970s, Sanguineti has used sequences of hendecasyllables in various strophic formations, often governed by the law of the acrostic or tautogram, such as the poem for Enrico Bugli in 1975 and the *Acrosticobatico* for Antonio Fomez in 1976. Balestrini also used some traditional forms in a way that was not naïve. By highlighting its fossilized departure, he used it as an element whose certainties and consolatory capacity could be liquidated, as an architecture to be consciously renewed by crashing its most canonical joints, and as a form with which to bring his varied levies into friction to realize that authentic linguistic—and poetic—adventure that he had illustrated in his programmatic writing *Linguaggio e opposizione* included in the anthology *I Novissimi*.

This work of continual manipulation of forms—even the ballads of *La signorina Richmond* (1977) presuppose traditional forms that are anything but respected—has yielded innovative results even in some recent "sestine," which are among the highest proofs of Balestrini and the poetry of the years closest to us. Already in itself, the sestina is an exceptional and cataphract structure, the most closed and dynamic in our tradition, because it is circular, claustrophobic, mobile, and fixed simultaneously. The earliest evidence of a pattern in the "odor of sestina" is *Tape Mark I* (1962). Although sestina *sui generis*, the most recent texts are in *Caosmogonia* (2010) or in a plaquette entitled *Contromano*, which appeared in 2015 for the Diaforia series edited by Daniele Poletti, where the *Sestina bugiarda* and *Sestina vertical* are collected, along with other compositions that, with zigzag typographic arrangement of stanzas, rework, circumvent, or negate the sestina form.

It is well possible that, despite the more establishment-accommodated culture pretending otherwise, the experience of the Novissimi and their subsequent practice of poetry have left a scattered legacy in younger generations. I will limit myself to a few names. On the one hand, some of these may be surprising because they are avowedly far from the proposals of the neo-avant-garde. On the other hand, others will appear more clearly approachable to a legacy of the neo-avant-garde that is not congealed and assumed as irrefutable and burdensome authorship but instead as a term of dialectical confrontation and as an example of awareness of the allegorical bearing that form can have or of the cognitive value that style possesses. To borrow a concept from the great Gianfranco Contini: "Style seems to me to be, without a doubt, an author's way of knowing things. Every poetic problem is a problem of knowledge. Every stylistic, or even I would say grammatical, position is a gnoseological position" ("Una lettura di Michelangelo" 243).

This—problematic and dialectic—legacy can be grasped in works that keep subjectivity at bay, grasp and highlight the most dissonant and broken aspects of reality, and make pragmatic and countercultural use of metrical structure. Here are a few hypotheses. Among those who have reflected, prodded by the crumbling of forms to propose alienated ancient ones as emptied structures shown in their historical distance and re-functionalized, or stimulated to look for others with historical ones in friction, is Lorenzo Durante, whom Tommaso Ottonieri has called, with Dantean echo, the "miglior fabbro" (*Purg.* XXVI, v. 117). He is the author, among others, of algid and merciless operations, that is, of memorable sestinas obtained by means of grammatical and punctual casts starting from Dante's sestina *Al poco sole e al gran cerchio d'ombra* and Petrarca's *A qualunque animale alberga in terra*, and continuing, from model to model, century by century.[9]

Also worth mentioning is Gabriele Frasca, who imparts to poetry by means of style a memorability not unlike, in concept, that which Sanguineti recommended in the recipe of *Postkarten 49*:

> concludo che la poesia consiste, insomma, in questa specie di lavoro: mettere
> [parole come
> in corsivo, e tra virgolette: e sforzarsi di farle memorabili, come tante battute argute
> e brevi: (che si stampano in testa, così, con un qualche contorno di adeguati segnali

---

[9] EN: See Lorenzo Durante, Tommaso Lisa, and Federico Scaramuccia, alias I Perversi's *Trilorgìa*. Editrice Zona, 2006.

socializzati): (come sono gli a capo, le allitterazioni, e, poniamo, le solite metafore): (che vengono a significare, poi, nell'insieme: attento, o tu che leggi, e manda a mente): (209).[10]

Frasca, too, who is also theoretically far from the neo-avant-garde, worked on formal structures not by slavishly adopting them or resurrecting them *tout court* but by making them return in new guises, colliding their rhythm with typographic composition, loading them with meaning, exposing them, making them also a vehicle, according to his poetics, of recognizability, memorability and—not least—morality. Moreover, Frasca often referred to Weinrich to link memorability, morality, and style (as sharp as a "stiletto"): "As Harald Weinrich used to repeat: 'Only those who wish to lie will eschew style. Those who wish to deceive want oblivion, not memory'" (n.p.).

In turn, Frasca's baton has passed to younger authors, such as Adriano Padua, whose poetry in *La presenza del vedere* offers readers an interesting sequence of increasingly abraded, uncertain, lacking, broken, and decayed sonnets. An *allegory of patterns*[11] may work in this way. Mention should also be made of two rather secluded Genoese authors of the same generation as Frasca. The first is Marcello Frixione, author of *Diottrie* (1991), a very beautiful book according to Sanguineti, and, more recently, *Naturama*, which collects his texts from 1981 to 2019. The second is Marco Berisso, who proposed the conspicuously artificial, critical, very virtuous, and, above all, de-sublimated reuse of literature in a book like *Annali* (2002), where what appears to be language waste stands instead in opposition to the clarity inherent to the language of power.

Tommaso Ottonieri and Mariano Bàino also need to be mentioned. Both also partook in the Gruppo '93 debate, which had with Gruppo 63 a dialectical relationship, at times not peaceful but always fruitful, capable of taking into

---

[10] EN: "I conclude that poetry consists, in sum, in this type of work: putting words like / in cursive, and between quotation marks: and forcing oneself to make them memorable, like so many witty and brief / replies: (that are printed in front, like that, with some contour of adequate signals / that have been socialized): (in the same way as headings, alliterations, and, one posits, the usual metaphors): / (that come to signify, then, all together: / careful, oh you who reads, and memorize):" (Translated by de Thomasis).

[11] AN: I gladly derive the expression "allegory of patterns" from the title of a section by Filippo Bettini and Roberto di Marco in *Terza Ondata. Il Nuovo Movimento della Scrittura in Italia* (1993). Moreover, in the section "Allegory of Patterns," the *Sestina [first]*, *Al poco seno e ai gran cerchi del culo*, and the *sette haiku del Golfo* by the aforementioned Lorenzo Durante was anthologized.

account the ancestors' lesson (the reduction of the I, a schizomorphic vision, formal awareness and metric manipulation) without, however, being crushed by it. Both are "shapers" (in Italian, "plasmatori"), to use a beautiful, evocative, and simultaneously material definition. Both are persuaded of the "manuality" necessary to art, of poetry as *poiesis*. Both worked by reusing and liquidating forms in verse and prose, working even in fractured narrative forms, allegorical in its stylistic structure. See, for example, *Prova d'inchiostro e altri sonetti* by Bàino (2017). Quite different from each other, Bàino and Ottonieri are also linked by multilingual experimentation that also becomes an intellectual understanding between them, although declined in different ways. See Bàino's *Fax giallo* (1993) and Ottonieri's *Le strade che portano al Fùcino* (2007).

In some cases, authors of later generations have confronted the possible legacy of the neo-avant-garde in an opposite manner. Some who identify themselves with the so-called "research writings" have reacted by disentangling themselves from inheritance etiquette, by trying to reset too recognizable characters of poeticity—assimilating certain lessons of Balestrini and Ponge, with their due differences—and reduce assertiveness, and looking to transalpine experiences such as Gleize's prose in prose or, in Italy, the work of Carlo Bordini, in ever-renewed ways. This is the case with Marco Giovenale and Michele Zaffarano, to name but two. Vincenzo Ostuni combines the lessons of Pagliarani and Sanguineti: attention to everyday life, the presence of biographical elements that try not to jolt the self narcissistically, the use of long, "accordion" verses, a Marxist perspective, etc. Pagliarani's own formal conception of breath seems to act in Vincenzo Frungillo's *Ogni cinque bracciate* (2009). This text has as its fulcrum the breath taken after every five strokes by swimmers. The metrical construction is the octave with alternating rhymes: a way to realize a text that was, says the author, "a symbiotic connection between the body of the protagonists and that of the author, my breath was the breath of the swimmers" ("Autoantologie-1. Vincenzo Frungillo" n.p.). To conclude, Ivan Schiavone must also be mentioned. He is a poet who reflects and works on form. It is a cornerstone of his poetics, convinced—like Pagliarani—that language should be maintained in efficiency for all, in the sign, and that a shared code, a code of shared practices, as Frixione noted, is indispensable to the literary text.[12] But even in this case, the work on forms is not an expedient or has

---

[12] EN: "The meaning of words is in the shared practices, and knowledge distributed among speakers, the same is true for the meaning of a poetic text" (1988; *Gruppo '93*, 1990 112).

a restorative intention. It does not bring back to life wrappings of the past with naïve, decorative, or reassuring intentions. Instead, it shows their irreducible fall. He concurs in liquidating them by proposing, however, new and elaborate forms in the project of a programmatic, structural complexity that is inquiry, vision about the world—the example of the irritating, innovative sestina "se confluisse il senso della presenza" in *Tavole e stanze* (2019) suffices. A reflection by Umberto Eco, who participated in Group 63, does not seem alien to this complexity: "Art knows the world through its own formative structures (which are therefore not its formalistic moment but its true moment of content)" ("Del modo di formare come impegno sulla realtà" 270). And here, in the belief that formal structure has programmatic and conscientious value, Balestrini's parable seems to gather, certainly deprived of irony. In fact, poets receive "la qualità dai tempi" and "le condizioni esterne esistono realmente," to use two famous quotes inserted by Sanguineti in *Laborintus' incipit*. However, it is an entire trajectory that from *Il sasso appeso* arrives at the extraordinary *Istruzioni preliminari*, which, by altering the "returning" sestina form, closes *Caosmogonia*. However, we could also say that it arrives at the iron mechanism of *L'esplosione* (2019). Thus, it seems to this day valid, and valid for any written expression, even where the pattern is renounced, what Eliot stated: "There is no escape from metre; there is only mastery."

Gianluca Rizzo

A Violent Inclusion: Translation as Composition (or What Cannibalism Has to Do with Poetry)

> Cannibalism alone unites us. Socially. Economically. Philosophically.
> — Oswald de Andrade, *Cannibalist Manifesto*, 38.[1]

> The individual can never become the measure of all things.
> — György Lukács, *History and Class Consciousness*, 193.[2]

The following remarks were initially presented at a panel called "Translation as Composition." At first, I thought I had come up with a rather clever title, but then, to my great relief, I found out that Jerome Rothenberg had already used it for an article he published in 2004. Having narrowly avoided that most bourgie of sins, originality, I was also reassured by discovering, upon reading Rothenberg's essay, that his ideas are entirely compatible with those expressed below.[3]

Before we get on with it, there is one more intertextual interference I would like to highlight: a few sections of this essay had a previous life as part of an "inchiesta" (survey) initiated by Lorenzo Mari and myself. The survey, which is being published in installments by the Italian online magazine *Le parole e le cose*, focuses on the use of the first-person plural pronoun ("we") in contemporary poetry.[4]

---

[1] EN: See "Cannibalist Manifesto." Translated by Leslie Bary. *Latin American Literary Review*, vol. 19, No. 38, July—December 1991, pp. 38–47. Translation of Oswald de Andrade's "Manifesto Antropófago." *Revista de Antropófagia*, 1, 1, May 1928.

[2] EN: See *History and Class Consciousness. Studies in Marxist Dialectics*. 1968. Translated by Rodney Livingstone. The MIT Press, 1972.

[3] EN: See Rothenberg's book *Writing Through*, whose preface is a reworking of said article "Translation as Composition / Composition as Translation," originally delivered as a talk on his receiving of the Alfonso el Sabio Translation Award from San Diego State University on March 22, 2004. AN: The essay can be read online, here: https://www.cipherjournal.com/html/rothenberg_translation_composi.html.

[4] AN: Available here: https://www.leparoleelecose.it/?p=45566.

Since the "inchiesta" is in Italian, I will take this opportunity to translate it into English and weave the relevant parts with the remarks prepared for this panel presentation. Thus, in the span of a few pages, I will model the kind of choral voice, intertextual hospitality, and unprejudiced openness to all forms of translation, interpolation, and textual cannibalization I will advocate for.

At the origin of that *inchiesta* is a sense of discomfort I experience in my own writing whenever I try to use the word "we." At best, such a collective entity seems purely aspirational. At worst, it feels like the marker of a bad conscience, of a repressed reality. Most times, I cannot shake the suspicion that by writing and saying "we," I might be trying to claim an unearned plurality. The survey, involving several contemporary poets and critics, tries to dig a little deeper and expose, as much as possible, that "Real," to use Lacan's terms, that lies beneath the veneer of our shared "reality," that is, the obscene, unbearable thing that underpins the world we all inhabit. The difficulty in saying "we" is a symptom of something more consequential and recent than the garden-variety anomy endemic to modernity. It indicates an anthropological change. Naturally, I am not the only one saying this, nor am I the first. To help construct this argument, I turn to a brilliant essay by Mark Fisher, *Capitalist Realism* (2009), that details the changes caused by capitalism in all of us, at both the biological and psychological levels. The difficulty of saying "we" is a consequence of these changes.

Other symptoms of this epochal, anthropological transformation can be observed in the debate over climate change, where much work could be done to establish a "we" that really includes all living humans—and not just rich Western countries—as well as future generations and non-humans, such as animals and plants. Additional clues can be found in the analysis of technology's influence on society and the arts: think of the role of social media in shaping *algorithmically* our "we" or the possibilities offered by AI technology in augmenting that "we" to include a non-human, electronic entity, which in turn can become a means of interaction between authors and audiences, a distinction that is, now more than ever, utterly obsolete; more on this in a few pages.

This essay's first half analyzes the current political, psychological, and poetical landscape. In the second half, I will try to indicate the direction of a possible way forward (at least in poetry).

Axioms and Prolegomena (A Pseudo-Manifesto)

1. Politics is politics, and poetry is poetry. If you try to use poetry (the tools of poetry) to do the job of politics, you'll demean both politics and poetry, which doesn't mean that poetry has nothing to do with politics, quite the opposite! But if the goal is to organize and mobilize voters, regulate access to power, and reform institutions, then poetry isn't the best way to go about it.
2. Reducing poetry to lyric poetry has damaged it and has limited its margins of operation within society, painting it into a corner. An exclusively lyric poetry is doomed to be perceived as either the product of a small cultural elite, difficult and opaque, or a playground reserved for delicate souls and diaphanous feelings. This position appears even more untenable if you compare poetry to other genres and artistic mediums that proved more effective in creating opportunities for the emergence of the "Real," thus allowing their audience to observe and study it better. Fisher reframes Lacan's term in the context of politics: that "traumatic void that can only be glimpsed in the fractures [...] of apparent reality"; more on this later. Furthermore, the reduction of all poetry to lyric poetry is, in and of itself, a symptom, a *figura* of that Real suppressed by the Capital, built on atomization, isolation, alienation, and the failure of those social structures intended to organize citizens in the pursuit of the public good. Poetic genres like invectives, *satura*, and epics have been neglected or completely pushed out of the artistic discourse. Thus, precious opportunities for communal reflection, conversation, and dialogue—in other words, for maintaining a "political we"—have been lost.
3. Framing the issue in terms of "creating a 'we' in poetry" rather than as an issue of "poetry's audience" makes a huge difference.[5] The word "audience" implies a passive dimension, one of exclusive reception. The distinction between producers and consumers of culture has long been obsolete, at least since the aesthetic revolution carried out by the Avant-gardes at the beginning of the 20th century (although we can trace it even further back to Rimbaud's "objective" break); since the second and third waves of Avant-gardes in Italy (think of the stochastic

---

[5] AN: The reference here is the influential (and controversial) anthology *Il pubblico della poesia* [Poetry's Audience], edited by Alfonso Berardinelli and Franco Cordelli, first published in 1975.

model of text composition derived from the Dadaists and revived by the *Novissimi*); since the digital revolution whose proselytizer, Mosaic, the first modern browser, opened the doors to the world wide web (it was 1993). Such a distinction is even more obsolete in the era of social media when everyone is a writer—more or less. What's needed today is poetry capable of turning the new reality to its advantage rather than complaining about it in a nostalgic and fruitless voice.

4. Establishing a new political subject (or restoring an old one, as unlikely as that might be), creating a "political we," if you will, is not a task any single actor can carry out. Such a hypothetical entity (the starting point for any discourse regarding the *State*) can only be born of a convergence of powers, institutions, and strategies deployed by various groups acting in unison.
5. Question: what's the role of poetry in this process?
6. Let's begin with the obvious: this is not an issue that an individual can tackle; a statement of poetics cannot resolve it; it cannot be settled through any given stylistic posture. It's an issue for the community of those who write and read poetry. Thus, here I am, promoting this conversation through the two traditional tools of the trade: the essay and the survey.
7. More questions: why is it so hard to write and read "we"? What do we mean when we say "we"? We who? We Italians? We the middle class? We seasonal workers? We Southerners? We immigrants? We women? We who write poetry? We who read it? We the electorate? We who? How can one escape the feeling that by saying "we," one is pointing to a void, an absence that, in the best of cases, marks a mere aspiration to establish a community of peers; at worst, conceals stereotypes and prejudices stemming from an idea of collective identity predicated on exclusion—an obsolete, backward, and regressive one, if not openly reactionary (or racist)? And even after finding adequate answers to all these questions, how can that "we," so painstakingly constructed and clarified, be translated into stylistic, rhetorical, and poetic terms?

Clearly, this is no small feat. It might be helpful to move the conversation forward by taking stock of the present landscape and identifying some major transformations that took place over the last few decades.

Anthropological Mutation/Crisis of The Democratic System

Deleuze, Žižek, and Fisher, to name a few, investigated and documented the physical, psychological, and spiritual changes caused by late capitalism.

> The symptoms of the failures are everywhere [...] what is required is that effect be connected to structural cause. Against the postmodernist suspicion of grand narratives, we need to reassert that, far from being isolated, contingent problems, these are all the effects of a single systemic cause: Capital. (Fisher 77)

We are witnesses to a paradoxical process that, on the one hand, homogenizes horizons, imaginaries, perspectives, stories, dreams, and aspirations and, on the other, isolates and atomizes the population, locking them in their individuality, confining them to their own very private interests. To overcome this paradox, we need to expand the horizons of the imaginable and, at the same time, include within the confines of our awareness the desires of others—both human and non-human. We must come to terms with their presence, validity, urgency, and substantial equality to our desires. "To reclaim a real political agency means first of all accepting our insertion *at the level of desire* in the remorseless meat-grinder of Capital" (15, italics in the original), Fisher writes. Poetry can help in the process of modulation and reconciliation of desires at the level of the community.

The most uncomfortable truth is perhaps the realization that, despite all our illusions concerning the differences that appear to divide us, we already are constituted, in the deepest, anthropological sense, as a unified "we": "What needs to be kept in mind is both that capitalism is a hyper-abstract impersonal structure *and* that it would be nothing without our co-operation" (15). And thus, since we are all complicit in Capital's "planetary networks of oppression," we are already part of *that* community; we are constituted as *that* kind of "we."

Alienation is one of Marxist criticism's most effective, precise, and long-lived diagnoses. It is much more difficult to accept and recognize the responsibility that each of us shares in the perpetuation of the very system that isolates us and causes our unhappiness: "There is a sense in which it simply is the case that the political elite are our servants; the miserable service they provide for us is to launder our libidos, to obligingly re-present for us our disavowed desires as if they had nothing to do with us" (15). Such an invasive and consistent influence *at the level of desire* has had an intergenerational impact. Its consequences accumulate and multiply, like genetic defects passing from parent to child. They have finally crossed the threshold that marks an anthropological difference. Contemporary human beings differ substantially from those who lived half a century ago. For instance, antagonism has been moved from the space between classes to inside the individual.

> Antagonism is not now located externally, in the face-off between class blocs, but internally, in the psychology of the worker, who, as a worker, is interested in old-style class conflict, but, as someone with a pension fund, is also interested in maximizing the yield from his or her investments. There is no longer an identifiable external enemy. (34)

But that's not all; that same system—Capitalism—that in the past was just one among many ways of organizing economic production, has become, in recent decades, the only, and, therefore, "natural," "necessary," "neutral," and "immutable" system for organizing all aspects of social, moral, and affective life. As Fisher puts it:

> In the 1960s and 1970s, capitalism had to face the problem of how to contain and absorb energies from outside. It now, in fact, has the opposite problem; having all-too successfully incorporated externality, how can it function without an outside it can colonize and appropriate? For most people under twenty in Europe and North America, the lack of alternatives to capitalism is no longer even an issue. Capitalism seamlessly occupies the horizons of the thinkable. (8)

This failure to be there for oneself despite—or perhaps because of—a complete homologation with the others is the Real (obscene, in the sense of unthinkable and impossible to describe, in Lacan's sense) that underpins our inability to say "we" in poetry. The only traits that unite us all beyond our narcissistic traps and individual interests, shaped, as they are, by common sense, that is, by Capital, seem to be instability: this transformation currently in progress, the uncertainty and unpredictability of the inner landscape inside each of us, especially when contrasted with the apparent immobility and universality of the system of values in which we are immersed. This is our starting point. This is the situation. Where do we go from here? I suggest we make two moves, different but complementary.

First Move: The Tools of Kinship Studies

On the one hand, we should revisit the tools offered by anthropology, in particular, the tradition of kinship studies, from Levi-Strauss to Viveiros de Castro, as an ideal place, a disciplinary environment, where the philosophical instruments needed to overcome the impasse we are facing can be built. I mention Viveiros de Castro because of his efforts in *Cannibal Metaphysics* to free anthropology—and himself—from a Eurocentric point of view, to turn his discipline into a device for the "permanent decolonization of thought" with the secondary goal of "creating other means besides philosophy for the creation of concepts" (47–48). With marginal modifications, both tools and programs can be adopted by poetic writing and literary criticism toward a "permanent decolonization of *language*."[6] Perhaps the answer to establishing a "we" in poetry comes from focusing on the transformation process inevitably involved in artistic creation rather than on the final products. Jamille Pinheiro Dias reflects on the use in literature of ideas explored by Viveiros de Castro:

> In the conceptual language mobilized by Viveiros de Castro, poiesis / creation / invention / production belong to the same paradigm, one that presupposes a primary cause, while praxis / transformation / exchange / transfer belong to a different one, pertinent to the Amerindian world, which presupposes a constant dynamics of differential unfolding—"production creates; exchange changes," as he sums it up ("Exchanging" 478). What I am referring to as *creativity*—and *creativity* in Amerindian *poetics*, specifically—[…] points to poiesis or 'making' precisely as a mode of transformation through an engagement between humans and non-humans. (409)[7]

---

[6] AN: And the connection between capitalism and colonialism is by now sufficiently clear and well-understood that it doesn't really need to be discussed here.

[7] AN: The quotation Pinheiro Dias incorporates in this paragraph comes from Eduardo Viveiros de Castro, "Exchanging Perspectives: The Transformation of Objects into Subjects in Amerindian Ontologies." *Common Knowledge*, 10.3, 2004, pp. 463–484. The following passage from this same article by Pinheiro can help clarify and appreciate the demarcation between Western and Amerindian epistemologies and worldviews: "To what extent, though, does this choice lead us to reconsider the Aristotelian distinction between *poeisis* (production) and *praxis* (action) that Viveiros de Castro evokes? Although my goal here is certainly not to offer an in-depth comparison between scholarships on Amerindian thought and Classical Antiquity, it is important at this point to note that *praxis*, according to Aristotle's *Nichomachean Ethics*, finds its telos (fulfillment, goal, purpose) inside itself. Above all, what matters is performing a particular activity in a certain way. In contrast, the completeness that poiesis seeks lies outside the activity, i.e., it finds its telos in an exterior product. In Aristotle's consideration of praxis and poiesis as mutually exclusive, the key issue has to do with locating the telos inside or outside activity. Both action and production are subjected to the dualistic constraints of interiority and exteriority. While collaborative studies between ethnologists and classicists would be necessary to subsidize a more consistent comparative approach to this matter, one may notice that in the highly transformational dynamics

This way of thinking of creativity as a praxis rooted in collaboration between humans and non-humans (not only animal but also vegetal, electronic, etc.) is a crucial element, one that should be kept in mind, especially as we discuss the climate crisis and the changes due to technology. In fact, before moving on to the second strategy announced above, it might be a good idea to take a detour and face head-on the implications (for poetry) brought forth by these two issues.

Climate Crisis

The climate crisis is to Capital what reality is to the Real (to use, once again, Lacan's terms). This is how Fisher puts it:

> For Lacan the Real is what any "reality" must suppress; indeed, reality constitutes itself through just this repression. The Real is an unrepresentable X, a traumatic void that can only be glimpsed in the fractures and inconsistencies in the field of apparent reality. So one strategy against capitalist realism could involve invoking the Real(s) underlying the reality that capitalism presents to us. Environmental catastrophe is one such Real. At one level, to be sure, it might look as if Green issues are very far from being "unrepresentable voids" for capitalist culture. Climate change and the threat of resource-depletion are not being repressed so much as incorporated into advertising and marketing. What this treatment of environmental catastrophe illustrates is the fantasy structure on which capitalist realism depends: a presupposition that resources are infinite, that the earth itself is merely a husk which capital can at a certain point slough off like a used skin, and that any problem can be solved by the market. (18)

Here, one could add the work done by Naomi Klein on how the idea of "crisis" is used by Capital to implement radical reforms that repress democracy and concentrate privileges.[8] Clearly, the remedy must include the creation of a "we" that is capable of discussion, of rational decision, of facing that polit-

---

of Amerindian creativity—in which action and production are given not as essences that have an inside or an outside, but rather as collective assemblages that are not co-optable as demarcated products by an individual subject—it is debatable whether poiesis and praxis would be antithetical to one another – if these terms are to be considered as counterparts to Indigenous modes of making and doing. In other words, what happens is that creativity and transformation are here tied up in an inextricable knot" (410).

[8] AN: See Naomi Klein's *Shock Doctrine. The Rise of Disaster Capitalism.* Knopf Canada, 2007.

ical Real described by Fisher, and, more importantly, of imagining a future that is substantially different from the present: a social, moral, and economic order that is a complete alternative to the current capitalistic system (as Klein suggests). When referencing a "we" in today's poetry, this entity should also include the descendants (human and non-human) of those currently alive. If it is true that decisions made today will determine the destiny of the next 3, 5, 10 generations, then the responsibility each member of the "we" must shoulder is proportionally increased.

Technology: Social Media

> If the figure of discipline was the worker-prisoner, the figure of control is the debtor-addict. Cyberspatial capital operates by addicting its users [...]. If, then, something like attention deficit hyperactivity disorder is a pathology, it is a pathology of late capitalism—a consequence of being wired into the entertainment-control circuits of hypermediated consumer culture. Similarly, what is called dyslexia may in many cases amount to a post-lexia. Teenagers process capital's image-dense data very effectively without any need to read—slogan-recognition is sufficient to navigate the net-mobile-magazine information plane. "Writing has never been capitalism's thing. Capitalism is profoundly illiterate," Deleuze and Guattari argued in *Anti-Oedipus*. "Electric language does not go by way of the voice or writing: data processing does without them both." (Fisher 25)

When practiced as a reflection on and through language, writing is an intrinsically critical activity. The type of self-aware, deliberate, vigorous, and creative reading that poetry demands is also a form of writing. However, if incentives (social, technological, cultural) are aligned in favor of a superficial, instrumental, and narcotic fruition of the text, how can one reach out to the post-lexic population described by Fisher?

There is a "we" that is constantly created by those algorithms that govern social media platforms. Should one resign to this "we" as the only one possible, a "we" built on the figure of the "debtor-addict"? Absolutely not: a better way must be found, a way of piercing the social bubble enveloping us, of silencing the echo chamber deafening us. This matter becomes even more urgent if one considers how social groups formed on digital platforms are more united and resilient the more their identity is predicated on a shared sense of contempt or hatred. Groups rooted in a common interest and a sense of compassion are much weaker and have a shorter lifespan. Everyone experiences this sad situation in their own daily life.[9]

The "we" of social media is created every minute, one way or another, whether we like it or not. Its *modality*, the control over this instrument of social aggregation, must be wrestled out of the claws of the algorithm, of neoliberal capital, and given to… whom? To "us"? Us poets? Yeah, right! To whom, then? Perhaps to this "we" that I have been painstakingly describing and is yet to emerge. Meanwhile, as we try to figure this out, control over these important tools must be kept beyond the reach of those nostalgic for the good old days who would like to shut them down or establish centralized control over them. The techno-utopians who see direct democracy as the panacea to all evils should equally be reined in and kept under check.

As far as poetry (and literature more in general) is concerned, this is an urgent, practical issue that must be faced with political acumen and a pragmatic approach: how can one build a rhetoric of the "we" that is not based on hatred? A rhetoric not based on the sense of identity that comes from a misunderstanding (a simplification, a purposeful misrepresentation) of history? One must work on the planning of new meanings, "planning and not creating," as Elio Pagliarani wrote more than half a century ago:

> Many of the most engaged intellectuals of the avant-garde […] believe […] that the final goal and/or purpose of art is *opposition* […]. But here it is important to note how opposition is a *modality* not a finality. […] Looking at the big picture, […] the negation is better specified as protest. A protest against received meanings, the ones that are completely worn out and belong to the *langue*, and the *planning* of new meanings. I speak of planning new meanings, and not of creating them, because the creation of new meanings, when it comes to language, should be left to the community, society in history […]. It's a matter of planning the new, because negation is not enough […]. ("For a Definition of the Avant-Garde" 314)[10]

In other words, we need a poetics of the first-person plural, a "poetic we," to oppose the "algorithmic we" pushed by social media platforms. Without

---

[9] AN: For a poetic equivalent in the Italian context, see the recently published *Nuova poesia troll*. Edited by Federico Ronconi. Argolibri, 2022.

[10] AN: Pagliarani, Elio, "Per una definizione di avanguardia." *Nuova Corrente*, 37, 1966; now in *Gruppo 63. Critica e Teoria*. Edited by Renato Barilli and Angelo Guglielmi. Feltrinelli, 1976; Testo & Immagine, 2003, p. 314. The translation is mine.

a rigorous critical assessment of this issue, we would run into a double and somewhat specular risk: on the one hand, we might not recognize ourselves in the group we have been assigned to by the various algorithms that rule our lives (with the resulting sense of disorientation, depression, and isolation). On the other hand, we might end up identifying too closely with the ideology of a group built on a commercial (that is, created by corporate marketing) basis that is beyond our control and does not align with our best interests (economic, social, spiritual, etc.), nor our emotional needs.

Technology II: Artificial Intelligence

The presence of Artificial Intelligence in the space of literature can no longer be ignored. The same applies to that system of tools, genres, conventions, and traditions that Leonardo Flores calls "distant writing."[11] Especially in English, certain AIs have reached a level of sophistication that must be considered and put to good use. See, for instance, *code-davinci-002* or Google's experiment *Verse by Verse*, even though the most promising results can be found in David (Jhave) Johnston's (relatively) recent work.[12] Soon, the misunderstandings and the prejudices that limit these systems and force them to produce a mere mockery of human writing (and, more in general, of human mediocrity) will be dispelled. At the same time, various modalities of distant writing are reaching a growing level of maturity and independence. These trends are being affirmed as a rich, layered, and vital tradition that brings a message of undeniable relevance. Could this be another way of putting a "we," an alliance of human and artificial, at the center of poetic creation? Possibly. This could be a way of bridging the distance that seems to isolate us, a resource that could help mitigate those adverse effects of technology (and capitalism) discussed above.

In short, the "poetic we" described thus far should also include its electronic, computational, and algorithmic counterparts, both in their incarnation as social media platforms (with all the challenges and opportunities they pres-

---

[11] AN: Two lectures by Leonardo Flores on this very topic are available on his website: https://leonardoflores.net/blog/presentations-2/two-recent-lectures-turning-the-page-and-distant-writing/.

[12] AN: More on these AI-powered poetic projects is available at the following links: https://www.newyorker.com/culture/culture-desk/the-new-poem-making-machinery?utm_medium=social&utm_brand=tny&utm_source=facebook&utm_social-type=owned&mbid=social_facebook&fbclid=IwAR3L-nCmZ8jjuvbHjhP-cWM4yz6DumRLpAwhDqpzvYbH_v-piJ7sM2IXeG0 ; https://sites.research.google/versebyverse/; http://glia.ca/index_Digital_Poetry.html.

ent) and in the form of artificial intelligence. The latter provides access to several invaluable tools that can enable us to cope with the huge quantity of information making up the infosphere in which we live. At the same time, this approach would allow us to create a kind of programmatic art capable of exploiting the obsolescence of the distinction between producer and consumer of culture, between artist and audience.

Second Move: Translation, Transcreation, Cannibalism

The first of the two moves I wanted to suggest was resorting to anthropology and kinship studies to rethink creativity and how it binds us together rather than sets us apart. The other move I would like to sketch out is internal to poetry and has to do (as anticipated) with finding a strategy to re-modulate the structure of desire so that it may include the "other," be it human or non-human (that is animal, vegetable, electronic), to form a "poetic we." And here, all the various threads that I have been unraveling will (hopefully) come together.

The first step must be pushing poetry beyond the confines of the lyric. That is more easily said than done. Centuries of tradition and critical prejudices stand in the way. Where to turn? Where to find a way beyond lyrical poetry and toward a new modulation of desire, predicated on a "we," the first-person plural, rather than on the atomized and narcissistic "I"?

The one solution I see lies in the way of the cannibal, the kind of "transcreation," to use de Campos' term, that combines translation and creation. Just to be clear, I am speaking here of an entirely metaphorical cannibalism.

> In an early assessment of the poetics of *antropofagia* [cannibalism] in Brazilian literature, Randal Johnson[13] observes that, Oswald [de Andrade, the Brazilian poet and critic, author of the *Manifesto Antropófago*] valorizes the cannibalization of the colonizer by the Indian. Initially, then, cannibalism is a form of resistance. Metaphorically speaking, it represents a new attitude toward cultural relationships with hegemonic powers. Imitation and influence in the traditional sense of the word are no longer possible. The *antropófagos* do not want to copy European culture, but rather to devour it, taking advantage of its positive aspects, rejecting the negative, and creating an original national culture that would

---

[13] AN: See Johnson, Randal. "Tupy or not Tupy: Cannibalism and Nationalism in Contemporary Brazilian Literature and Culture." *On Modern Latin American Fiction*. Edited by John King. Hill and Wang, 1987, pp. 41–59.

be a source of artistic expression rather than a receptacle for forms of cultural expression elaborated elsewhere. (Cisneros 31)

This is what is meant by translation as composition, that panel title mentioned at the very beginning of this essay. Translation is always a communal enterprise: it presupposes a multiplicity of entities, a concurrence of authorities, and a reconciliation of aesthetic sensibilities. Translation, even the straight-up translation that Jakobson called "interlingual translation or translation proper" (233), is a locus where a complex "we" is established, the starting point of an aesthetic and political "we." It is the place where something weird and magical happens, something that calls into question key ideas at the core of our society (read Capitalism): property, ownership, authority, originality, authenticity, all concepts that on the surface seem to be meant to elevate us, but that are actually the bonds that keep us subservient and quiet.

From an establishment's point of view, translation proper is a necessary evil: eerie and disquieting as it is, it's a temporary measure while we all wait for the coming of the universal language (English? Russian? Chinese? Math? You pick it!). Now imagine a kind of translation that challenges and even disregards ideas of authorship, authenticity, propriety, and property: that would be outright dangerous! That is poetry, first-person plural! It is what Haroldo de Campos called "transcreation." But also, elsewhere, "transluciferation," a "satanic enterprise."[14] I will quote from a couple of sources to clarify what I mean. But think: isn't the cannibal already constituted as a "we"? Isn't the translator already a "we"? Aren't translation, appropriation, manipulation, and interpolation of texts places where a "we" can be created? Where can an author, a translator, and a reader convene to build a literary and political program together, through and with language? This is, I think, the way forward. Whether we'll reach our destination remains uncertain. Odile Cisneros describes "transcreation" as follows:

> In "transcreation," the translator becomes in effect a co-author, his or her role being creatively at least equalized to that of the author. More emphasis is laid

---

[14] AN: For "transcreation," see Haroldo de Campos, "Translation as Creation and Criticism." Translated by Diana Gibson and Haroldo de Campos, in *Novas: Selected Writings*. Edited by Antonio Sergio Bessa and Odile Cisneros. Northwestern UP, 2007, pp. 312–326. For "transluciferation," see Haroldo de Campos, "Transluciferação Mefistofáustica." *Deus e o Diabo no Fausto de Goethe*. Editora Perspectiva, 1981, pp. 179–209.

on the agency of the translator, on the role of the translator as an independent agent rather than a subservient passive force. Nowhere is this more evident than in the postscript de Campos wrote to his translation of Goethe's *Second Faust*, an essay entitled "Mephistofaustian Transluciferation," where, instead of "transcreation," he calls his translation a "transluciferation." (29)

Campos' ideas of anthropophagy, translation, modernism, and cannibalism are directly linked to the work of another master of modernism, Ezra Pound, whose thoughts on how to make creative use of tradition have been a consistent point of departure for numerous critical reflections and aesthetic experimentations. On this, see Medici Nobrega and Milton, who writes:

> Translation […] combined the concept of Anthropophagy […], and the Poundian idea of "Make it new," reading and translating the authors of the past, remote or not, modernizing them in such a way that they live and breathe again in a new cultural context. Both Anthropophagy and "Make it new" take on a synchronic, critical view of the literary tradition. (272)

But we can quote from de Campos himself, from the article entitled "Anthropophagous Reason: Dialogue and Difference in Brazilian Culture":

> Oswald's [de Andrade] "Anthropophagy" […] is a theory proposing the critical devouring of universal cultural heritage, formulated not from the submissive and reconciled perspective of the "noble savage" (idealized following the model of European virtues […]), but from the disabused point of view of the "bad savage," devourer of whites, the cannibal. This last view does not involve submission (conversion) but, rather, transculturation, or, even better, "transvalorization": a critical view of history as a negative function (in Nietzsche's sense), capable of appropriation and of expropriation, of dehierarchization, of deconstruction. Any past which is an 'other' for us deserves to be negated. We could even say, it deserves to be eaten, devoured, with the following clarifying proviso: the cannibal was a "polemicist" (from the Greek *polemos*, meaning "struggle, combat"), but also an "anthologist"—he devoured only the enemies he considered courageous, taking their marrow and protein to fortify and renew his own natural energies. (159–160)

And who are these cannibals de Campos speaks of? They are the "Alexandrian barbarians," intellectuals such as Octavio Paz and Jorge Luis Borges, extremely refined, nimble, and sophisticated practitioners of the fine art of chewing Europeans:

> They [Alexandrian barbarians] have long been resynthesizing them [the Europeans] chemically, through an impulsive and uncontrollable metabolism of dif-

ference [...] equipped with chaotic libraries and labyrinthine card catalogs [...]. For some time, the devouring jaw of these new barbarians has been chewing up and "ruining" a cultural heritage that is ever more global. In relationship to this heritage, the barbarian's ex-centrifying and deconstructing attack acts with the marginal impetus of the carnivalesque de-sacralizing, profaning anti-tradition, evoked by Bakhtin in counterpoint to the main road of Lukácsian epic positivism, to monologic literature, to the closed, univocal work. In contrast, the combinatory and ludic poly-culturalism, the parodic transmutation of meanings and values, the open, multi-lingual hybridization, are the devices responsible for the constant feeding and re-feeding of this baroquizing Almagest: the carnivalized transencyclopedia of the new barbarians, where everything can coexist with everything. They are the machinery that crushes the material of tradition with the teeth of a tropical sugar-mill, transforming stalks and husks into bagasse and juicy syrup. (173–174)

This type of carnivalism, cannibalism, assimilation of a tradition that is "other" and is made one's own through a systematic inversion of values, a radical alteration of the linguistic code and the macro-structures of genre, character, etc., are all stylistic strategies that are not unique to the colonies, and colonized literatures and peoples. Instead, this is what oppressed people do no matter where they are, no matter who the oppressor is, and no matter what culture is being wielded against them as a weapon of subjugation. For instance, we find similar rhetorical, aesthetic, philosophical, and political solutions in studying macaronic literature in the Italian Renaissance. I am referring here to Teofilo Folengo and his *Opus Macaronicum* (that is to say, Merlin Cocai and his *Baldus*): the same multilingualism, the same carnivalism, the same inextinguishable hunger for words, genres, characters, and, why not, food!

Anthropophagy is a violent form of inclusion or, even better, a violently inclusive practice, one that is absolutely unpalatable and undigestible to the Capital. It is rooted in the first and best part of the historical avant-garde movements. Think of Alfred Jarry and his *Pere Ubu*, always on the verge of swallowing wealth, objects, other characters, and others' texts.[15] Think of F.T. Marinetti in his 1909 *Foundation and Manifesto of Futurism*: "Verranno contro di noi, i nostri successori; [...] protendendo dita adunche di predatori, e fiutando caninamente, alle porte delle accademie, il buon odore delle nostre

---

[15] AN: Regarding Ubu's intertextual hunger, see, among others, Linda Klieger Stillman, *Alfred Jarry*. Twayne Publisher, 1983, p. 43.

menti in putrefazione [...]."[16] Before closing, I would like to make a suggestion and warn about a potential risk.

De Campos and de Andrade didn't consider the reader's role in this process of cultural cannibalism, of linguistic transcreation. There's room for improving and updating their theories. The reader must be part of this creative process because there is no longer a distinction between producer and consumer of culture, as we observed earlier, and because aesthetic (literary) thought can aid political thought only when they are both professed *as praxis*, as a craft that exists in the linguistic labor applied to the text. Because this is the age of social media, and we can't pretend it is not. Because AI technology gives us the tools to make this dream a pragmatic reality that anyone can experience.

The potential risk is that this cannibalistic practice could create a refined, sophisticated, and precious pastiche that pushes away readers because of its exquisite complexity and subtlety. The cannibal translation I am advocating for must be digestible to the audience. In the 80s and 90s, postmodernism attempted a similar path, and it was readily assimilated and neutralized by Capital. The "remorseless meat grinder," as Fisher calls it, gobbled up all the antagonism and criticism implicit in those pastiches and neutralized them, rendering them just another "flavor" to choose from and be added to our global ice cream bar of the pacified arts. The type of cannibal translation I am describing (and advocating for) should be easily assimilated by the reader and indigestible to the Capital.

To avoid a proper conclusion on this topic, I will transcribe a quote from Benjamin that de Campos used to open his essay on anthropophagous reason, the one I've referenced many times: "Genuine polemics," Benjamin writes, "approach a book as lovingly as a cannibal spices a baby" (*One-Way Street*. Qtd in de Campos, 157). By this, I mean that we not only need a fully developed cannibal gastronomy but also cannibal cooking classes that are easily accessible.

---

[16] EN: "They'll come up against us, our successors; [...] extending hooked, predatory fingers, and sniffing canine-like, at the doors of academia, the sweet scent of our putrefying minds" (Translated by de Thomasis).

Charles Bernstein

An Intervention and a Brief Foreword

Perhaps I can react right away to Gianluca Rizzo's talk because it fits into what I want to say. I have already spoken in this room at the Italian Cultural Institute for the launch of the first volume of a great translation project, and it is great to be back here. I want to go back to yesterday and to Marjorie Perloff's wonderful talk when she mentioned the realm of younger, post-conceptual poets who appropriate news events and incorporate them into their work, making me wonder whether that's possible. I wanted to link this to Paul Bové's talk, which I greatly appreciated. He specifically talks about Reznikoff and Holocaust testimony. The word testimony is taken from court documents of the late 19th century and refers to violent crimes. Reznikoff reworks them, but the language comes from the Holocaust documents from the Nuremberg Trial, which were not written in English. So, I think there is a great difference, and I also think that what Marjorie Perloff is talking about can be talked about in terms of Reznikoff and the difference between those two things. Paul Bové made this difference very clear regarding the aesthetic of historical representation. Reznikoff's work is a translation of those legal documents.

Gianluca Rizzo's talk resonates with what I think about translation. You did not mention Gertrude Stein, but it's implicit: *Composition as Explanation* is a crucial work for many of us, and it is foundational.[1] You are bringing in, with your intervention, Pound, whom I welcome. Obviously, Pound is an American Modernist poet and has a great influence in terms of thinking about translation and transduction (especially Haroldo de Campos, who is really a transcreation coming out of Pound). But I think Stein is quite interesting in her own intervention before the flowers of friendship faded, and she completely

---

[1] EN: "Composition as Explanation" was originally a lecture Stein gave at the Cambridge Literary Club and Oxford University in the summer of 1926. It was published later that year by Leonard and Virginia Woolf's publishing house, Hogarth Press.

rewrites the poem she is putatively translating. I also want to mention Dennis Tedlock and Jerome Rothenberg's *Total Translation*. One thing that Dennis emphasized when he was my colleague at Buffalo and translated the *Popol Vuh* (the most remarkable and knowledgeable of Mesoamerican languages) was that he always made fun of the idea that when the Europeans and Americans translate things, they like to make them look the same: the line has to break visually the same, and then the translation has to look the same. He ridiculed that idea: in other cultures, retelling has nothing to do with reproducing the actual look of a work of art.

Talking now about cannibalism, which was at the center of Rizzo's intervention, in 1999, I published an anthology of poetry called *99 Poets 1999* together with the journal *Boundary* 2, edited for many years by Paul Bove. In that anthology, I included an essay by Haroldo de Campos on cannibalism, which is a great essay, but it took me a long time to understand it from a Brazilian point of view. There is one last thing that has to do with America, Italy, Europe, and power dynamics: one of the things that formulates this Brazilian idea of cannibalism is not to allow your work to become a local color for export. You want to preserve what is yours, even if it makes it opaque, so cannibalism is a way to avoid becoming an export product. It also has to do with the influence of what it's outside, but it also is to protect itself so that it doesn't become simply an extension of European culture. That power dynamic always becomes crucial in translation because translation is never neutral, as I tried to prove in a poem about translation, which I have published in my bi-lingual book *Eco/Echo* (2022), translated by Carla Buranello and five other people, one of them being Haraldo de Campos (who made a transcreation of my poem about translation that many Portuguese speakers told me is better than mine).

Before talking about my book *Eco/Echo*, I would like to address the logic of translation. Consider A as the source text and B as the destination text. A can never be B; it never wants to be B and refuses to be B, but it is B in its own beasting way. When we did this book, we assembled several people's translations. Carla Buranello and I said we did not want facing pages because I did not want the English texts in the Italian edition. So, I proposed it to Barbara Anceschi, but she refused. So, we came up with this idea, like what happens in Westerns and romances: when you read it one way, it is in Italian, and the other is in English. I am going to read now a sort of poetics of translation, a kind of dialogue between Italian and American poetry that fits into the topic of this panel. Marjorie Perloff wrote the foreword to the first volume of a wonderful collection of Italian poets, and this is for the second volume of *Those Who from Afar Look like Flies*, a massive anthology of materials that maybe someone already knows in Italian, but I am sure not so many know in English. The title, *Playing Cricket without a Paddle*, refers to Frost's comment about poetry when he famously said that free verse is like playing tennis without a net. But it also would like to symbolize the Italian American exchange.

Charles Bernstein

Playing Cricket without a Paddle[1]

1. Novelty

The complexity and scope of this volume will be a pure delight for readers coming upon some of these poets for the first time, fully as much as it wins over readers familiar with the company here presented. *Those Who from Afar Look Like Flies* presents an immense and polydictory set of poems inside a vast and complex conversation among poets, critics, translators, poetics, transcreations, and poetry.

I'd put it this way: poetry is what is found in contradictions.

In the previous volume, the editors emphasize "research" as a key term for the poetry presented. For this next volume, I would modify that and say *searching* might be a key. In the wake of the powerful models for Italian poetry achieved in the previous decades, this period is marked by working in, about, and around—in and out of the shadow of—the poetry of poetics not only of the immediate postwar period but of Italian modernism.

This anthology covers the period of my writing life, since I published my first poetry collection in the mid-70s. It's striking how little known we have been to one another, we American and Italian poets of innovation and invention, during this period. But insofar as we are in touch, a signal person to thank is Luigi Ballerini, for both his anthologies of American poetry translated into Italian and his anthologies of Italian poetry translated into English. That Ballerini has swung both ways—if I might be permitted to put it that way—is extraordinary and it speaks to a kind of intimacy with both American and Italian poetry that benefits us all. Still, it's an uphill battle, mostly because of the cultural insularity of U.S. American poetry, which is so vast that it is hard for

---

[1] AN: Published as the "Foreword" to *Those Who from Afar Look Like Flies: An Anthology of Italian Poetry from Officina to the Present*, vol. IV, tome II (University of Toronto Press, forthcoming).

most of us to climb out of its abyss. Framing our work as poets only in terms of U.S. history and culture might have worked through the mid-70s (though probably not); after that it has been crippling.

Of course, there are many significant American poets and poetry scholars who have worked hard to bring voices outside the U.S. into our poetry. Perhaps the richest exchange between American poetry and non-English European poetry has been with French poetry. Firmly rooted in the nineteenth century, this relationship has flourished through the reciprocal engagements of poets creating translations that have significantly affected the poetry of each other's language.

Alfredo Giuliani's 1961 anthology *I Novissimi* is a touchstone for postwar Italian poetry. The influential English translation, edited by Ballerini and Paul Vangelisti, was published by Douglas Messerli's Sun & Moon Press in 1995. An expanded edition, edited by Ballerini and Federica Santini, with an illuminating new introduction and an additional section of poetics, was published by Agincourt Press in 2017.

I Novissimi was published just one year after the iconic anthology of U.S. novel/young poetry, Don Allen's *New American Poetry* (1960). The radical potential of both, and some of the limitations, might well be compared.

I am particularly grateful to the other Italian translators with whom I have been in touch over the years, in addition to Ballerini and Vangelisti: Lawrence Venuti, Carla Billitteri, Susan Stewart, Jonathan Galassi, Lawrence Smith, Thomas Harrison, Richard Milazzo, Jennifer Scappettone, Paolo Verdicchio, and Peter Valente. These are just a few of the many translators who work in this field; I mention them because I want to acknowledge the supreme value of such personal points of contact.

2. Three Points of Contact

In September 2013, Rainer Hanshe, of Contra Mundum Press, wrote to ask me to write a foreword to a major Emilio Villa collection he was publishing in an English translation. Hanshe attached a photocopy of a letter I had written to Villa on February 13, 1978:

> Dick Higgins suggested I write you. I am a writer interested in many of the concerns I understand (from Dick) that you've made part of your work. In fact, I am co-editing a newsletter L=A=N=G=U=A=G=E that brings together texts, reviews, and short essays to writing which concentrates in some primary on

language, featuring people like Jackson Mac Low, Bernadette Mayer, Ron Silliman, Tom Raworth (I don ' t know how many of these people you would know of). I will be in Italy in early April and would like very much to meet you if this was possible. Do you have a phone where I might reach you when I am in Rome? I'll look forward to hearing from you, if you have the time to get back to me.

Unfortunately, I never got to meet Villa, nor to write the foreword to the Contra Mundum book. But it was an early point of contact. Villa's work remains a powerful presence for me, and I regret we didn't find a way to include him in $L=A=N=G=U=A=G=E,$ as I had intended.

But on that trip to Italy I did meet Milli Graffi and she was the Italian poet, apart from Luigi, with whom I have been in closest contact over these many years. She was in $L=A=N=G=U=A=G=E$ and I was a contributing editor for her magazine *Il Verri*. And it was, at least in part, through Milli that I met Marco Giovenale, with whom I remain in touch. Through *Il Verri*, I became better acquainted with Nanni Balestrini's exemplary "nonconformist ethical imperative"—as Cecilia Bello Minciacchi puts it.

I last saw Milli in the Fall of 2015. We met at her apartment before going to dinner. Milli suggested we go to a barebones Chinese place near her apartment. I said I would prefer the most "typical" Italian restaurant (I live in Carroll Gardens, New York's "Little Italy," where Italian American restaurants and shops are the most local). Milli seemed a bit disappointed but headed for a nearby spot. As we got near, Milli remembered it was closed.

Since the Chinese place was on the same block, we ended up in a booth there—Milli, her daughter, and me—sitting on the hard wooden benches, spending the night drinking cheap wine (though high-end from a Carroll Gardens point of view), and talking in broken English mixed with the lingua franca of a shared life in poetry. I knew right away that this was as local for Milli as it was for me. We said goodbye for the last time as I headed back to my hotel by the Duomo. Milli died at the end of this past Spring.

My third close encounter with contemporary Italian poetry had two parts. The first was in 1979, just a year after I had written to Villa. In March 1979, Ballerini invited me to be a respondent to "The Favorite Malice," a conference he organized at New York University, which brought to New York several of the key poets included in this collection. Bruce Andrews and I liked Gianni Vattimo's talk so much that we published it in our final volume of $L=A=N=G=U=A=G=E$. The second part was more than a decade later, in October of 1991, when I met Amelia Rosselli. Well, if truth be told, I didn't speak to her, she seemed splendidly unapproachable, but I did hear her read. Ballerini invited Rosselli and a number of other Italian poets to the Casa Italiana Zerilli Marimò New York University for a conference called "The Disappearing Pheasant." He also assembled a stellar group of American poets and critics to participate in the event, and I remain grateful to Luigi for including me. Listening to Rosselli, I recognized how shot with light, with life, a poetry so rife with strife could be. In a moment like that—I still recall the newly minted auditorium, the lighting, the feeling—the distance between poet and listener, American and Italian, disappears in a flash, reforming, within that aesthetic encounter, into a new, ever sharper delineation of distance and connection, one through the other.

3. The Mix

In 1999, I edited *99 Poets 1999* as a special issue of *Boundary 2*. For the collection, Carla Billitteri introduced a short selection from Renato Barilli, Mara Cini, Gianni D'Elia, Flavio Ermini, and Graffi. Billitteri's tripartite schema of different "frequencies" in that selection is a good one to begin to approach this volume: Ideolect/dialect, experimental, ontological.

What's striking in reading the poems and poetics gathered here is the way these frequencies merge, clash, and morph. Linguistic materiality rubs up against semiotic indeterminacy; affective flashes are laid bare by their conceptual grounding; and lyric diction is highjacked by hijinks.

Here are a few of the frequencies I hear in this grand collation:

Commingling lucid confusions (contusions), heterogeneity of enunciation (emancipation), mystic erotica, mannerist imprecation, Janus-charged pyrotechnics, syntactic detonation (desolation, denotation),
    Hecuba's hiccups,
    counter-hermeticism, counter- counter-hermeticism,
    fractured silence, inclement noise (lost, missing, vanished, scattered, dispersed), unpredictable,
    perimedidated,
    microtraumas, lyric embossing, laboratories of inextricable mediation
    (meteors), diffraction of ideological orientations, weak verse / strong poems, almost nothing, reversal of frames, cruel explosion of rejoicing, *rauca socius compellat voce*,
    what's me to Latin or Latin to me?,
    atlas of mimetic nonsense, Lucretian vernacular, ancient becomes the revenge of new, new's not news, nearly boreal auroras, downpour of infatuations,

sleep-green-ideas-colorless-as-water, castles on clouds, tipsy, scattered in laminations and withheld sighs,
    smoked tongue,
    lighted windows on rainy days,
    rinsed in blue fog, fake ruins, looted snares, puppets without strings, blurring the soul (soil), cosmic crises, an abyss that pulls, diving into frozen horizon, completely inside entropy,
    a body without armor (amour, ardor, honor),
    strange unrememberings (forgetting forgetfulness), tremulous murmurs, residual and indeclinable, discordant aligning, solitary war, epigrammatic longing, aphoristic Eliotics,
    modern classical / classical modern,
    disfigured decadence, figuratively ritualist, bewildered, bewilted,
    allegorical lipstick,
    elliptical symbolism, cups stained with saturation, Sardinian watches and Neopolitan teapots, neo-neo-neo-avant-avant-avant-garde-garde-garde, metropolitan envoy,
    Gruppo 2 - 4 - 6 - 8 - HIKE,
    puncture, pulse, elusive allusion, macaronic splendor, dialect/ic (vernacularity), subalternity (the subaltern sublimed), rhyming images, ironic systems of falsifications and lyric utterance,
    caducity, informalism, rubble of words, steepness of time passing, mind-tossed frisbees, net of the eye translated to parataxis of the ear,
    Polly Phonic and the Red Devils,
    sonnets to the right of us / sonnets to the left of us,
    velvet aromas of ludic semantics, socialist chimeras and capitalist dystopias, infractions of indispensable arrhythmias, false spells, true shells, shadows of voices averting the standard, legible illegibility, bringing high down low, polyglottalism, skewed mannerism,
    O! obliquity,
    woven warps, whimsical deliriousness, flow of discontinuity, materialist spills, orphan contusions, hypotactic camouflage, emblems of make believe, void in void out, voracious layers of flocks upon flocks, grazing disgrace found by chance, after insomnia,
    as when Pasolini was around,
    the ancient smell, murmuring half-lost fissures, patina of taint, amalgamated binds, upside down stars, apophantic drapes, sleds three millennia high shuddering with tactile impertinence, Gramsci's tears . . .
    schizo-orphic . . .
    in a web of infinite possibilities.

In other words: poetry is like playing cricket without a paddle.
    Che la poesia prosegua! Let the poetry continue!
                                            Brooklyn, November 3rd, 2020.

Luigi Bonaffini

Translating Dialect Literature[1]

Any critical discussion of works written in dialect is destined to run against the heavy legacy of prejudices and misunderstandings that have historically weighed upon literature in dialect, often considered a "minor," subaltern, and marginal language, even coarse and plebeian. These are misconceptions that the recent, and, in many respects, exceptional, flowering of dialect—or neo-dialect—poetry in Italy has put into a much different perspective. The absolute parity of vernacular poetry with Italian, for a long time maintained by some enlightened critics, Croce is a case in point, has gradually gained universal acceptance to the extent that it is now an established and irrefutable tenet of contemporary criticism. Dialect poetry has even penetrated those prestigious editorial circuits from which it had always been excluded, bolstered by the recognition and encouragement of influential critics, even vying with Italian poetry for the attention of a readership that is no longer local or regional but national and international. Very significant, in this respect, was in recent years the candidacy for the Nobel Prize of two poets who, in a way, embody this fundamental dichotomy of Italian letters: Mario Luzi and Albino Pierro. This is all the more remarkable considering that the latter wrote in one of the most archaic dialects in Italy, that of his native Tursi (which Contini defined as "proto romance"), without any literary tradition and extremely limited in its diffusion.

There are many reasons why so many contemporary Italian poets (the neo-dialect poets) are turning to dialect nowadays rather than standard Italian as their medium of expression, which carries far-reaching and deeply rooted implications (literary, psychological, political, existential, and anthropological). Recent dialect poetry is part of a vaster reaction to the alienating effects of post-war industrial society, which, especially in the Seventies, has meant

---

[1] AN: Parts of this essay already appeared in *World Literature Today*, 71, 2, 1997, pp. 279–288.

rehabilitating ethnic history and memory. In the face of an increasingly complex reality, one rediscovers the universal potential in every human. Hence, the recovery of personal history and roots, which the impersonal language of mass media cannot recognize or transcribe. This also means the recovery of one's native place, the place of origin, as an alternative to a monotonous and meaningless reality.

Perhaps the role of the dialect poet, as Brevini notes, reveals its deepest meaning in the struggle against the imposition of a super-language, English (this is particularly relevant in the case of poets who live in the United States and also write in English, such as Giose Rimanelli and Joseph Tusiani), and at the national level of a standard emanating from the productive industrial centers of the North.[2] Dialect is posited then as the language of concreteness and difference, in direct opposition to the flat homogeneity of the language of TV and advertising, and therefore offers a greater potential for individual creativity. The strength of dialect lies in its essential "otherness," in its position of eccentricity to the national language, in its different history, predominantly oral, which has saved it from the process of erosion that always attends literary languages. For this reason, contemporary dialect poets have tended to accentuate this difference in many ways, usually opting for more archaic forms, farther removed from standard Italian, even in spelling (Pierro, Bandini, Loi).

Along with sociocultural factors, psychological motivations also account for the choice of dialect. Not only can dialect be a maternal tongue, as in Pasolini and Zanzotto, but also a forgotten truth, a sacred, archaic language that can reveal our hidden being. Through dialect, the poet represents the places and events of his memory and a conception of the world closer to their own experience. To contemporary men and women in danger of being swallowed up and obliterated by post-industrial society, dialect can offer the support of a culture that, while threatened with obliteration, radically differs from the dominant culture. Dialect is the linguistic testimony of a cultural heritage, a collective patrimony, and an anthropological condition condemned to extinction. De Benedetti has called dialect   the painful conscience of history because only dialect, as opposed to the language of the ruling class, can bear witness to the injustices of history and give a voice to the excluded and the oppressed.

It was again Contini, recognizing the importance of dialects for Italian literature, who pointed out that Italian literature is the only great national lit-

---

[2] AN: Franco Brevini, *Poeti dialettali del Novecento*. Einaudi, 1987, p. x.

erature for which dialect literature is an integral part; yet dialect poetry, for reasons stemming from its traditional condition of subalternity and limited diffusion, but also due to objective difficulties inherent in the translation itself, given the scant knowledge of dialects outside of Italy, until very recently has been mostly ignored by translators, with the result that it remains largely untranslated, particularly the most recent output. There are, nevertheless, some notable exceptions. After the publication of the landmark anthology of dialect poetry edited by Hermann Haller (*The Hidden Italy*, 1986), more anthologies appeared in translation.[3]

First, it should be noted that the problem of dialect does not concern Italy alone, although in Italy, the phenomenon is much more extensive than in any other Western country. Since most of this essay is devoted to translation from Italian dialects, a good starting point might be an American writer well-versed in vernacular speech, Mark Twain, who prefaces his masterpiece *Huckleberry Finn* with the following remark:

> In this book, a number of dialects are used, to wit: The Missouri Negro dialect, the extremest form of the backwoods Southwestern dialect, the ordinary "Pike County" dialect, and four modified varieties of this last. The shadings have not been done in a haphazard fashion or by guesswork, but painstakingly and with the trustworthy guidance and support of personal familiarity with the several forms of speech. I make this distinction for the reason that without it many readers would suppose that all these characters were trying to talk alike and not succeeding. (193)

John Du Val, who translated from Romanesco both Trilussa and Pascarella, in an article in which he discusses Miller Williams' translation of Belli's sonnets and which begins with the above quotation from Mark Twain, advises any hypothetical translator of *Huckleberry Finn* not to translate the author's explanation at all ("Translating the Dialect: Miller Williams' Romanesco" 27). Of course, this would not solve the problem of translating all the varieties of dialect mentioned by the author, which not only pertain to the depiction of local color but also have a key role in distinguishing and individualizing the various characters. The use of dialect in *Huckleberry Finn* is more complex

---

[3] AN: See *Poesia dialettale del Molise. Testi e critica / Dialect Poetry from Molise Texts and Criticism*. Edited by Luigi Bonaffini, Giambattista Faralli and Sebastiano Martelli. Marinelli Editore, 1993; *Dialect Poetry of Southern Italy*. Edited by Luigi Bonaffini. Legas, 1997; and *Dialect Poetry of Northern and Central Italy*. Edited by Luigi Bonaffini and Achille Serrao. Legas, 2001.

than it might at first appear from the author's preface because the characters' vernacular speech is dynamic, not static; that is, it tends to adapt itself to different situations, and its use is complicated by a moralization of the linguistic act, which privileges some varieties over others. The hypothetical Italian or Spanish translator of *Huckleberry Finn* who wished to reproduce the multiplicity of local linguistic forms would be forced to let the characters speak Neapolitan, Sicilian, Galician, or Catalan, with all the resulting problems of incongruity and misplacement. It is not surprising, then, if the complexity and semantic richness of the language appear sharply diminished in the Italian translations, where the local and individual varieties are, in effect, erased and substituted by a generically colloquial and idiomatic form of speech, as, for instance, in the following speech by Jim (chapter VII), in the bilingual edition with Giovanni Baldi's translation:

> I tuck out en shin down de hill, en 'spec to steal a skift 'long de sho' som'ers 'bove de town, but dey wuz people a-stirring yit, so I hid in de ole tumbledown cooper shop on de bank to wait for everybody to go away.

> Mi sbatto giù dalla collina e penso di sgraffignare una barca lungo la riva sopra la città, ma c'era ancora in giro della gente, e allora mi nascondo nel vecchio negozio del bottaio, quello tutto a pezzi che sta sulla sponda del fiume, per aspettare che se ne vanno. (4)

Jim's dialect, strongly characterizing and quite different from the other characters' speech, is flattened in the translation, eliminating the most markedly idiomatic and vernacular elements by transferring it to an area of uncertain colloquialism. Moreover, the idiom *"sgraffignare"* translates almost incongruously one of the few standard words in the passage, "steal." At the same time, all other linguistic peculiarities, which are phonetic as well as grammatical and syntactic, disappear entirely from the Italian text.

Mark Twain himself criticizes the French translator of his famous tale "The Jumping Frog" for having used standard French without any understanding of the importance and the implications of the use of vernacular: "Benzon has not translated the story at all: he has simply mixed it all up; it is no more like the *Jumping Frog* when he gets through with it than I am like a meridian of longitude" (Sewell 67). In other words, when translating into a standard language, the translator cannot capture the eccentricity of vernacular speech, its function as an alternative, non-normative deviation from the norm. While reflecting on this concept of deviation, inescapable in any discussion of dialect literature, one must, however, consider the substantial variation in meaning that the very term "dialect" undergoes in Anglophone areas, where in effect, it stands for abnormality, a departure from a well-defined linguistic standard, so that even a local or regional pronunciation can be regarded as a form of dialect. The "vernacular" style is therefore designated by a deviation from a standard, where there is no multiplicity of autonomous idioms as in Italy:

> Vernacular style may, of course, be defined in a number of ways, but in the following I shall take it to mean a special category of "substandard" or "common" usage that serves as a marker of class, regional, or age-group affiliation and that includes such speech-oriented lexical and grammatical features as colloquial formulas and epithets, slang, obscenities, and other vulgarisms, and certain kinds of allusive or elliptical morphological and syntactic arrangements. (Rosengrant 16)

This definition could be suitable for the various American "dialects." Still, it would be inadequate to describe the phenomenon of vernaculars—and thus related questions of style—in Italy, where dialect is understood not as a simple divergence from the national standard but an autonomous linguistic system, historically determined through well-known mechanisms, as all linguists recognize. Conversely, as we shall see further on, several translators acknowledge the inevitable validity of this principle, and not only do they reject the notion of dialect as a deviant and eccentric language but consider it instead the place of naturalness and spontaneity, the linguistic norm of a determined community and, therefore, in keeping with a seemingly paradoxical methodological criterion, the exact opposite of deviation.

An Italian example of using multiple dialects in a work of fiction bears the prestigious signature of Carlo Emilio Gadda in *Quer Pasticciaccio brutto de Via Merulana*. In this expressionistic and baroque detective story, Gadda mixes Romanesco, Neapolitan, Venetian, Milanese, Molisan, and Sicilian with the bureaucratese of the various offices, police jargon, and several other sectorial languages. To guarantee the authenticity of the various dialects, Gadda consulted several people; for Romanesco, for instance, he turned to the dialect poet Mario dell'Arco. *Quer Pasticciaccio* is at least as refractory to translation as *Huckleberry Finn*: the translator must consider not only the complex interaction of the various dialects but their expressive and structural function as well, as in Mark Twain. It would be impossible to recreate the individualization of the characters through language carried out in *Quer Pasticciaccio* by assigning each, say, an American vernacular variety, and the translator, William Weaver, does not even try, with the same effect of expressive impoverishment and depreciation noted above. In "Translating Dialect Literature: The Paradigm of Carlo Emilio Gadda," Brian Altano takes the translator to task for not having used a sufficiently colloquial, vernacular language in the translation and cites, as an example, the following passage describing a seller of *porchetta* in a market:

> "La porca, la porca! Ciavemo la porchetta, signori! la bella porca de l'Ariccio con un bosco de rosmarino in de la panza! Co le patatine de staggione!... V'oo dico io. Asssaggiatele!" Posava un attimo a riprender fiato. E poi a scoppio: "Uno e novanta l'etto, la porca. È 'na miseria, signori! a chi venne e a chi compra! Uno e novanta l'etto, più mejo fatto che detto. Famese avanti co li bajocchi a la mano, sore spose! Chi nun magna nun guadagna." E poi sottovoce a una belloccia: "A voi ve do er mejo boccone, v'o giuro! Me piacete troppo! Sete troppo bona!"

> "Get your roast pork here! Pork straight from the Areca with a whole tree of rosemary in its belly! With fresh, new potatoes, too, right in season!... I'm here to tell you. Taste them for yourselves." He rested for a moment to catch his breath. And then, exploding: "One-ninety the slice, roast pork! We're giving it away, ladies! It's a crying shame, that's what it is, ladies! You ought to be ashamed to buy it so cheap. One-ninety, easier done than said! Step right up, cash in hand, ladies! If you don't eat you can't work." [...] Then, to a local beauty, lowering his tone: "What about you, pretty girl?" The girl, at that tone of authority, couldn't restrain her laughter. "A half pound of pork?" and, sotto voce, to her, but with a glance at the penniless tooth-puller: "I'll give you the best part, that's a promise. You're my type, all right. You're too pretty! (Translated by Weaver. Quoted in Altano 155)

In translating this passage, according to Altano, the translator should consider three important factors: 1) the lively jargon used by the youth to attract the crowd; 2) the sense of breathless excitement of the original; and 3) the nuances of tone, especially the spicy allusions of a fourteen-year-old.

Weaver's translation is quoted in its entirety in the note, but here, it will suffice to read the last sentence, namely: "A voi ve do er mejo boccone, v'o giuro! Me piacete troppo! Sete troppo bona!" Weaver renders it as "I'll give you the best part, that's a promise. You're my type, all right. You're too pretty!" "You're too pretty!" has nothing of the sensuality of the original, perhaps because the translator is not aware of the erotic connotation of the adjective "bona," the spicy allusion mentioned by Altano. The latter proposes his translation of the passage, using a much more colloquial and idiomatic language:

"I'll give you the best mouthful, I really swear. I really like ya a lot! You're really good lookin'" (156). But even here, something is missing, and the original's tone, its expressive specificity, remains remote, beyond reach.

Huckleberry Finn and *Quer pasticciaccio*, however, are extreme examples of the literary use of multiple vernacular codes; the norm is instead the use of one vernacular—Belli's Romanesco, Meli's Sicilian, De Filippo's Neapolitan—that can nevertheless be articulated in several expressive registers that indicate social position, cultural level, place of origin, and so on. All dialectophones know these linguistic levels in their dialect and can immediately distinguish slightly more archaic or peripheral forms. It must also be added that the same dialect is not necessarily identical for all and can be employed in very dissimilar ways by various authors: Basile's Neapolitan is quite different both from Di Giacomo's and from Serrao's more recent one, and Trilussa's Romanesco is different—much more neutral and closer to Italian—from Belli's. To return to the latter, let's read the preface of his translator, Miller Williams:

> There is in some quarters an assumption that because Romanesco is looked upon as a dialect by those who don't speak it, Belli's poems can't be truly translated unless they are rendered into some sort of patois, some special language spoken by a people outside the center of culture and mostly deprived of whatever the culture offers; people, that is, like the Romani of Trastevere. The truth, of course, is exactly the contrary. If we render the poems into any kind of dialect, slang, or jive talk, we hear them only as the middle- and upper-class Roman would have heard them and hears them now. If we are to come to them as the people of Trastevere did, then we have to hear them as they did, in the plain language of our own conversation. The simple fact is, to those who live in Trastevere, the language spoken in Trastevere is the way people talk. (xxii)

Suppose it is true that every dialect, as Williams notes, is merely the natural way of speaking for people who speak dialect. In that case, the problem of translating dialect poetry is made considerably simpler because it does not require the translator to employ a strongly connoted language other than and different from the language of ordinary conversation. Du Val points out, for instance, that, in Belli's time, the political and cultural power in Rome belonged to those who spoke Latin and Italian and that the sonnet was the literary form par excellence. Writing sonnets in Romanesco was, in fact, a violation of the traditional sonnet. Therefore, Belli's Roman readers saw in every sonnet an act of literary and linguistic impertinence, as well as political (Du Val 27–28). To translate dialect as was perceived by those who spoke it, Williams was obliged to translate its impertinence and potential for sedition.

Besides using dialect, Belli desecrates the sonnet with obscenities, depicting popular scenes and commenting on the church, philosophy, theology, and biblical history from a low, popular perspective. These other subversive factors come to the translator's aid because they tend to retain their iconoclastic force in the new linguistic context, where they can sound just as out of place and irreverent, especially in the dignified literary garb of the sonnet. A few examples of Wiliams' translation cited in Du Val's article will suffice: the pope "fiddles around, snacks, debauches a bit"; "instead of making a tower they made a mess"; "one of the angels had a charley horse" and so on. Du Val points out again that it is more difficult to render the complex play of words that often mixes obscenity and religion (28). He cites as an example the following closing tercet of a sonnet:

> San Giuseppe tratando s'ariscarda:
> Doppo leva ar somaro la bbardella,
> E appoggeno tre mmesi la libbarda.

The last line, "e appoggeno tre mmesi la llibbarda," literally means "for three months they put away the halberd," which means that they sponge and freeload for three months, but also implicit is the idea of sexual abstinence and, therefore, a negation of the Catholic doctrine of Mary's perpetual virginity. Williams translates it this way:

> Saint Joseph, meanwhile, rubbed away the cold
> beside the fire and saddled up the ass
> and put his tools away for a long time. (28)

The last line remains a strongly ironic comment on the Virgin's chastity, retaining the original's subversive force (31).

If Romanesco impresses translators with its impertinence, what should one say of Neapolitan, its uncontainable expressive richness and proteiform embodiments in poetry, theater, and narrative? One of the first works in Neapolitan dialect to be translated was *Il Pentamerone* of Giambattista Basile, published in 1634 and translated for the first time in 1713, curiously not into Italian but into the Bolognese dialect, by Maddalena and Teresa Manfredi, and then anonymously into Italian in 1754. It was later translated into German in 1946 and English in 1848, 1923, and 1983. In his long introduction to the

1925 translation of the *Pentamerone*, Benedetto Croce finds the German and English translations generally better than the Bolognese or Italian ones and then explains the criteria adopted for his translation:

> I have been very faithful to the words of the text, trying not to diminish the quantity, and to alter as little as possible the quality, of the images they contain; but I have acted freely in reworking the syntax, which in Basile is defective and often very bad, mainly perhaps because the work was published while still unfinished and, in many parts, still in the draft stage. I resisted the temptation, to which someone else would have given in, to substitute Neapolitan idioms with equivalent words and phrases of current Florentine usage; and I have tried to preserve not only the baroque adornments, but also a certain Neapolitan flavor of the book. (30–31)

Norman Mosley Penzer's English translation of 1932 is mainly based, but not exclusively, on Croce's Italian translation. In his premise, the translator wishes to display a certain familiarity with the complex relationship between standard Italian and dialect, taking care to convince the reader that he also knows the original in dialect and going as far as criticizing some of Croce's translations:

> I have endeavoured to keep two main objects constantly in view: first to translate literally, taking noun for noun and verb for verb, and secondly to preserve all the puns, local allusions, similes and metaphors of the original. Before speaking of the style of language adopted, I would like to give a few examples of the difficulties of translation. Take, for instance, the string of vile abuse that pours out of the old woman's throat when her pitcher is smashed by the court page (*The introductory tale*). She starts off as follows: "Ah zaccaro, frasca, merduso, piscialietto, sautariello de zimmaro, pettola a culo, chiappo de mpiso, mulo canzirro!" The first four words present little difficulty, but what is the meaning of "sautariello de zimmaro?" Croce gives it in modern Italian as "salterello di cembalo," and "martellino da cembalo" something moving very quickly and causing a lot of noise, possibly our "madcap". But figuratively "martellino" can mean "torment," and "cembalo" can mean "ugly." (viii)

He goes on in this vein for quite a while, at the same time examining the previous English translations and finally concluding that Croce misread the text and that "zimmaro" really means "billy goat"; he then proceeds to reveal his translation of "sautariello de zimmaro," namely "jumping he-goat." Having demonstrated his knowledge of dialect, at least theoretically, Penzer states his methodological criteria, that in a way, place him in the same line as Williams and Du Val:

> In the present edition, I have decided to employ modern rather than archaic Chaucerian or Elizabethan English, which might be supposed to be the equivalent of Seventeenth-century Neapolitan. My theory is that the modern reader in reading modern English will obtain a much better idea of what the Neapolitan book meant to the Seventeenth-Century reader than if I attempted to preserve a mock-archaic atmosphere by dragging in early English words and phrases. (viii)

What is lacking here is any reference to the uniqueness of dialect, to the latent dialectical tension between dialect and standard language, so that Penzer does not attribute any specific difficulty to the translation of Neapolitan that could not be resolved with a good dictionary.

In the Sixteenth century, the most renowned dialect poet of his time is a Sicilian, Giovanni Meli. Meli's Sicilian is a very particular language that shows how the question of dialect is so intimately connected to Italian literature and requires a specific treatment, as Gaetano Cipolla explains in his introduction to his translation of Meli's *Don Chisciotti* e *Sanchu Panza*, first published in 1787:

> While Meli may have intended to create an "illustrious Sicilian," the result of his efforts was a mixture of the literary idiom of Italy, that is, Tuscan, especially in its Arcadian tradition, and of Sicilian. The interrelationship between these two components represents an essential feature of Meli's language. This interrelationship may be articulated along an axis that includes a highly literary Tuscan (a direct quotation from Petrarch, for example), passing through a line of expression that is structurally Tuscan but with Sicilian superimposed on it. A third point of the axis might consist of "illustrious Sicilian," that is, purified from its local Palermitan dress and distilled from a variety of idioms spoken in Sicily, and finally there might be a line or expression which comes from the every-day jargon of the streets. I have tried to reproduce such sliding along the axis whenever possible [...]. Consonant with the tone of the original which obtains comic relief by mixing a highly dignified language with popular speech, I have tried to maintain the same combination in English, allowing myself to slide in the direction of archaic terms or slang, according to the situation. (xxxi)

I have quoted Cipolla at length because, unlike Penzer, the latter takes on directly the problem of the various expressive registers, of the tension generated by the relationship between language-dialect, dialect-dialect, and popular language-literary language, proposing various concrete solutions in his translation. Consider, for instance, the mixture of styles in Sanciu's answer to the lofty "bel morir tutta la vita onora":

"Comu! rispusi Sanciu, e chi scacciati!
Ch'aju a muriri pr'esseri onoratu?
Pirdunatimi, è grossa asinitati;
mi sentu megghiu eu vivu, sbrigugnatu,
chi Achilli e Ulissi morti, decantati;
pirchì eu, o tintu o pintu, avennu ciatu,
la cìnniri di st'omini valenti
la scarpisu, e perciò sù chiù potenti".
[Canto I, 11]

"What are you telling me?" then Sanciu asked,
"Am I to die so honor can be mine?
Forgive me, but that's really asinine!
Alive, though in disgrace, I feel much better
than both Achilles and Ulysses, for
they're honored but quite dead, and since
         [I breathe,
good man or bad, I am the stronger, then,
for I can tread the dust of those brave men."

In more recent times, one of the most interesting phenomena in contemporary Italian literature is undoubtedly the current flourishing outcrop of neo-dialect poetry, exceptional in so many ways. I would like to dwell briefly on two of the best neo-dialect poets, Giose Rimanelli and Achille Serrao, whose work I translated into English. Rimanelli recently published *Moliseide*, a book of poems in the Molisan dialect with my English translation in which the problem of dialect is complicated by the extreme literariness of the text, systematically contaminated by references to troubadour poetry, medieval Latin poetry, American and French poetry, jazz and blues. It is a text characterized by diverse languages and styles and a rich variety of meter, from free verse to the ballad, from hendecasyllables to double seven-syllable lines, with abundant rhymes and assonances. Therefore, the dialect is the trunk on which multiple linguistic and literary experiences are grafted. The search for dialect thus becomes a search for the poetic word, with the awareness that the greatest difficulty lies more in the cultural and literary layering of the text and the pursuit of a rhythm suited to the internal movement of the verse than the peculiarity of dialect.

 The untranslatability of dialect, its semantic opacity, is proportional to the idiomatic use of words, slang and jargon, limited to local color. On the question of the untranslatability of dialect, Hermann Haller, who translated into English the poems of his important anthology *Hidden Italy*, insists on opting, however, for a literal, rather than literary, translation: "I have chosen a literal prose translation at the cost of some stylistic and rhythmic elegance, aware of the difficulty of translating the unique expressiveness of each of the dialects" (22). And further on:

> The result of this pluralistic operation is a poetry that can barely be translated. Words such as the Milanese *cagabizet* or *cagoni*, the Piedmontese *brandèv,* or the Triestine *povaro can* cannot be rendered accurately […]. The sound of each

dialect is different, the phonosymbolism of each adding a special musical effect: the rather somber, melancholy sounds of Sicilian; the happy tonality of Neapolitan, expressing love for life; the cordial timbre of Romanesco and the airiness of Venetian; the powerful gallic intonations of Milanese. (45)

Conversely, as Franco Brevini points out in a fundamental study of dialect poetry, *Le parole perdute. Dialetti e poesia nel nostro secolo,* the translatableness of dialect depends precisely on the elimination of the more strictly vernacular elements, the overly pronounced idiomatic peaks, as is the case with Giotti, Marin, Noventa, and, finally, Rimanelli. Let's take as an example the very first stanza of the first poem in *Moliseide*:

Quanne t'èzzíccche a i vríte du pènziére	When you get near the glass panes of your
e fóre chiagne u sole, ze fa' nòtte,	[thoughts]
u sanghe te ze chiátre, sie' strèniére:	and outside the sun weeps, and darkness falls,
a vije da terre tíje dónde sta'?	your blood turns into ice, you are a stranger;
	the road back to your land, where can it be?

It should be noted that, in this stanza, no word or expression presents particular difficulties for the translator. Instead, they are hidden in the tone, rhythmic modulation, and metrical structure so that, in the translation, I was forced to leave out the rhyme, which would have considerably affected the possibility of following the subtle musical patterning of the text.

To remain in contemporary dialect poetry, for a trilingual anthology of the dialect poetry of southern Italy that I edited, I asked some translators to provide a few observations on the difficulties they encountered in translating dialect. It must be premised that, from the translator's perspective, the problem of translation is affected by their knowledge of the dialect in question. Those who do not know the dialect must avail themselves of the Italian translation and remain essentially outside the dialect experience. The best situation is that of the dialectophone who is also Anglophone and can, therefore, deal with dialect from the inside. The ideal situation might be that of the bilingual writer who translates himself, as we shall see in Zanzotto's case. For Michael Palma, translator of Gozzano and Valeri, who translated Neapolitan and Calabrese poems for the anthology, poor knowledge of dialect is a determining factor:

> I would point out two immediate problems that I have encountered in translating dialect poetry. The first is my unfamiliarity with the dialects in question. There

is always a concern with what is lost in the translation process; under these circumstances, there is a concern over a potentially double loss [...]. The other problem occurs at the other end of the translation process. Obviously, there is no equivalent in English for the Italian tradition of dialect poetry. Translating into slang or any other non-normative English dialect—"So I says to him, I says," or some such thing—would be totally inappropriate; it would fail to catch the spirit of the original and it would make for some rather bizarre-sounding English poetry. The only real solution was to translate these poems in the same idiom as any others: if there was any concession to the supposed flavor of the originals (and even this notion of "flavor" is debatable, if the dialects are in fact the normal language of their speakers), it was a slightly greater tendency at moments toward more informal expression.[4]

Palma's remarks are along the lines of those made by Miller Williams, as he considers dialect the norm for dialect speakers, so translating into slang, that is, deviating from the norm, would be inappropriate and out of place.

The ideal situation perhaps occurs only when the bilingual writer becomes a translator of their own poems. In an essay on Zanzotto as a translator, Giovanni Meo Zilio remarks that

> [T]he translator of someone else's text, even in the best of cases, namely when he is perfectly bilingual and effectively possesses the *"internal form"* of the language from which he is translating (which is not very frequent) runs into every kind of semantic difficulties (which are added to stylistic and melodic difficulties), such as polysemy, ambiguity, intentional obscurity, contextual reference of a historical, sociocultural, biographical nature, etc., which do not exist for the translator of oneself. (n.p.)[5]

Zilio provides a long and very detailed analysis of Zanzotto's Italian translation of one of his stories in the Venetian dialect entitled "La storia del barba zhucon / La storia dello zio tonto" (The Story of the Witless Uncle). He concludes that Zanzotto adopts a criterion of rigorous faithfulness but that within this fundamental faithfulness, there are here and there in his translation certain stylistic choices (lexical, syntactic, melodic, etc.) that depart from the original text and that in such a careful and controlled writer cannot be accidental. These differences are grouped into two categories:

---

[4] AN: In a letter to me, answering a few questions on translating from the dialect.
[5] EN: See Zilio, Giovanni Meo. "Come un poeta veneto traduce se stesso (Per una critica stilistica della traduzione)." *Quaderni Veneti*, 14, December 1991, pp. 95–107.

a) *Deviations from literariness:* in the choice of words or syntagms (less familiar or less plebeian or less rural than those of the original text).
b) *Deviations from essentialness:* in the sense of a greater sobriety (restraint, expressive discretion), which includes simplification, rationalization, and downplaying (anti-theatricality), with respect to the original text.

As for the greater literariness of the Italian text, Zilio concludes that, while the original is taken from the dialect folklore of Treviso, in the Italian text the author is less conditioned by the psycholinguistic and sociolinguistic forms with which that folkloric material was handed down. However, there is another mechanism at work,

> which acts more or less in all dialect speakers when they go from dialect to the national language. It can be articulated, with various results, under the label of "*hypercorrectionism*" (stylistic, in this case) and it consists, as is well known, in a psycholinguistic reaction that produces effects of excessive self-censure towards the natural tendency for contamination. (106)

It should be noted that this difference in literariness between Italian and dialect texts in Zanzotto occurs in the translation rather than in the original writings since his dialect poetry is no less literary than the Italian.

It would be useful, in further studies, to analyze the texts in translation to measure and evaluate their literary and stylistic rendition concretely. In the end, however, we are forced to acknowledge the obvious, namely that it is very difficult to find a conclusive answer to the problems of translating dialect. I have pointed out some possible paths to explore, but the success of any attempt can ultimately only depend on the linguistic and literary sensibility of the translator.

Thomas E. Peterson

The Imperfect and the Ideal: On Poetic Translation

> A real translation is transparent.
> — Walter Benjamin, "The Task of the Translator," *Illuminations*, 79.

1. Dante

Even if Dante were to claim that poetry is untranslatable since poetic translations cannot replicate the "sweetness and harmony" of the original, the same poet seemed to recognize the inevitability of poetic translation when he presents, in *De vulgari eloquentia*, an array of poetic samples from diverse Italian dialects and assesses their relative merits.[1] Dante's goal was to conjure the idea of the "volgare illustre," a vernacular language that is not only illustrious (giving luster to its user) but "cardinale" (pivotal, as the hinge about which other dialects turned), "aulico" (regal), and "curiale" (courtly) (*De vulgari eloquentia* I, xvi, 6).[2] Even as the father of the Italian language conceived of a *koine* that would serve as the ideal language for Italy—metaphorized as a panther whose perfume is emitted everywhere but is nowhere to be seen—he set out

---

[1] AN: See Dante's *Convivio*: "E però sappia ciascuno che nulla cosa per legame musaico armonizzata si può de la sua loquela in altra transmutare sanza rompere tutta sua dolcezza e armonia" (I, vii, 14). ["Therefore everyone should know that nothing harmonized according to the rules of poetry can be translated from its native tongue into another without destroying all its sweetness and harmony" (Translated by Lansing)].

[2] EN: "Itaque, adepti quod querebamus, dicimus illustre, cardinale, aulicum et curiale vulgare in Latio, quod omnis latie civitatis est et nullius esse videtur, et quo municipalia vulgaria omnia Latinorum mensurantur, ponderantur, et comparantur." ["So we have found what we were seeking: we can define the illustrious, cardinal, aulic, and curial vernacular in Italy as that which belongs to every Italian city yet seems to belong to none, and against which the vernaculars of all the cities of the Italians can be measured, weighed, and compared" (Translated by Botterill)].

to formulate that language—however imperfectly—in the *Commedia*.³ He did so fully aware of the historical mutability of the vernacular languages, which were protected from the danger of losing touch with the languages of antiquity by the existence of an immutable "grammar":

> This [awareness of language's mutability] was what inspired the inventors of the art of 'grammar,' which is nothing but a particular constant and unchangeable usage unaffected by time and place. Since this was settled by common consent of many peoples, it then became independent of the individual judgement, and thus incapable of variation. (I, ix, 11; translated by Purcell)⁴

When Dante poet invokes the "gloria della nostra lingua" in *Purgatorio* XI, he again refers to the historical mutability of the Italian language and the evanescent fame accorded to those who are its purported masters: "così ha tolto l'uno a l'altro Guido / la gloria de la lingua; e forse è nato / chi l'uno e l'altro caccerà del nido" ("So did one Guido, from the other, wrest / the glory of our tongue; and he perhaps / is born who will chase both out of the nest") (vv. 97–99; translated by Mandelbaum). When Dante formulates the "volgare illustre," he cites, by contrast, several poets from the Italian regions, arriving at only a small number—Guido, Lapo, Cino—whose language could *approach* the ideal idiom he has in mind, the translator's dream of an illustrious, curial, aulic, and cardinal language.⁵ Dante's point of departure in his linguistic trea-

---

³ AN: See Dante, *De vulgari eloquentia*: "Postquam venati saltus et pascua sumus Ytalie nec pantheram quam sequimur adinvenimus, ut ipsam reperire possimus, rationabilius investigemus de illa ut, solerti studio redolentem ubique et necubi apparentem nostris penitus irretiamus tenticulis" (I, xvi, 1). ["Now that we have hunted across the woodlands and pastures of all Italy without finding the panther we are trailing, let us, in the hope of tracking it down, carry out a more closely reasoned investigation, so that, by the assiduous practice of cunning, we can at last entice into our trap this creature whose scent is left everywhere but which is nowhere to be seen" (Translated by Botterill)].

⁴ EN: "Hinc moti sunt inventores gramatice facultatis; que quidem gramatica nichil aliud est quam quedam inalterabilis locutionis idemptitas diversis temporibus atque locis. Hec, cum de comuni consensu multarum gentium fuerit regulata, nulli singulari arbitrio videtur obnoxia, et per consequens nec variabilis esse potest."

⁵ AN: See Inglese, Giorgio, in Dante Alighieri, *L'eloquenza in volgare*: "Ammesso [...] che Dante abbia intuito l'unità linguistica delle parlate italiane [...] si dovrà tuttavia riconoscere che ha cercato di fondare e svolgere tale intuizione come identiifazione e deduzione di una 'lingua-uno' esistente accanto e simultaneamante ai 'volgari-molti'; e che, mentre il momento identificativo si è realizzato nella assunzione di una certa lingua pooetica duecentesca come documento di volgare illustre, il momento deduttivo non è approdato a risultati coerenti" (24). ["While Dante intuited the

tise was the two-part identity of the verbal sign, constituted by the sound of its utterance and the reason of its sense.

The art of poetic translation is immanent in the art of poetry. If the worthy poem conveys a truth or mystery, the translator must preserve that truth or mystery by whatever means necessary.[6] Such an assertion is implicit in the ontology of relations established by Dante in his recognition of translation's imperfectability and the desirability of an ideal language—the model for which is present in the underlying grammar of the classic languages—capable of ennobling and dignifying the mission of poetry and resisting the Babelic multiplicity of tongues that threatens it.

2. Translation as Adaptation: Steiner, Tynianov, Ortega y Gasset

There are as many obstacles and filters to comprehension when translating poetry as there are cultural and linguistic (syntactic, semantic, lexical, phonetic) factors that constitute it. The poem is a rite that reveals its secret through the reading by crossing over some degree of foreignness. It is a *traslatare* between different codes (oral/written, objective/subjective, intellective/affective), times, and spaces. Since Darwin's time, the concept of adaptation has been of fundamental importance to the sciences. By considering poetic translation as a form of adaptation, one acknowledges its cognitive-epistemological import and the desirability of translations that approach the goal of suitability rather than the much more constricting goal of mimetic identification or replication of the original.

Perhaps the theorist who gets us closest to this concept is George Steiner. In contrast to the customary three-part approach to the translation debate—"The perennial distinction between literalism, paraphrase, and free imitation, turns out to be wholly contingent" (*After Babel* 319)—Steiner offers

---

linguistic unity of the spoken languages of Italy [...] one must recognize that he sought to found and develop such an intuition as an identification and a deduction of a 'singular-language' existing simultaneously alongside the 'many-vernaculars'; and that while the identifying moment was realized in the assumption of a certain 13th century poetic language as a document of the illustrious vernacular, the deductive moment did not arrive at coherent results" (author's translation)].

[6] AN: Theorists of poetic translation have mapped out their positions according to a model organized around such polarities as fidelity/freedom, fidelity/beauty, service translation/creative translation, literality/rifacimento, target language/original language. Benjamin speaks of the outdatedness of the fidelity model, or rather the dependence of fidelity on freedom and vice versa.

a four-part sequence of organic operations: trust, penetration, embodiment, and restitution.[7] In this process, the translator first assumes the source text has something to say, investing themselves in its value. Then comes the phase of appropriation, of "encirclement and ingestion," that results in a "comprehension" that is in part instinctive and involves an "aggression" toward the text. This is followed by an incorporation by which the poem is brought back to the translator's own cultural and linguistic milieu: "Here two families of metaphor, probably related, offer themselves, that of sacramental intake or incarnation and that of infection" (315). While this stage comports the risk of imbalance due to the individual stylization of the translator, the fourth phase of restitution aims to achieve parity between the source text and translation (314–315). It does this through interpretation and by pushing the language of arrival toward the structures and logic of the language of origin. Steiner's is an organic conception of the text as a living thing, concerning which a negative entropy factor indicates a successful translation.[8] Therefore, its four phases are hospitable to the paradigm of translation as adaptation.

In his final chapter, "Topologies of Culture," Steiner examines the larger anthropological milieu and cultural humus in which translation occurs, and specifically the middle ground between "translation proper" and "transmutation," which he labels "partial transformation" (437). Here, one confronts a "multitude of means," including "paraphrase, graphic illustration, pastiche, imitation, thematic variation, parody, citation in a supporting or undermining context, false attribution (accidental or deliberate), plagiarism, collage, and many others" (437). Citing the ubiquity of these linguistic and communicative practices, Steiner asks, "To what extent is culture the translation and rewording of previous meaning?" (437) Adopting such a line of inquiry, he cites several practical analogies between translation and music; just as multiple translators will tackle a version of the same work, so too do multiple composers set the same texts to music. Steiner's concept builds on the mathematical discipline of topology that deals

---

[7] AN: See also: "The theory of translation, certainly since the seventeenth century, almost invariably divides the topic into three classes"; these are: (1) "strict literalism," the "interlinear crib"; (2) "the great central area of 'translation' by means of faithful but autonomous restatement; (3) "imitation, recreation, variation, interpretative parallel" (256).

[8] AN: See also: "Fidelity is ethical, but also, in the full sense, economic. [...] There is, ideally, exchange without loss. In this respect, translation can be pictured as a negation of entropy; order is preserved at both ends of the cycle, source and receptor" (318–319).

with those relations between points and those fundamental properties of a figure which remain invariant when that figure is bent out of shape. [...] The study of these invariants [...] has shown underlying unities and assemblages in a vast plurality of apparently diverse functions and spatial configurations. Similarly, there are invariants and constants underlying the manifold shapes of expression in our culture. (448)

Steiner addresses the multiplicity of translational phenomena to view them in a relativistic network of intercultural communications. The "partial transmutations" of culture relativize the language of translation, accounting for contingencies of transmission and reception, and the shifts in historical sensibility. The artifact is freed of presumed criteria of aesthetic purity or perfection as the translator recreates some essence of the original.

A second theorist who contributed to the idea of translation as adaptation is Yuri Tynianov. For this Russian formalist, poems are constructions whose "elements" exist in "reciprocal correlation"; a poem is born out of everyday consciousness and is the result of a "struggle" and "the pushing forward of one group of factors at the expense of the other" (*The Problem of Verse Language* 33).[9] The proper view of poetic language is not in isolation or statically but in terms of its networks of interactions, lest one arrive at a poetry of mild harmonies and simple musicality or the idea that character is immutable. It is useless to focus on a single factor to the exclusion of the others insofar as the worthy poem is dynamic and fluctuating, yielding a flow. What Tynianov calls "motivated art" has the fatal defect of denying this flow. If the translator intends to yield a flow and not falsely separate form from content, they must recognize that the respective merits of poems rest on their systems of "dominants," the marked features and style of their authors. The translator is responsible for recognizing these and generating a similar flow, recognizing that the dominant constructive factor is rhythm or the dynamic grouping of verbal material.

A third theorist for whom poetic translation is a form of adaptation is José Ortega y Gasset. In his "The Misery and Splendour of Translation," Ortega stipulates that the translation is neither a text nor the mold of a text but a journey toward a text.[10] Positing that "language is the original science," Ortega

---

[9] AN: The proper view of poetic language is not in isolation but in terms of its networks of interactions. Otherwise, writes Tynianov, one arrives at a poetry of mild harmonies and simple musicality, or at the idea that character is immutable.

[10] AN: "It is well worth stressing this and affirming that translation is a literary genre apart,

states—with reference to Schleiermacher's essay "On the Different Methods of Translating"—that "it is only when we uproot readers from their own linguistic habits and compel them to experience those of the author that there is true translation" (Translated by Boyd, n.p.):[11]

> Science today would be impossible without language, not because of the truth of the platitude that to do science is to speak, but quite the reverse, because language is the original science. It is precisely because of this that modern science lives in a perpetual polemic with language. Would this make any sense if language were not a science in itself, a knowledge which, because it seems inadequate to us, we try to overcome? (n.p.).

The translation genre assumes a cognitive-epistemological responsibility when language is understood as a science. Finally, Ortega confirms the reasons why the reader of a translation prefers hearing their language stretched into new territory:

> [I]t is clear that a country's readers do not appreciate a translation rendered in the style of their own language. [...] What they appreciate is the opposite: by carrying the possibilities of their language to the very edge of intelligibility, the particular form of expression of the translated author can be made transparent. (n.p.)

3. Benjamin, Terracini, Poggioli

In "The Task of the Translator," Benjamin distinguishes between the "meaning of the original" and its "mode of signification," where only the latter is the translator's concern. Benjamin advises the translator to adhere to the syntax of the original, not its meaning. By so doing, they will succeed in "making both the original and the translation recognizable as fragments of a greater

---

different from all others, with its own norms and ends. And this is for the simple reason that a translation is not the work itself, but a path towards the work. If it is a poetic work, the translation is really an apparatus, a technical artifice that draws us close to the work without ever attempting to repeat it or replace it" (n.p.).

[11] AN: "It is well worth stressing this and affirming that translation is a literary genre apart, different from all others, with its own norms and ends. And this is for the simple reason that a translation is not the work itself, but a path towards the work. If it is a poetic work, the translation is really an apparatus, a technical artifice that draws us close to the work without ever attempting to repeat it or replace it" (n.p.).

language" (78). The yearning for the language manifest in translations characterizes a philosophical genius. "The language of a translation" should be seen as "[giving] voice to the *intentio* of the original not as reproduction but as harmony, as a supplement to the language in which it expresses itself, as its own kind of *intentio*" (79). Thus, the two languages share the intention of participating in a pure language: "[A]ll supra-historical kinship of languages rests in the intention underlying each language as a whole—an intention, however, which no single language can attain by itself but which is realized only by the totality of their intentions supplementing each other: pure language" (74).

Basing himself on the "truth" of a source text and the "pure language" in which it participates, Benjamin enunciates a rudimentary theory of language as constitutive of the human being and, therefore, something humans cannot entirely comprehend. He speaks especially of poetry, as poetry is not invested in communication but expression. If translations were made for those who don't understand the original, they could only mediate the communication of sense, "that is, something inessential" (69).

In Benjamin's view, the more elevated the poem, the more translatable it is (a position also taken at the end of the 18th century by Novalis).[12] He disregards the traditional opposition of fidelity and freedom (also phrased as fidelity and beauty) since these terms only pertain to the reproduction of meaning, and "poetic significance is not limited to meaning" (78). Fidelity and freedom (or beauty) are partners not adversaries, as translators are free to act on their own language in the name of the pure language, employing the source text as a stimulus. This is seen in the need for German translators not to Germanize the foreign languages but rather "[turn] German into Hindi, Greek, English" (80). In contrast to the "humanistic" translator, who "preserves the state in which his own language happens to be," Benjamin urges that one "[allow their] language to be powerfully affected by the foreign tongue" (81). Inevitably, the translator's goal—to release the pure language imprisoned in the source

---

[12] AN: See Risset, Jacqueline: "[M]i viene da pensare a Novalis, a quel passo in cui egli afferma che gli autori 'grandissimi' sono più traducibili degli altri, perché prendono la lingua alla 'radice' e la muovono in una prospettiva così carica di tensione e di energia che va anche al di là della loro lingua e dei loro testi" ("Il rischio della scrittura, intervista di Filippo Bettini," *Rinascita*, 44, 1982, 23). ["I recall that passage in which Novalis affirms that the 'very great' authors are more translatable than the others, because they seize the language at its 'roots' and they move it in a perspective so charged with tension and energy that it also goes beyond their language and their texts" (author's translation)].

text by recreating it in the translation—is difficult, contingent on the historical phase of one's own language. The translator must not attempt to resolve the poems' ambiguities or accept the devil's bargain of 'reading into' the text a sense that is not there. "The Task of the Translator" does not take us into the translator's workshop but establishes an ontology of relations within which the translator can pursue a form of the ideal language present in those few poems of universal importance, not unlike the "panther" pursued by Dante in his formulation of the "illustrious vernacular." Optimally, a translation is a flowering, with the high purpose of expressing the central reciprocal relationship between languages. The kinship between languages does not involve likeness but lies in the *intentio*, which the skilled translator can identify in the source text and transfer, as a kind of echo, into the translation.

Benvenuto Terracini also sunders the dichotomy between the faithful and free (or beautiful) translation: "A beautiful translation is always faithful" ["Una traduzione bella è sempre fedele"] ("Il problema della traduzione" 103). Terracini outlines two contrasting but equally plausible ways for a translator to be faithful. The first is the "critical and realistic genre" of translation, which "stimulates the reader's critical faculties and doesn't avoid what is unusual and difficult. The mental form of our age, still saturated with history, our habits of philological exactness, render us very open to developing this genre" (90). This second type is adopted by "writers who prefer to seek their expression by submerging themselves in their language and simply interpreting its expressive interiority [...] without desiring to leave a visible trace of their own person" (90). This "idealistic translation of the romantic type only looks at the inner form of the original which it seeks to transpose without residuals or shadows in molds familiar to its own spirit and that of the reader" (90). As an example of this latter, Terracini cites Giacomo Leopardi: "La perfezione della traduzione consiste in questo, che l'autore tradotto, non sia, per esempio, greco in italiano, greco o francese in tedesco, ma tale in italiano o in tedesco, quale egli è in greco o in francese. Questo è difficile, questo è ciò che non in tutte le lingue è possibile" (*Zibaldone* [2134-2135] 925).[13] A 20th century version of the same philosophy of translation is found in Salvatore Quasimodo's transla-

---

[13] AN: "A perfect translation consists in this, that the translated author is not, e.g., Greek in Italian, Greek or French in German, but the same in Italian or German as he is in Greek or French. This is the difficulty; this is what is not possible in all languages" (qtd by Terracini, 90, author's translation).

tions from the Greek lyric poets, *Lirici greci*. In his "Introduction" to the volume, Luciano Anceschi states that Quasimodo's translations "interessano per lo straordinario sforzo di alta contemporaneità artistica nella ripresa di testi aspri e lontani" (45).[14] In addition, Quasimodo embodies "la distinzione romantica, per cui gli antichi sono un ideale che sta davanti a noi non per una passiva imitazione [...] quanto per un'attiva emulazione" (46).[15] As Quasimodo himself would write, he intended to avoid the floral and "aromatic" lexis (such words as *opimo, pampineo, rigolio, fulgido, florido*) that had been customary for Italian translators of the ancient lyric poets (133).

The great scholar and translator Renato Poggioli also dismisses the fidelity-freedom or fidelity-beauty dichotomy: "beauty is the highest kind of fidelity"; "what moves the genuine translator is not a mimetic urge, but an elective affinity: the attraction of a content so appealing that he can identify it with a content of his own" ("The Added Artificer" 359). Poggioli writes of the key role played by translators in society and the rarity of great translators:

> [T]ranslation is, both formally and psychologically, a process of inscape rather than of escape; and this is why, of all available aesthetic concepts, the best suited to define the activity and the experience of the translator is that of *Einfühlung* or "empathy," which must not be understood merely as the transference of an emotional content. The *disponibilité* of the translator is primarily formal precisely because an external formal sanction is the main object of his quest. (360)

The critic's clarification that a translator requires "an external formal sanction" is especially useful as it reminds us that in the absence of such a sanction, the translator risks descending into subjectivism. A failed translation is analogous to an organism that doesn't adapt to its environment. In the conclusion of Poggioli's essay, one hears a reminder of the critical debates surrounding the topic of translation in the early 19th century, which gave new life to Italian national literature.[16]

---

[14] AN: "stand out for the extraordinary effort of a high artistic contemporaneity in the recovery of distant and difficult texts" (author's translation).

[15] AN: "the romantic distinction, for which the ancients are an ideal that stands before us not for a passive imitation [...] so much as an active emulation" (author's translation).

[16] AN: "Translators are [...] the most cosmopolitan among the citizens of the Republic of Letters; their absence from the scene, or their presence in a too limited number, may mean that the literary tradition will rest all too easily within the Chinese wall it has erected around itself" (366, author's translation).

4. The Romantic Age and Leopardi

In her 1816 essay "On the Manner and Utility of Translations," Madame De Staël urged Italians to translate their European neighbors' literary works and to end the mythological imitationism of their literary culture. She impugned the Italians for using the theater as a social meeting place, not a venue for high art, and argued that there are so few great works that it is incumbent on nations to share them through translation. As is known, the many responses to the essay ranged from highly critical to highly favorable. Unique in this regard were the contributions of Giacomo Leopardi, whether in his "Discorso di un italiano intorno alla poesia romantica," where he defends the imagination of the ancient fabulists, in his translation work or his theoretical observations on language differences and the feasibility of translation, given the root differences between languages. The young polyglot had himself mastered numerous world languages and engaged in a steady activity of translating classic texts. Leopardi does not accept the positions of the Romantics or the Classicists; instead, he elevates the ancient poets, especially the Greeks, making the integration of classical sensibility and modern consciousness possible.

Leopardi distinguishes ancient classical works (such as Homer), which are "all style" and lose everything in translation, from modern classical works (like Cicero), which are "all content" and lose nothing in translation (*Zibaldone* [3475-3476], 1420–1421). Since the poet's style invariably marks poetry, one must acknowledge the "impossibility of a perfect translation, especially with regard to books whose chief worth, or whole or a good part belongs to the style, to the extrinsic, to the words, etc., which must be more or less all books of true poetry in verse or in prose" ([3954] 1652). This leads inevitably to the problem of the translator's style, viewed by Leopardi in terms of the opposition affectation/naturalness:

> You can see, therefore, how difficult a good translation is where literature is concerned, a work that must be composed of properties that seem discordant, incompatible, and contradictory. And likewise the soul and wit and intellect of the translator. Especially when the principal or one of the principal merits of the original likes precisely in its being unaffected, natural, and spontaneous, whereas the translator, by his nature, cannot be spontaneous. But on the other hand the affectation I have described is so necessary to a translator that when stylistic merit is not the strong point of the original an unaffected translation according to what I have said can be called a slicing in half of the text, and when stylist merit constitutes the main attraction of the work (as it does in a good part of the ancient classics) the translation is not so much a translation as

a sophistical imitation, compilation, residue, or, if nothing else, a new work. The French easily dispose of this difficulty because they are never affected at all when they are translating. So they have no translations..., but only summaries of the contents of foreign works, or else new works composed of other's ideas. ([319-320] 201–202).

In response to De Staël's opinion that the German language was more fit for translation than Italian, Leopardi states that the German language's ability to replicate each and every factor of a poem results in a "copy" rather than a true translation, for which Leopardi uses the term "imitation," the latter being more pregnant with emotions and freer to capture the interiority of the source poem without sensing a slavish adherence to the technical aspects of its composition.[17] Italian, like Greek, is an aggregate language, a fact that explains its flexibility in this situation. French, in contrast, is a unified language, which makes it more difficult to move the language of the translation toward the language of the source text. Fittingly, Leopardi ties this fact to the greater adaptability of the Italian language: "Hence in Italian there is perhaps a greater capacity than in any other language to *adapt* to foreign forms" ([964] 456, emphasis added). Another factor Leopardi refers to in this regard is the dichotomy of the (poetic) word (*parola*) and the technical term (*termine*), with the latter being more prevalent in the French language. In Leopardi's view, this amounts to an obstacle to translating poetry.

5. Poetic Translation as Lectio Difficilior

If the theorists I have cited remind us of the difficulty and risks of poetic translation, this problem is only compounded in an era when the language of ordinary communication is exiled from the poetic text due to a breakdown in confidence in the public language:

> From the beginnings of Western literature until Rimbaud and Mallarmé [...] poetry and prose were in organic accord with language. [...] With them Western literature and speech-consciousness enter a new phase. The poet no longer has or can confidently hope for tenure in a generalized authority of speech. [...] Established language is the enemy. (Steiner, *After Babel* 185–186).

---

[17] AN: See [2845-2846] 1178–1179.

In such a situation, the *lectio difficilior* becomes more of an obligation than a choice as the poets' rupture with the linguistic status quo causes translators to confront poems pervaded by obscurity and imaginary flights, silence and reticence. The following paragraphs provide several examples of poetic translation as adaptation in the last century.

In 1929–1930, Federico García Lorca visited New York City and wrote the tumultuous poems of *Poeta en Nueva York*. The following passage contains the closing lines of "Tu infancia en Menton" ("Your Childhood in Menton"), a haunting remembrance and love poem, alongside the translations of Ben Belitt (1955) and Edwin Honig (1961):[18]

> — *García Lorca*
> No me tapen la boca los que buscan
> espiga de Saturno por la nieve
>
> o castran animales por un cielo,
> clinica y selva de la anatomía.
>
> Amor, amor, amor. Niñez del mar.
> Tu alma tibia sin ti que no te entiende.
>
> Amor, amor, un vuelo de la corza
> por el pecho sin fin de la blancura.
> Y tu niñez, amor, y tu niñez.
>
> El tren y la mujer que llena el cielo.
> Ni tú, ni yo, ni el aire, ni las hojas.
> Sí, tu niñez ya fábula de fuentes.
>
>
> — *Ben Belitt*
> Do not stop up my mouth, you who seek
> Saturnalian wheat in the snow,
>
> or unsex the created of heaven,
> anatomy's groves and dispensaries.
>
> Love! Love! A childhood of ocean!
> Your spirit's lukewarmness, that cannot construe you, still lacking you.

---

[18] AN: *The Selected Poems of Federico García Lorca*, 112–113 (Honig); *Poet in New York*, 14–15 (Belitt).

Love! Love! A running of deer
through an infinite bosom of whiteness.
And your childhood, beloved, your childhood.

The train and the lady who overflows heaven.
Not you, nor myself, nor the wind, nor the leaves.
Yes, your childhood, now fable for fountains.

— *Edwin Honig*
Don't let them gag me, they who seek
the wheat of Saturn through the snow,
who castrate creatures in the sky,
clinic and wilderness of anatomy.
Love, love, love. Childhood of the sea.
Your tepid soul without you which doesn't understand you.

Love, love, a flight of deer

through the endless heart of whiteness.
And your childhood, love, your childhood.
The train, and the woman who fills the sky.
Not you or I, not the wind or the leaves.
Yes, your childhood now a legend of fountains.

The sense of Belitt's translation is that of an embellishment. He makes the third-person "los que" into "you"; he adds five exclamations not present in the original and introduces the ethereal "heaven" for "cielo" ("sky"), "ocean" for "mar" ("sea"), "infinite" for "sin fin" ("endless"), the bland "unsex" for "castran" ("castrate"), "lady" for "mujer" ("woman") and "running" for "vuelo" ("flight"). Honig's translation, following the literal translations placed in parentheses, is elegant, evocative, and avoids any false afflatus or poeticisms.

Let us now consider two translations of the first section of Eugenio Montale's "Iride" ("Iris") (from *La bufera e altro*).[19]

---

[19] AN: See Montale's *L'opera in verso*: "*Iride* è una poesia che ho sognato e poi tradotto da una lingua inesistente; ne sono forse più il medium che l'autore" (962) ["*Iride* is a poem I dreamed and then translated from a nonexistent language: I am perhaps more its medium than its author"]. Translation by Sonia Raiziss and Alfredo de Palchi in Eugenio Montale, *Selected Poems*, 127. Translation by Jonathan Galassi in Eugenio Montale, *Collected Poems 1920-1954*, 355.

— *Eugenio Montale*
Quando di colpo San Martino smotta
le sue braci e le attizza in fondo al cupo
fornello dell'Ontario,
schiocchi di pigne verdi fra la cenere
o il fumo d'un infuso di papaveri
e il Volto insanguinato sul sudario
che mi divide da te;

questo e poco altro (se poco
è un tuo segno, un ammicco, nella lotta
che mi sospinge in un ossario, spalle
al muro, dove zàffiri celesti
e palmizi e cicogne su una zampa non chiudono
l'atroce vista al povero
Nestoriano smarrito);

è quanto di te giunge dal naufragio
delle mie genti, delle tue, or che un fuoco
di gelo porta alla memoria il suolo
ch'è tuo e che non vedesti; e altro rosario
fra le dita non ho, non altra vamp
se non questa, di resina e di bacche,
t'ha investito.

— *Sonia Raiziss and Alfredo de Palchi*
When suddenly St. Martin's summer topples
its embers and shakes them down low in
Ontario's dark hearth –
snapping of green pine cones in the cinders
or the fumes of steeped poppies
and the bloody Face on the shroud
that separates me from you:

this and little else (if very
little is in fact your sign, a nod, in the struggle
goading me into the charnel house, my back
to the wall, where the sapphires of heaven
and palm leaves and one-legged storks don't shut out
the brutal sight from the wretched
strayed Nestorian);

this is how much of you gets here
from the wreck of my people, and yours,
now that the fires of frost remind me of your
land which you've not seen; and I have
no other rosary to finger, no other flame
has assailed you, if it's not this,
of berries and resin.

— *Jonathan Galassi*
When suddenly St. Martin shunts his embers
down his sluiceway, stirring them
deep in Lake Ontario's dark furnace,
the popping of green pinecones in the ashes,
or the steam from a fume of poppies
and the bloodied Face on the shroud
that keeps me from you:

this and little else (if a sign,
a wink from you is little, in the struggle
that shoves me in a charnelhouse, back to the wall,
where sky-blue sapphires and palms
and storks aloft on one leg
can't hide the atrocious view
from the poor dismayed Nestorian);

this is all of you that reaches me
from the shipwreck of my people,
and yours, now an icy fire
recalls the land of yours you didn't see;
and I hold no other rosary in my hand,
no other flame than this of resin and berries
has given you form.

Galassi interpolates "Lake Ontario" (from "Ontario") and adds "sluiceway" (which has no equivalent); he renders "infuso" ("infusion") as "fume," resulting in the redundant "or the steam from a fume of poppies" and personalizes St. Martin ("*his* embers"). He translates "vampa [...] t'ha investito" as "flame [...] has given you form." In contrast, Raiziss and de Palchi translate "flame has assailed you," where the violence of the verb captures the impact of the sacrificial flame striking Clizia, taking charge of her, a meaning reinforced by the rhyme "smarrito"/ "investito" that aptly concludes this "passional" half of the obscure poem. Raiziss and de Palchi render "Ontario" literally, which is where Clizia now resides. Not attempting to embellish or explain, they allow the autumnal setting's fiery imagery and emotional tenor to emerge in all its intensity. As for the Dantean epithet "smarrito" for Nestorian-Montale, "strayed" conveys a sense of spiritual desolation and loss that is not captured by "dismayed."

During the years when Hilda Doolittle translated Euripides's *Ion* (1920–1937), her relationship with Freudianism intensified, exerting a transformative impact on her work. If in the early drafts, Doolittle hewed closely to a minimalist diction and wholesale elimination of rhetorical excess, a 'bare bones' version of the play, as her study of Freud deepened, she realized that she must find equivalents for the "repetition, *remplissage*, or sentiment [in Euripides' text]. Associations must here not be cut away, dismissed, paraphrased or omitted, but dealt with, searched out until they yielded under new orders their meanings" (Duncan 384). This transformational process valorizes the original play's sacred inspiration by finding equivalents for its only implicit stagecraft: "Not only has H.D. articulated the play into felt sections, but she is also concerned with interpreting her aesthetic feeling. Once the psyche of the person has been analyzed, a new sense of the psyche of the poet arises along analytic lines as well as the pure stroke of the original inspiration" (382). H. D. searches out the "workable stuff of Euripides' text, not the manner that made for a new style in poetry, but deeper, back of that, for the level at which manner and style are seen as form and meaning" (384). She projects the play's organization into nineteen sections based on the entrances and exits of characters and the Chorus. In this way, she merges the inner and the outer, the upper and lower realms of Euripides' inspiration. She transfers the play's revolutionary meaning to posterity by arriving at an essentially synchronic and classic style purged of her more radically modernist beginnings.

In the following rendering of the Chorus's anticipation of Creusa's bitterness when she finds the youth in her house, as she believes she is childless and that Ion is her husband's child with another woman, H. D. inserts the direct discourse of Creusa's imagined speech:

> Tears, tears / wild grief, / pity, / pity my mistress; / O, what will our lady / think, / when she sees her husband / and asks, / "Who is this, / this beautiful youth? / what is it / the prophet / grants? / a child to his house; / I am left / deserted / and childless; / who is this child? / who left / this waif / on the temple steps? (*Ion* 58)

The immediacy and pathos of H. D.'s rendition contrasts with the prosaic character of a "meaning-based" translation of the same passage:

> Tears and grievous cries, / a seizure of lament, / will take my mistress when she learns / of her lord's fruit / and her unbroken barrenness. / Oh prophet son of Leto, what harmony is this / that you impose? / Whence came this boy that you have bred / familiar to your shrine – / what woman gave him birth? (Euripides, *Ion*. Translated by Anne Pippin Burnett, 73-74).

Thanks in part to her study of Freud—who praised her translation of the *Ion* in a letter—and to her meditation on the process of translation, H. D. frees herself of the earlier constrictive style and becomes open to broader influences, as is appropriate for the cultural and not merely philological-literary nature of the project she is engaged in: "*Ion* is not only a translation of Euripides but a translation of Freudian thought. It stands as a statement opening toward her analysis with Freud, a preparation, an expectation. It was, in this sense, away from style itself toward the act of writing itself that Freud helped H. D." (Duncan 385).

In roughly the same years as Doolittle translated the *Ion*, Eugenio Montale and Giuseppe Ungaretti translated William Shakespeare's sonnets.[20] Here again, we have late modern poets addressing a classical (if not ancient) poet and confronting the difficulties of language and form. Here is Sonnet 33:

> — *William Shakespeare*
> Full many a glorious morning have I seen
> Flatter the mountain-tops with sovereign eye,
> Kissing with golden face the meadows green,
> Gilding pale streams with heavenly alchemy;
>
> Anon permit the basest clouds to ride
> With ugly rack on his celestial face
> And from the forlorn world his visage hide,
> Stealing unseen to west with this disgrace.
>
> Even so my sun one early morn did shine
> With all-triumphant splendour on my brow;
> But out, alack! he was but one hour mine;

---

[20] AN: See Toulmin, Rachel Meoli. "Shakespeare ed Eliot nelle versioni di Eugenio Montale," *Belfagor*, vol. 26, no. 4, 1971, p. 467.

The region cloud hath mask'd him from me now.
Yet him for this my love no whit disdaineth;
Suns of the world may stain when heaven's sun staineth.

— *Eugenio Montale*
Spesso, a lusingar vette, vidi splendere
sovranamente l'occhio del mattino,
e baciar d'oro verdi prati, accendere
pallidi rivi d'alchimie divine.

Poi vili fumi alzarsi, intorbidata
d'un tratto quella celestiale fronte,
e fuggendo a occidente il desolato
mondo, l'astro celare il viso e l'onta.

Anch'io sul far del giorno ebbi il mio sole
e il suo trionfo mi brillò sul ciglio:
ma, ahimè, poté restarvi un'ora sola,

rapito dalle nubi in cui s'impiglia.
Pur non ne ho sdegno: bene può un terrestre
sole abbuiarsi, se è così il celeste.

— *Giuseppe Ungaretti*
Ho veduto più di un mattino in gloria
Con lo sguardo sovrano le vette lusingare,
Baciare d'aureo viso i verdi prati,
Con alchimia di paradiso tingere i rivi pallidi,

E poi a vili nuvole permettere
Di fluttuargli sul celestiale volto
Con osceni fumi sottraendolo all'universo orbato
Mentre verso ponente non visto scompariva, con la sua disgrazia.

Uguale l'astro mio brillò di primo giorno
Trionfando splendido sulla mia fronte;
Ma, ah! Non fu mio che per un'ora sola,

E dell'umano clima nubi già l'hanno a me mascherato.
Non l'ha in disdegno tuttavia il mio amore:
Astri terreni possono macchiarsi se il sole del cielo si macchia.

Both translators retain the fourteen-line sonnet structure, but Ungaretti, who seeks a complete semantic equivalent, allows the lines to balloon to an average of sixteen syllables and abandons the rhyme. His at times awkward interpolations of the Elizabethan English are contrasted by Montale's version, in regular hendecasyllables with a regular rhyme scheme (allowing for assonance), which yields an altogether more satisfying version of the sonnet and its meditation on the imperfections of love as metaphorized through images of solarity and clouds.

In addition to the above examples, let us recall Steiner's premise concerning "partial transmutations" (in his chapter "Topologies of Culture" discussed above). Examples of this hybrid practice are legion, but just limiting ourselves to the illustrious case of Dante, we could mention Pasolini's aborted 'rewrite' of the *Commedia*, *La divina Mimesis*; the theatrical *rifacimenti* of *Inferno*, *Purgatorio*, and *Paradiso*, by Edoardo Sanguineti, Mario Luzi and Giovanni Giudici; Louis Zukovsky's "Mantis," an imitation of Dante's use of the sestina; or Mary Jo Bang's versions of *Inferno* and *Purgatorio* in contemporary American vernacular. The spirit of these and many other poetic experiments in the larger "topological" field delineated by Steiner is captured by Octavio Paz's remarks about the *Renga* project he undertook with Sanguineti, Jacques Roubaud, and Charles Tomlinson when the four poets adopted the Japanese genre of a collective 'chain' of poems written and translated in four languages: "For us translation is transmutation, metaphor: a form of change and severance; a way, therefore, of ensuring the continuity of our past by transforming it in dialogue with other civilizations (an illusory continuity and dialogue: translation: transmutation: solipsism)" (Paz 18).

6. Conclusion

In this essay, I have addressed the "imperfect" and the "ideal" as intrinsic aspects of poetic translation. After a summary reading of key theorists, all of whom stress the need for the language of the poetic translator to be strongly impacted by the language of the source text, I described the sea change in poetry that began in the early 19th century with the debates concerning the classics and the desirability of the diffusion of major literary works across linguistic boundaries. I posited that the romantic era provided the substrate for the more radical overturning that occurred later in the 19th century when the stature of the poet in society and the bond between canonical poetry and linguistic norms began to erode, leading to a lapse in confidence in the established poetic language. This led to new problems and opportunities for translators, who stand as always at the fulcrum between language's development and its involvement in the most serious human questions of tension and conflict:

> In a very specific way, the translator 're-experiences' the evolution of language itself, the ambivalence of the relations between language and world, between 'languages' and 'worlds.' In every translation the creative, possibly fictive nature of these relations is tested. Thus translation is no specialized, secondary activity at the 'interface' between languages. It is the constant, necessary exemplification of the dialectical, at once welding and divisive nature of speech. (Steiner 246)

When the poets who anticipated the historic avant-gardes became active, they created a private language to counter the public language of ordinary discourse, which they see as hollow and bankrupt. By the same token, the 'private' language cannot exist without its 'public' counterpart as a reflective mirror, so when the translator approaches the most radically disruptive of texts, they will continue to make judgments about the beauty and merit of the work, its ethos and its reason.

Given poetry's semiotic density, material grounding in a single sign system, and its intention to transmit something universal, the theorist of poetic translation is necessarily led to consider the ontological nature of that art. The theoretical debates about the aims and strategies of translating poetry need not be settled; indeed, they cannot be settled programmatically. It is sufficient that the artful translator, who succeeds in integrating the oppositions between linguistic codes, historical periods, cultural intonations, and other factors, remain attuned to the affective language of poetry, the irradiations of its connotations, its self-similarity in form and theme, and its mystery.

Poetry

Mary Jo Bang

from *Romanzo in tre capitoli*
This Supposed Alchemy

What you took was: an arm, a hand, a face
 from an out-shining mirror.
We were carried away in the trunk of a hollowed year.
Not whole, never were, with skulls still amiss,
 draped windows through which one can't see.

And after the violent begin, the seeking:
 veil after unlifted veil, acolytes trailing behind, foot drag
and dream, while someone crooned some Gregorian.
The flock in the dove-cote asleep. *Nestle, my sweet,*
here beside me.

Love as lapsed, as indifferent. Moon as an end.
Appeasement turned bitter by cultured contempt.
Nestle, my sweet, here beside me. The hand opens
to show its new tooth. Can you believe?
In these arms you were once

a birthright eschewed, a Duchess of Windsor, a *Darling*.
The cheek will always be proffered, but the seam,
 it no longer meets.

The Year Chases Its Tail

When it's April in the eye, it's December elsewhere.
In the air, a sent satellite is traveling faster
than anyone ever expected, causing a state
of fret among flight controllers.

What is acceptable speed for crossing the bridge,
sliver of silver, between notions of gravity?
Windows allow the street to come through
in a city dressed for evening or earthquake.

Neon knocks, but refuses to enter.
Imagination is a yardstick, the sun its dead center.
Pitiful eye, inheritor of vain insistence, take heed.
The horse running by is not that of a different color.

It's the rider who changes:
Trade his orange and black satins (October is over)
for street clothes. He says, It's a marvelous thing
to be watched. The pleasure's enormous.

He says, We are each a megadose of our own making,
an almost in the off-and-running. In November,
a barrel of monkeys was dropped onto an unruffled incline.
By June, it had come to a halt.

Some called it time, others argued, compulsion.

In the Book of All That's Befallen

There were one hundred eighteen miniatures,
index and prologue, blue and vermillion,
all bound arabesque. A single edition, with a map

at the back: a mapamundi del Milenio
with five fish in a fountain, a forest
of fern taking root and cherries galore.

The text? Pure art,
part drawn with water, part taut repetition
with a twist of sediment, particles floating

on the surface like ice floes facing extinction
in the matte shadow of a hot four o' clock.
(Tom, it means twin don't you know?).

What train ride, she asked, can escape
what's befallen? What lark in a riverside park
can sing us up out of this pit?

Knowledge was knowing
what would behappen. The fire was a case of negligence
unleashing the literal

edge of a glacier, and ergo—the flood.
The air was thick with switches. She said, said she.
All had befallen, and someone was sobbing.

The Downstream Extremity of The Isle of Swans

In the window a jacket cried, *Wear me, wear me,*
on a street of tall houses, all showing teeth (ash white of ice rut,
of water on rock)—
many their eyes, all shaded by marmalade hoods. O cobra.

I was foreign then, living in a limited range.
Disavowal lodged here and there; everyone was saying:
I would never   I would never

> *In the distance was a sapphire city: part early invention,*
> *part aviary. Everything depended on perspective.*
> *A viper's tongue could upend such a place,*
> *a blown leaf could bury each and*

At night: opera wind raked through a field of hollow reeds,
the song of disquiet dogs from doomsday's third circle.
The raging distemper finally force me to breed
a new brand of silence.

(The singlet before it is distichous, doublet.)
We meet again, Moriarty, one said to the mirror in the morning.
One said to the friend on the street.

> *every embassy and chancellery, shop and legation.*
> *Gone. To what? A gash, a flat field.*
> *A field, as far as the eye could*

See how all that has been amended? Though nothing attenuates
the hour of late gray, spittled rain, slip chain and bolt,
the nights in a family of dreams: slaughter of heathen,
falcon-headed henchman.

What was you that I stood waiting for sky
to become chintz over swiss—dot after dot measuring an immense span
of glass—mouth tasting the burnt sun, the black sea.
Heart thumping behind its insensible hoof.

> *see. And who would know it had ever been?*

When Meeting Beauty

What must we do?
Nothing is clear, not since a vroom swept the sky
raising dust clouds, drizzling grit down to veil our small minds.
Something seen against a grave stone.
Something with a deadly center.
In this center of November, a dog bows its head and howls.
Leaves cling to the fence's faux diamonds.
What isn't dead is dying.
Everywhere the eye discovers fortune. Take it
on faith. A gray stone adhered to green lichen,

like the skull with its spare coat of reason.
A wall succumbs to its brick: at the brink, fourteen windows,
three tiers. It fascinates, this glass triangulation: sky, window
and which. Can you tell me, Marco Polo,
is this gray butter dish a bridge, or a narrow waterway?
A lock, or the long door behind which everything comes clean?
I need to know, if only as a forewarning
of weather. As a possible key
to the fore-court of heaven. *What* can be counted
upon? Now, back to the exhausted topic.

The Constant Bride

Do you understand the concept? The marvel? Tender at the neck,
shoulder at turn. Water freezes like this, bent and ready
to thaw. We are entering the realm of winter
 but this is the exciting, awful, now. Remember dancing?
Audacity's threat: that it could make us fall?

Both body and soul have been sewn strict to the lining,
seam to seam. Needle curved, minuscule stitch.
 Pearls furrow the bodice—hives adhered.
 Then there's the bangles, the serpentine
garter wrapping the calf. O decision,
with which word will *very* now link arms?

The bridal veil draped the bed. Worn it would turn
 to a rustle of besotted birds. That night, the mechanical
garden—the lych-gate, a hinged iris. And only one wish
from which to choose: sleep and may she never wake.

A Case of Asymmetry

In this case, the right eyes sees better than the left yet not enough
to rapture a glimpse of the Hudson gleaned between two trees
or to have augured what would come of this

telephone all, its curious kiss.
Last night,

an ice-cream dream where three flannel mice
 grew dauntingly larger and less and less gray.
 Morning was equally surreal, but life-like and fused.
Someone too free with her utterances stopping to ask, *You do believe me,
don't you, Dearie?*

Freud makes much of the mice and never forgetting.
*Man is mad as the body
is sick, by nature.*

Meanwhile passion's falcon refuses the wrist and dim hood
and takes to the forest instead
 in search of attachment equally morbid, muddled and cruel.

When the sun's hot on the face of two places, it's never an equal
divide. No and not was all she heard.

Poor eye, she said from the off-center door of her head.

The Mouth in Clarity

Is criminal to itself: add to silence the human
(not only the throat, anatomical suctions
and removals but the impulse

of a woman letting down her long hair,
 or a girl mourning in a glass of milk—
 tired the eyes, ragged the nails and chipped).

Tell me a story of a second-floor floor
 that couldn't be cleaner, a house that wouldn't fit
back in its box but succeeded in eating

its way to the edge of a lot.
The system is what we pay for, brown of burnt copper
coating the eave and a rococo wreath

ringing the circular window
 inside an untimely now. Coming back at the end
to an aisle of red-vested archers.

To wit, to woo. Certain, what does it mean?
To be most urgent, a moral generosity,
 a discarded modesty.

Leaping from the page to break into the heart
of a choice: dull love or love-
 ly opulence. O flamingo.

On This Late Stage

She said, It's true, my turtle dove, trucks do roll
 on the highway in the pie and tigers will imbibe
 their own stripes if thirst requites it.
 Re-belief is a tender trick but if you can *touch* the object,
can see the scarf that muffles the score of an engine
(and yes, yellow mean more than mere cowardice
although it's a cupboard color if ever there was one).

Now don't you believe the taxi man. The *Amalfi* doesn't really
mean *mafia*: we can eat any where you wish and we can drink
any little rivulet that washes our way. We're just fine
 living in an unlabeled box where the blond puffs her cheeks
on the beach of a truffle pig's ear and throws us
 a look every once in a vile. Doubtless, she thinks she knows us.
She knows us not at all.

The What Within

In this sober domain, the first girl's name was Cookie.
 The brune had no name now and wanted one. She went by
Honey. She went by my little lamb,
 she went by the last to enter the boat. She went by.
 It is not a deficiency. Not a coarse necessity. It's good, she said,
to enter a circular road. A festive occasion.
 The blond disputed nothing. She was old-fashioned. She had features.
But her tics were becoming unraveled.
Can such an assault be avoided and if so, how?

To get closer to sensation, the two women pressed against a third
possibility. Eidos. Certain things are undeniable:
 jug, axe, a pair of shoes—impenetrable, sufficiently hard,
elastic while firm. The blonde wore red
 shoes. Soles made of leather and the upper surface made of leather
cobbled by thread and nails. Glue. What will you preserve?
Only (see fig.) a simple something. A Simon.
Whatever we are at home with:
 Nearness. Exact determination. Strife.

The brune said, You have your norm. The blond felt she didn't,
not really. She had refusal, privation. She preserved the dis-
 of distance in two modes. She had deeds.
 But did she have direction? Did she have design?
I'm made of wood, she said, and warp.

Maria Grazia Calandrone

Translated by Nicholas Benson

(°) – seed

you have the fragility of an ear of wheat,
the muscles of a mare, the heat
of beaten sand
in your spine
and a plowing furrow,
the loneliness of a holy beast in the far
right corner of your mouth, where a newborn
intelligence grazes you
almost without awakening you

put your finger in the furrow of your heart, point to me

you discover your crease where my blood
drops on the forest of symbols, and in sleep may some kind
of love
spill over
onto the objects surrounding

    (whatever exceeds
the limits of the body activates
between the electric ligaments of the world
like the burning
of everything neutral – the beginning
of anonymity – it leans all its weight
on the Foreign Land of your body – *please
don't say it – close your mouth*)

because your right eye brushes the water
of a buried sea
                       – deep
bramble and crown,
seed of
an unknown
species –
            silent as bronze out in the open, walk
in the now
as in a temple, as in memory –
                         until from the depths,
from the theater of the sea
an adult creature rises,
unarmed, believing in your mercy

5.23.13

© – fossil

put a hand here like a white blindfold, close my eyes,
fill the threshold with blessings, once
you've passed through
the green gold of the iris
like a queen bee
and – straw
upon straw,
of gold and threshed wheat –
you've made me
your honeycomb of light

a constellation of bees swarms on the linden
with inhuman wisdom, a whirlwind of intelligences doesn't leave
the honey tree
                – it would be reductive to call love
this necessity of nature –

                    while an anterior void heals
between flower and flower, leaving no trace:

                                use your mouth, pull from my heart
the golden stinger,
memory of a flash that seared my human form
in some prehistory

where the mad caress stones like they were children's heads:
                            come closer, like the first
among lost things
and that face rises from stone to smile again

5.24.13

○ – clearing

scent of wild honey
when you awaken to the sound of the shaker
like horse and woman combined, throughout
                a silent damnation: a beauty
simple and without sacrifice – shedding
of honeydew and lymph, out in the open –
                with sunburned shoulders, you say
I am immortal
        and all around there is light
like water inhabited by a biological entity
red and flickering
        a vein that, rapid on the neck
                      is pushed
                              from the deep
drum of blood

the whole earth imitates the word, adjusts to the secret confidence of man,
bends the bushes
on the border of the field, so they resemble a human face

when laughter spills into tears, and tears into a fleeting
look that contains
in itself all the forsaken ones

       what perfect dominion over the clouds and what memory
life has: *now*
that it contains you, it attains particular unsayable strength
because it let everything go, and
your face,
so alone

within, embodies
the human type, shines
in the void like a golden coat of arms, as one praises, in the fire of the clearing,
the ferocity of the sun, all this rebirth
                             now
               a white technique of rising up
something like watching you lift
                    – radiant
and undone –
               from the cursed fields,
               to no longer have a name,

serious as a mass of splendor, saying
               I'm already singing – can't you hear me?

5.30.13

Ω – throne of the sun

love
       – hieroglyph
and sprout –
             you occur:
                    you cross
the threshold, barefoot

and without will – and the more
you unexpectedly arrive, the more you burst and transform
memory in the Present,
carrying within yourself the theater of distance – and so

> it's June:
> a dark power

is stamping its hoof, touching infected painful areas, and other
usual feelings

> (it's so serious and sweet
> and doesn't hurt, and stays all night
> bent over the dark red of your organs, prepares the furrows
> where it will sow

joy+joy, joy² = to approve

the splendor of the constellation, intently
blowing it over the surface of the world like the silence in a quarry):
> what bloodshed
on human heat, like fireflies on the countryside
at night, razed by the planetary wind:
> *open your eyes* – I tell you – *and make me miss you,*
inscribe
with the golden ink of your gaze the bulb
of my eyes, make them flower
the broom's tongue
of fire, after
we've lived
> – alone
as stars – the ephemeral
grace of a world fated to end
> (on the shore, a reed bed worn down
> by the smoothing wave of the Nile)
> with the stone of the heart
hidden: what
opened the curtain, what face

appears again, unexpected and already
discerned as
indispensable, from the rugged scenery of the rocks
and brambles

and suddenly drags across the earth
all the emptiness of the sky, all the hard

work of the heart, acute as a spring fever, ascensional like this prehistory
ossified now
so close you can brush it
with your lips, the origin
of the world, this dry matter
free of death, clean
as the root
and like the root, intensely
founded
in
the future

6.1.13

* – reborn, without an I

I recognize your white flank, your black animal beauty, I loosen all your living
filaments

                                                      so that

you are entirely new, you shine in the grass like an apple
just created – you are the light of dawn and you are the apple
and the simple act of plowing:
                       male, female, shadow:
                             I recognize, here,
on the lips, the exact point of the interruption – you feel

                    the nostalgia of the prey outside
          the moist chewing of your mouth, covered with gold
                      and salt from the deep

and, to the right, the lightning bolt, the split, something like
                              a cry: *on the eyes*

I bear the weight of all this sky
rough and grave, of late spring,
                I have the pain of having reigned
over a forsaken kingdom

            – so the Edenic monkey
                              leaves
                                        – for you –
                                                  separates

from the botanic strength
of the forest, grows from the horizon
out in the open –
              reinforced
              and exposed, it plucks
                              from the air the honeyed fruits
of words,
          weaves the bridge of rejoining, not
for any purpose
but to make that rejoining possible:
                    word

after word, he forges the spear of your fulfillment, he fine-tunes you like shipyard
gear under the millstone of the sun
and the black vectors of wings: swallows awakening
over the boat /
              / slip, against shoulders of white concrete, dense
                                        with nets (within

flickers the silvery *catch*, a harvest of uranium and pallor,
of platonic sirens)

the animal rages, does not yield,
does not concede, it glows,

it hammers, melts: it is manufacturing, it is karst, it desires
to deliver you – word upon word – the world
entirely split by your eruption, subdued and shaken by the heel
of the demigod, it desires

to put in the palm of your hand
like a red apple, the fiery beauty
of *this* world
dripping with heaven's amnion, it keeps saying:
                take it, it was always yours

6.5.13

Θ – for dawn

my soul is a human god,
        a bird of the heights
that every night nests in the clear
of your chest
like a perfect hendecasyllable
    (thing) white and ample, a slender wing – rose
    and bramble, ash – *parva*
    among profuse stars,
         white blood
of tubular sponge
in the white planetarium, white tiger
sitting by the side of the white road free from pain

my soul grows from your bones
like a rose from a living tongue
   – in drops,
      in gushes
        – from your unimaginable
            alphabet

but it is from this body,
from its silent harvest
that the word comes,

this absolute bread
that I offer you, this living
beauty, made for you

6.6.13

α – **aurora sickness**

                in what white noise, on the surface of what altar,
                                    in what profanation

you deposit the unknown value of the body
constricted
by the snow – equinoctial
body,

        numinous – a thought
        thing –

        – α (alpha) –

                      – prime number – thing

supple and soaked,
earthly genius,
earthly step of a bird
swoon, thing
that happens without will,
brown root of star and wolf
under the apple tree

                (if we love him, he will become docile *)

a dog nose
sniffed out
what's left
of the lost body

      in the folds of the world, in what rumble
      under the earth
      hatched the same root

                                      and grew

      so much in the sun, and ended up in my hand

              I climb the Cartesian axis of a cherry tree laden with fruit,
                        pull down the sun in a blue water
                            of irregular vastness,
                    from the midnight blue chalice
                      of the gentians
                        I lift

an adult heart

without a claim,
              something
                        that decided
to tend
            always
                      to your amazement

6.14.13

☼ – nihil umbra

when you tilt your head toward your shoulder
you expose the radial parabola
of your neck
to the summer afternoon light, which limns with gold filigree
evidence of your hips

and your arms,
        bright in the spiritual
                lime of the sun,

                  high above the phosphor of the grass,
in the air they write a word never before conceived, an alphabet made to unfurl
in this afternoon canticle

naked and simple, you draw
the chemical force of your hands
to the muscles of the chest, almost to the heart
                                      – and the open
                                              body

drips albumen, a secret
communication of stars,
antral fluid sweet as apple

in common you have the smile, the deep
odor of absolute
dawn, virgin honey and milk
that foams
from the living body
after the silence of reproduction

                  and the adductors tremble
                      like grass in a breeze
and you are reborn secret as the flower of the linden where I am reborn, now
that the roots
below us drink the warmth of new life

                I who thought I knew everything and didn't know anything
                            about this love
on the threshold, you have the light
at heart level, dawn
bride, made of pure air, with your
                      whole body you say *behold, no longer do the dead*

return, I am as simple as love, I
       am here
       and transparent: present and alive as life

       9.15.13

on water-lilies

and it goes on, goes on
as if it were flesh, but it is dream matter that inclines
over my body,
                hair
in slight disorder, puts numbers on my mouth and numbers
are the form of its beauty

                      you were here with your real mouth, dark
                          as a wild blackberry
                          and I was a desert
                              slaked
                      by wounds in the living flesh
                      and the berry of the heart
                            dripped
                          bitter honey

oh! continue—continue
from the instant of the tear, come as though descending stairs, as though no longer afraid

                my love is a membrane that adheres to the liquid
                    sound of the matter that you are, to your voice,
                        which is a vibration of childhood
                            strings and echoes
                                in the rib cage
                        so close to the heartbeat
                    of a mother, to the pancreatic fluid
              dissolving sugars behind the tissue of the abdomen
                while you smile like a little secret blessing

start over, from where
you stopped, then
get up!
like a strip of wind up high causing
a procession of bright clouds, rise like a true sister, take me away

from the parched cries
of the monkeys
and the thirst of beasts forsaken
in their fur, away from the disaster
of falling aslumber
without waiting for sunrise, no longer waiting

1.20.14

Ϋ – tree, fossil

you will be fed
well, all through
your life, with the fruit
of an ancient apple. in a future April, you will rise
with your spine fed
by a new lymph,
you will remember the sweetness of the tree that did not want to die, and revived, and blossomed again, every time
you cut it down. you will turn back
your head, you will stretch out your hand, the beautiful hand that with such tenderness caressed
the open branches of the apple tree
and you will eat. then I will return to your mouth with the weightlessness of light. and again,
in the white heat of our summer time, you will eat
the apple found
on the bottom of time, the fruit plump and red
as an artery, flowing
from my life to your life,
but far away, down below, where reason can not reach,
in implacable places. forget
the tree. don't think about anything any longer, puff me away. let only life remain for your life,

8.24.14

Vincenzo Frungillo

Translated by Christina Vani

from *Every Five Strokes. A Five-Canto Poem*

Canto 1
Sequence I
Ute's Promise

The time of memory drips from the foot
in regular circles of water and chlorine
Ute reopens the space of history.
Tired, at the edge of the pool, she recalls those
who showed her the way,
the escape route from poverty, yelling all together,
in a burst of joy, "pushing with our arms
we will tear down this titanic cage!"

They shouted loudly at the red spray
on the primordial bricks of the highest wall;
she, still a child, burdened herself with that yell
and chose to take on the hardest task:
"I'll save these voices from the stench of piss – I can! –
I'll take them with me to a place that is free and safe,
I'll make their body out of my own,
I'll make their flight out of my gestures!"

Free from the bias of those who are in the wrong
she now swims in the blue water of the pool,
transparent to herself, in her sharp-edged strokes
on the surface that shines like hoarfrost,

she listens to the splashes of the water she cuts
and measures the rhythm of life on her temple.
No defeat now, no victory, her life story, she decides,
will be measured in hundredths of a second.

Ute knows she is the best and keeps training,
without pause, three hours in the morning and three
at night, her body grows, adapting to the strain,
and each day the shape that was slight and bony
under the pale blond of sorrow changes.
What doesn't disappear from under her eyes
is the look of a girl who burns slowly when alone
and watches others who chat and do not train.

Ute is strict with those who stay on dry land
and don't understand the need for a flipper hand,
of those who seize the water's resistance beneath their chests,
she is strict with herself and thus she strives
against the unmoving randomness of her land.
She feels alien but decisive against the masses who threaten her.
Ute is the blue proof of a pledge,
the liquid crystal body of a champion.

Sequence II
Lampe and the Team

Lust for victory gets stronger in the team
the only comradery she is allowed to claim,
in the relay she takes turn with those who share
her own euphoria. Lampe who's got something unknown
to Ute, the linear joy of life, the stimulus of glory.
Lampe is the apple of everyone's eye,
Ute's not the only one to notice the brightness
of her skin, its rebellious and aggressive elasticity,

while she watches her fly above her head:
taut are the muscles of her perfect thigh
when she enters the water and after a quarter
of a lap, stops to begin the butterfly stretch
and her back stands out erect amongst the curved
arms and the crest of pale-blue foam.
Life lingers sometime out of the water
but it quickly disappears and Ute feels done in.

In her eyes, Lampe is never passive
when she talks with another teammate
or when she laughs without an alibi and secretly
comes back to herself, to the bathing suit that soaks her
—she pulls it aside to let out the air—and then, unhurriedly
to the locker room and her patient chaperon.
Lampe is like water, her absence pressing,
her intensity, sweet and unreachable.

It is only silence that complains,
in the empty awning echo the screams
for her who has no one calling her,
in the small water vortices, in the moistened air
the day re-weaves its plot. Those who remain
endure the weight of challenge, having to feel again
on their tongues and in their noses the fear
and the anxiety of those who do not wish to exit.

The buildings house the days and the days and the days
of faces, lights, advertisements
recorded on the *Strassenbahn*, napes and returns
stations with pillars and garbage (and you who refuse to give up)
shutters pulled down on the clothing shops and the outlines
of dirty snow (and you who pronounce
with your eyes as if they were close friends)
"in this neighborhood even shop dummies are alienated."

Canto 2
Sequence I
Generation

On both sides of the sun there vestiges
of other worlds, like satellites, suggestions,
directions drawn from uncovered rays
—"the silences of fathers will be visited on their children" —
prophesied her paternal grandparents
in the afternoon, the perpetual yawns,
when a veil over the pupil
hides from everyone that which shines.

A whore noticed his white hair
she was the first, while riding him,
with tired eyes she told him
"here on your temple. Do you want me to cover it?"
She pushed harder with her hips
avoiding all words,
she wanted to silence him,
make him nameless. He climaxed.

His memory is vast as his pain,
a failure in his repression,
all is viewed with the eyes of lethargy
and he pours water at the nation's feet.
Swears on his honor,
repeating it is his opinion,
saying he belongs to the social body,
without feeling any symptoms of it in his flesh.

Through blue-collared metaphors
he enunciates prophetic theories,
speaks of rules as if they were crash doors,
for the masses are always hysterical
and can be juggled around reminding them sadistically
of the nuclear threat, the psychic blackmail,

urging people to escape from themselves
and put the Party in control of the gates.

Such emptiness captured him, kept him at bay,
involved him in one too many discussions,
where no one offers the sympathy of a hand,
but merely the reverberations of the sounds
uttered by a man who has lost his mind.
He repeats "History is like thunderbolts,
sudden bursts brightening the sky
and the darkness following those bright veils."

Sequence III
Renate's Body

Renate sees him, seated on his stomach,
the imperturbable air of an absentee,
one who swallows his own history while
singing the loser's national anthem,
and collects one by one his forevers.
His head, like a weeping willow,
falls into a pond of arms that capture quiet,
"this is the tomb of the hero, his Lethe."

The Nazis chose grooves in the rocks
for their Aryan rituals, they slept in them for hours,
my arms is all I have,
look, Renate, how porous
the banks of this sea, spreading like a stain,
I could drown in it!" His postures
are proof of a deeper silence,
the promise of a new pain.

Her father swings from hysterical laughter
that fills the eye with a tear,
to the sternness of a sermon,

against the regime of absence: "Once
Germany's body was shaped like a sphere,
flowing as in a rhyme.
The law of the nation was its plenitude,
everything plotted to make us skin and bones"

Captured in some form of warmth
she sees herself in the crowd wearing
nothing, covered only by her blushing:
"Us, we are a patient race
though we live by counting hours
and love our nothing.
In time of piece this is the only way
to build a regime: we must vanish."

Thus, his prophecy was never dismissed
nor did Renate cease to feel naked,
she was also visited by the police
and asked about her father, his escape.
She whispered, "I am not a spy,"
and it was as if she had not spoken.
Her father was never found
and any material evidence disappeared with him.

Sequence IV
The Confession

"My father would blow into his cupped hands
and rip off the skin from his mouth.
They said he felt some kind of anxiety for the future
that sooner or later depression strikes everyone
if you spend your life watching the shadow that eats sofas,
if you keep watching how its space overflows.
My father, however, tried to,
he would always say that he would leave.

He would say so spitting venom, to my mother,
returning from his night shift,
he used to bring home sugar cubes, neatly arranged,
with on top, every time, the face of a different animal
then he stopped laughing, my father,
he started to be ill,
twice they caught him curled up
like an old rag in barbed wire.

He did not apologize, he did not cry,
he just kept staring at the ceiling like a boy.
At times, he talked about his father, of how
he had suffered seeing him die, stricken
by the same illness, yet he had not cried,
he thought only that he had not been defeated,
that it wasn't true, that his father was a legend,
his father was as strong as a rock!

Then one day he began to use my hand
like the valves of an imaginary solfeggio
or like an ancient Roman's accounting boards,
he let the days drop like the grains of an almanac
between his fingertips and the back of my hand.
He counted, he counted, fearless,
tightening his lips between his teeth,
and patiently complied with the losers' lot.

My father passed away, faded and thin,
without an illness to speak of, he died
without screaming, exhausted, tightening
his fist in mine, determined, it might be
that my father has run away, someone said
that it is as if he killed himself, leaving me
alone with a great remorse, that's why, when
I compete, I squeeze my lips between my teeth."

Canto 3
Sequence II
Competing

Renate tightens her lips, she is the most determined,
and thrusts her chin beneath her knees,
ready for the initial stretch,
she dives curving her body in mid-air, springing
—tension embalms the stale swimming pool—
then she stretches out as a true backstroke swimmer
and spies in the air her point of gravity,
then make the turn toward victory.

A touch and she senses above her the flight of the breaststroker,
the yells of the crowd reverberate in the water,
she is in the lead!, but Karla is already in the spotlight,
she gathers basins of water between her legs, rolls
her limbs while giving power to her trunk peeping at the track,
no one's close! Moves her arms in semicircles and plunges
under water, extended like an eel,
she turns, rises, dives back in, and shines at her finish line.

A touch and the butterfly soars and rises
and arranges the lap around her hips,
Lampe swells like a powerful wave, clean,
she sinks her wing that act like a hook
when she harpoons the watery mass and hurriedly
relinquishes it to make room for the dolphin kick,
a perfect synthesis that becomes harmony
when she turns and heads for her finish line.

A touch and Ute is free to spread her arms
to loosen her shoulder, break with her hand the straight line
grab time in a clamp of air
in her lungs, her mouth, in the squeeze
of her chest and elbow, to grab history,
for a fraction of a second in the rush

of her embrace all faces wait patiently,
suspended they find shelter beyond deadlines.

Ute is free, at long last free
to see her friends in turmoil at the edge of the pool
celebrating the breaker of their mold,
the figure who only lived once
in another world, another era
as though her were not the same heavenly dome
enfolding the stands and the pool, as if she didn't have to walk
on earth, and to arrive first was not a must.

***

During the 1980 Olympics in Moscow, the women's swimming team of the DDR amazed the world on a count of the impossible records they established and the young age of their athletes. The bodies of these young girls had something mythical about them: they were a synthesis of masculine strength and feminine harmony; they were the face communism wanted to show the world; they were aliens. Their triumphs were striking and mysterious. In the West, no one knew anything about their training. The girls remained locked behind the Curtain. Just as soon as they appeared, they disappeared with the end of an era and with the turmoil of the 1989 revolution. Only recently have they re-emerged. Their silhouettes had drastically changed; they were as unrecognizable as their country, which extended without borders in the middle of Europe. With their swollen faces and bull-like chests, they told about the strange blue pills that they had to ingest every morning before training; they talked about the color that had served as the backdrop of their lives—the melancholy, the pool, and the steroids, all of the same shade. The swimmers from the east were History's surplus. This epic poem is inspired by the experiences of these champions, gives them names, retraces the chemical dosage of their victories, and acknowledges the irresponsible behavior but, at the same time, affirms the impossibility of exhibiting sufficient evidence to explain the mystery of those teens' life.

from The Pauses of the Evolutionary Series

7.
Today I'm waking up later than usual
and ask myself if all of this is true,
if the present state still exists,
if there is room for its kingdom,

for the voices of the masons
that build scaffoldings in the sky,
if each of their actions is not a way
to quiet the dogs that I dreamt about,

and I ask myself if the animals—
if it's true that dogs
have no memory,

if it's true that they don't suffer,
do not feel pain,
like people who can't remember their dreams.

8.
They leave the seats of their trips
like live nerves from rotten teeth,
they sport messy hair on their heads
like a wrinkle that betrays their sleepiness.
It is theirs and it is the foreign hairdo
of people who know what it's like to move,
the crossroads from which every accent is born.
They take note of the wind,

because it is impossible to stop it,
hold it back, they blow it out rather
in a gust of ice, in the space of a countenance,

disappearing, each day,
at dawn, once again,
in the yawn of the world.

10.
Now I live where the elephants lie.
There, behind the chimney stacks, amongst the bales of iron,
you can find their cemetery;
their rib cages still swollen with breath.

There are carts that climb slowly,
they carry coal to the sky,
from their odor you can smell how black it is.
A worker walks toward me, shakes my hand,

says that he fell down on the job
—ghosts have the soft fingers of doubt
like people greeting without wanting to—

he is the custodian of this place,
he makes sure that no one touches the ivory,
says that I'm the only one allowed to see it now.

11.
You bequest the barest instinct,
little trifling things, the newspaper typos,
to those who still believe in emendation
and you stare at the horizon,

its belly pregnant with waves;
you stand on the sandbar, a sole stares at you,
nature stays mute, everything around retreats
with the breathing undertow.

"Come back, come back."
Someone shouts from the shore,
but you know the tide is coming,

that your final challenge is
to regain volume, rise up to the surface,
see the end again.

12.
Now that mornings have turned white,
they leave the sting of nighttime,
now that we might be able to widen the shadow,
we go back to the usual agreement.

It was Rilke who said,
"I'm not interested at all to be right."
Reality does not gather these pearls,
they remain virginal like pebbles on a grave.

"Burn down what remains,"
someone responded,
"burn down the Great Wall of China as well."

Because one day there will be no border
between those who attack and those who defend themselves.
Prehistory includes us.

Disappearing

1.
The bend in the coast has only now reached
Its perfection, now that the waters are retreating,
the natural apex of destruction.
Maybe you heard about it,

observing the opalescence of pebbles at the shoreline,
that was the first revelation.
Then came the Manneristic attempt
to enclose the strength in the basin of a pool.

You opposed a life that was too exposed
to emptiness's meek cause,
pressure versus pressure,

or the idea and its dispersion.
All this from infancy to the present day,
all this as its shape.

3.
If these stones could feel pity
for my wounds, I would be right,
as an animal amongst other creatures,
for the accent you notice, the pain,

it is only memory deteriorating
and, just think about it, it is worthless.
Now, my way to speak up
is a wheeze that doesn't belong to me,

that distracts me from my heart beat.
And you, too, on the other side,
will resign yourself to the power erupting

in the final moment of the hunt,
from the prey that does not hide,
that is no longer extant on the face of the earth.

(Second Part)
The End of Lucretius

To end is not leaving life,
it is forever staying
in its climatic scene,
a weakness of sight,
which we do not choose but simply endure,
and can be seen only by those who know how to look
at our mortal wound.
The pause in the vertical collapse
bents every discovery to an external light,
the spiderweb behind the door,

and the spider, hypnotized by its prey,
they obey a single rule.
The light, I mean, the light,
is the apex of the species,
and light is not a natural source,
though it is the eye that sees
the nebula of ash over the crater,
and it is the word of the poet
that captures every particle of it.
It would be moon dust
without the sound of his voice.
It is that word that unveils
the origin, the atom hesitating
before the fall, that sees the void
and the elementary shaping of the mortal
crossroad, Heracles' doubt,
the Y of the decision;
it gives power to that sling,
and pain to that cross.
The sublime is precision.
But now, what will I have to say,
what will I have to tell,
how to reveal the sublime,
the iridescence of the clinamen?
After seeing the view,
I can only remain silent.
The raw material is the cloth
that dries the poet's tears,
this fabric of parchment
translates the song of the cicadas
from the hollow of their larvae,
when, at the foot of the olive trees
everything becomes peace: death
is right there, but the buzzing
of their wings resumes.
Knowing you are constant mutation
beyond caste separation,

although the world,
orphan of the sublime,
sees everything deprived of its end.
It draws a sphere on paper,
eats into its shape,
matter loses blood,
this atom hopes
for a fission that is not happening.
God is silent. Acknowledging his absence
is the winning proof!
No one is forced to educate
this gentle rain,
to know that it has been saved from the swamp
of streets while the ash
threatens to fossilize
the brothel: an eternal cast.
Now I feel matter growing,
under the tip of the ballpoint pen,
I feel the word scratching the parchment,
a concrete semiosis reawakens.
Indeed there's no exit from life
that is not as well an entry
into the mortal fold of the clinamen.
From the noise in the streets,
a single voice arises,
the octopus hangs from the canes,
its sucker brings
the littoral onto dry land,
the shoreline touches the town,
a vendor sells fresh eggs,
the nucleus is suspended in its albumen,
analogy pervades us.
Hen, flesh, lubrication
of the vagina attracting the erected cock
into its ovaries the semen,
the patient uterus awaits
—the rooster is born not of an egg

not of a hen, but out of pleasure,
out of a moment of suspension.
Venereal influence of the species
the wound generates milk and urine,
it infects our Latin soul.
Beauty, certainty of a life lived
on the edge, to be a poet is to climb rearward
to the goddess' temple, the Etruscan Venus,
mistress of the carnival, who gives not away a single measure,
entrusts each body its own downfall.

Memmius, my son,
my only disciple,
my only counsel,
before all others you understood,
the message is all yours,
in the teacher's house
you destroyed the peripaton,
the garden devastated
by your youthful hands.
You will not hear their chatter
growing in your chest,
like larvae of flies
causing my look to age.

One
is the rule,
but the measure varies,
bodies return to the source,
then, repulsed, they distance themselves from it,
likewise the stars, and the light, and the sun
repeat the revolution, the fundamental principal of all generation
and though the volcano would eventually prove me right,
only ash and destruction will surround us,
I don't wish to share Empedocles' end,
but a life worthy of Hyperion.
As there is only one rule,

         and only one source
            look, Memmius,
               the sun.

Rosmarie Waldrop

Object Relations

How differently our words drift across danger or rush toward a lover. Meaning married to always different coordinates. I married a foreigner, in one sense. In another, no word fits with another.

Your smile breaks from any point of your body. I need a more complicated picture. This falls among crow's-feet and bears no fruit. What did it try? Replace your body?

My doubts stand in a circle around us. Like visitors around the well under the house. They advise to board it up. Dampness unhinges. And decay of fish.

It would mean all night. Hands scraped on rough surmise. Remembering I too am a monster.

The objective character of statements has shifted to relations. Boiling water and the length of a column of mercury? Or that you mean me when you say "you"?

When I say "we were standing close" am I saying: we were not touching? To replace a laugh. Which could be described as: wish, yellowfish, fish.

What if there is no well? What if language is not communication? If facts refuse coordinates? Detachment vanishes, as if thinned.

Meaning you consists in thinking of your body. There are no fish in my mouth.

We Will Always Ask, What Happened?

Imagine a witch in the form of a naked girl. Now say her name. Is it foreign? Was the idea of the witch complete before you named the girl? Did you go down a passage that does not exist toward a well of dark water?

Your mind makes small rudimentary motions. Because the joke is against it? Because it does not know which way to turn and keeps reviewing the field of possible actions? Aches? Actresses?

I hear you sighing. Intention is neither an emotion nor yet lip-synch of longing. It is not a state of consciousness. It does not have genuine duration. I say, are you alright? Can you have an intention intermittently? abandon it like a soldier paralyzed the moment before battle? and resume it?

Could I order you to understand this sentence? just as could tell you to run forward? into the fire?

Would the understanding cast a shadow on the wall even though a premonition is not a bullet hole?

One symptom is that space is forced into a mirror. As if the event stood in readiness behind the silver. You move your hand, and it goes the other way. Then the earth opens up and you slide down your darkest desires.

Witches were killed by fire, by water, by hanging in air, burying in earth, by asphyxiation, penetration, striking, piercing, crushing in a thousand and one ways.

What was the name you gave her?

Isomorphic Fields

Thinking is not an accompaniment. The fluttering of eyes and long pauses of lovers. Your attention wanders with your hands.

Unhinges the confines, and your name, trembling slightly, turns membrane. No other space permits such a glow from under the skin. As in Florentine painting?

If my idea of thinking is modeled on breath does it imply opening my lips? Moving with the wind?

We lean toward each other and don't know what will come of it. Like an electric charge? The pull is toward loss of balance. The word "pull" already throws its shadow toward other uses, other possible attachments.

If you do not look at your feet you begin to sway. As in a gale? So while I push my image toward marriage, you stand with your legs apart and wear dark glasses.

My image, on its way to the thalamus, gives off branches forming a net. For further entanglement?

A high wind of thought? Particles with velocity but no location? Or is that geometry itself is altered next to a warm body?

The way you seem to hover above your seat. Like a hummingbird? And our gestures remain hanging, careless of the fact that visual evidence compels belief.

Is love impossible where we are in it? Do we hope it might be? Am I using words to say something quite different?

Intentionalities

My hand moves along your thigh. When we describe intentions, is the ventriloquist taken over by the dummy? Or pretending to be a ghost?

Instead of "I meant you," I could say, "We walked through wet streets, toward a dark well." But could I speak of you this way? And why does it sound wrong to say "I meant you by pulling away?" Like lovers caught in headlights?

If I talk of you it connects me to you. By an infinite of betweens, not by touching you in the dark. Touch is the sense I place outside myself for you to ride.

When I mean you I may show it – if we stand close – by putting my head on your shoulder. You can show you understand by describing the well under the trap door. What will you say? Don't be frightened?

The feeling I have when I mean you draws an arc of strength between my hips and the small of my back. It doesn't follow that "meaning you" is being exhilarated by terror. Of course not, you say: We need a red thread to run through, but it's entangled with space, form, future. Is this true?

It would be wrong to say that meaning you stands for a forgotten part of myself, a treatise on labyrinths, a path leading nowhere. Am I living in a shell where the sea comes in along with its sound? And drowns us?

I was speaking of you because I wanted to think about you. "I wanted" does not describe a general before battle. Nor, on the other hand, a ship heading for shipwreck. There is no way to decide whatever this is an autobiography or a manifesto.

Enhanced Density

Should it worry me that thought, in my sentences, seems never wholly present at any one moment? Let alone love, in my life? Even my skin has no precise shape, that is unless touched. By clothes?

There seems a brownish mist under construction. From forest fires?

My feeling for you seems to flow (like traffic?) under my skin. I want it to break through the pores and touch you. Inflict wounds so small you don't know what's killing you?

The way a word can pierce? Because of the use it has had in your life? Because it comes out of a deep well? Because war follows the opening of mouths?

You are never in front of me, like an object. And if I try to hold you sideways the melody slips away leaving a single note. Like a reflection in a shifting mirror? A phoneme escaping between the sutures of my accent?

What can I do but let my thoughts roam in the field around a word. The way desire roams through my body? It's called the meaning of the word because we cannot touch the groundwater in any other way.

Are we making an object when we make love? Do we hope it'll stay in front of us and allow us to observe it?

It may not be enough to look at a surface I love. Or parts adjacent.

from *Slowing Perceptions*
Photo
for Alan Lebowitz

definitions
abbreviate your face

you walk into abandoned

reasons
directly, driftwood
some trick of the current

eyes strange
like natural processes

openwork

between balance and precarious
a dancer
off a step

Time Ravel

1

With the mind's eye. We see against the light. The way we see the dead. My father reading at his desk. Read, road, door. Remains unclear how my brain chose to store this image rather than another. Or how it veers toward the surface. Ulysses fights his way back to an Ithaca with four-lane highways. Where serfdom has been replaced by alienation, anomie, anxiety. Returns, reverts, replies. A borrowed book, the sword to its scabbard, in recompense, response.

2

The assumption is that the sirens have drowned in the alphabet. And been replaced by warnings, war, warp. My father's stopped reading to watch a magpie rising black and white against the sky. Memories are many. Glitter in the brain, ready to be pilfered. Does this fit my image of the real? Where the norms of social interaction have multiplied, and spontaneous acts come back as mistake? Or combustion? Natural feeling, temperament, disposition, impulse, energy all lashed fast to the mast. The rubrics of the dictionary meaning business.

3

The crew were afraid they would not come back, unable to close the loop time won't permit, but sometimes a ghost or shifting winds. Or the memory of a big slab of ice that a man with leather mittens splits across the middle. To reveal the time hidden within where I might not find my body for the cold. And though my mother wraps the slab in a rag before putting it in the icebox, it would not warm me enough to have a self. Same, identical. Interest, confidence, esteem, reliance, respect. Skin, though it takes pains to remember caresses, is marked by the roads that pain takes.

4

Color of fables, the Indies, scarves, curves. Every island Columbus found was a vow kept toward a map with no elsewhere. High spirits and cloud theory reflect in the sea and stitch coordinates toward a flight of gulls, of stairs. America becomes a continent while numbers pass through the air, soar out of bounds. Or run from danger, flicker of fear. How can I remember my parents if I need to run my hands over my body to make sure it is there. Or lean forward to brace against *our element*, deflect its head-on force into a more general time. Where God for love of us wears clothes.

5

I can't hear my father's voice, moored as if among antipodes, articulation hindered by head hanging down and a spill of oceans. Spell, sperm, spatter, splash. If the mechanisms of subjectivity are disturbed it requires total restructuring of the world. As when I first learned that the earth turns on its axis, that spleen, n., is a highly vascular ductless gland which serves to produce certain changes in the blood. Merriment (obs.), caprice, spite, anger, malice, moroseness, melancholy. Most marked in complex civilizations where the pace of events and cordless voice exceeds all the running one can do just to stay in one place. Though silver, on clear days, is the light.

6

In haste we now blast ourselves beyond the clouds, and get lost in skies behind the sky. It's hard to rescue time from such a sight. And though they cast a shadow, perspective has no power over clouds. "Bodies without surface," they vanish the moment before the move into abstraction. The way my mother's large body evaporates before I can ask her to show me the breast I did not take. Columbus, though, Magellan, Vasco, in the name of Christ and King took firm hold of new markets. A mirror for a parrot, scissors for cinnamon, a playing card for a girl naked to the waist, a kingdom for a horse. And dust in everyone's eyes for private purchase and sale. What does it mean to recall the past if I have little sense of the present?

7

Names multiplied in the wake of caravels, clippers, communicating vessels. The spelling capricious (see spleen) as the winds. Track itineraries, track vanished and erased, track how many pages between Circe's island and Charybdis. It is not that our sensations need to match images in the brain, but that the brain needs a body for frame of reference. No matter if it be square or cant, short, squat, parts fitted together to enclose a window, door, picture or disposition of the mind. Just as emotion shows if we're ready for the future hovering at the edge of our eye.

8
Great beginnings too can end up a small world. Whorl, old. Set sail on the power of imagination for hearsay geographies and real dangers. With greed as secret motor. It drove them back home to cities crazy for spices and gold. In between, waves and more waves. When I think of my mother I am heavy in the pelvis with the children she wanted, and begin to sing. A complex song of if and though I never had a voice. To introduce an exclamation, condition, stipulation, untenable argument, or wish. On condition, in the event that, allowing that these long-term memories are abstractions, a different mode of thought from short-term ones. And that their differences shape my sense of time. A violet's blue as a sign of distance.

from *Driven to Abstraction*
The One Who Counts, Who Paints, Who Buys and Sells
ZERO, THE CORROSIVE NUMBER
Impossible. Without the idea of counting. To imagine numbers. Repeating an identical act, a particular mark. Over and over.

Like languages that express a plural by repeating the singular. Or a man with a woman, and another, and a third, a fourth.

"Etc." prolongs its shadow, its mathematical imperative. The idea that ceaselessly. A string of beads. Of follies. Of particles. Elementary? as long as the momentum. Zero as trace of one-who-counts. Is-under-the-spell. Of women? Naked. Infinite progressions. Delirious possibility. Offspring.

I dig a hole, he said, and then dig another and fill it with the soil I took out of the first hole.

A system of numbers instead ties a knot around nothing. Of abbreviations, conventions of syntax and grammar. Conventions instead of. Notch, tally mark, or pebble. Instead of. Thou shalt not make unto thee any image, no likeness of a thing. No catalogue of ships. No list of wars.

Imagine counting emptiness. Fearless the mountain people cross the abyss on a flimsy bridge. Finger the empty space on the abacus. Has no value but colors what's around it. Like a premonition. Nudges other numbers into place. Origin and starting point. Position without precedent, as if being in the world without being born.

Once we have eaten of the fruit we cannot be. Like one who has not. Cannot vomit up the fruit and kill the ox that drank the water that put out the fire that burnt the stick that beat the dog that bit the cat that ate the serpent that crossed the coordinates.

Laura Liberale

Translated by Murtha Baca and Federica Santini

from *Livid Dance Song*
Dreamlike
(Homo Bulla)

We walk close together and you tell me you've been spitting up blood.
"How so? Since when?" I grip your forearm more tightly.
"But you should"
(stop spitting up blood?)
I once believed
(when I was a little girl? until a moment ago?)
that thought could be focused
into a bubble of health
(of love, just love)
smash it where it hurts, where the pain is
pop it and heal it
(yes, come on, let's try that right now)
"But you should try."
Then we break apart, a sentence stuck in my head:
I leave you at dawn in the city that smells of ethylene.
(has it got to do with chemistry poison cancer?)
But before this (or is it right after?)
we are (I am you no longer are)
in the temple and my voice is steady:
Alberto
Alberto
Berto
Alberto

It's you.
The bubble of your name
that explodes in our ears.

***

The rock is slanted, slippery
like in an abandoned washtub
seaweed-slimy land of a sodden
crèche. The youngest daughter
enters treacherous waters, there she is
with the sudden jolt that can kill
children. She does what a mother
needs to do and stays splayed
like a sodden rag on the green rock.
Run, big sister, cry out for help
oops on the rocks, stunned cricket
reaching your father stretched out on the beach
(can you see the blue blob of his swimming trunks?)
beyond the pools overflowing with garbage
the tarred fish gasping makes
your Mercury-like foot
slip away from the carnival mask
that you leave behind, cast off as a splinter.

Your eyes, two badly cut holes.

***

(To Maurizio, who came before you)
Do not promise me an afterwards.
A presence of braided air and light
to be poured over you.
It is to my flesh that I had to tie my children
to carry their growth every day
like a wreath shielded from the mother.
So don't promise me an afterwards.

Cut out your tongues along
with my youth cut short.

***

Being overwhelmed with words	Being wordless
Accumulating/ Self-accumulating	Dispersing/ Self-destratifying
Settling down	Disintegrating
Being immanent	Being absolute

> If life and death were this
> (an imitation of an action
> held in the verbs: such a way to die)…
> The fact is that on the left you also find:
> drinking milk in the morning
> sticking one's hands in the grease of the earth
> pedaling up and down
> making love and entwining tongues
> when they aren't speaking
> laughing until you cry
> like when the child plunges out of the womb.
> There is no active opposite of these verbs.
> Only a not. Negation.
> Thus one trembles.
> *To tremble*
> a verb of suspension
> between our life and our death.

***

To go out
like from the fence of a campground
what's been used is all organized

what was rented
with the idea of leaving it in better shape than when you got it
so no one can complain afterwards
among those who remain
among those who will come afterward
(and they'll pull the same handle
they'll drag the same chair
only after wiping them down
because everyone likes a bit of protection
the idea of making a new start
terse and oblivious
as if arranged just for that from the beginning.
Only later to wonder
when that gouge got there
that dark stain that persists
the deep nick on the cutting board.)

To go out
like one gets out every day
with and without the same things
identical steps
no new pose to try out.
No longer worrying
about photos
the camera left on the table
terse and oblivious
like a gift.

from *The Availability of Our Flesh*
You cut your hair
refused to blandish the air
with the blond volutes of your head.
Upturned, you grow downward
under the earth.
Bulbs sprout from the soles of your feet.
Roots that grow longer, to suck
the lasting keratin of the dead.

***

Tell me about this beyond.
If, our former self worn down,
the ego abraded, scraped away
the slag of tamas, of nigredo
the nugget shines
it sparkles again.

But he cannot respond.

To know, he says, *would freeze your blood.*
Let this be enough, he says:
the scent of the flesh
borne in the embrace.

***

He bears the fateful fruit of pomegranates twisting him
leading him off the path
and his breath comes out of a thousand slits.
Every awakening is a leap off a cliff
clinging to himself as to an enemy.

***

They dig the earth with their jaws
they sink their tomblike nests into it
honey in the stone
stone honey that does not preserve.

They are the mother bees of craters
they possess the vault of free will
and are possessed by it.

Therein are mixing bowls and jars of stone, and there too the bees store honey.
Odyssey XIII, 98-101
(Translated by A.T. Murray)

***

The first time was for the farewell
that February condensed upon the glass.
Your hands, he implored
and took root in you.
The second time, the puppet
dismembered by your use
overflowed in the little
of yourself that you conceded.

Both times, you commanded
a storm upon that seed:
Come, disaster, reap the harvest.

***

This is a blue that frightens
and its mane has eight rays.
At the end, like baubles, hang your legs
which twice you opened to the void

struck by the light.

***

From the dry friction of bodies
with the inexact rhythm of rubbing
from the fallacy of your wood
you generated a primitive ardor
a fire of ruin.

It burned, the bait of flesh.

Guilt, inextinguishable.

> *The two pieces of wood with which the Ashvins generate fire are gold.*
> *Brihadaranyaka Upanishad* VI, 4, 22

***

To the exact turn of lunations
—body divided in two:
your before and all of the after
the nebris of white leather
the translucid skin of your son—
he came to graze on ashes
the beasts of panic howling.
Someone said:
Did you perhaps think there was no price to pay?

***

Our arid hips will besiege us
never orbiting over the sternum.
Bees of pure desire
will smash against the pubis again and again
each time seeking, in the honey of a new coitus
the availability of our flesh.

***

Count your steps from when you threw
your eyes into the pool, the woman dressed in red
her tongue to lick the earth
for the weight of the dead words
in the broken vase the unburied placentas
the blade hidden out of pity.
In no place will the pair of skulls
separate from you. Bone beads
fingered like a rosary.

> *Brahmahatya held in her hand a knife and a cup, she had terrifying,*
> *piercing eyes the color of bronze, and then all of a sudden she roared.*
> *Skanda Purana* IV, i, 31, 56

***

In the waters inside I immerse you
in the tumult of the corporeal water
in the ford that takes one's breath away
and rejoins it to the Breath.
In the pools of the belly I drown you
in the tremendous, in the black of the water.

There is breath for only one in this water.

> *One after the other, she throws her sons into the water.*
> Mahabharata I, 98, 13

***

For us whose teeth chattered in our beds
there was the visit of the pale women
horrible feet twisted backward
their veil of skin, their arms outstretched toward the blood
that gushed from our nipples.

***

The god who dissolved the waters
slipped in while you were asleep
and wreaked havoc there.
It wasn't enough for you
to secure the precipices
the stairwell
the holes in the ground
the pools, the chasms
nor to invoke it, the void:
the pulp was already singing

infinitesimal, tenacious tremor.

> *The Lord of the yoga, having entered the womb of Diti, by means of a thunderbolt cut into seven pieces the fetus that shone like gold.*
> Bhagavata Purana VI, 18, 61-62

***

You did not deposit the pieces
in a pot of honey
after having struck your womb.
No beast cried out
ominous against the dawn.
But the Black One, she, remained
to watch you bleed
with a strand of heads
adorning her throat.

> *Gandhari pounded on her belly and gave birth to a piece*
> *of flesh similar to an iron ball.*
> *Mahabharata* I, 114, 12

***

Reconstitute me
the one who was cut into pieces repeats
to the fire turned toward the South
that gave a military beat to the blood.
Return me to myself.
And the blood abandons itself to its own loss
it dissipates, impotent.

Some women believe that by solidifying
their blood they can give birth to a son

> *When they dismembered the Purusha, how many parts did they cut him into?*
> *Rigveda* X, 90, 11

***

Among all of the rooms, this one:
the green sororal hospitalization
that germinates losses, recissions
and gathers your time in the dead hour.

Miliary flesh will scan you from now on.
Miniscule vermilion gravestones.

***

In a dreamless sleep
the pain of the fathers is silent.

Their seed was cooked.

Vulvas rusty
like altar stones.

> *You women with your rusty pudenda.*
> *Rigveda* X, 155, 4

***

She hung her slippers on the branches
of the bronchi. In her bust the confines
from which to crouch down and spy on time.
Cold comes out of her feet, but it has already been.
Outside, cracks and a bare skull.

***

Grown for days to die
the body of pain nourished
with the sesame of the ancestors:

devoured food that devours.

> *In nine days and nights, the body is fully formed.*
> *With the first rice-ball, the head of the departed is formed.*
> *Garuda Purana* II, 5, 33

***

Since he didn't stop you then
in his evil he now feared
an elemental retribution.
Your heartbeat became darker as you walked
and gently you disengaged yourself from his arm.
In the metaphysical silt of the father
something of you gave in. Defeat.

He said, "And me, father, to whom will you give me?" and he repeated it a second,
a third time. Then his father answered: "I will give you to death."
Katha Upanishad I, 1, 4

***

In this cathedral of the West
tolerated only in the feasible
vision of a vegetable
phagocytosis, here where what is human is forgotten
and the only daughter is celebrated
with liquid, vertiginous coils
they also appear to you, pallid, androgynous
adolescents. They chant vague
words beyond your comprehension:

their" look tells of the betrayal of the water.

***

Not outside, the walls of the massacre but inside, in the cavity of an organ.
That's why with her you feared a mechanism of waves
the propagation of evil without time on the amnion veil.

The flesh of both claimed by ghosts.

***

Are you still asking to feed her
to celebrate the rite of care?
This table is an altar, dig
two furrows, fill them with milk and water
pile up clods of earth to make a barrier
erect the mound, the closed-off garden
savor in the sun that shrinks the outline
of the size of spring.

***

The mother is the black lion
that tears apart with his claws
the cupola of childhood.
To know if to pierce the light
to open the gates of shadow.
These scattered pieces
are the ultimate measure of damage.

***

In the ear of the dying man
because in the ears of the extirpated
reconciliation should be poured
in the ear of the dying man
you blew the unabsolvable
murmured what can do nothing
on their uninterrupted rise to the belly
grab the laces of your shoes
nothing on their pretense of fulfillment.

***

To grow there, new moons
to submit to the fullness
to bring swallows to the season
plundered of fruit.

Small red fruits
aged blood.

To protect in the palm of one's hand
a redemption of wings.

***

The nest of the grebe that you protect in the reeds
the bee that struggles in the water, plucked out to dry
the ant that has lost its way with the honey
the snail fed with leaves and, even before
the cemetery flowers, straightened up after the storm.
To portend guilt in death
to expiate by taking care of little creatures.

***

But that which was another and was us
barred the nine gates at the word "I"
freed himself from waiting for the name
stopped the wheel.
The snakes that we threw upon his sleep
found an empty room, uninhabited.

> *In the city of nine gates, in the body, there is the hamsa, the spirit, the lord of the entire world, of that which is motionless and that which moves.*
> *Shvetashvatara Upanishad* III, 18

***

With the Swift One you entrusted the words to the circle of blood
upon evil the Black One spread sleep
the Terrific One tore bodies limb from limb
the Glittering One left the mark of her cautery
the Deep Red One was the law of not forgetting
the Smoke-colored One made the world flow again

and the Dazzling One is the faces that the world has given
with which it has survived.

> *Kali, Karali, Monojava, Sulohita, Sudhumravarna, Sphulingini
> and the divine Visvaruci: these are the seven flickering tongues of fire.*
> *Mundaka Upanishad*, I, 2, 4

***

Only on the third night did you learn
in the cavern of your own womb
and further inside, in the generated womb.

Child who grew inside you
golden embryo to transmute the lead inside you.

> *For three nights the master bears the disciple in his belly.*
> *Atharvaveda*, XI, 5, 3

***

The unrestrained hooves of the mares
the waters consumed by their breaths.

To put a halter on the word is what remains.

That fire in the form of a mare penetrated into the ocean.

Maria Grazia Calandrone

Writing Poetry is a Political Action

Poetry is activism, mainly for two reasons:
1. The fact that it exists outside of the market economy, resisting (either with its simple existence or by being overtly opposed to it) the capitalist norm, which today seems to be dominant over the intention of building a just world to live in.
2. In its highest moments, poetry becomes—or it convinces itself of becoming—a collective human voice, displaying and hence proving a radical kinship to the writer before all others.

This radical kinship is the base of politics in the absolute, as it is free of the restrictions of time and space. Poetry's social and political power elicits a similar response in the reader: it evokes a feeling that we can call compassion, which is, in fact, the first indicator of civil, social, and political collective life.

Having posited this imperative premise concerning an obsession of mine, it seems that there is greater attention to the deconstruction of language in American poetry compared to contemporary Italian poetry, often with political intentions being accompanied, at the content level, by a greater conviction of being able to impact reality, even economic reality, a persuasion that can at times become explicit and striking social critique, as it happens in the works presented by Susan Briante.

The experience drew me in so much that I decided to host a radio *reportage* of the New York meetings in five takes on Radio 3 Suite. I knew this poetry would be radically new to Italian listeners, making it necessary to explore known ideas at first and then evolve into these uncharted ways of understanding and desiring poetry. Discovering any similarities became necessary for presenting them in the best of ways.

It seemed to me that I found two fundamental influences working undercurrent: the first one is the domestic, ironic, disenchanted, and mature legacy of Edgar Lee Master's *Spoon River Anthology*, with the second being the subversive and destructuring heritage of the Beat Generation poets, the bad guys dreaming of a new world, without wasting time in giving too many explanations about sentence structure and moral constructs.

Two intentions, then, chronologically opposed even, two different representations of phases of human development that contrast in a paradoxical harmony, resulting in the landscape of writing appearing torn, burned, and brittle by a live turmoil. The constant is always the *fil rouge* of irony, sometimes raining in sarcasm or a bitter laugh.

And, talking about bitter laugh, it seemed to me to also have intercepted a subtler trace of the well-known *confessional* poetry, as it's called, that overexposed intimacy, real as apparent as it is, that intimate life becoming a shadowy and effervescent fiction of the art, as it did with greats such as Anne Sexton and Sylvia Plath during the second half of the Nineteenth Century. It is a case in which irony transforms into sarcasm and sometimes loud accusations. There is no absence of lyrical, classical tones resembling European and Italian writing, the latter soaked in the amnion of its literary history.

I go back home having been enriched with unprecedented information on extra-national contemporaneity and, just maybe, having been authorized to practice more real and subversive poetry by my colleagues overseas because the new note sung by the American poets - compared to the Italian ones - reverberates a tragic lightness, sometimes doing a flip into the more confidential tones of friends talking, with that written confidentiality asking for absolute faith in (human and intellectual) comprehension. And I will want to have trust in that, too.

Vincenzo Frungillo

Poetry between the End of History and the Determinism of Nature

1. A Theoretical Premise

The end of history prophesied by Francis Fukuyama in one of his famous books (*The End of History and the Last Man*, Free Press, 1992) resonated powerfully in literary and cultural circles between the end of the 1980s and the 1990s when the fall of the Soviet Union seemed to have reduced the world to a single flat dimension. After that epochal event, there was the illusion, in a certain sense, that no serious upheaval could touch Western people anymore. This *Weltanschauung* might suggest that the end of the dialectic between capitalism and communism coincided with the end of the dynamics of history; so, we would have gone from an ideological reading of history, i.e., Hegelian-Marxist, to an equally ideological reading of globalization. On the literary level, the consequence was the crisis of poetics that made poetry the privileged place of internal contradictions in Western society. Postmodernity has somewhat sanctioned this phenomenon even if there would be an exception for the so-called "critical postmodernism" of the neo-avant-gardes of the Nineties, for example, the work of Gruppo '93. In turn, mainstream literature, and in part poetry, aimed at an effective grip on the spectator-reader. As in a dark fairy tale, the writer and the reader stared at each other as if they were looking in the mirror and became trapped in what they saw. Someone would have said their spectral image no longer felt the traumas and jolts of events. This inhibitory phenomenon is perpetuated by authors of fiction or poetry with the nihilistic attitude of those who see the destiny of the land of sunset in an emotional stalemate. The underlying assumption seems to be that Westerners have become passive observers of events; they no longer enter the game of history. As Karl Löwith helps us understand, Fukuyama's theory, which also captured a widespread feeling of a postmodern matrix, contains only the latest in a series of illusions (disguised as rationalist and ruthless recognitions on the present) indebted to Judeo-Christian eschatology (*Sul senso della storia* 91).

As a linear and progressive process, history is realized thanks to the reduction of possible worldviews into a single interpretation. Consequently, kairological categories (past, present, future) can tend to coincide with an absolute present. The same misunderstanding could include all those writings that allude to a zero degree, i.e., to a zeroing of the diaphragm existing between the world and the subject: those who allude to the idea of a zeroing of the difference between facts and the self, to the depression or implosion of the subject on the world, risk considering this partial vision as an eschatological and therefore ontogenetic condition.

On this aspect, Byung-Chul Han said some interesting things about the radical mutation that the digital revolution would have brought in a person's perception of their own self. This aspect refers in particular to the work of Vilem Flusser, for which the philosopher of Seoul uses the expression "messianism of the network connection" (*Nello sciame. Visioni del digitale* 63). This misunderstanding confuses the great game of history with a single application of it.

2. Poetry and Testimony

Poetry can remedy this misunderstanding by bringing into play our temporal nature as mortal beings; it can be the right tool for this operation. In this case, the experience is not the trauma of novelty but the basic and original relationship with our temporal nature that literally has no end. From this point of view, poetry, even before having a moral task, is the very condition of memory. Benjamin said the philosopher's mission "consists in comprehending all of natural life through the more encompassing life of history" ("The Task of the Translator" 71). If history is made up of collective and imponderable events, nature is immovable, that which cannot be removed: sex, violence, fear, etc. On closer inspection, these aspects of the human being define us as a species and not as individuals; they express a common code and environment. Nature is the root, but Benjamin seems to tell us that both history and nature, outside of a reciprocal relationship, are liable to a deterministic interpretation: eschatology leads to a reductionist vision of history, nature defines us as a species indeed, and not as single individuals (71–72). This risk is always present, even if in a negative key, when it is commonly said that "nothing makes sense" and life is the "brute animality of a species" (it is certainly no coincidence that the words "nature" and "species" are so present in new Italian poetry). Benjamin's sentence thus indicates a relationship between history and natural life, even if it puts the latter in the wider circle of the former.

This describes the same scheme that Contini uses regarding Dante and the *Divina Commedia* when he speaks of the relationship between "frame" and "life" (*Un'idea di Dante* 71–72). For Contini, the frame is the events that condition and change many people's lives, events of paradigmatic value that the poet must confront, even before a civil or ethical dictate, to clarify the profound dynamics motivating writing and textual space. Here we are at the point: there is, therefore, an essential link between *bios* and history, not a historical frame to which the *bios* adapts, not natural life on which the historical frame adapts, much less the exclusive presence of one or the other, but a relationship between the two dimensions. This relational relationship can be reduced and forgotten but not canceled. The illusion of being able to lift ourselves from the constraint of this "relational logic" removes the fact that we are the very reason this relationship exists as eccentrics to the purely natural sphere and on this side of the absolute objectivity of the facts that occurred.[1] This ontogenetic datum made Blanchot speak of the "vertigo of spacing" (*La conversazione infinita* 57). Poetry, or poetic praxis, is "giving place" to this truth. The authors grappling with this task emphasize the diaphragm that approximates nature and history; rather than being a reminder of what passes, their texts are a memory of what remains. Therefore, the space emerging in these works is an allegory and a concrete space where an experience takes place.

To be clearer, let's use an example from fiction: it would be absurd to reduce Roberto Bolaño's saga to the historical novel genre; we all agree on this, yet the Argentine writer addresses the historical theme. To explain his job as a writer, he uses a simile: he says he feels like a detective who returns at night, alone, to the crime scene when all the others have gone away. By crime scene, Bolaño means Western history with its load of violence and crimes. The author investigates the scenario, goes to the bottom, studies the traces of a certain event that affects his life, and, at the same time, analyzes the imagination of an entire generation. As well as being the detective, he is also the witness, participant, and co-responsible, and his writing is the practice that allows us to

---

[1] AN: The expression "relational logic" (xv) is used by Giovanni Bottiroli in his preface to the Italian translation by Roberta Ferrara (Einaudi, 2015). On this matter, I would like to refer to my essay "Lo spazio della poesia nel tempo della dispersione," in *Teoria e poesia*. Edited by Andrea Inglese and Paolo Giovannetti. Biblion Edizioni, 2018, p. 38.

distinguish the chronicle—the simple listing of facts—from the investigation. His novels entrust the victims and perpetrators to the gloomy light of time, and they live thanks to the breath that transpires in the gap between the indeterminacy of extra-subjective events and the determinism of the law of nature. The organic remains, the bones in the desert of the women murdered in the novel-poem *2666* (2004), altogether do not constitute the clue that leads to the discovery of a culprit but will be redeemed by the textual space offered by the plot of the characters. Their story is the breath of the victims. At the same time, we think of the voice of one of the most touching characters of the Argentine writer and poet, Auxilio Lacouture, respectively a character and protagonist of the novels *Los detectives salvajes* (1998) and *Amuleto* (1999). She is a woman who calls herself the "mother of Mexican poetry" and who, having taken refuge in a bathroom in the Faculty of Letters of the National Autonomous University of Mexico during the 1968 coup, remembers and tells us the story of a generation of poets.[2] Poetry is born and transmitted from unusual places. Auxilio's voice prevents time from crushing itself and compressing individualities in a form of absolutism. The protagonist's name in this touching story better clarifies her role. This is the messianic function, however, in Benjamin's sense, of the literary text and the angel, the one who brings help to poets and all living beings, is not an abstract metaphysical figuration nor an ethereal figure born from the solitary imagination of a poet, but a concrete, real person, who has become a character, who acts in an exemplary way. Acting exemplary means bringing out what we have sheltered inside: in this case, the faculty bathroom. This is the painful task of one who is out of place both in absolute evil and in absolute good.

3. Ogni Cinque Bracciate

I have tried to do the same with the characters of my poetic production, such as the swimmers of the former DDR, victims of heavy state doping. Ute, Karla, Renate, and Lampe, in particular, are precisely emblematic bodies that bear the signs of time's passing. Still, they are also irreducible characters to the totalitarian and all-encompassing vision of communist or capitalist ideology.

---

[2] EN: This character is based on Alcira Soust Scaffo (1924–1997), a Uruguayan teacher and poet whose fifteen-day stint in the university bathroom became a notable anecdote of the 1968 Mexican Student Movement and Bolaño's novels.

The bodies of these champions are an attempt to make an ideological vision of history coincide with nature's determinism. This project's failure and their testimony are highly allegorical. Poetic writing does nothing but record these toil appendages of the century. In the case of *Ogni cinque bracciate*, a text begun in 2002 and concluded around 2006, this occurs with a poem in octaves: the text is made up of five cantos, and each canto is made up of five sequences, and each sequence of five octaves. The book was written within the framework of a cultural context outlined in the first part of this essay when the new generations of Italian poets mostly followed lyric poetry in its pop or late-romantic, confessional, or nihilistic versions (according to a Beckettian or Celanian canon); or it was poetry directed towards the unconditional acceptance of the "sea of objectivity" that submerged everything and everyone, so much so that the poem inevitably veered towards humble prose surrendered to the laws of the new technological context. Within this framework, we can summarize the research poetry developed between the two centuries, which took up the lessons of the most prominent poets of Gruppo 63. *Ogni cinque bracciate* (2009) intended to allegorize a common destiny in the body of swimming champions, but, at the same time, it was dealing with a specific phase of history. The songs that make up the poem and give shape to a deteriorating Western culture also constitute a descent into my personal unconscious. Not having lived the life of a Berliner between the Seventies and Eighties, the years that corresponded to my childhood and adolescence, I had to adapt the Eastern part of my city to those alienating scenarios. I had to look at hidden Europe through the veiled Naples filter. It was not the heavenly city, bathed by sea and sun, but the city of factories and industrial warehouses, the same city I frequented as a kid. The Soviet bloc of Europe thus overlapped with the working-class world that had been the backdrop for the first part of my existence. The book's historical framework was instead documented thanks to research carried out at the headquarters of the BSTU in Berlin, the Stasi archive. There, I consulted the file that informed me of the decades-long state doping program in the former DDR, and I obtained the photos that close the volume published in 2009.

At the center of the vision, there was also a father figure, strong and normative, who marked the border, the space within which reality was played out. In the poem, he corresponds to the father of Renate, the backstroke of the group who advances "with his back turned to the future," an old worker who has seen the mutations of contemporary Germany. When I wrote these sequences, the eastern area of Naples, where the city's industrial sector lays, had been abandoned for years. The octaves on Renate's father, placed at the book's center, represent the vault of a cathedral about to collapse. With the fall of the Berlin Wall, the indistinct magma of neoliberalism would have flooded even the part of the continent resilient to advanced capitalism. The idea of purity cultivated for too long turns into rot, so after the collapse, the champions are back in the headlines with their bodies deformed and corrupted by performance-enhancing substances: the East and the West show they are suffering from the same disease. However, the swimmers do not obey a destiny of decline; they are reborn in a new body; however, this time, welded by the common experience and the possibility of obtaining an original feeling, an alternative way of looking at the world and history.

From this point of view, even the love affair between Ute and Lampe, two of the protagonists, is emblematic. Therefore, the poem's characters are historical and real but also emblematic; they carry a shared destiny in and on the body. These characters are also the emblem or allegory of what the poetic word can and must do. The verse takes up the tradition of Italian epic poetry and formalizes the protagonists' fate: the verse in classical octaves allegorizes the condition of subjection to a national and nationalist project and the will of the swimmers to reflect this imposition of time in their gestures and bodies. The melting of the octave, after the fall of the Berlin Wall, is instead an allegory of personal and national decadence but also the beginning of liberation from both an ideological and deterministic vision of life. Therefore, the swimmers carry the double meaning of words and languages, always ambiguous and risky. As such, the swimmers' story must be read in its entirety and complexity to understand its meaning. The first and second parts of the poem mark the game of victory and loss in their ambiguous meaning: victory is also a loss, and defeat is also a liberation and victory. The poetic word grasps and insists on this.

4. Martina, Lucrezio, Stephan, Epaminonda, and The Other Poems

With the following poem, *Il cane di Pavlov* (2013), in the form of a theatrical monologue and divided into four parts like the phases of Pavlov's experiment, I tried to express in poetry "the extension of the domain of struggle" after the fall of the Berlin Wall and the imposition of a single development model.[3] The

---

[3] EN: This is a reference to *Extension du domaine de la lutte* (1994), the eponymous novel by the French novelist Michel Houellebecq.

parable of Martina and Bruno manifests the microphysics of power grafted onto the most intimate sphere, the erotic one, to make it a laboratory of domination and oppression. The protagonist is the clerk Martina, a twenty-first-century *ragazza* Carla,[4] who experiments with the Pavlovian phases of the stimulus-response on her shy colleague Bruno. The text is also an account of a psychiatric report inspired by a true news story. The link with Eastern Europe remains, as made evident from the title. This relationship continues throughout the text due to the apparent references to the Russian poetic tradition, particularly Pushkin's *Eugene Onegin*. At one point in the text, Martina and Bruno (a clear reference to the protagonist of Houellebecq's *The Elementary Particles*) have just consumed their first night of sex.

We are in the first phase of the four foreseen by Pavlov's experiment. Bruno is the laboratory guinea pig who savors a desire conditioned by the object. The motto of the Stooges, *I wanna be your dog*, here becomes a pretext for an analysis of the Western subject, or rather of the Western province that instinctively re-proposes the models of the most advanced capitalist countries (the reference to Bret Easton Ellis' *American Psycho* is explicit in the poem). In this prosodic monologue, even desire and sex lose their nature to become pure functional artifices of the system. The lovers will be taken away from their natural fault, but when they prepare for manipulation, Bruno amazes Martina with an unexpected choice. Both in *Ogni cinque bracciate* and in this text, there is a way out of the mechanism of oppression and domination that is revealed only at the end of a vexatious dynamic. The breaking of the octave in the book on swimmers and the ending of the 2013 book allude to the impossibility of a deterministic or ideological reduction of human affairs. Ultimately there is a principle of freedom and indeterminacy.

Therefore, the composition behind these works cannot be assimilated to lyrical afflatus, to the expression of an interiority. Incidentally, as Martina points out in a passage from *Il cane di Pavlov*, naive lyricism expresses a strong-willed (narcissistic) desire dictated by the machine of control. In these works, I wanted to stage the mechanics and systems of power, considering the trap and the deviation from the norm contained in it. The poem acts as evidence of the exceptionality of the individual from technological, scientific, or evolutionary determinism. Beyond a simplistic first impression, which could

---

[4] EN: Elio Pagliarani's *La ragazza Carla* (Mondadori, 1962) is noteworthy for signaling the transition from neo-realism to the experimental poetry of the neo-avant-garde.

reduce these texts to the epic-poematic genre, they must be cataloged as tools for verifying powers.

Le pause della serie evolutiva (2021) takes up a sentence by Osip Mandelstam on Lamarck and underlines precisely the suspension from the machinic law of the evolutionary chain. If the poetic word recognizes the urgent need of history, it also knows how to find a counterpoint. The poems' characters, the Latin poet Lucretius, the French shepherd Stephan, and Epaminonda, a member of the Spinalonga leper colony in Greece, are figures who, on the one hand, represent the victims of the dominant historical forces but, on the other, also the emblem of a possible response to them. These three historical characters stage the conditioning of a deterministic vision of nature or an ideological and absolutizing vision of history. Still, they are also an allegory of an escape route: Lucretius embodies the clinamen, painful fold, which prevents any consolatory vision of life. Stephan stands in the short-sightedness of an absolutizing reading of history but is also the voice of the missing. Epaminondas is the last patient of a leper colony, an exponent of the extreme corruption of the West who finds a fault in which to let shine the singular exceptionality of mortals.

The bodies of all these characters are where the tragic relationship between history and nature manifests itself, the place of poetry as memory and testimony. Moreover, they are also an allegory of the historical time in which we live and which aspires to erase the mortal matrix of every single subject supplied with speech.

5. The Space of The Word

The latest text, *Prime scene di caccia e di morte* (2021), a plaquette that anticipates a larger work, *La luce dell'eclissi*, focuses precisely on the "spacing of the word." There are no real characters but two anonymous protagonists of a drama who stage the word's very meaning as a reminder of and defense from oblivion and the indistinct. This text uses theater and theatrical staging to speak of space and plot in their ontological sense. The two voices are A. and a., i.e., Author and actor. One of the models is Samuel Beckett, recovered here as the playwright who could look at the extreme limit of the word. In any case, the aspiration remains for a composite and structured text with the prevailing sonnet form, as in the case of *Le pause della serie evolutiva*. The two protagonists seem to cross the ages and confront each other on the archetypal value of the challenge of the poetic word.

6. Conclusions

As Heidegger wrote in the famous essay on Hölderlin, "Why poets?": "[E]very entity, the objects of consciousness and the things of the heart, men who impose themselves and the most risky beings, all beings, each according to their own way, are in the region of the tongue," and then adds "the most risky are those who, in the absence of salvation, realize that they are without protection" (*Sentieri interrotti* 287, author's translation).[5] In poetry, therefore, it is not a question of being romantic supporters of the reasons of the heart or, on the contrary, apocalyptic accelerationists; rather, for the German philosopher, poetic writing is the technique that, more than others, records the movement of the species and its own caducity.

The books I have published since the early 2000s present themselves as parables, even narrative ones, or emblems of this. The profound dynamics of language, which specifies the genetic character of humans, cannot, therefore, be fixed once and for all either by scientific determinism or utopian ideology, including that of the end of historical events. Any ideological vision of poetry, and with it the sociological reduction of the function of poetic writing, must be examined against this underlying condition.

If the poetic references I adopted during the Noughties were different, they were all used for this purpose. Poetry was the place of verification or, better yet, the fallibility of things. In conclusion, we can speak of a philosophical poetry that also owes much to the most recent analyses of anthropology and biology but remains a poetics of the "first things," of the human condition.

---

[5] AN: See Heidegger, Martin. *Holzwege*. 1968. Klostermann, 1984; and *Sentieri interrotti*. Translated by Pietro Chiodi. La Nuova Italia. 1991, p. 287.

Research Poetry between Utopias, Metaphors, and the State of Things. Part II. A Conversation with Fabrizio Bondi

During the three days of the conference, Professor Bondi delivered two different talks on two different topics. The second and last of them, during the second day of the conference at the Italian Cultural Institute, was part of the roundtable "Research Poetry? A Poem by any Other Name." Professor Bondi ad-libbed his speech; for this reason, I interviewed him via email. In this way, I could focus on some of the most relevant aspects of his speech, as well as expand on topics and perspectives that he didn't have a chance to focus on during the conference.

IM: The second talk you gave was part of the roundtable "Research Poetry? A Poem by Any Other Name." How do you think your talk connected with the other speakers (Marco Giovenale and Daniele Poletti)?
FB: I think that both the talks by Giovenale and Poletti have been very idiosyncratic (*absit iniuria verbis*).[1] On the one hand, in Giovenale's talk, he referred to an idea of poetry (influenced by Gleize and others) that was a declaration of "poetica" (to use an old Italian critic keyword) undoubtedly shared by other poets and critics but, in my opinion, very related to Giovenale's own poetic work (one that is very valuable, without any doubts). On the other hand, Poletti fiercely claimed his newly found category of "poetry of complexity," with which he would replace the old labels of avant-garde and research poetry. Moreover, Poletti relies, for his idea of poetry, on the tireless work of his publishing house, focused on the writers of complexity of today and the past. Last but not least, Poletti is himself a poet. My talk connected with the others for the common idea of the necessity to defend, on every level and in every situation, the kind of poetry that can be considered as complex, multifaced, self-aware, ironic, unconventional and, I'd like to say, reckless—which the conference

---

[1] EN: I.e., "let injury be absent from these words."

represented in such memorable ways, both on the critical and the poetic sides. Nonetheless, my concern is that this kind of poetry needs a commitment of the reader that nowadays is almost impossible to reach because, on the one hand, of the lack of appropriate skills and, on the other, the lack of time. This second issue (sometimes used as an excuse to avoid challenging and difficult readings) is rooted in the deep structure of psycho-technical mechanics of work organization in the age of late capitalism. I quoted the paradoxical (but maybe not so much) statement by Mark Fisher, according to which, today, the only readers who really have enough time to read are the inmates.[2] In fact, after the fall of the classical opposition between working time and free time (the latter being time that workers could fill with vacation, family, fruition of the products of mass culture, and free explorations of art, culture, or politics), the subsequent ideology of the worker as entrepreneur-of-themselves, the smart working, and other forms of subtle colonization of time have turned the so-called free time in a void full of anxiety, vague senses of guilt, and depression. Also, the crisis of traditional scholarly education has deep roots, linked to the general crisis of knowledge. In this case, the crisis involved both the historical-nationalistic way of teaching literature and the American model, based on rhetorical clashes and debates. Because Poletti has already fully investigated this phenomenon, I don't want to talk here about the leveling of publishing houses due to the development of a cartel-based model that started more or less forty years ago. The "great readers," whom Walt Whitman preconized in a famous poem as the correlative of "great writers," would be possible only if the entire society will be taken into a "revolutionary-becoming," a *devenir révolutionnaire* (Deleuze). In fact, the very roots of the so-called Tradition of the Avant-garde are intertwined with periods of rebellion and insurgency: the reformation of language through the means of poetry dreamed by Rimbaud is contemporary to the Paris *Commune* of 1870.[3] During Russia's first revolutionary period, arts had an incredible development, and poetry wasn't certainly subordinate to cinema or painting. I disagree with Rimbaud, who refused to work (as a poet)

---

[2] AN: "Only prisoners have time to read, and if you want to engage in a twenty-year long research project funded by the state, you will have to kill someone" (2012, n.p.).

[3] AN: See, on this topic, the wonderful course given by Michel Butor in 1982 at Genève University, available on YouTube: https://www.youtube.com/watch?v=DAHluqDDJNs.

under an unfair government: we must continue to experiment in our corners because the Messiah can also enter through a minuscule breach. *Estote parati.*[4]

IM: The purpose of this roundtable was to investigate the definition of contemporary poetry: do you think that Research Poetry can be a good way to define it? And, whether yes or no, why?

FB: I'm less interested in a label *per se,* but more interested in the label's historical meaning and, obviously, the more-or-less developed concept that it summarizes. The label "research poetry" has some historical reasons that we can investigate. The previous label for this kind of poetry was "avant-garde," a metaphor referring to the semantic field of war.[5] In the 19th century, we witnessed a real battle of poets to conquer a free space in the market of literature, as Benjamin and Bourdieu explained so well.[6] See what Sainte-Beuve said about Baudelaire: "la Folie Baudelaire" was something totally new, a kind of original and strange music-hall, or an exotic, uncanny space within a universal exhibition.[7] Like a brave soldier, Baudelaire reached a territory never occupied before. In the 20th century, even before the Atomic Bomb, Science began to lead the war-politics dynamics, and it gained enormous importance in the power relations between branches of knowledge. For this reason, the semantic field of the metaphoric operation (implicitly finalized to give prestige to an art whose social importance seemed to be decreasing) switched from military to scientific connotation: the poet was doing research just like the scientist, so the poet (I simplify) was as important as the other researchers. In a similar way, Poletti's proposal of a "poetry of complexity" is a result of the discourse field of "complexity" (used for example in the theory of systems) developed after the two globalizations: the economical one and, the other, due to the spread of the World Wide Web.

IM: Months after the conference ended, what has been its impact on your work and your research?

---

[4] EN: The Scout Motto and a reference to the Gospel of Matthew: "Ideo et vos *estote parati*: quia qua nescitis hora Filius hominis venturus est" (Vulgate, emphasis added).

[5] AN: See Sanguineti, Edoardo and Jean Burgos. *Per una critica dell'avanguardia poetica in Italia e in Francia*. Einaudi, 1995.

[6] AN: See Benjamin, Walter. *Baudelaire*. Edited by Giorgio Agamben, Barbara Chitussi, and Clemnes-Carl Härle. Translated by Patrick Charbonneau. La Fabrique, 2013; and Bourdieu, Pierre. *Les règles de l'art: genèse et structure du champ littéraire*. Éditions du Seuil, 1992.

[7] AN: See Calasso, Roberto. *La folie Baudelaire*. Adelphi, 2008.

FB: I could mention a very long list of suggestions, ideas, discoveries, and conversations that I picked up during the three days of the conference, but a general idea has touched me for its importance: the necessity to overcome the distance between poets and poetry on the two sides of the Atlantic, and, even more generally, the necessity of overcoming cultural nationalisms. In the present age, when the most terrible nationalisms are coming back with their bloody parade of war and destruction, a concrete dialogue between languages and cultures is absolutely necessary. Poetry, with her capacity to exceed the mere mechanics of language (only bad poetry is untranslatable), can help. But, like huge collective enterprises as the anthology of *The Flies* and this conference demonstrate, all of us "workers of the words" must thoroughly employ our energy and creativity. The effort is hard, the times are harder: but what is at stake is crucial.

IM: The title of this conference wished the poetry (the pheasant) to reappear: do you think that poetry manifested itself in those days? And how?

FB: Yes, I felt the presence of the poetry in those days, sometimes strongly and other times less intensely. What I constantly felt was the energy fueled by the enthusiasm of every participant, both between speakers and audience. Maybe it was because of the contagion—a good one, in this case—emanating from Professor Ballerini, a man for whom the adjective "charismatic" is not merely a rhetorical cliché. Sorry for the mystic metaphor, but those who receive the charisma speak in tongues and must spread the Word.

Marco Giovenale (Translated by Nicholas Benson)

An Effects Machine. Some Spare Parts for Descriptions and Theories of Contemporary Writing

0. Preface

If a text is written by a poet, it's customary to say that it is a piece of writing *en poète*. But, like Artaud with God's judgment, perhaps the time has come—even in 21st-century Italy—to begin questioning the legitimacy of attempts to do away with the judgment of Poetry, with canonical poetry, and perhaps even with Poetry itself, at least if that "self" insists on the capital "P," or employs a false lowercase. This is not to say that resisting "doing away with it" implies an evangelizing movement. It is always subjective, of course, but poetic expression is part of a very crowded and maybe even dangerously international network of subjectivities.

1. Introduction

This will not be a piece of writing *en poète*. Each machine (meaning *machine* in an eco-compatible and human sense: I'm not contrasting the machine made with the organic) produces a series of effects, which obviously act on it in return. So, what does this essay's title mean? An *effects machine* is:

- contemporary criticism, and the criticism of contemporary writing, in precise, explicitly phenomenological examples;
- a machine that would like to have an effect (calming but not necessarily so) on the controversies → factions and fractions (which have always manifested themselves) in Italy;
- a machine made up of different pieces that may be thought of as premises of analysis and as the beginning of refinement of the same → to then generate other effects of critical re-reading of "research" (i.e. "experimental") texts by the authors themselves, or by authors more linked to some specific tradition (but, I fear, to no avail when it comes to adverse critics);

- text or rather writing (not only contemporary), before—well before—language, in general, without connotation, unaccompanied by any adjective, fragmented into sets, currents: its effects can be affective, or logical-mathematical, or of another nature, such as reasoning, deceptive, sapiential, exhortative, ornamental, time-wasting, gap-creating, and so on. (On the net, one hears *research poetry* accused of anaffection / poverty of emotion, with startling frequency. Experimental writings may be anaffective, perhaps, but they cannot be—and no article of language can be—ineffective. They have effects. They cannot fail to have them);
- always the relapse into structures (plastic or rigid) of texts and criticisms. The structures can be found online (for example, the Ex.it symposium / series of reading, which exists both as a hard copy and online; or the hard copy anthologies like the one by Vincenzo Ostuni, *I poeti degli anni Zero* (2015) or others, more recent or remote, e.g. *Parola plurale* (2005), or even born of meetings documented (with critical materials) as a pdf on the net (*Prove di ascolto*, edited by young poets and critics Fabio Teti and Simona Menicocci).[1] In the latter case, there were no typological distinctions.

2. Spare Parts

If one wanted to change some critical presumptions (not necessarily "categories") or poetics, or even broader segments of "what is thinkable as literary," at least in the West, at least in Italy, now, the way would be open to do some things. One advances a few steps on unsteady planks, which may not necessarily hold up but that some (including this writer) have set up between one page and another, one kind of research and another:
- The possibility of attenuating or seeing disappear (behind horizons of another nature, to be studied) the attribution of a value-trait to the phonosemantic and rhythmic qualities of the text, or even indifference to these qualities. The poems of Michele Zaffarano can be cited as an example.[2] Or a part of Gherardo Bortolotti's prose.[3] I'd also refer to

---

[1] AN: See slowforward.net/2018/05/09/prove-dascolto-link-ai-testi-degli-autori-della-rassegna-a-cura-di-simona-menicocci-e-fabio-teti/.

[2] AN: See slowforward.net/tag/michele-zaffarano.

[3] AN: See slowforward.net/tag/gherardo-bortolotti.

Fabio Teti's essay on poet Niccolò Furri's textual or, more accurately, verbo-visual work, an essay read at the Hungarian Academy in Rome in 2017.[4]

- [unlike works by authors central to literary research in Italy, especially in the second half of the twentieth century: from Gianni Toti to Emilio Villa, from Edoardo Cacciatore to the Sanguineti of *Laborintus*]
- Because of all that has been mentioned here, the invariable temporal measure of the writing is diminished or disappears. First, I'd point to the case of *Retro*, by poet Corrado Costa (1929–1991), and his audio track of about eight minutes in length.[5] What prevents us from thinking of the recorded piece as shorter, segmentable, or even reworkable? It can be cut. Its durability, its texture, the materials it includes, everything can be shortened, lengthened, varied. There are no rigid strictures to do with its "integrity" (that must be subjected to a "stylistic analysis"). (One can begin to deviate from stylistic analysis in the twentieth-century sense).
- Perhaps the recent electronic poems by Fabrizio Venerandi (b. 1970) cannot be circumvented in terms of "graphic evasion" (as well as temporal).[6]
- This aversion or rather indifference to rhythms can gather in masses, such as the irregular appearance of segments or blocks (rhythmic neither for the eye nor ear) of different lengths, tissues of repetitions, intentional paralogisms or sophisms, obsessive phrasal returns, as in the prose of Christophe Tarkos (1963–2004) or in *Prati* (2007) by Andrea Inglese (b. 1967).[7]
- The opposite of an ornate, rhetorically enhanced, perhaps hyper-cultured discourse (with broad ramifications in the connotative) can be read in the flat, dry, and "literal" denotative and in the very idea of *désaffublement* (as Jean-Marie Gleize would say; or "of integral nudity," or

---

[4] AN: See nazioneindiana.com/2017/06/22/prove-dascolto-7-niccolo-furri. See also vimeo.com/190696192, and the footnote-comment at the end of golfedombre.blogspot.it/2014/09/niccolo-furri.html.

[5] AN: See youtu.be/TLoKkRAUcZk, or also youtu.be/XmA3caVDu5M, which offers the following information: "Recorded in Parma and Brescia in 1981 and published posthumously in the magazine *Baobab. Phonetic information of poetry*, edited by Adriano Spatola."

[6] AN: See for example quintadicopertina.com/fabriziovenerandi/?p=945.

[7] AN: See gammm.org/2007/01/04/prati-andrea-inglese-2006.

littéralité).[8] Stripped of complications and embellishments. Without the moves of the reader, the barker, or the fine speaker, whether oral or moved to the page (assonance, rhyming, rhythmic speech, wordplay, etc.).
- Babbling, losing coherence within the text (as in Luc Bénazet's works, in Emilio Villa's lallations, and back to Antonin Artaud's intentionally incomprehensible litanies). And, beware: it is not a child's language (Andrea Zanzotto's *petèl*), nor is it plotted with semantic references. It is not his intention to reconstruct a healthy text in which stammering would be corruption. It is really, originally, inherently crushed.
- The uncertain irony found by poet Vincenzo Ostuni in texts by Michele Zaffarano,[9] similar or equal to that found by critic Luigi Magno in Nathalie Quintane's texts.[10]
- The idea of installation, not necessarily as an opposite but certainly as *another* possible praxis with respect to performance.[11]
- The maintenance of prose (in works of prose): *completely and firmly unable* to be summarized and recast into a novel. Short prose as an internal detonator within a poetic flow—photographic elements as, essentially, an optimal, extremely changeable interlocutor of and between forms and codes, such as the prose of authors like Elisa Davoglio, Giulio Marzaioli, Manuel Micaletto, Mariangela Guatteri, and Fabio Teti (*Spazio di Destot*, Diaforia, 2011).[12] An absolute disconnection from the syntax of narrative, especially if it is all-encompassing. (In the case of Teti, the disappearance of causality, or generally of hypotactic syntax).
- *Suspension of the tragic* and emergence of *parody*, without either of the two mechanisms crystallizing into style or norm.[13]

---

[8] AN: See Gleize, Jean-Marie. *Sorties*. Questions théoriques, 2009, pp. 40, 175, 293.

[9] AN: For example, see *Cinque testi*: issuu.com/benwayseries/docs/zaffarano_cinquetesti_anteprima_en.

[10] AN: For example, in Magno's talk on June 5, 2015 at Teatroinscatola: gammm.org/index.php/2016/05/26/luigi-magno-presenta- Osservazioni-di-nathalie-quintane-roma-giugno-2015.

[11] AN: See the text by Bortolotti and this author, *Tre paragrafi su scritture recenti*, in gammm, July 16, 2006: gammm.org/2006/07/16/tre-paragrafi-gbortolotti-mgiovenale, and various other references, including *Veil* by Charles Bernstein, 1976, or *Le drame de la vie*, by Valère Novarina, 1984: see slowforward.net/2009/06/30/inst-txt.

[12] AN: See diaforia.org/floema/2015/11/11/spazio-di-destot-fabio-teti.

[13] AN: As in Carmelo Bene: read Maurizio Grande's introduction to *Nostra Signora dei Turchi* in the Bompiani edition of 2005.

- Suspicion cast onto logos (this is nothing new, of course, but *repetita iuvant*). Apposite quotation, from Carmelo Bene: "In cinema, I certainly faced the use of the image in ways I always refused and found unbearable: a servile, decadent cinema, a cinema of the literary provinces, where progress depends on the reliability of the story, of logos etc. etc." (*Sono apparso alla Madonna* 88–89. Translated by Benson).
- Orality is in play in some new writing—and not as a substitute, origin, or point of antagonism towards the written—as some write and say, from time to time, whether or not with polemical intent.
- If desired, a possible modus of speech metamorphosis is on the field and at stake: marked, écrit. In the end, it is the great discovery of Céline—but in some respects, also of Bene. In other words, the game (and what's at stake) is still and always *the saying*, not the said; it is the speaking, not the reporting. The clear disappearance of the Ego in *saying* (not in *the said*, which is always something else) and the deletion of the same moment of speaking from time, history, chronos, which, if anything, flashes only to immediately vanish, to slip away (into) itself, like *aiòn*.

At work is the exhaustion of meaning through its wearing down; by massive molecular infection and perhaps the denotative saturation of the signifier. An example is Mario Corticelli's volume *aria (comunione)* (2014) where we find what was outlined above: parody, suspension of the tragic, the signified multiplied to wear down the signifier and 'exhaust' the sense, not full orality therefore, not full, assertive 'song,' if anything detached from itself, as has been said already, and from the risk of spectacle (a single listen to Corticelli, and one realizes this).

The new writing completely avoids the dimension of parenetic, moralizing, assertive, posture / imposture. On the contrary, the sayings of the *fini dicitori*, the critic-clowns of (assertive) Poetry, are the sayings of the desert fathers. The desert is still there, but the fathers are not. *Pas d'orphanage*, of course: there have never been fathers. So, nothing is reported or said. If anything, there is saying that has stopped summoning us to a scene. Therefore, there is no show. (And, consequently, every possibility falls short of making a show=rhetoric, a concertino arising from pain, so to speak). (For the purpose of saying *something beautiful and memorable*).

Just as for Carmelo Bene, the theater is without spectacle, so writing is without the spectacle of the writer staging the writer, the scribe, who dictates jurisprudence or rather applies its laws: he writes in public (he holds the phallus-pen in public, the microphone of the poet) and, in short, offers the pop spectacle of the worst orality, neorealist (or rather: of an oratory and oracularity of a certain type that says prayers, counts the rosary, very possibly melancholy-social-sociopathic, whether euphoric or dysphoric).

If there were more time or space, I would approach the relationship between announcing/enunciation (and to being spoken), a reference to the (virtuous) practice that I have elsewhere referred to as *loose writing*, as mimesis or quasi-mimesis of the regular effects of anacoluthon, idiom, family lexicon, implication, accidental slippage, error, all of which normally occur and recur in our conversing, our mis-telling, ill-seeing, ill-saying.

2017–2023.

Daniele Poletti (Translated by Sandro-Angelo de Thomasis)

Breaking Fences and Putting Up Barricades. "Scrittura Complessa" as Overcoming and Resistance. Between Formlessness *and* The Continuous Word[1]

New York, November 12th, 2022

"Scrittura complessa" is not intended as a category since it would be tantamount to including the new label in the myopic diatribe among fighting factions, or even worse, it would be stating a certain power or empowerment to form a category. However, we don't have to relinquish ourselves to dialectical relativism because this would be counterproductive. Why? Because of the state of emergency of language, the situation today is that language is trampled upon; language, in general, is under attack. We are in flux today, and language is downgraded into a precarious state.

Instead of all this, it is necessary to start from the real context from which writing proliferates, disseminates, and moves to overcome the sterility of a specifically confrontational behavior (see the lyrical versus the experimental, research versus mainstream, etc.). Instead, what is needed is a broader vision that makes possible the approach to art and to writing as a social and intellectual necessity, unshackled by pre-established positions, as a political act coextensive with the formation of free individuals.

I coined the idea of "scrittura complessa" almost indolently in 2014. It is neither a critical category, a clearly identifiable school of thought, nor a manifesto (although the literary situation would benefit from it if it were), but an observation point on those types of writing that cannot be reduced to precise, comforting categories. These are the very reasons why it is neither possible nor beneficial to give a standard definition of "scrittura complessa": it is constantly evolving; in the words of François Julien, it is "de-coinciding." Obviously,

---

[1] EN: For ideological reasons, the author of this contribution has opted for a style of citations that refuses academic standards. To respect his choice and to provide the reader with all the necessary information, when possible, we have tried to provide information on the sources.

simplifying with a definition something that presents itself as irreducible by nature would be a contradiction. As such, "scrittura complessa," or "neo-complessa" or "della complessità," does not exist. It is precisely the opposite, for instance, of the experimental writing of the Sixties and Seventies, to which it is, however, only connected insofar as the established, fixed, grammatical rule of opposition to the fixed order and an aesthetic philosophy turned toward the progress of art and individuals.

Therefore, there is no such thing as a "scrittura complessa" programmatically given as a *modus operandi*. Still, some writings could be identified as complex through a lens that first recognizes a non-accessibility to consumption and through a biological deferral of "senso" and "segno." However, these writings opposed the immediacy of consumption, and, therefore, what they do is a political move to reappropriate the differential function of art and writing.

Furthermore, the paradigm of "complessità" (complexity) does not distinguish between different types of writing: prose, poetry, theater, concept, and performance; they are all under the same kind of attention. At the same time, though, when we speak of contemporary writing, we can diachronically see that complexity existed since the beginning (from Dante to Burchiello, passing through Rabelais, Folengo, Leporeo, Garzoni, etc.).

Short Methodological Follow-Up
Today, we find ourselves in an anomalous situation in which epistemology and philosophy of science have redefined the individual as co-individual ("co-individuo"). In the millennium of biology, ours, there is the affirmation of a new idea of the individual. It is becoming the subset of a superorganism called "olobionte," formed from the combination of our body and the community of microorganisms living in it, such to make doubtful the certainty of a single, specific individual self. Even more so, we cannot ignore the post-humanist turn, from anti-speciesism to transgender identity, that deflates the importance of the anthropometric vision of the world. Therefore, it is apparent that a de-location, a moving elsewhere, a radical shift in the point of observation toward otherness is occurring. Still, it is also clear that the political Right has gained traction in the last thirty years. In light of these considerations, though brief, there seems to be an undeniable, paradoxical fracture between social behavior and scientific discovery. This is not the time for a sociological disquisition; it is sufficient to affirm that the cultural and intellectual formation of individu-

als has regressed, at least since the Nineties. This is a regression that I would define as a true and proper "regressus ad uterum," where desire is wholly substituted with availability. Or, to say it in the words of Mario Perniola, "the basic tonality of 'performative culture' is no longer oriented toward pleasure but maintaining excitement." The typical hedonism of the Eighties has disappeared; it was the last impulse of a structured desire. We are today in a condition of widespread addiction, that is to say, an uninterrupted chain of offers that deprives individuals of the possibility of reflecting and choosing. This state of things inaugurates a transmutation of linguistic values such that inconclusiveness, retraction, and confusion turned from weak points into challenges that replace education and instruction with "edutainment," politics and information with "infotainment," art and culture with "entertainment." Perniola summarily defines all this as "democratainment," a situation in which language is, consequently, euphemized (*Contro la comunicazione* 2014). In other words, it is a displacement that dissimulates a disengagement that unmoors meaning in favor of sense, which may be more articulated but nourished by an apparent and presumed morality of rights and duties. The result is a flattening of differences, the horizontalization and impoverishment of experience, and the imposition of a "neo-language" comprised of periphrases and acronyms that appear as coming from a benevolent government for all intents and purposes.

Retrospectively, one can hypothesize that this state of things comes from the emergence of the "ordinary individual" and mass society that symbolically goes back to the advent of statistical science in the 19th century by Adolphe Quetelet. Individuals progressively accepted being computed, surveyed, and manipulated, transforming themselves into "types" and becoming abstractions, followed by an immense acceleration of the phenomena in the era of advanced technology. Being uniformly subjected to the same means of production and commodities, and thus being drawn toward the same labels, is a very efficient way to rigidify and uniformize thought. The theory of consumer economics tends to create a self-referential *habitat*, an *hortus conclusus*, that produces a serialization of behaviors, castigating individual reactions and personal reflections, inaugurating what Marcuse used to call the "language of total administration" (*One-Dimensional Man*). In this type of language, the tension between appearances and reality, fact and factor, substance and accident, it tends to disappear, promoting the immediate identification of reason and facts, truth and established truth, essence and existence, and the thing and its use. The elements of autonomy, discovery, demonstration, and criticism recede before designation, assertion, and imitation. The reduction of everything to a commercial fact ends up unifying previously antagonistic spheres of existence. The union expresses itself in the fluid linguistic conjunction of parts of speech in conflict with one another. Therefore, the universe of speech that characterizes commercial and political style, in which opposites reconcile, is one of the most efficient ways to make language and communication incapable of expressing protest and refusal. In this context, ruled by standards and patterned phenomena, efficiency has absolute precedence over function. *Repressive democracy* dispenses immediate answers for immediate comprehension as an instrument for amniotic capture and control of the masses, understood as cannon fodder for consumerism and productivity. The step toward achieving fascism is short. In fact, one could speak of a dissimulated congruence, that is, to render impracticable the freedom that language enables thanks to the ambiguity of words to the power of association of ideas inherent in it and the poetic enrichment of meanings. Under the banner of democratic progress, technological mass communication hides a resurgence of populist obscurantism apt to cancel cognitive aspects and promote emotionality and limitless availability and, thus, once again, depriving individuals of the capacity of ethical and aesthetic judgment and making pedestrians out of them that can be pointed wherever at will.

"Complessità" as an Anticommercial, Antiacademic, and Antimechanical Proposal

The categories of "experimental writing" and "research writing" (except for, at least in part, that of "literary research," for its semantic perspective of dynamism) are now empty slogans.

The former, coming from past experiments (alas!) still not taken for granted, crystallized itself into a museum-like idea, entomological or etymological. The latter is born from trying to indicate the new path of "literary experimentation" through clear stylistic examples and some genealogies. However, all of this is still done under the banner of an unproductive antagonistic posture against the literary *status quo*, which must, of course, be opposed. Most of all, this ought to be done by becoming mindful of both the limitations of the hyperspecialized perspective of "genres" and the inefficiency of critical tools, which are now insufficient to give an account of new experiments in writing.

The concept of "post-" undoubtedly aggravates this interpretive stagnation. After the long century of "–isms" (a suffix that in the 19th century acquired the abstract meaning of faction or doctrinaire system), which coincided with the most significant moment of fracture in art and literature in concomitance with the avant-gardes, there is a reversal in direction starting from the Sixties. We go from the suffix to the prefix; as such, Surrealism, Dadaism, Orphism, etc., are replaced with neo-avant-garde, trans-avant-garde, even post-neo-avant-garde, post-poetry and, at last, post-humanism. The era of "post-" and "neo-"—as such, of a society of prefixes—seems to me to be a clear symptom of the inability to individualize, analyze, and gather those aesthetic experiences that are set outside the ordinary, imperturbable course of tradition and that need no definition other than themselves.

Furthermore, applying this concept to any type of presumed fracture—provoked by saturation, thickening, loss of meaning, and the consequent necessity to overcome—denotes, on the one hand, a willful surrender to one's condition of marginality and, on the other, a constant state of desiring the right position, the necessity of colonizing a place that, by nature, is fluid and jagged, at the risk of obscuring those experiences that lie outside the posthumous. Therefore, "post-" becomes *posture*, the inauguration of a *status*, and, finally, "posteggio" (parking). However, before formulating a proposal to identify a trend of new writings capable of transit, infraction, and reorganization of current artistic-literary conventions—which, given the present situation, can no longer be postponed—it is necessary to posit a question: where does experimental art fail (not that it errs, let's be clear)?

The issue is not the predominance of one genre over another, of a trend, or a penchant—instead, this is an outcome of the issue—but, as mentioned earlier, the focus needs to be placed on the voluntary servitude of individuals. The intrusion of consumer capitalism has been so ubiquitous that it globally deprives individuals of the cognitive and critical capacity to assess reality with diverse nuances, reaching even into the so-called intellectual class with an unprecedented intensification caused by the advent of technological mass communication. Besides, the subversive charge of thought and the once-upon scandalous character of art appear today co-opted, almost in real-time, by what can be defined as a "progressive digital sponge." The system of digital organization that endlessly develops has become an incessant accumulation of information, to which the concepts of "post-something" pale in comparison, giving a direction to the inclinations of the "hyper-," a space of acceleration where, as argued by Byung-Chul Han, "we no longer content ourselves with passively gobbling down information, but we want to produce and communicate it actively; we are simultaneously consumers and producers" (*Nello sciame. Visioni del digitale*). If, on the one hand, citing once more Han, "the digital connection encourages symmetrical communication, no univocal hierarchy separates the addresser from the addressee"; on the other hand, the pervasiveness of democratic transparency of the web creates a spontaneously enslaved population of individuals progressively enslaved by immediate, swift, destratified, and impoverished codes. Without delving into theories of power, the immediate consequence is a flattening, not so much of communicating possibilities but of the complexity of language, to the detriment of its determining function as clinamen. In this kind of framework, the aspect of artistic experimentation and the search for a new, fertile, unhabitual language create three obvious effects: 1) the continuously expanding digital sponge appropriates radical instances of research and neutralizes them, filtering them out and representing their most superficial aspects through a process of destructuralization, typical of the avant-garde; 2) the code adopted by "experimentation" is asymmetrical with respect to its users, communication is halted, even when the aim is to shock; 3) in digital democracy, anyone is capable of becoming the center of attention of a virtual audience, determining the end of aesthetic orientation in favor of an ever-increasing spectacularized subjectivity.

After having said all this, it seems apparent that the majority of this society is misaligned with the expressive codes that require an interpretive effort and are beyond the statistical threshold of attention. This occurs understandably for the indistinct mass of consumers, but the same behavior afflicts poetry readers and the so-called "strong readers."

There exists an inventory compiled in 1971 by Anna and Martino Oberto and cited by Spatola in *Verso la poesia totale* (1978), referred to as "poesia sperimentale," which gathers 67 diverse types of poetry: phonetic, gestural, symbiotic, electronic, concrete poetry, etc. It is important to underline through a simple taxonomy how, in those years, the effervescence around experimentalism (not only literary) was active and, I would say, somewhat natural and taken for granted. With the relinquishing of perspective and the advent of relativity and dodecaphonic, art could no longer be as before. Today, things have really changed, first and foremost, from a social point of view. The types of writing that do not result as performative on the level of consumerism and emotional satisfaction are almost entirely rejected. A refusal to experience that which diverges from one's own certainties to the point of paradoxically negating the ontological status in which one lives. To this purpose, I believe it would be opportune to add to the Oberto list even the category of "poesia dogmatica," that is, "dogmatic poetry," as a further example of this rejection. By now, a matrix-prejudice is well rooted, assimilating art to its "communicative function." Therefore, structurally, in literature, a page, which is the frame *par excellence* of writing, is experienced as an infallible device in which readers reposit their own horizon of understanding to obtain a result that, if not similar, is incongruous to their own desires, with the minimal effort possible. As such, even "from poetry's side," so to say, we bear witness to a process of simplification that alters the differential function of art (and writing) necessary to provide a dysmorphic, polymorphic, and polyphonic point of view on reality, that is to say, an aesthetic refinement that nourishes a sense of critique and the consequent formation of free individuals.

In such a context, where the great mass of consumers does not enter (for algorithmic reasons) or is unsuccessful in making contact with aesthetic factors that are not immediately consumable and where even the readers of poetry, and literature in general, end up responding solely to the dogma of hyper-codification of genres and content, the spaces that remain to engage in "arte complessa" are diminished and powerless.

At this historical juncture, despite the disproportion or, should we say, precisely because of it, pitting the highest degree of complexity of reality against a retrograde social and political nadir becomes a necessity, a factor that opposes uniformization and lack of difference that surrounds us.

Elsewhere, and as mentioned above, I have sought to delineate what is meant by "scrittura complessa." It remains an open field with various declensions that, for me, preferably borrows concepts from other disciplines to be refashioned critically. The term "complessità" already refers to the theory of complexity in physics and science in general, as well as epistemology and sociology. To paraphrase Edgar Morin, it is a "problem-concept," not a solution concept. It derives from the Latin verb "plectere" (to weave) compounded with the preposition "cum" (with). The word is practically an oxymoron, two things that are traditionally thought of as opposites: a plurality of components, of elements, but also a unity (*unitas multiplex*).

Given that literature, like the other arts, is always the expression of a society and the times in which it is moored and grounds, even anticipating at times, the Weltanschauung, "scrittura complessa" has the duty to resist and contrast with the reduction of linguistic factors to minimal terms, typical of the everyday life but also contemporary writing. Particularly in writing and its reception, this manifests itself with a dynamic of immediate identification and understanding. It is germane to an advanced form of emotional illiteracy that does not correspond to ignorance due to a lack of tools but to a knowledge unable to savor wisdom. After turning the corner, the course is once more toward ignorance. Complex writings have been practiced since time immemorial; however, today, they are necessary to re-establish an equilibrium to demonstrate that writing cannot simply belong to the unilateral exigencies of comprehensibility, of decoding at all costs but must create a margin of unavailability and unbelonging that reverberates potentially as a cornerstone of an ulterior cognitive structure for its users. The word must transform itself into an *event* to carry out these functions and make it such that it fulfills its epistemological role, fleeing the prison of codes and becoming reversible material. As Paul Ricoeur writes: "The word must not become a relic, but must evolve itself thanks to a constant reinterpretation. For the word to be actual but also significant, it must transform itself into an *event*, a non-preordained space of possibilities, an open and multiform space" (*Per un'utopia ecclesiale*). I have defined, on this matter, three descriptive modes as examples of complex approaches to writing, above and beyond that of "perennial subtraction" from univocal and superstitious signification.

1. Disjunctive function of language

Although the functions of language organized by Jakobson exhaustively contemplate all the articulations of language, one can dare to add another layer to the pre-existing and well-known "poetic function." The anthropologist Massimo Canevacci writes that

> the disjunctions are all fractures of experience [...]. The disjunctions are also cognitive fractures: something is broken in the acquired ability to orient oneself, to classify, to elaborate models. Strange creases cut across diverse and oppositional parts of what is referred to as the 'I,' the unified 'I.' Slowly, we perceive it more and more endowed with striations (*Sincretismi. Esplorazioni diasporiche sulle ibridazioni culturali*).

With the "disjunctive function of language," every sign rebels against its specialized and static role, claiming a production of meaning that exceeds, by a short-circuit, through hybridization and contradiction. Even the architect

Bernard Tschumi busied himself with disjunction and, heeding to his ideas, if we replace the word "architecture" with "literature," we would obtain an enlightening result:

> The concept of disjunction is incompatible with a static, autonomous, and structural vision of architecture. However, it is not against autonomy or structure; it simply implies constant and mechanical operation that systematically produces dissociation in space and time, where an architectonic element functions exclusively by butting against a programmatic element, against a mass movement, or something else. This way, disjunction becomes a systematic and theoretical tool for architecture (*Architettura e disgiunzione*).

To pivot onto the next coordinate, it is necessary to briefly reference two concepts that result from the act of disjunction.

a) Lacuna. According to Nicola Gardini, this means "not speaking for the purpose of speaking. Lacuna participates in representation: it is an essential motor of both form and meaning; actually, the source itself of the literary, there is no textual omission that does not point toward an extratextual wholeness" (*Lacuna. Saggio sul non detto*). To recognize the value of omission means searching for the meaning of a work.

b) This strenuous search for meaning is directly related to Duchamp's *infrasottile* (infrathin), which is a category that gathers all the substances, states, minimal differences, sharings, and metamorphoses to the limits of perception. The 'infrathin' indicates what dwells at the extremes of perception, of the discernable, of difference. This does not mean being invisible or indiscernible, nor transcendental, but instead a presence at the limit, a possibility that is also real, or a copresence of two statuses that "wed one another," according to Duchamp, giving life to a third waiting to be gathered. An example of this concept could be "the space between the sound of a gunshot and the appearance of a bullet hole on the target." Still, in abstract terms, one can argue that writing, in general, through the dissipation of meaning and form, is a great 'infrathin' device that leaves behind a trace of ineffability. This invites an attitude of pursuing a duty that one knows is endless but eye-opening, constraining one to observe, search, and remember.[2]

---

[2] AN: See Elio Grazioli's *Infrasottile. L'arte contemporanea ai limiti*. Postmedia books, 2018.

2. Formlessness

As mentioned earlier, art and writing today are subjected to transaction mechanisms, like any other commodity. One attribute that successfully removes them from the monetization of value is the dimension of formlessness. For Bataille, formlessness is the category that allowed the deconstruction of all categories. Being allergic to definitions, he does not so much specify the sense of formlessness, preferring instead to assign to it the task of negating that everything has its own form and positing the possibility of achieving a formless sense. The goal is to put the relationship between subject and object into crisis. Subjects lose their capacity for perception and are no longer at its origin. Space swallows their gaze, abandoning it as an object among the objects of the gaze, thus totally destroying the rigid integrity of individual identity. This is a clear-cut opposition to anthropological idealism and the cultural one that derives from it, and based on which form is imposed by an idealistic logic, in an absolute manner, onto reality to be able to dominate it. De-sublimation is the main feature of formlessness, acting as an enzyme that undermines the primacy of sight in favor of a visceral coactivity of the senses, causing a loss of the center and a diffused perceptive status.

3. The continuous word

The endpoint of this brief excursus of a motivational character is a coordinate of motion and dynamics. Given for certain that the system of representation of the world is, for the most part, articulated according to antithetical categories so that, in the opposition between *Identical* and *Different*, the latter ends up transforming itself into the former, it is necessary to propose what can be defined as a *Permanent Revolution of Writing*. In 1965, Dick Higgins coined the concept of "intermedia," for which every distinction between various cultural forms must vanish so that the idea of "category" must be substituted with that of "continuity." But, beyond the exigency of mixture, fusion, and interference, the concept I am proposing of the "continuous word" is a sample taken again from architecture. In particular, it comes from *Monumento Continuo* by the group Superstudio. The word and writing make themselves the radical paradigm of an unrelenting metamorphic movement that, through various intermediaries, adapts itself to the landscapes it traverses, transforming itself and the landscape. This gives place to a spatiality destined to host new "truths" unbounded by the logic of consumerism. In the continuous beyondness of sense and form, a type of renewed word emerges that inaugurates with that established word a dialectic of inclusion and separation. Therefore, the "continuous word" suggests the necessity of memory of the most diverse traditions in the face of the pathological amnesia of contemporary society and prefigures incessantly the remoteness inherent in the unbounded tension of discovery.

The words of Coleridge about the reader of poetry seem to me apt both as an absolute metaphor for literature and a demand for forgiveness for that which you have just heard: "[T]he reader ought to be pushed forward, at least not merely or principally, by the mechanical impulse of curiosity, nor by a restless desire to get to the last act, but rather by the pleasant activity of the journey itself" (*Biographia literaria, ovvero schizzi biografici della mia vita e opinioni letterarie*).

Viareggio, October 25th, 2022.

Day 3 – Sunday, November 13, 2022

Giorgio Patrizi (Translated by Sandro-Angelo de Thomasis)

"And the Avant-Garde Found Something, Right?"

Andrea Zanzotto asked himself this very question, opening a poem from his collection titled *La Beltà* (1968) with this ironic or, better yet, sarcastic query. Obviously, Zanzotto was looking at Gruppo 63, and at that season, rich in *Sturm und Drang*, that had marked a decade and breached the most traditional bulwarks of poetry. These, in turn, were defined, by the end of the 50s, on the modalities exemplified by the people at *Officina* of the interweaving of experience and ideology. This rupture brought about a new, and in various modes disruptive, practice understood as taking on the duty of a radically critical outlook toward the language of literature and late-stage neo-capitalist society. The adventure of the neo-avant-garde was a strongly innovative experience for those who lived the tension of twentieth-century poetry as a search for a new language capable of managing expressive and communicative tools in ways that transgress the habits of literary institutions. Therefore, in its increasingly radical and novel experimentalism, or better yet, in its establishment of a "tradition of the new"—as would have written Harold Rosenberg[1]—the question as to what precisely the avant-garde found could not exhaust itself in an answer that did not presuppose the stubborn continuity of a search for unusual solutions.

In this way, during the 70s, a maturing vision of the poetic text came about, seeking to settle the score with these two antithetical perspectives and be capable of articulating the gesture of contradiction. This vision dominates the historical anthology *Poesia italiana della contraddizione* (1989), edited by Franco Cavallo and Mario Lunetta, that summarizes the tensions and moods of an entire decade according to two binary perspectives: first, the destructuralization of the poetic subject and expressive and communicative language,

---

[1] EN: For Harold Rosenberg, see *The Tradition of the New*. Horizon Press, 1959; later published by Feltrinelli in 1964.

removed from its positive function and re-dimensioned into an area of combinatory play; second, a ludic sense that could find justification in the search for new linguistic dynamics.

In 1981, the Roman collective Quaderni di Critica put forth the following hypothesis: "Il linguaggio, riconosciuto nel modo di sviluppo capitalistico strumento e luogo specifico di produzione [...] slarga la dicotomia di significante e significato [...] e pretende che l'uso della letteratura non sia più unilineare e positivo, ma frammentario, negativo, fortemente autocritico" ("Per una ipotesi di scrittura materialistica" 21).[2] This hypothesis is based on the theoretical and creative work that, since the 70s, projects itself onto the following decade, looking at the work of the neo-avant-garde and their fellow travelers. Born in contrast to the peculiar textual work of the neo-avant-garde, of more traditional and ideologically compromised modalities of poetic work, these *ipotesi* are but one of the various examples of theoretical engagement that is antagonistic to a restoration. The restorative anthology of *La parola innamorata. I poeti nuovi, 1976–1978*, edited by Giancarlo Pontiggia and Enzo Di Mauro (1978), was answered by the articulation of new modalities of poetic research. The "Lecce Theses" of 1987 (with Bettini, Leonetti, Luperini, Lunetta, Giuliani, Sanguineti, et al.), summarizing a long phase of gestation, were again putting forth spaces of experimentation intended to give momentum to a project and then from there, "a trend, that is, the selection of a field and travel trajectory," and "avoiding surrendering to the blackmail of the only ideology that is not casually spared from the pullulating neophytes of the 'end of ideologies' [...]. Today, the correct trend cannot be anything other than a critique of the crisis" ("Progetto, tendenza, allegoria" 60).

In that passage between decades, from the 70s to the late 80s, the voices that made themselves heard were many and active. In this perspective, it is necessary to underline the multifaceted renewal effort achieved by reformulating already neo-avant-garde techniques. At times, these reformulations went in the direction of an accentuated and grotesque connotation capable of disarming

---

[2] EN: "Language, recognized within the framework of capitalist development as an instrument and specific site of production, [...] broadens the dichotomy between signifier and signified, [...] and lays claim to the use of literature no longer as unilinear and positive but fragmentary, negative, and intensely self-critical" (Translated by de Thomasis; unless stated otherwise). Later republished in *Gruppo '93: La recente avventura del dibattito teorico letterario in Italia*. Edited by Filippo Bettini and Francesco Muzzioli. Manni, 1990, pp. 20–24.

cultural and social themes most typical of the 80s through a comic key: from the cultural industry to Bell's so-called "end of ideology,"[3] weak thought to globalization, themes found in that war of ideas, which was the typical modality for polemics in that decade.

On this matter, Muzzioli notes that "[u]na letteratura di ricerca sperimentale comincia innanzitutto col mettere in dubbio e rendere problematico il suo stesso statuto e ruolo sociale [...]. Lo stesso termine sperimentalismo indica la presenza di un controllo razionale (quasi scientifico)" that intervenes on the language of the community "con il giudizio sulla posizione e sul rigore (sulla "tendenza" e "sulla qualità," per usare i termini cari a Benjamin)" (45–46).[4] This experimental modality

> tende ad incrinare l'identità centrale dell'io, che rappresenta il marchio della proprietà privata del tessuto poetico [...]. Il testo si apre all'inserimento di 'voci' diverse e anche all'intersecarsi e mescolarsi dei generi [...]. La scommessa sta nel conservare un preciso riferimento ai significati, magari mediante il ricorso a termini obsoleti (arricchimento del vocabolario, quindi, contro l'impoverimento dei *media*. (47)[5]

The so-called "Lecce Theses" refer to the programmatic writings elaborated at an encounter in April of 1987 held in Lecce under the banner of the publishing house Manni. It is a fundamental reference point for this phase of theoretical and textual work, and we find in it the central value of *trends*: "La tendenza non può essere oggi assunta e rilanciata, se non a condizione di essere intesa e vissuta come presa di posizione e *critica della crisi*" ("Progetto, tendenza, allegoria" 60).[6] From this angle, what affirms itself is the radical choice of

---

[3] EN: See Bell, Daniel. *The End of Ideology. On the Exhaustion of Political Ideas in the Fifties*. Free Press, 1960.

[4] EN: "before anything else, experimental research literature starts with the doubting and problematization of one's status and social role. [...] That very term *experimentalism* indicates the presence of a (quasi-scientific) rational control" that intervenes on the language of the community "judging the position and rigor (on the 'trend' and 'quality,' to use the terms dear to Benjamin)."

[5] EN: "tends to compromise the central identity of the 'I,' which represents the mark of private property of the poetic text. [...] The text opens itself to the insertion of diverse 'voices' and the intersection and mingling of genres. [...] The bet is on maintaining a specific reference to what is being signified, perhaps by having recourse to obsolete terms (a lexical enrichment against the impoverishment of *media*."

[6] EN: "trends today cannot be undertaken and relaunched if not on the condition of being understood and lived as a stance and a *critique of the crisis*."

refusing to construct the practice of writing in the name of the symbol that "holds everything together"—as one can infer from the etymological construction. It does this while evoking a transcendent value where allegory calls on the essential requirements of that which we have elsewhere indicated as a possible "materialistic writing." This historical-ideological adjectivization recalls a fundamental instance of a philosophical, epistemological, and linguistic style. It pivots onto allegorical procedures as a modality of textual play that moves within an antagonistic universe, responsibly understood by a realization of contemporaneity, with the awareness of the strength of a language mobilized in an effort of innovation and anti-conformity.

Among them, we may recall two particularly active groups that worked on such problems: the Neapolitan group K.B. (Kryptopterus bicirrhis, with Gabriele Frasca, Tommaso Ottonieri, and Lorenzo Durante) and the one gathered around the pages of the journal *Baldus* (with Mariano Bàino, Biagio Cepollaro, and Lello Voce). There was an outlook of "elaborazione di strategie di contaminazione ed ibridazione (allegorica) che nel pluristilismo e nella polifonicità dialogica potessero trovare uno strumento d'espressione che parta dalla coscienza dell'impossibilità per un unico stile di costituirsi in *altrove* rispetto all'esistente, di essere, di per sé, oppositivo," this being the result of a "una disarmonia dialogica, di una contaminazione" (Baldus 122).[7]

Alongside the widespread—and often solipsistic—individual practice mentioned earlier, what characterizes the experimental scene of the 80s is the blooming of numerous schools or groups connected by contiguous environments other than research. It is in this way that the experience of the Neapolitan journal *Altri termini* (1972–1991), led by Franco Cavallo, unfolds diverse and, at times, parallel trajectories. There are interesting experimenters of words and rhythms, such as Biagio Cepollaro, who interpreted a position of the subject as decentered and splintered, narrated with a plurilingualism constructed with loan translations of period phrases, or broken words, allusively truncated. At the same time, Mariano Bàino shows himself active in a mixture, often playful and parodic, of low-level languages, dialectal constructions, neoplasia, and onomatopoeia. Lello Voce is very active in the passage from "classical" plu-

---

[7] EN: "elaborating strategies of contamination and (allegorical) hybridization that, in the dialogical plurality of styles and sounds, could find an expressive instrument cognizant of the impossibility of a unique style constituting itself *somewhere else* in respect to existence, of being, in and of itself, oppositional," this being the result of a "dialogical disharmony, a contamination."

rilingualism to the one found in *Baldus*, citing Folengo's mock-heroic poem *Baldus* (1517) as a typical modality of an antagonism of style and narration. Voce points to the weaving of various lexicons and registers, with the expressive deformation of words, but also the phonic articulation of the signifiers, rhythms, and sonorities that are grasped expressively, even deploying musical supports to the texts. On this subject, Cecilia Bello Minciacchi writes:

> Potrà dirsi allora dialettica, la relazione che il Gruppo '93 ha teso a stabilire con il Gruppo 63, data la dinamica di avvicinamento e allontanamento delle posizioni teoriche e della progettualità letteraria. Data, anche, la diversità delle premesse e degli esiti raggiunti dai più giovani. È negli intenti dei critici, soprattutto, che si potrà individuare—comunque perseguito, da parte di alcuni o anche solo di pochi o pochissimi, e comunque portato a compimento—il tentativo di fondare una avanguardia altra. (17)[8]

Thus, there is a new wave, third in the ebb and flow of Italian literary avant-gardes. But, let us stay, for now, with the facts of history. Gruppo 93 was a locus of debate and cooperation between individual authors—mostly gravitating around the above-cited *Poesia italiana della contraddizione*—and other pre-existing groups already launched into experimentalism. First of all, the K.B. collective—Durante, Frasca, Frixione, and Ottonieri, mentioned earlier—gave its adherence to singular voices ever since the beginning; so did the Genoese group behind the journal *Altri Luoghi*, born as a Collective of Emergency Poetic Intervention—Marco Berisso, Piero Cademartori, Guido Caserza, and Paolo Gentiluomo; as well as the collective Baldus, promoter of the homonymous journal, formed by Mariano Bàino, Biagio Cepollaro, and Lello Voce. Therefore, these previous and very diverse experiences converged into Gruppo 93. As mentioned, Baldus was the collective that gave the name to the journal *Baldus*: "Baldo ha tre voci. Sia chiaro: non è uno. È triperuno. È Limerno, Merlino, Fulica" (Qtd. in Minciacchi 36).[9] In 1992, the editorial group

---

[8] EN: "Therefore, it could call itself dialectical, that is, the relation that Gruppo 93 tried to establish with Gruppo 63, given the to-and-fro dynamic of the theoretical positions and literary projects. Also taken as a given is the diversity of the premises and the output of the younger generation. Overall, it is in the critics' intentions that one can individuate—in any case, undertaken by some, or perhaps a few, or even by very few, and even so, rarely brought to a conclusion—the attempt of founding an*other* avant-garde."

[9] EN: "Baldo has three voices. Let it be known; it is not one. It is Threeforone. It is Linmer, Merlin, and Fulica."

underscored its three voices in this manner amid the discussions held within Gruppo 93 and not without friction. As Minciacchi explains:

> Alla discussione dell'89 nella libreria Buchmesse di Milano, là dove il Gruppo '93 si era costituito, Baldus, che non aveva ancora dato alle stampe il suo primo fascicolo ma esisteva come collettivo, in consonanza con le riflessioni teorico-critiche proposte da Bettini e Muzzioli, sostenne il ricorso programmatico all'allegoria, figura retorica privilegiata "per la conservazione e lo sviluppo del rapporto del testo poetico con la dimensione extraletteraria." (37)[10]

Adding that: "[L]a prassi della citazione, in facile odore di postmodernismo, ma intesa invece rigorosamente come 'un lavoro di contaminazione tra diverse realtà linguistiche che si ponga come obiettivo la trasformazione e la torsione dei materiali utilizzati a livello di micro e/o macrostrutture linguistiche'" (37).[11] The Baldus collective efficiently interpreted the instance of a research capable of confronting the themes of Postmodernism without demonizing them, but with the necessity of overcoming them: under the tagline of critical postmodernism, the techniques of macaronic comedy, seeking in Folengo's materialism the suggestions of a blended poetry, in which linguistic play be functional toward a critique of ideology.

I cite once again Minciacchi, who notes how:

> Altri autori, altri critici o teorici diedero vita, immediatamente a ridosso dei lavori del Gruppo 93, all'ipotesi di un nuovo, 'terzo momento' dell'arte d'avanguardia in Italia. L'operazione *Terza ondata. Il nuovo movimento della scrittura in Italia* [2016], una volta messe in luce e interpretate alcune caratteristiche comuni nella produzione letteraria coeva, molte delle quali riconducibili a un ambito di esperienza d'avanguardia, mirava a raccogliere sotto una coesa dialogicità oppositiva e innovativa tendenze anche nettamente diverse tra loro. (51)[12]

---

[10] EN: "In 1989, during the discussion held at Buchmesse, the Milanese bookstore where Gruppo 93 had gathered, Baldus, which had not yet printed its first volume but existed as a collective, following the critical and theoretical reflections proposed by Bettini and Muzzioli, argued for the programmatic recourse to allegory, a privileged rhetorical figure "for the conservation and development of the relation between the poetic text and the extraliterary dimension.""

[11] EN: "The practice of citation, with its facile postmodern odor, is, however, understood rigorously as a 'work of contamination between diverse linguistic realities that posits for itself the objective of transforming and distorting the material used at the level of linguistic micro- and, or macrostructures.'"

[12] EN: "[O]ther authors, critics, and theorists had given life, immediately following the work of Gruppo 93, to the hypothesis of a new 'third moment' of avant-garde art in Italy. The work *Terza*

The Gruppo 93 is called as such in echo to the movement from thirty years prior and fixed itself onto the proximity of the term to the verification of its operations, precisely 1993, which would have marked the conclusion of the group's activities. That same fateful year also marks the appearance of an anthology edited by Filippo Bettini, who had the Roman experience of Quaderni di Critica behind him, and Roberto Di Marco, who, together with Michele Perriera and Gaetano Testa, established themselves into the so-called School of Palermo, the backbone of the neo-avant-garde. *Terza ondata: Il nuovo movimento della scrittura in Italia* is a direct result of the theses of Gruppo 93, which, already in its martial title, indicates the bellicose intention of promoting conflictual ideas and writings of a third phase of the twentieth-century avant-gardes. In the theoretical part of the book, the prospects of contestatory writing are recalled in the awareness of a marginal but also peculiar collocation of literary discourse in the environment of the dynamics of the global market and new media. The editors remark that

> [L]a contraddizione letteraria non la si intende appieno se la si percepisce riduttivamente come "letteraria," cioè solamente come interna alla tradizione-istituzione delle lettere. Essa invece è innanzitutto una contraddizione sociale, essendo il sistema letterario vigente e il movimento extrasistemico della scrittura due soggetti sociali e culturali specifici della postmodernità capitalistica. (Di Marco 21)[13]

The radical character of the linguistic processes, the direct connection with current events, the re-reading of the past with the "alienating" spirit of the present, and the same combination of criticism and poetry all re-enter exactly inside a framework that is both historical and ideological, which can be described only with the now standardized formula by Rosenberg of the "tradition of the new." And here returns, once again, the strong and articulated recall to "allegory." Allegory is the great figure that this antagonistic practice

---

ondata. Il nuovo movimento della scrittura in Italia [2016], once having shed light and interpreted several common characteristics in contemporary literary production, many of which are retraceable to an avant-garde, experiential environment, aimed to gather under a cohesive, oppositional, and innovative dialogue trends that are even sharply different from one another."

[13] EN: "[L]iterary contradiction is not fully understood if reductively perceived as 'literary,' that is, solely as internal to a tradition or a literary institution. It is instead, and foremost, a social contradiction since the current literary system and the extra-systemic movement of writing are two social and cultural subjects specific to capitalistic postmodernism."

of literature recalls; allegory as a communicative rationality of the mechanisms of semantic and representative production, the imposition of a projected discursive structure, and its ideological-cognitive ends. The adherence to the historical and socialized meanings of *la langue* [the abstract, systematic rules and conventions of a signifying system] and the tensions rising out of conflict and breaks, and therein lies the refusal of lyrical subjectivity, the recall to the objectivity of events, the principal attention to the discontinuities 'submerged' by temporal processes.

The problem of the avant-garde—of its possible repurposing or its definite death—occupies a good portion of debates surrounding poetry in the last decade, registering answers that situate themselves between experimentalism and the market, with attention given to novel youth languages and linguistic creativity that often draw more from extraliterary codes, visual and musical than traditional verbal writing.

Yet again, all this does not exhaust the key themes to a confusing but most vital and significant form of experimentalism. Alongside the names and dynamics we have spoken about, one discovers a most animated territory traversed by new and unusual outlooks on many of the abovementioned problems. Women writers who retrace traditional themes and codes, under the light of their intense rethinking, belong to this area. Since the 70s, the time of women's poetry has been experienced as witnessing a peculiar and widespread realization of problems related to gender roles and conflicts. In the decades that accompanied the turn of the millennium, a wide and varied area of women authors continued to do poetry with a diversity and multiplicity of perspectives but also with a recurrence of stylistic registers and modalities of symbolization. This area ranges from the precursor Frabotta, one of the apexes of poetic work from this long and complex phase—to be recalled, now, alongside Patrizia Cavalli, in the sorrowful disappearance of exemplary voices, potent and penetrating, like the excellent "outdated" Anna Maria Ortese—to other protagonists of those years, from Mariella Bettarini to Antonella Anedda, Iolanda Insana, Gabriella Sica, Giovanna Sicari, and Rosaria Lo Russo.

I have sought to sketch this experimentation that marks fundamental socio-cultural transitions and that, although suffocated by the involution experienced in the new millennium, remains a strong voice, antagonistic and beneficially practical. Indeed, one cannot conclude an account of poetry in the last decades without retracing the observations of critics and historiographers who situate the parabola of research poetry of this phase in a downward curve, destined to founder in silence or, its equivalent, a massive confusion of languages. But it must be said that the concern with a dissolution of the *rules of the game* has governed the trajectories of twentieth and twenty-first-century versification; the assessment of exclusion from the historical publishing industry suffered by the most unclassifiable of authors; the rebuke of the plurality of voices and languages as a confusion to be exorcised or the outcome of a practice in the name of the worst form of narcissism. Stefano Giovanardi, one of the most lucid voices surrounding this debate—too quickly silenced by destiny—affirmed that "[D]a una decina d'anni a questa parte le manifestazioni di poesia si sono fatte improvvisamente rare, episodiche, discontinue, come se alla diffusa, debordante creatività degli anni Settanta e primi Ottanta fosse repentinamente subentrata una devastante aridità, un deciso rigetto della comunicazione in versi," of which the cause is, other than the unprecedented editorial crisis, the fact that "gli orientamenti generali della civiltà dell'immagine [...] tendono evidentemente a relegare il fatto poetico in una zona di marginalità assoluta." ("Introduzione" lv–lvi)[14]

All this seems to stem from judgments on the dynamics of the poetic universe often derived from a much too general vision of the phenomenon, from a distrust in entering texts and the peculiarities of authors, from the temptation to dissociate oneself when challenging to fit within twentieth-century schemas. Suppose the last frontier of poetic *samizdat* has become, for some time now, together with the online publishing industry, the occupation of Internet sites with verses by novices and critical discussions dedicated to them. In that case, it is indeed, so to speak, a *multiethnic* and *multicultural* poetic society, this panorama in which unfold the most diverse discourses on poetics, for the most part, associated—to upper-intermediate levels—by the instance of a renewed language distanced from the consumption of everyday life and enriched by the *pathos* of experimenting new expressive forms. These are widespread writings that situate themselves in a great unguaranteed territory, outside of any market and exchange value, at times specimens of a mode of rethinking speech and

---

[14] EN: "[F]rom about ten years ago to now, the manifestations of poetry have made themselves suddenly rare, episodic, discontinuous, as though in response to the widespread, overflowing creativity of the 70s and early 80s a sudden devastating aridity followed, a decisive rejection of communicating in verse," of which the cause is, other than the unprecedented editorial crisis, the fact that "the general leanings of an image society [...] obviously tend to relegate the poetic fact in a zone of absolute marginality."

producing meaning to find once more novel potentialities, discover new resources and rare significance from it.

But here, unlike the previous decades, some design of progress is no longer in play but rather a recovery of the voices and experiences snatched away from market and mass media logic. It is the recovery of a possibility of experience and discourse about experience, a possibility for knowing and interpreting that is *other*: against the process of neutralizing languages from memory and tradition, of both old and new. The language of poetry renews its very own disquiet universality, not in positing itself as a language of the sublime, but instead, in showing itself as a "tongue set free" to echo Elias Canetti. And here, one comprehends again the exactitude of Adorno's warning on the necessity of always being, as an ethical choice, on the side of obscurity. This "awareness of suffering" intends to speak, even from the most cryptic expressive decisions, even from the harshest verses. Whoever recognizes themselves, even if taking on different paths or places of artistic work, cannot but sense the urgency of questions formulated by the poetic discourse that do not require answers as much as, and most importantly, the maintaining of the possibility itself of continuing to posit questions, perhaps even conserving the utopian premonition of the dying Isidore Ducasse, Comte de Lautréamont: "La poésie doit être faite par tous. Non par un" (371).[15]

---

[15] EN: "Poetry must be done by all, not just by one."

Ugo Perolino (Translated by Nicholas Benson)

For The Reappearing Pheasant

Latent movements of revision and subversion of poetry's language and institutions marked the 1950s. Not only the first experiments of the Novissimi—*Cronache e altre poesie*, the first collection by Elio Pagliarani, was published in 1954; *Il cuore zoppo* by Alfredo Giuliani in 1955; and Sanguineti's *Laborintus* in 1956—but, more generally, due to a mutation internal to language and its poetic use. In this perspective, the theoretical moment (reflections on code and language) assumes new relevance for expression: poetics expands, adopts new techniques, and is secularized; the lyric proceeds towards prose, narration, commentary, or auto-commentary; it is imbued with terms from the new languages of technology and science. It is a fact that, in *Officina* and the *Novissimi*, the paratext and notes have as much weight as the texts in outlining a reading horizon, a code, and its rules; the "Piccola antologia neo-sperimentale" presents itself as an appendix to "La libertà stilistica," as realization and exemplification of Pasolini's discourse.[1]

In the criticism of the 1950s, a restrictive judgment of the post-war generation became established, identified as the condition of "epigonism," a term used in various circumstances by Macrì, Anceschi, and Pasolini. In reality, the pressure to renew language and stylistic institutions manifests itself in a capillary and widespread manner, producing innovations that can be documented in the texts of the younger poets. The *Seconda antologia di poeti nuovi* (1951) collects the unpublished works of authors debuting in the 1950 "San Babila" Prize competition. Antithetical approaches and attitudes can be detected: "[T]

---

[1] EN: "La libertà stilistica" is an essay written by Pasolini and published in the journal *Officina*, 9–10, June 1957, pp. 341–346. It is followed by the "Piccola antologia neo-sperimentale," which includes Alberto Arbasino, Edoardo Sanguineti, Elio Pagliarani, Brunello Rondi, Mario Diacono, Michele Luciano Straniero, and Massimo Ferretti (347–358). See also Pasolini's essay "Il neo-sperimentalismo." *Officina*, 5, February 1956, pp. 169–182.

he quiet yet relatively skilled craftsmen who make use of given materials and a good knowledge of existing tools, on the one hand; the dissatisfied and restless aspiring pioneers, who seem primarily concerned with forging new means of work, on the other" (10).[2] The anthology promotes an interesting excavation of the poetic subsoil, revealing submerged materials that are in some cases difficult to extract but useful for measuring, beyond purely aesthetic and evaluative judgments, the exhaustion of the twentieth-century *koiné*—identified in particular with Hermeticism—founded on the "ontological quality of the poetic word" (Romanò, *Discorso degli anni Cinquanta* 26).[3]

The "San Babila" selected Andrea Zanzotto as the winner, but the as-yet unpublished works of the prize selection testify to an overall linguistic restlessness ("forging new means of work") that provokes a widening of the boundaries of lyrical discourse. In this perspective, Enrico La Stella's versification exercises—under significantly "exotic" titles such as *Do* and *Guernica*—reveal (the latter poem in particular) the influence of Lorca's poetry, projected onto a non-introspective rhythm: "Avevi calze di seta Guernica / e

---

[2] AN: See the unsigned introductory text of *Seconda antologia di Poeti Nuovi (Premio "S. Babila" 1950–Inediti)*, pp. 7–11. The jury consisted of Eugenio Montale, Salvatore Quasimodo, Emilio Sereni, Leonardo Sinisgalli, Giuseppe Ungaretti, and the promoter of the prize, Germana Marucelli, financier of the event and secretary of the jury. In the 1950 edition of the "San Babila," Andrea Zanzotto was the winner with some compositions (including the fourth movement of *Montana*) destined to merge into the debut collection, *Dietro il paesaggio* (1951), published in the interval between the award ceremony and the publication of the anthology. The poets of the second anthology were: Ninya Anfossi, Gino Baglìo, Silvio Bertoldi, Armando Biselli, Gian Piero Bona, Giancarlo Buzzi, Orlando Pier Capponi, Giuliano Carta, Enrico La Stella, Toti Mannuzzu, Biagia Marniti, Geri Morra, Giulio Nascimbeni, Graziana Pentich, Alessandro Peregalli, Luciano Bocca, A. M. Z. Tomsich, Fiore Torrisi, Paola Viviani, and Andrea Zanzotto.

[3] AN: This is a reflection that Romanò had already published in *Officina*, which represents a lucid contribution to the understanding of a generation that had to deal with industrial development and post-war social changes to a late-idealist, mainly literary culture. Looking back on his own experience, Romanò writes: "It was difficult for us, and for those of us even more involved for reasons of age and formation in that 'position' (I use the term in the sense adopted by Pier Paolo Pasolini in no. 6 of *Officina*) to understand how the end of Hermeticism meant something more than the decline of an avant-garde, a selective, closed stylistic *cursus*; of a theme of poetry imbued and influenced by decadent values; of a circumscribed, mythical parnassus, carved out within the parameters of a Platonic formal typology; it meant the conclusion, or the beginning of the conclusion, of a much wider literary cycle" (35).

fiori di chitarre alle finestre / quando esplodevi nelle tue canzoni / tristi e gaie di amore spogliato" (vv. 1–4).[4]

The Catania poet Fiore Torrisi (b. 1918) is also stylistically restless, subsequently given ample space in Quasimodo's anthology *Poesia italiana del dopoguerra* (1958), but not in the one edited by Falqui (1956).[5] Torrisi hopes for a return "alla rima, al verso / del dolce ottocento" (*Fuga dal collegio*, vv. 1-2), on a lexical basis of anti-hermetic extraction, underpinned by crepuscular twilight: "Non sono un crepuscolare, / non sono un assassino, / non un mentecatto un miscredente / non sono che io ma senza risultato" (vv. 44-47). The result is a strident and sarcastic recitative, which recalls certain comic and clownish mannerisms of Palazzeschi: "La provincia che guarda il deretano / delle turiste, il cui palato adesca / parata e festa con giornali esteri" (*Fine della provincia*, vv. 1 -3). The real bursts onto the page as a journalistic headline: "Truman apre una campagna / contro i sovieti ecc. ecc. ecc. / Non è Eliot che comanda qui / non è Strawinsky, né i vivi né i morti" (*Subsidia*, vv. 19-22).

Note also the poems of Gian Piero Bona, anthologized in *Quarta generazione. La giovane poesia* (1954) as well, and later in *Giovane poesia* (1956); Orlando Pier Capponi and Geri Morra, both included by Enrico Falqui and symmetrically oriented towards late-Hermetic (the former) and neorealist (the latter) solutions; and Alessandro Peregalli, present in the anthology of Salvatore Quasimodo.[6] The case of Biagia Marniti is interesting: already recognized by the Saint-Vincent Prize of 1948, in the San Babila anthology she published the first lyrics of her little songbook, *Nero amore rosso amore* (1951), with which she made her debut. More compact and secure—but less stimulating

---

[4] AN: Journalist, storyteller, and poet, Enrico La Stella (1926–1999) worked for newspapers such as *Epoca*, *La Fiera Letteraria* and *Il Mondo*. In 1957, he won the Bagutta Prize for his first work with the novel *L'amore Giovane* (Mondadori, 1956).

[5] AN: These are two anthologies of great use for understanding the fluid development of language and poetic values over the course of the decade. See Enrico Falqui, *La giovane poesia. Saggio e repertorio* (Carlo Colombo, 1956); and Salvatore Quasimodo, *Poesia italiana del dopoguerra* (Schwarz, 1958). For a "contrasting" reading of the two anthological proposals, see Ugo Perolino, *La ricerca poetica da 'Quarta generazione' a 'Officina'* (Carabba, 2022), especially pp. 49–65.

[6] AN: Geri Morra and Alessandro Peregalli were very active during the fifties. By Morra, the following collections should be noted: *Solstizio d'estate* (Gastaldi, 1951) and *Parole udite domani* (Schwarz, 1953). By Peregalli: *L'altopiano* (Guanda, 1955). By Orlando Capponi, we should note: *La nave* (Il canzoniere, 1952), *La veglia* (Il canzoniere, 1952), *La trilogia* (Il Presente, 1954), *Addio ad Erato* (Leonardi, 1955), *Il fiume tra i morti* (Roma, 1958).

as a revelation of novelty and ferment—is *I poeti scelti* (1949), the anthology of poets of the 1948 Saint-Vincent Prize edited by Giuseppe Ungaretti and Davide Lajolo.[7] The winners were Sergio Solmi and Alfonso Gatto, while the figures recognized just behind the winners were the emerging Pasolini, Spagnoletti, and Spaziani. These anthological repertoires have important documentary value, as they contribute to determining the synchronic context and detailing, through the movement of single personalities and single groups of texts, the contingent fluidity of the canon, even before the crystallization of a historical and critical perspective.

With *Linea lombarda* (1952), the most successful of the militant anthologies of the decade, Luciano Anceschi interpreted the renewal of the forms of poetry in the sense of an ontology centered on the opaque evidence of objects that refers back to Montale and Gozzano.[8] In the preface, Anceschi underlines the "particular Lombard disposition of the new work" nourished by trust in a "poetry that rediscovers objects" (8) through carvings and engravings in the real that maintains its resistance to dissolving in the word. There is no compulsive turn to realism; the critic admonishes: "[T]he object is always a free, unexpected construction, an intense charge of internally organized forces" (22).

In discontinuity with Hermeticism, but even more against post-war realism and its ideology,[9] the poets of *Linea lombarda* trust in the "poetic possibilities of the presence of objects," favoring "full-bodied allegory over diaphanous analogy" (6). Of the six anthologized authors, Risi, Orelli, Modesti, and Sereni had made their debuts in the 1940s, Rebora, in 1939, while the youngest of the group, Luciano Erba, had published *Linea K* (1951) only a year before

---

[7] AN: See *I poeti scelti*, edited by Giuseppe Ungaretti and Davide Lajolo (Mondadori, 1949). The jury of the 1948 Saint-Vincent Prize was comprised of Giuseppe Ungaretti, Pietro Bargellini, Elio Vittorini, G. Titta Rosa, Natalia Ginzburg, Lorenzo Gigli, Mario Bonfantini, and Davide Lajolo.

[8] AN: For the connection to the literary experience of Eliot and Montale, see Tommaso Lisa, *Le Poetiche dell'oggetto da Luciano Anceschi ai Novissimi. Linee evolutive di un'istituzione della poesia del Novecento* (Firenze UP, 2007), in particular pp. 43–53.

[9] AN: "One does not expect that this small collection will clarify what the newspapers, in the somewhat coarse tone of political language, call 'the situation of poetry'; nor is it expected to offer one of the usual and not always congenial 'anthologies of new poets.' I'm not sure what an expression like 'poetry situation' means; as for anthologies, even if they are of some use, there are so many ways and rationales for their selection! It truly does not seem easy to find *poeti nuovi* in Italy after 1942. We have probably seen *nuovi poeti*, but certainly not—and there is a difference!—*poeti nuovi*" (6).

the publication of the anthology. Vittorio Sereni was designated the leader of the Lombards, whose inspiration "always presupposes a certain condition of prose" (19). Anceschi notes how "in his poems, Objects, the moment they become images, immediately become symbols" (15). In fact, in his first book, *Frontiera* (1941), the poetic language of Sereni seems to pass through Montale's *Ossi di seppia* (1925; 1928) and *Occasioni* (1939) and trace the course of the twentieth century since the "bequest of Gozzano" (19). The author of *Frontiera* devises a "contemporary symbology," degraded in accordance with a prosaic, non-poetic lexicon: "E quei *velocipedi*, e *siluri* dell'*Avus*, e *sottopassaggi*, e *semafori*, e *binari*, e *fari*!" (19). Therefore, poetry *in re*, in a lyrical geography, "not at all Lombard (and Emilian) of certain places that are always familiar and recognizable" (19).[10]

In Sereni's second book, *Diario d'Algeria* (1947), Anceschi detects "a new tension" and "a more resolute order, a man's decisive commitment to himself" (20–21) with the intention of highlighting a peripheral dislocation of the poetic self—of the *io poetico*—represented in a condition of existential uncertainty and bewilderment.

In his third book, Sereni multiplies the enunciative levels. Rather than designating semantic or pragmatic values, in the poetry of *Gli strumenti umani* (1965) the *verba dicendi* are signs that mark the "ontological levels" (dialogue, indistinct sound, incomplete perception, semi-conscious murmur, reported speech) through which the experience of language is subjectively realized. The finest reader of *Gli strumenti umani*, Eugenio Montale, recognized in Sereni's major collection "a series of soliloquies or appeals or observations" and "meditations that retrace the thought from within" (*Sulla poesia* 330–331). Retrace—"ricalcano"—Montale specifies, like a mask, a hollow and empty space that adheres to an object. In fact, the presence of an interlocutor in the 1965 collection is thematized in the titles (*Comunicazione interrotta, Intervista a un suicida*) and is, above all, noted in the opening lines: "Meno male lui disse, il più festante: che meno male c'erano tutti" (*Nel vero anno zero*, v. 1); "Non era un sogno, vi dico" (*La speranza*, v. 1); "Ma senti—dice—che meraviglia quel cip sulle piante" (*Pantomima terrestre*, v. 1); "Sono andati via tutti— / blate-

---

[10] AN: "La poesia di Sereni è poesia *in re*, si muove soprattutto alla sollecitazione degli oggetti del tempo, nasce da un reame di immagini quotidiane e fedeli in un'aria riservata di ripiegato sentimento: e la geografia lirica è affatto lombarda (e poi emiliana) per certi luoghi sempre consueti e riconoscibili, con un vago presentimento d'Europa" (19).

rava la voce dentro il ricevitore" (*La spiaggia*, vv. 1-2). Through this "very subtle *imitation of intonation*," noted Franco Fortini, "the introduction of a theatrical element, the insertion of a second or third voice in the dialogue" (170) is achieved so that dialogism is, in reality, a movement of decomposition of the planes of enunciation, a phenomenon of repetition and specularity.[11]

Returning to *Diario d'Algeria* (1947), it is important to underline the value Sereni's second collection assumes within *Linea lombarda*. Favoring the figure of the prisoner, the survivor, "dead to war and to peace" and interpreter of an experience of segregation tormented by remorse and sloth, Anceschi opposes the rhetoric of engagement and political realism with a poetic model based on the traumas of individual conscience. The interpretation of the war, Nazism, and the post-war period, subsequently motivate the interdiscursiveness of *Gli strumenti umani* (joy, the socialist city, the dead who speak at the end of *La spiaggia*).[12] But what is of interest here is the context of synchronic relationships, the contemporary framework in which Anceschi's critical operation acts and creates a system by opposing other facts and trends active in the culture of the 1950s, in a perspective attentive to the public discourse on poetry.

In the first half of the decade, at the center of the period under consideration, *Quarta generazione* (1954) configures a "return to order" whose program rests on two pillars: reaffirming an idea of poetry as lyric and remov-

---

[11] AN: As Pier Vincenzo Mengaldo wrote, recurrence and specularity "are the dominant thematic matrixes according to which the vision of reality is organized in *Strumenti umani*. Two fundamental variants of the phenomenon can be distinguished: the theme—on the temporal level—of the recurrence, of the re-emergence in experience or awareness of events, objects, characters; and on the other hand, the theme of the mirroring, or doubling, of the ego" (106). See Pier Vincenzo Mengaldo, *Iterazione e specularità in Sereni*, in the postface of *Gli strumenti umani* (Einaudi, 1975), pp. 89-116. Mengaldo's essay was previously published in *Strumenti critici*, VI, no. 17. February 1972, pp. 19–48.

[12] AN: On *Strumenti umani*, the pages of Fortini, a closely involved reader of the poem, are fundamental: "Da un oggettivo concorso, da una grave collaborazione fra la sconfitta europea della tradizione democratica e socialista e la vittoria individuale d'un lirico post-simbolista su se stesso—combattuta con tutti i sotterfugi e le desolazioni di chi vorrebbe giocar perdente—questo libro di versi mi pare abbia ricevuto, anche più che l'origine, la compiutezza. Di esso l'elogio probabilmente maggiore sta nel confessare che la sua comparsa è postuma a buona parte di noi stessi. Come una luce polarizzata, la poesia di questi versi infligge una decolorazione spettrale al nostro già invecchiato diagramma di profitti e perdite, indica vuoti nel repertorio dei nostri luoghi morali, sembra accennare altre possibilità d'uso alle nostre esistenze" (*Di Sereni* 173).

ing post-resistance ideological tensions.[13] The title of the collection edited by Chiara and Erba derives from an intervention by Oreste Macrì in *Paragone* (1953).[14] In those pages, Macrì noted the absence of emerging voices who had marked the post-war period in terms of quality and originality:

> We waited some years for young post-war poetry to mature and explode under the banner of the new political and ethical-social reality: we felt it in the air, it intimidated us before it existed, like something that could bring about a clear break, a radical reform in theme and style. But instead, nothing of the sort happened. (45)

In Macrì's entirely negative assessment, the young post-war poetry left no tangible signs: "[W]hat this generation lacks is a sure and objective set of textual values in the clear light of readings and criticism. And we are in 1953: one could jokingly say that there are three years before the naturally and historically established age expires, after which we move on without regrets into a time of passive squalor" (51). To order poets and works of the twentieth century chronologically, the critic adopts a rather complex "generational scheme" that should be reported in detail. Each generation comprises a space of seven years; this interval of births corresponds to a ten-year rhythm of "creative youth." Specifically, the first generation includes poets born between 1883 and 1890: Saba (1883); Jahier (1884); Rebora, Campana, Onofri (1885); Cardarelli (1887); Sbarbaro, Ungaretti (1888); Comi and Fallacara (1890). The second generation covers the period from 1894 to 1901: Vigolo (1894), Montale (1896), Grande (1897), Pavolini (1898), Betocchi and Solmi (1899), Quasimodo (1901). Whereas the third spans from 1906 to 1914: Penna and De Libero

---

[13] AN: The "Prefazione" (pp. 7–15) must be attributed to Luciano Erba (the quotations are taken respectively from pp. 9 and 10). See also the valuable volume of correspondence between Chiara, Erba and Anceschi, full of notes and information on the publishing affair, internal relationships, and cultural context: *Gli anni di "Quarta generazione". Esperienze vitali nella poesia.* Edited by Serena Contini and with a preface by Giorgio Luzzi. Nuova Editrice Magenta, 2014.

[14] AN: The essay by Oreste Macrì, "Le generazioni della poesia italiana del Novecento" (1953) provoked reaction and controversy. Among the young poets mentioned, and largely anthologized later in *Quarta generazione*, were Pier Paolo Pasolini, Alda Merini, Gian Carlo Artoni, Bartolo Cattafi, Andrea Zanzotto, Biagia Marniti, Elio Filippo Accrocca, Gaio Fratini, and Bruno Conti. An overall positive assessment was made of the poets of the *linea lombarda*, "amorosamente curati da Anceschi" (46), and who, moreover, would be amply represented in *Quarta generazione*. Among others, Vittorio Bodini replied to Macrì in "Risposta a Macrì" (1954).

(1906), Sinisgalli and Pavese (1908), Gatto (1909), Bertolucci (1911), Caproni (1912), Sereni (1913), Luzi, Parronchi, Bigongiari (1914).

For the first generation, the "creative youth" covers the period 1911–1922, full of works capable of renewing the poetic system and literary institutions: Saba's *Poesie* (1911) and *Canzoniere* (1921); *Con me e con gli Alpini* (1919) by Jahier; *Frammenti lirici* (1913) and *Canti anonimi* (1922) by Rebora; *Canti orfici* (1914) by Campana; *Orchestrine* (1917) by Onofri; *Prologhi* (1916) by Cardarelli; *Il porto sepolto* (1916) and *Allegria* (1919) by Ungaretti; *Poesia (1918–1928)* by Comi (1929).

For the second generation, the period of "creative youth" extends from 1923 to 1933 and includes, among others, the following collections: *La città dell'anima* (1923) and *Canto fermo* (1931) by Vigolo, *Ossi di seppia* (1925) by Montale, *Fine di stagione* (1933) by Solmi, *Realtà vince il sogno* (1932) by Betocchi, *Acque e terre* (1930) and *Oboe sommerso* (1932) by Quasimodo.[15]

From the blossoming of the third generation, from 1934 to 1944, Macrì singled out: *Poesie* (1939) by Penna; *Solstizio* (1934) and *Eclisse* (1940) by De Libero; *Lavorare stanca* (1936) by Pavese; *18 poesie* (1936), *Campi elisi* (1939) and *Vidi le Muse* (1943) by Sinisgalli; *Sirio* (1929) and *Fuochi in novembre* (1934) by Bertolucci; Luzi's *La barca* (1935) and *Avvento notturno* (1940); *La figlia di Babilonia* (1942) by Bigongiari.

It's hardly necessary to point out the contradictions of the "generational method": the presence of Pavese among the Hermetic poets or the omission of some non-secondary names in the history of twentieth-century poetry. But what characterizes the last decade, Macrì reiterates, is the absence of a coherent movement, such as the Hermetic one, or of texts capable of founding a canon and a lasting line, such as *Le occasioni*: "Almost non-existent is the imprint of the fourth post-war generation," is the lament of the critic, "which should include the decade 1945-1955, corresponding to the seven-year period of births between 1922 and 1930" (51). Except for a few names—Pasolini and Alda Merini, anthologized by Spagnoletti in his *Antologia della poesia italiana 1909–1949* (1950); Cattafi, Zanzotto, Marni, Artoni, Conti, and Risi—"what this generation lacks is a secure and objective set of textual values in the clear light of reading and criticism" (51).

---

[15] AN: Macrì notes also *Avventure* (1927), *La tomba verde* (1929), *Nuvole sul greto* (1933) by Grande; and *Poesie* (1923), *Odor di terra* (1928), *Elixir di vita* (1929), and *Patria d'acque* (1933) by Pavolini.

The anthology of Chiara and Erba responds to this critical intervention to reveal a dense fabric of presences and individual initiatives, some of which had reached maturity, although not in an organic framework or ordered along recognizable trends and formal hierarchies.[16] The apparent arbitrariness of the resulting design did not escape the editors; however, they looked above all at the restoration of lyrical and stylistic values as the common denominator of the fourth generation. Luciano Erba, who signed the *Introduction* of the anthology, stated that the post-war generation is oriented towards the "rejection of a new rhetoric *in fieri*, which the exceptional circumstances and the red-hot climate had seemed to favor for some time" ("Introduzione" 13–14). In this way, neo-realist poetry is rejected altogether, to instead revitalize the poetry of the *entre-deux-guerres* as "the only vital strand, albeit restless and not always easily recognizable, of tradition" (10). The reader is also informed that "1945 was not a literary date: similarly, neither was '14, or 1989" (11). The new Italian poetry is directly linked to the "overflowing pre-war poetic season." The poets between the ages of thirty and forty were not influenced by the "grotesque attempts at nineteenth-century restoration" (11) nor by the "strident grafts of modern poetics on classical trunks, not even in the form of poetic realism or neo-realism" (11–12).

The anthological selection responds to this prohibition against any form of ideological contamination of lyrical discourse. As has been rightly observed, of the thirty-three authors included in it, only one or at most two "can be ascribed to the line of commitment, to civil poetry"; the range of dominant registers admits "at most slight changes in the specific weight of the components of the twentieth-century canon" (Giovanardi ix–x).[17] The *Quarta generazione* poets, Erba notes again in the "Introduction," find themselves in the "discourse on the return to origins, roots, *terroir*," a sort of "*Italic revival*, however unaware of oratory casts and cultural contaminations" (13). On a theoretical and historical-literary level, the preface's contribution is modest. It does not deviate from the uncritical re-proposition of a precise and traditional

---

[16] AN: "A noi sembra che l'intento del pur sottile e attento studioso—altre sue affermazioni, sempre riferite alla poesia dei giovani, parlano di 'vuoto pauroso,' di 'passivo squallore'—si muova dal presupposto assai arbitrario secondo cui i poeti cosiddetti 'postbellici' avrebbero forse dovuto farsi interpreti della nuova età e inoltre portare una decisa innovazione di temi e di stile. E perché mai?" See Luciano Erba, "Introduzione" to *Quarta generazione* (7).

[17] AN: See Giovanardi's "Introduzione" in *Poeti italiani del secondo Novecento* (2004).

idea of poetry, also on the level of content responsive to "a surprising ability to listen again to the irreducible voice, to refer to the perennial sense of *terra italica*, as ancient and true as the world" (13).

In the correspondence between Erba, Chiara, and Anceschi, the uncertainties and progressive adjustments of the project emerge in the advances and second thoughts that mark the entrances and exits of individual names and authors in the long preparation phase of the book. A list of names, drawn up in its first draft in September 1952, was affected by numerous solicitations. Spagnoletti proposes Pasolini and Michele Pierri (b. 1899), whose presence is also supported by Anceschi.[18] The insertions of Umberto Bellintani and Vittorio Bodini are decisive. Bellintani's contribution "in the current development of language and poetic form" is reiterated by Chiara also on another occasion.[19] Bodini[20] ironically updates a surrealist line merging with the experience of southern Hermeticism.[21] Both born in 1914, Bellintani and Bodini were forty

---

[18] AN: Although far from the poets of the *quarta generazione* by birth, Pierri made his debut in 1950 with a collection championed by Carlo Bo. The critic's interest in Pierri is documented by Spagnoletti's letter to Chiara dated 12 January 1952, in *Gli anni di "Quartagenerazione"*: "Ti renderai conto che si tratta di un uomo d'una certa età, ma d'una sensibilità molto giovanile. Egli è apprezzato molto non solo da me, ma da Ungaretti e Bo, il quale in una raccoltina di due anni fa volle presentarlo simpaticamente" (70). Spagnoletti refers to Michele Pierri's *Contemplazione e rivolta* (1950).

[19] AN: Encouraged by Lamberto Pignotti, Piero Chiara wrote a critical essay entitled "Consenso per Bellintani" for the magazine *Stagione* (a. IV, no. 14, 1957), which dedicated a monographic issue to the poet of S. Benedetto Po. See *Gli anni di "Quarta generazione"* (126–127).

[20] AN: In the 1950s, Bodini translated Lorca's dramatic works (1952) and Cervantes's *Don Chisciotte* (1957) for Einaudi; between 1954 and 1956, he founded and directed the magazine *L'esperienza poetica*, with contributions by, among others, Cattafi, Chiara, De Libero, Erba, Pasolini, Sciascia, and Zanzotto. In 1956, his second collection, *Dopo la luna*, was published by Salvatore Sciascia. His last poetry collection, *Metamor*, appeared in 1967. See the complete collection of texts in Vittorio Bodini, *Tutte le poesie* (2015). A broad critical perspective can be found in the volume *Vittorio Bodini tra Sud ed Europa (1914–2014)* (2017).

[21] AN: A southern line of poetry, with its own characteristics, was consolidated between 1938 and 1943, when almost simultaneously Sinisgalli, Gatto, and Quasimodo "raccoglievano in volume la loro produzione ermetica"—Gatto, *Poesie* (1939); Quasimodo, *Ed è subito sera* (1942); Sinisgalli, *Vidi le Muse* (1943)—starting a new phase marked by a more open and declared ethical and civil commitment. Alongside the names mentioned above, Rocco Scotellaro (who died in 1953, but whose collection of verse È fatto giorno came out in 1954), Vittorio Bodini (*La luna dei Borboni*, 1952), identified as the leader of the 'fourth generation,' Raffaele Carrieri (whose debut, *Il lamento del gabelliere*, dates back to 1946), to constitute the most significant nucleus of a southern line identified by "una comune matrice antropologica, che si rivela nella presenza genera-

at the time of the anthology's publication. Although they did not belong to the 'fourth generation' by birth, they had both made their debut in 1952–1953 with two collections—respectively *Forse un viso tra mille* (1953) and *La luna dei Borboni* (1952) —which suggest their enlistment in a leading position. It is assumed that the order of succession followed in the anthology also represented, with some exceptions, a hierarchy of values. Following the two leaders are the most celebrated names among young poets of the decade, almost all of them around the age of thirty (except for Turoldo, b. 1916): Risi, in 1920; Zanzotto, Orelli, Marniti, and Guidacci, in 1921; Pasolini, Cattafi and Spaziani, 1922; Scotellaro, 1923; Volponi and Budigna, 1924; Merini, the youngest, born in 1931.

The coherence of the selection is guaranteed by the quality of the individual voices, especially in the first part, which can operate originally in the worn-out language of the lyrical *koinè*. But by gradually scrolling through the book's pages and proceeding in one's reading into the minor zones, the sensation is confirmed of semantic wear and tear on the language, primarily composed of an inert mass of repeated stylistic elements and ossified syntagms. "Macrì was perfectly right" (417), writes Sanguineti polemically in his review of *Quarta generazione*, "[W]e are really in a time of 'passive squalor'; and the fourth generation indeed appears, thanks to the eloquent panorama now offered, to its diligent precision, to be essentially a generation of epigones" (416).[22]

After all, even a non-systematic survey would be sufficient to account for the repetitiveness and monotony of an exhausted, crystallized, and largely fossilized poetic language. See, for example, the invariance of some metaphorical plexuses: "l'ombra silenziosa / di quest'ala smarrita" (242); "l'ombra

---

lizzata, in quanto poeti, di alcuni elementi caratteristici […] della civiltà meridionale" (Giannone, *Recognizioni novecentesche* 186). These "characteristic elements" are reflected in the structure and composition of the verses; they reconnect thematic and formal constants, among which the religion of the dead and the rituals of mourning have specific weight, in a broader ethnographic sense. It is a "constant, almost palpable fact" (195), Giannone notes, in the typical manner of a peasant culture in which "the magical element merges with the religious" (197). At the same time one can see in the poets of the South, in the attention paid to the "human and social data of reality," which "does not disdain to address themes drawn from history and even from the news" (190), a gaze that extends over the horizon of time, the intuition of an accumulated past that bears the signs of successive and profound stratifications of different cultures (Greek, Arab, Swabian, Spanish).

[22] AN: Note the definition of "epigoni" ["followers"] which will later be adopted by Pasolini in his speech on *neo-sperimentalismo*.

odorosa / dei primi passi" (243). And again on the same metaphorical register: "Un'ombra / che si confonda con la nostra" (245); "ombre inseguite invano" (271); "l'ombra dei compagni" (320). Furthermore, the predictability of the adjective-noun pairs is especially acute: "muto aprile," "ala gioiosa," "dolce amore," and "dolci mattini d'estate" (242, 269) The rigidity of the language is the result of a process of "stylistic fixation," an effect that, due to its mechanical nature, extends to the rhythmic line of the septenary lines: "lenta città sul fiume"; "l'ombra azzurra sui monti" (246). Finally, constructions proliferate that emphasize a deliberately embellished and ornate syntax blending the abstract and the concrete: "terrazze / della fanciullezza"; "strade del ricordo"; "chiese grevi / di fiati e di miserie"; "buie litanie / di sassi"; "alture dei sogni"; "primavera degli anni"; and so on (232, 249, 250, 262, 297).

The ideological perspective in which Erba and Chiara recognize themselves and intend to position 'the fourth generation' emerges above all as a polemical reaction against post-war poetry. The editors' response to the news of the imminent publication of the anthology directed by Quasimodo, *Poesia italiana del dopoguerra*, is symptomatic: it is inspired, according to Erba, by "real-social-communist criteria."[23]

---

[23] AN: In a letter to Piero Chiara, dated 6 July 1953, Erba noted: "Anceschi confirmed that he is very keen on the anthology, especially since Quasimodo is preparing one according to real-social-communist criteria, which could keep some poets from us, and block our way" (*Gli anni di "Quarta generazione"* 83).

Poetry

Mariano Bàino
Translated by Gianluca Rizzo and Dominic Siracusa

Scraps

usable, greasy, gray
days: eggwhite in which to drown, my hypocrite
reader, my brother
: eggwhite that scrambles
every standard beare
*

spring-driven devil the clock
watches us (you, lover, pick up
passion and dress like lightning)
: a policeman slips out
of the enchanted plaster
*

prostrated (you on the perch
I on myself), we twaddle
to each other: I ask you if the mud
that splatters us is dark or light: you ask
if I'm jaundiced like the other parrots
*

who knows if this tinkling (tempter,
psst psst in the dark) is chatter
of coins or fretfulness
of the nail where we hanged
our itch to contradict

*

the spiders in this house
are blind drunk: in one spot
of the web they're meticulous (ah!
to a painstaking fault), in an another
they leave a gaping hole
*

phew, what a mess: the kernel
of nerves deflects the knife
(surgeons turned beginners again)
: aslant and aslant in the belly
of things, a hundred skins
*

the world's tailor shop is huge
(skeins of lost time): to hoodwink
the tailors and the mathematical
thread
it takes the lampblack in the needle's eye
*

the tickle moves the hand
of an unintentional memory
: at random the thread of time
breaks through
the needle's fog: it sews back the shreds
*

a dolphin looks at galleons on the bottom
(a heap of rotten bones
in the greenishnesss): then jumping
and pirouetting he leaves this dead
cornucopia: he looks for the she-dolphin, the wave, the struggle
*

I always loved this hilltop
where things get smaller now and then
or seem to grow (an ancient game,
a waste of time): a nice view
the cross-eyed tangle of the city
*

after sex every animal is dreamy
and sad: my reward
for the frenzy is a turning of your eyes
(when they see
who knows what chimera)

from genius loci

a)
I don't know which saint it was, not even his name, what miracle
he had done: and: saint aniello said looking out
the small window: screw yourselves poor people: and: saint anthony
fell in love with the pig: and: saint oliver saint oliver
today is not like yesterday: and: saint miserino: naked, skinned,
and without a cent: and: saint clid-clad patron of clods:
and: saint glutton was born before saint just:
and: saint callistus didn't find a rose in the whole garden
of christ: and: saint vitus with saint vitus's dance: and: saint martin
throws me a pear, a perkly pear, a wedge and a shoot
a shoot and a wedge, a quincely pear: and: all the saints together:
orapronobis:

b)
a throw of dice (you already know, my reader) will never
get rid of
chance,
even if you're a keen prepared wily astrologer
machiavellian seasoned ensnaring composed level-headed wise
wry lean hunchbacked graceful drunk
greedy tight-fisted frightened a slacker show-off oddball
infatuated befuddled ill-mannered
isn't it so?
*

b)
But who has died?
The Crooked puppet.

Who takes him away?
The Fate puppet.
Who makes the coffin?
The Velvet puppet.
*

b)
naples became palepolis necropolis nowhereopolis slumopolis
homunculi broccoli frogs dry branches
full of lunkheads
*

B
a)
I'll be marat, you'll be charlotte
corday? taking turns?
b)
naples's superego: milan

De comendatione
Mediolani ratione habitantium
Ratione habitantium considerata...
If we want to consider the people, I see
Milan as the most beautiful city in the world.
In fact the people there have the right
height, men and women:
a cheerful look, rather
good-hearted; they don't cheat, they don't
use guile with strangers, and this is why
people can tell them apart
from other people. They live
right, they know manners money
shrewdness, they wear clothes
that make you proud: at home or out, wherever they are
they're rather liberal spenders,
they appreciate and are appreciated, they know
how to live urbanely. And since the language

they speak is the language
that is better spoken
and understood, you immediately
recognize them too among any other persons:
just by the way they look! Are they or aren't they,

more than all others, those
more worthy of respect?

a)
thrown at noon inside the yellow bug (old type
of scrap metal the trambus, it picks up
different people and races, that keep
their distance, that suspiciously
mistrust each other, as they do
all society, do I find myself
in a complicated mess? doesn't
a long-necked blusterer with a hat bad-mouth
a complete stranger for the most trivial thing? Hey, doesn't he
pick a quarrel
because his big toe was stepped on?
He does! He bristles, suddenly brazen, with words
that spread black
with stubbornness... ah, the way we were
inside that trambus (my mind crawled,
hey, just like with skin, because nothing
frightens more than fright): ah what a weird
and snooty youth, who just wanted
to quarrel with this guy, (what a customer
this kid, he said,
having been brushed against): but I don't know who he was: he stood under
his two-pointed three-pointed three-water
three-wind hat shaped like a mushroom lantern sombrero like a cowl
turban pileus gibus kepi: the braggart's hat
seemed strange to me

b)
naples
                                          (and the thirty-six villages: belly
inside the belly
of the nation (the core and black hole
in the big doughnut)

a)
who knows what affliction and bewilderment snaked
through the psychiatrist's voice while
he murmured: "the fantasy of the child with shit
in his hand to snack on is the world,
the surprised wicked world" and suddenly
he swallowed a needle case, and his face
no longer looked like a deadbeat's, and it was no longer
the face of an astrologer, in the last
breath, with which he said: "I will make my own
nothingness, I want to give it
to myself"

from Pinocchio (Moviolas)

Persons

Arlecchino   (*Italian mask, he wears a costume all made of Italian patches*)

Pinocchio   (*Italian puppet*)

Mangiafoco   (*Italian puppeteer, Italian cyclops, he is afflicted by an Italian -type cold, his eyes look like two lanterns of red glass, his black bristly beard looks like a scrawl made with Italian ink*)

Chorus   (*Italian, of Italian puppets like gioppino, rugantino, gianduia, meneghino, pantalone, tartaglia, fracassa, rosaura, colombina...*)

Scene I

(Silence. An Italian pendulum clock strikes seventeen times. Italian style. The aforementioned silence was and still is an Italian silence)

(Arlecchino)   I am acting in this drama
and I'm the star of the show,
they want me to be an ardent hero aflame,
But am I blatant enough? I don't know...
*(he stops acting, turns toward the audience
pointing with his hand at someone in the back
of the orchestra, he starts to shout)*
Am I dreaming? Am I awake, Gods?
That guy down there is Pinocchio!
He is my brother! he is my wooden brother!
born from good wood... good to catch
fire... oh, the good sauce sucked
from a green teat, oh so many green flowers:
a seed bed! it's a story that will never
be untangled... do you want me to tell it to you?
do you want me to say it?

(The audience protests, they want him to perform, they want to watch what they thought they were watching)

(Mangiafoco)   I am acting in this drama
and I'm the star of the show,
they want me to be an ardent hero aflame,
But am I blatant enough? I don't know...
(addressing Pinocchio) Why do you
confound my theater? turn
ambiguous words into non-words?
would you open fire on them to reach
what's between them, in the white
shadows of the page? perhaps a reader's
need? what do you seek amid the shifting
sands, the movable soil
of a lexicon filled with and empty
of nouns?

(Pinocchio) I am acting in this drama
and I'm the star of the show,
they want me to be an ardent hero aflame,
But am I blatant enough? I don't know...
(*addressing Mangiafoco*) Excellency
leader guide bard author,
master of thespians y master
of rhetoric
y aguantador de los desnudos nombres,
I... know little of aparencias 'cause I come out
of small events very tough and true, under
translucid of the tongue...*' Xcellency,
I don't know anything anymore, and talking
seems a burden, even death
found me... disgusting....

(Chorus) I say curtain to mean that's the way
the Act must end, and they really
lower the curtain!

Scene II
(They all look in front of them)

(Arlecchino) *(with a spellbound voice)*
...and in summer... the moon. O
beautiful, blessed,
that go by shedding light, neither tender
nor hard, but who gave you
that round little face? O
what is the moon? honey?
poison? it's a white nothing or
a white all rolling in the sky?
where are you going all by yourself
venerable old lady?... or are you a wild
woman's soul that makes one lose his mind?
before the sun rises tell me a mountain
of chitchat, brand-new moon, bubble,
of brightness, white glow, eye

of night, luminous mullet, carnival
tear, light body... love..,

(a cold shiver is already running over me)

(Mangiafoco) *(turning to Pinocchio)*
Circus wood, moth-eaten knot
and yet sentimentuous of your signs
dreams lard, with one breath
that solum is mine I could make of you
fodder for my canon, my canon
redo in your ponderable matter,
in your ring shakes... with your crooked
squintered body make chests
or some soap... a sphere, one of pythagoras's cubes...
make you a square-shaped heart...

(Chorus) On the old man's flag we decipher
 rattled a new sentence
  o yea
Crushed we read something in it
that annuls the necessary peace
  o yeah

The old man has a mendacious nature,
malicious aginst the new, the fresh in years
  ooo yeah
 Shitmade we decipher

(Pinocchio) *(slightly timorous with fear)*
Cyclops,
in the horrorful world in which I unlive
wandering pensively amid
al golpear y al fontanal de sanghe,
only my hide, my thick skin, I
did not lose y kiss goodbye to, by sheer chance,
y I'm already used to chance y the rienvapplù!
Maybe it's to be a morituro heel

that I spit
on your feet, where a small marble tablet
repeats foscolian lines to bonaparte...
(*he reads*) and I see a warrior whose
golden locks are girted with blooming
laurel
and on them a purple wavering
of candid azure plumes...

Scene III

(Arlecchino) *(trembling more and more, maybe for fear of Mangiafoco or because of moon sickness, he puts his head into the prompter's box, and from there comes his voice, changing livery)*
Gee,
there is a moon here too,
in this upturned sky, and this one too
is a billiard
ball, bald, bald...
and this one too is a witch that could
bewitch me... no one's silver
drenched in cloudy anise water
and no one lives inside it ...wait! no!
it seems a flight of finches,
of humming birds...
Gee, even men fly,
look! grandpa! look! grandma!
my father... my mother...
and each flies all alone, shuffles cards
and plays solitaire... you have to resign yourself,
you can't bring them back to life...

(Mangiafoco) *(to Pinocchio, his eyes flaming red)*
Turn you into a thing,
like yesmen, yeti to be harnessed
ashen to a circle
of thoughts by the same hangup, by

rehashing idées fixes; of fixations
of my strings nailed to your twisted
shadow, to your soul; so much pulling,
from my fingers to the hand controller, to the cross
that will give simulated dexterity to your fake
limbs: reversible or
irreversible hands, flexible or rigid fingers
from the fixed wrist or with passive rotation
or articulated spherical passive with a cosmetic
blockage of skin or stretch nylon...everything
siliconed, from the coconut to the calcanear
spur with double suspenders
for the reinforced corset with tubular
femoral friction...

(Voice from
the hall)   Of carbon?

(Mangiafoco) It depends on my fancy!

(Arlecchino) *(As before)*
I'm in bewilderment, what do I see, beautiful roses
unthreading from a thread that shines
and unravels in a pearly hue...
it's already stretched, and it brightens
the sky with moonlight, you can read
the printed silence, printed
its enchanting voice...
and the silence is crawling with ants,
oh... there are so many small red ants
working as stone cutters underground...
millions every minute, a seething sea
and they don' get out of breath uphill...
the earth
is already a colander full of holes,
and... be still my lips
for I will give you a kiss...

Anselm Berrigan

Not all there

for Alice Notley

The whole time I lived in Buffalo
No one ever said lovely curious or extraordinary.
If they did I wasn't there at the time.
Who in New York ever says marvelous terrific or gorgeous?
I say terrific.
It was given to me to say terrific
By certain people who knew how to say terrific.
Elinor says gorgeous.
Alice says marvelous though she's usually quoting
Someone saying marvelous: You look marvelous, says Alice.
Bill says right on.
Allen says head trip - this poem is a head trip.
Eddie says fuck 'em but he's in San Francisco
Where I used to live
& where everyone says right on
Because not much in SF is right or on or both or neither.
And that's what San Francisco is like.
Like Darin DeStefano's dunhills.
Like not enough love poems.
Like the vegetarian meat restaurant
Which is in Buffalo
Where what the people do say is pop wings Bills homicide & no sun
& no one goes out until midnight.
Alice who says marvelous says it in Paris.
She also says My head is a block of ice

Which she says in French
When she means to say My hair is frozen
To a butcher with whom she is speaking in French, in Paris.
Douglas in Paris says A-lice to Alice.
Katy in Iowa says I'm scared of nuclear war to Elinor.
Dale in Texas says I'll serve tacos at Taco Bell to Hoa.
Johnny in New York says Covert tulips on the nape of the lowlands. AOA.
To no one in particular, including me.
I don't know what I say
& this has been pointed out to me
Though I think I said today
This train talks like I talk.
On a train
The first of three trains I rode today
I didn't say you are mostly beautiful
But I did say you'll never be yourself again anyway
Which isn't quite You are mostly beautiful
Or I am mainly an idiot
Both of which Alice said in New Jersey in 198S.
In 1985 I probably said I'm depressed.
I don't know what anybody else had to say in 198S
& I no longer wish to say 1985
Or anything else today Sunday.
Actually I haven't said anything since I spoke to Alice on Friday & said
Happy birthday!
Fifty-fucking-one!
What kind of present would you like?
& Alice said
Sweatpants
I don't know my size
Something like medium
Consult Elinor
Which I will tomorrow Monday work terrible freezing etc.
Horrifying things to say.
This may never end is something I know I'll never say.
So instead
Fixture

Falcon
Pablo
Highball
Ornery
Pig-fucker
Trellis
Doused
Kiss
Frame

The cultural revolution

If Willem Dafoe can be Jesus for Scorsese then Bobby DeNiro
can be Marty's Dalai Lama. They'll eat candy bars together
play basketball & speak of space-burning satellites. No more
bang-bang angst. Bobby having been taught English by Brad
the handsome Nazi who crossed the Himalayas chased
by redcoats & exploded conscience. Brad's tendency to haste
himself to bed hangs crookedly in the shop of his breast.
"A young man's psychology is always questionable. I should've
followed the path of love, like Bobby. The expense of spirit
in a waste of shame is lust in action. Must I shun the great nothing?"
Meanwhile, back west, the Santa Fe rail never was coming
from New Mexico. Outside Needles, CA an executive meeting inside
a boxcar enters session thusly: "Gentlemen, as to our project
enlightenment is a given. We didn't even need to hold a seance.
Our dilemma concerns pre-enlightenment purity & post-enlightenment
receipts: can one exist without the other?" As question & train
steam into ghastly night, five thousand miles east Brad sickens
to purge his calamity. "I am, myself, a motley to the view ...."

To what end is what we've got ...

To what end is what we've got
Sleep influences us, it makes us tired
& it's a total use of the body, for one

Where a myth begins is ashes on a tongue
but the black underbelly of the iceberg
I've become is not adrift. Honey
you're gonna have to come closer &
you'll never hold my word to your breath
or know why I keep calm. What else
is there for you from my being
but when I'm not, & not land enough?
Art is no consolation, but comfort
was never my intent. Composure
is meaningless when it's time to dive
into the starry grab. Signal yourself
to grow large for reckoning, there's an ocean
on the moon, & some thousands
of roles for us to decline today

Advice to a young philosopher

It should be in your nature to instantly trivialize anything
you read in italics. Everyone thinks they deserve a reward
for not dying, but there will always be someone availa~e
to hate you. Your reward can wait, can wallow in mud;
I love mud. That it's not quite the water & not quite the sh
This allows you to understand purgatory. Dilemmas
cause problems, cause auto-didacts. Have you ever met
a sultry philosopher? So, thanks. If a present is to be had
have it tied with a ribbon the color of the dress of God
& Howard Hawks' river. But the uniform you design
may still be stripped & not in some pleasant manner
by the frog of your choice. Your dilemmas will always fail
their physical, whatever roots you ingest. Waking up
is a nice way to start the day. When you think of order
think take out. It's always hard to get a perspective
from the inside. Measure the distance between dead
people & their existing stars. And vice-versa. You may
be killed by a random shot of a cannonball.

Ode to election day

Then to admire some beached whales
lights a cold. I run an ad agency on the side

& am a true blonde, with dirt; flesh rigged
for pressure I believe you must understand

in other people's brunch. There is an out here
slap the clever. A walking talking single-cell

grassroots activist finger fucking. The first part
was the disinclined moment. Then I wanted

to be Jane Eyre, in the third person on line
for a metrocard & chicken sandwich.

There is a stupid in my house & I'm not scared.
After many delayed probabilities we went right

for the essence of the matter. Who would
stand it? The orange wall, the green ceiling

the naked postcard coconut life saver. Xerox &
send, xerox & send! To make it easy we chose

bullfrogged detachment, no surprise, nooooooo
nothing. Verdict: robust, mellow, satisfying.

Looking up my balance

If I think you'll think I'm brainwashed
because I think I am. It's like having your belly
button on your big toe, & that was solace
'til I shut my eyes. Many constructors of chaos
are historically grabassy. Agitated
for lack of warmth & the answer is relax.

Off into orbit by merit of gratuitous misery
i.e., free long distance minutes inside.
Entering a mid-town diner & greeted by a sign:
Please wait for the waitress to be seated.
Logic dictates a reasonably healthy diet
but I read that one should undermine authority.
I left empty & thought about what I've stepped
on in the country. My brother said he called
Jesus but the outgoing message was too long.
He played Jimmie Rodgers over the phone & said
this man in this church with a chicken bone
in his hair was, like, totally no bullshit.

Fortune's drift

> for Jordan Davis

Hail Jordan & his little gold rook –
He walks it into Staples –
The staples attack his fingers –
His fingers fall off stapled –
Into a watertank full of clamshell
Tenements; No longer can I hold my pen –
Alaska, when will you let me know
If I shall ever write again?
It was great to be an intellect
It was like being a cow & going to the bank.
The farm had vanished.
Jeff and Maureen drove by
& wondered. Animals all gone.
Gone to the bank – volunteers -- wearing tin-foil
glasses. Carrying tin-foil laser guns.
Zap zap zap. Defeat is tender.
"I'm no way, you're no way"
Says vanished cow to vanished cow.

Security

I fly to Los Angeles. Come again? I walk to yon hot dog
srand, Grrrrrrrrrrrrrrrrrrrrrrrrr. The political implications
of hamburgers on the warpath. Think I shuttle around the track
'cause I like severe & uninteresting agony? I am not vague
I'm available, just not in the contemporary fashion.
In this office there are many post-its with your name on them.
There I was, there I was, there I was. Have we met?
No, but I was right there. We may not be the great loves
of each other's lives, but we don't see ourselves stranded
in each other's reflection now, do we? Cannot rescue or decide
well, I'm really very shallow over the phone. Buddha
why do you take my heart away? I shall wear my strength
tonight, my French birthday shorts with the green & blue squares.
The profound animation without which there is no originality
is my weakness. We will now look at some splendid
configurations: Miami, I fed you tonight. Send love soon.
Yrs., the Orphic Hatchet. Baby, I dreamt we had a big fight.
Enraging the cosmos was easier than I'd ever imagined.

John Latta

Morgenmusik

A syllabary of noise tending to white:
Behemoth gleeps and susurrus, the French
Word for key. Out of the din a tonality
Emerges, a series of probabilities we stake
High stakes to, betting that tempo itself
Points to recognition. Or we fall back to narrative:
A Polish girl with a straight smile
Gone nasty with drink. First she call the taxi
Driver a dirty Arab, second she loses her sandals
In the Parc de Vincennes, third she…
The sequence carries an emotional charge, something
We manipulate, divvying up events
As prior to a number of possible outcomes
And pointing to one in particular, a result
That makes necessary and defines the addends
That make it up. Frankly, mornings
I'd rather approach such a threshold
In oscillatory blink and bemusement, my vibrato
Declaring a dynamism I like to think of
As Einsteinian, voice expelling
A roll of units discrete and continuous as hubbub's
Own sown hubbub is, a business hard enough
To foster without exemplum and dash.
So a senator parks a Toyota under the dais, awestruck
By the pinch and release of the bunting's blue…
So two toy iotas of mischief invade

The blue eyes of an actress who is trying
To work up a sob, adding poignant bits
Of information briefly to the scene just before
The houselights come up and everything again goes white.

Elogio di Frank O'Hara

Now that I am up here in the sky I can see
The *mare di San Tommaso* is a puddle of ink,
A hierarchy of imperial blue tints, tempting
The way order often is. No stranger's foot
Weighs on my heart and the earth today, howsoever
Cloud-begrudged and fickle, in turning
Itself "to" the unbudging sun though we're slow
To end our geocentric habits of three meddlesome centuries
Of science leading us by the dirty hand and do not desist
In saying the sun "rises," inexpert with the language
That exists merely to placate our sensibilities,
Troubled by the evacuations of art, how it leaves
Adamant puddles in the landscape that go to work
On the imaginations of stragglers like you and me.
You go through it all through pure charm,
Like a little grinning quark, knowing bravado
To be as specious as any other absolute, dashing
Naked into the night-stormy ocean, the only man awake
On earth and nobody left up to play with.
If we make our own suspicious amusements up and leave
Too many things undone it's because life is a work-
In-progress like any work is, always open and remaining so.
So it transpires that we must needs fill somebody's shoes
With feet of clay, feet broken off a statue
We've been lugging around on our shoulders
For a number of decades now not knowing
Exactly where to put it, in the kitchen or out
In the dreary afternoons of Vaughan Williams and rain
And a caravansary of words all leaking largesse, ambassadors
Of a perception that arrives in pieces, the way

A walk up along the ridge above Fiesole
Makes the path drop away, invisible
As the angels, the spectators, the sky-
Borne millions though we see now how the path continues
As descent and know it and we and they and you are there.

Blank, with Blandishments

Something momentous and occasional
Like a sale in a French hardware store
Is about to reveal itself through the pettifoggery

Of itself, though, inevitably,
Interruptions'll hoosegow the business
Just to make it richer. Poor reader.

Just a telephone call away.
I am out here in the peripheries of the gorgeous
Word and there you are stuck

Centre ville where the tourist
Office stands empty though chock-
Full of brochures, maps and whatnot, all

Perfectly arranged by sites historical and near, marvelously
Illustrated, and set mostly in Garamond,
A roman-letter type first cut in the early 16th c.

And notable for its refusal to imitate handwriting.
It did become a standard, legible, clean, aligned
Often with "grace." I do so mind the fact

That you cannot be here with me, don't
Think I don't. It's what my peevishness is
All about, that and the inexpressible need I have

To pester the superfluous
In a terrible reaching after the absolute.
That same old same old. Thank God

The telephone is ringing now.
I know someone will get it, someone "unlocatable" perhaps,
Though reliable as a machine

Picking up by the forth ring
To announce calmly in a voice not unlike your own
That nobody's home right now.

It lets you know somehow
That home is here, reader,
Even if vacant, even if unreached.

Dirty Weather

The white fluff off the cottonwoods bordering the park
Marks the exact number of little local breezes
Out in the air today. Here on the porch I am stationary, just
A camera on a tripod, trying to figure out a link
Between *destiny* and *density* and thinking about a friend
Who's become a Pinkerton Agency man in Asia.

He's a talker, entirely "talk-oriented" as one says, a funny way to put it,
Seeing as I can't say I've heard much of him in a tortoise's life-
Span of years. How do the English call it? A spanner? What
I call a wrench and now need to undo the one large nut
That keeps my ass bolted down to the seat of my chair,
A folding metal model, rather like the aforementioned tripod.

Am I getting feedback? The vernacular always makes it appear so.
I remember when movies were mostly clever talk, rapid
Repartee and rejoinder. The set just sat there
Or a door made out of canvas moved occasionally

Ever so slightly, the result of a breeze. Weather-
Making machines were all the rage—the rain-

Stung or wind-lashed moor available at a nod.
I find it curiously sad that my friend the talker is a Pinkerton man.
It's as if he were now in a movie, something with Elisha
Cook as the oyster-eyed thug who steps out into the typhoon, out
Around the potted palm outside the Hotel Destiny
And into the dirty weather just in time to get his.

Somebody's turned off the wind-machine now and the cottonwood fluff
Is settling down, gathering its own density.
I could shoot the talker's adventures in Gstaad next—
The divorcee's champion dog, the revolver in the bathtub, the dropped ski-
Lodge book of matches... I could put it all in in one single take
And it would take a talking detective to figure out what I'm talking about.

Parisian miniatures

Ambulatory doubt, you
Step into radiance only because whose.
*
An occasion for thinking about the little executions of dusk, following
The summer's bigger.
*
You, trumpet of ennui in honey-
Yellow Hopper light aslant as an open door.
*
The kind of rumpled look all the post office clerks acknowledge,
With quick additions.
*
Preliminary to delineating,
Something major like a foot in a jackboot.
*
Writing under the imprimatur of the private culpability of.
*

Undeliverable, like that swastika
Appended to a postcard to Graham, unthinkingly.
 *

Of the maestro, no word, so you look at a program about bird dogs
In Normandy, and such gear.
 *

The Austrian boy translating a play by Sacher-Masoch keeps ordering stingers.
 *

Transistor radio underneath a pillow and here comes the BBC—*bong, bong, bong.*
 *

Every cahoots you get yourself into turns out to warrant
Some kind of impossibly wordy certificate.
 *

Around the fountain's periphery carp roll like oranges,
Like warnings, like signs.
 *

A girl in Codec is selling slices of blood oranges, lithe
Uninhabitable prize like a lighthouse.
 *

Understudy to an actor who threw a voice like a grappling hook
Up six stories of nineteenth-century wall.
 *

Alarming the way a clock bequeaths the day with slippage, brash
As a gangster, on the lam.
 *

Two episodes having to do with a sleeping bag
Lined with illustrations of duck hunters in red plaid caps.
 *

So what if you walk all the streets "in a doozy of a wine-blunt analphabetic god"?
 *

You, cabinet of curiosities—Street of the Woman without a head,
Street of the Man Who Waves and Waves.
 *

City of grit caught in the eyelid's watery, too distant horizon.

Rue Taitbout

Everything's about duration, like
The question invariably put first, a kind
Of poultice, a bandage to soak up our youth—

How long you been traveling?—though, in truth, we aren't.
Or I am, and you not. Traveling as a wound travels,
Or a mollusk or a scab: stuck

To an idea of something akin to motion,
Motionless, feeding. You are translating uncertainty
Into a love affair with a place

In that endearing and innocent more-French-than-the French way.
Or you reject that. Or I do. There are a number of possibilities,
All blind to the pretenses of narrative.

As narrative itself is blind and so possible.
You go off to the Schwarzwald, or to Norway and its fjords
And send back enigmatic postcards

About dropping acid near Ballon d'Alsace—
"I stand here like a semaphorist
Smack dab atop a pine-circled mountain and see

All the trees as one cubist tree, all
Overlay and disarray and simultaneity."
Or I return to the room, to the one window

Overlooking the one tree, a horse
Chestnut, courtyard straggler or emissary to some country
I do not know.

I pin a newspaper to the dormer-
Slant wall and draw a large rhinoceros.
I keep the rents

In the future pinned together, mending
My loneliness with flimsy blue *aerogrammes* I cover
With words that seem amiable enough

To be able to become whatever things they refer to—
And I don't even consider the audacity
Of one world outside becoming another one *in*.

Sad mottled city
Pigeons peck holes in the shiny tops of the yoghurt containers
I leave on the window's ledge.

The slanting sin turns
The clay chimneys to fiery copper, or sienna,
Colors I can reach with the paintbrush I have ready.

The world is moving on—traveling—
In a hundred directions *out*
Like the smithereens aftermath of an *attentat*, all

Fragment and trajectory while our long-winded lines
Of distress and conjecture provide no adequate
Order, just a salve, endurable, endured.

Reading Cicero's De Oratore

I
The edge of the text is where we sample the remarkable, as if gist were a king of outward drift, pith a sponginess only substituting for the absent center.

Ezra Pound, whom we forgive, knew this. He "tried to write Paradise" and found only wind—what goes and goes, ruffling the borders, the hedgerows,

tossing, like scrap paper, a flock of juncos (and the odd sparrow) into itself. Letting the wind speak *is* Paradise, that thing known only by its *passing through*, its *going elsewhere*, a shiftless continuum moving ever generously over unbordered mountain and forest and town. Cicero wasn't the first man to inhabit one of those towns though

town life agreed with a need to mark boundaries, to dispel the wild filigree of the countryside, that tangle, what he called "the rabble of rusticity," ever-

encroaching, unknowledgeable, uninstructed. He was the first man to use the word "urbanity" and mean not just "citified" but "refined

by means of proper confinement." For without the boundaries of knowledge, Cicero thought, discourse is only " an empty and ridiculous swirl of verbiage"—

that "empty" recalling the sweet captivating roominess, what lies around the rustic's camp, that "swirl of verbiage" announcing the dangerous thicket within.

II
I love the story of Themistocles, the Athenian endowed with an unstoppable memory, a monstrous city of memory, all of whose inhabitants, having one day entered its prodigious gates

were bound to remain, tearing about in toil and truckle, as if in a wilderness, wolf-haunted, unrent and rude. And I love how a man, a quack (he pulled a gilt cart, he did a little show)

"offered to impart to the Athenians the science of mnemonics, then being introduced for the first time." And Themistocles refused, seeking "the greater kindness"—forgetfulness.

Behind the story, of course, is a fear of disorder, a fear of a seamless world. A fear of going where the wind, ever-speaking, goes.

I remember a poet one day saying with only a trace of North Carolina raillery, with pale blinking innocence undone by a flicker of sass, not unlike a boy striking out for an excursion in the woods: "I think a poet ought to keep himself just a little stupid." Pure Cicero, really. For what is knowledge but a means of leaving some things out,

a sorting into unequal piles presumably distinct, a turning against unimpeded luxuriance? It is like saying we cannot speak as the wind speaks, all caress, all penetration, all uncovering.

And like the Greek tragedian who, each day, lying with the others in an orderly row, gradually raises his voice to the highest treble, who, after playing his rehearsed part slowly

brings his voice back to the lowest bass and "regains control of it," we know everything by its edge, by its limit, by its concomitant means.

III

Tonight, with snow finally unable to cover everything—that patch beneath the Norway spruce, for example—I think the "Greekling" Demosthenes' story is

the story oratory tells. Demosthenes the stutterer, he "unable to pronounce the initial *r*" in *rhetorica*, unable to name his only devotion, his only distinction. As Cicero asks somewhere:

"What is sillier than to talk about talking?" And so Demosthenes took to putting small pebbles into his oratorical mouth, took to marching up and down

the steep pebble-covered hills near Athens, talking pebble talk. Perhaps he knew the fragility of words and was comforted in spitting them, stone-like, into the silences.

It is as if all necessary eloquence could come only of rejection, of a *leaving behind*. And those real pebbles still burn on the path. They, too, mark an edge, a limit,

that spot where Demosthenes, done with the unseemly Paradise of the continuous remarkable world, turned, forgivably, back to town.

The Wag of the Inconsequent

A hullabaloo in the mist is missed
Due to other inner cadences
Only you seem party to. I mean I.

Attentive to the local,
The only thing to mock
Hereabouts in the mock hereabouts is mockery, so

Interruptions occur in the form of outer larks, a dog
Stopping mid-
Stride

To snap a loud fly out of the air.
No nourishment to it, just something to do
To insert a kind of punctuation

Mark
Into the shimmering text of the morning.
If you stumble against the *what*

In the midst of the *how*, processing the plaintive
Vocables into pure noise
Singular, even if only

For no moment's sustenance, they'll atomize the quick
Into diphthong and sequence,
Warring particulars, the great ha-ha-*haw*…

Off the jets of unintelligible truths
There's never no one thing like nothing arriving.
You know. You've scoured the sky.

No contrail scratches remain.
And I means I only by dint of this perfect mock-
Up of myself I's got sitting here

Socializing with the twentieth century, its dirt
Outlining the nail of a finger
Wagging emphatic an accusation

And pointing to the likes of words like *you*,
Unlikely though it is in such surroundings
To be you.

Explication de texte

It's about the wild tones ascending
With honk and clatter on the car-
Strummed avenues at the heated close of day...

It's about how one of you stood there
Knock-kneed, raving about inconsequentialities,
The refurbishing of a room.

You loved the soon-to-be-
Ordered disorder of it all
As much as you loved anything.

An historic mountain stood in the background,
Figuring in somehow, all tumulus
And talus, a bump on the hard line of horizon.

For one short period you lived up there
In a shack and burned firewood. The need
To say something—anything—caught

In the terrible middle of you.
In the uptake, in the winch, in the draft.
Something about two

Bluebirds nestling in a box out back.
Something about the box tilting crazy
Against the fence post.

One of you had to go
And name those birds—
Eliot, June—and not particularly aptly

You add to yourself.
It's about those kinds of additions,
The ones needed, the ones not.

Susan Briante

Love in the Time of NAFTA

For weeks it has been the same: the volcano spits steam without flame; the mountains stand useless; trees full of leaves and not enough sun to muster shade.

The rebels are captured on the cover of *Newsweek*, and nobody does anything about a waitress's salary, and the lemons getting sweeter, and the dusks ripening pink as wounds.

Driving north on the Periférico, a man looks up at a billboard and wonders about the name of the color being used to paint rouge on Brad Pitt's lips. (Vermeil.) He does not, however, notice his wife has not spoken to him for 3 hours.

The books she reads are getting longer. She has lost her faith in bottled water.

The coins she presses into his palm are worth exactly half what they were *y*esterday.

Eventual Darling (Galang Island)

Trees step out of the DMZ to be named. Vague branches smolder; ginkgo and lychee, royal palm and teak, rise like an alphabet. I prune a grammarian's path.

Leaves shaped like feathers, we call pinnate, palmate when shaped like hands. But nothing accounts for how we respond to their gestures. Silver backed, searing green. A meadow's edge is arbitrary. And patrolled. I witness close-cropped hills unfold, anonymous, as a page torn out, unable to conjure up a face that could move me.

At a detention camp on Galang Island, Vietnamese refugees sculpt a Statue of Liberty. Pure products of mother boards and strip mines. Welding awl and machete. Our lady smiles, wide-lipped, broad-browed and innocent. She clutches a crude pine bouquet instead of a tablet, a parrot where she should hold a torch. The bird draws out its wings. What stories should we read from its plumage?

And yet we are best when adulterous, when we mispronounce or break a phrase. On a day bed, we make love: eyes swollen, palms wide. And it is like clear cutting. It is like agent orange. Storms of seraphim. Clouds of flame.

Eventual Darling (Kinshasa)

Cables of dust bind the farmers' wives to plastic flowers, pesticides, bikes, to plastic sacks of cassava; in slip-knot and pitch, the present perfected voice of Agence France-Presse slingshots through east Kinshasa.

Inside the canvas, a picture does not finish.

Shepherds of reflex and deviation with preferences for "sticks trowels, knives," with preferences for nipple clamps and half-light, chase flocks of pandemics across withered earth

to swat and prod at syphilophiac scars, while the rooftops of a processing plant glisten like hand mirrors, while the tanks of a refinery shimmer like a silver-backed brush and comb.

The Cartographer's Son

They come down from the mountains like clouds, like christs, and wander into the cities. In addition to the difference in sea levels, there is the stark gap of languages. A new vocabulary writhes in the hard center of the jaw:

mirrored building, carburetor, safety pin, glue.

Much will go unwritten, read only in the pucker and slack of lips. Many objects get named twice:

a plastic bowl, a plastic bowl with a slender crack.

Translations swell until the lyric is sung to the wrong woman, brown instead of black, velvet instead of cotton, some shallow veil of crepe, or not a dress at all, the water at certain times of the year like gauze, like the blurred lines of age or the lines that were forgotten the last time someone sang it, making her much less.

And where he had written Uxmal	*ruins*
And where he had written Aquiles Serdán	*mine*
And where he had written Taxco	*historic church*

There is a time when you realize that anything can be produced in Mexico: wheel chairs, action figures, rice paper, lime. There is a time when you realize that for everything you are thinking, there is a word, sometimes two.

Alive in the hard center of the jaw,
you spell them the way they sound

And where he had written Jojutla	*sugar refinery*
And where he had written Xochimilco	*floating gardens*
And where he had written La Fundición	*sulfur baths*

There was nothing
       a bowl could not carry.

The Groom Stripped Bare

The hero flies through the air
    on a steed; on a raptor; in the form of a falcon; on an '88 Harley-Davidson; on board of a flying schooner; on her flying carpet; on the shoulders of a giant; in the wheel casing of a 747

He travels on the ground or over water
    on the back of a horse or wolf; on the over pass; along an underbridge; in a green Volkswagen taxi with the meter whirring; in a stifling boxcar over the Rio Grande; a handless soldier carries a legless one

He is led
>a coyote ushers the hero through a desert; a red cotton thread unwinds like a clock from his lady's hem

He makes use of stationary means of communication
>he climbs a stairway; he finds a subway passage; he walks across the back of an enormous pike as across a suspension bridge

He follows bloody tracks
>to the cougar's lair; to a rusty tin; to the pulpit; to the villain; to one cardinal flame above the charred door of her hermitage

7th Day of the Rainy Season

Between the window washer and curb, a galaxy swirls.
Between windshield and rag, office towers sway.
Old ladies pluck orange candies from pink market tubs.
Passionflower vines capture red and blue wavelengths of light.
Any search requires a preposition as in: "Estoy buscando a mi amigo."
Tradewinds skirt a Flamazul truck with its license plates from the interior.
Water trembles in a cistern with nothing to heat it.
The frigid woman, writes André Tridon, is a cripple or a neurotic.
Jacaranda trees bloom like lightning strikes.
"To the girl with the prettiest eyes," he says handing me his knife.
Nutrient cycling occurs through a process similar to valet parking.
Between my lover and myself, a preposition stiffens like cinderblock brick.
A guard in a bulletproof vest hoses a pick-up.
Every time he's out of my sight: "Estoy buscando a mi querido."
The window washer slaps a twisted red rag against the curb.
A broom licks the sidewalk. A slice of flesh-red mamey slips from his blade.

15th Day of the Rainy Season

Dusk falls through willow trees off the Pan American, traffic snags.
Mexico City turns to mountain, turns to cornrow in the middle of a sentence.
Here you see very few birds.

A Nahua woman opens her arms like wings to display a tablecloth bestiary.
A little something for a soda, a little something for a sandwich.
More Zacatecans live in the United States than in Zacatecas.
The sun smells the same on our skin regardless of pigment.
Its dusty rays pour through streets thick with cinderblock houses.
In Renaissance paintings, this kind of feathered light symbolized God's grace.
I see the face of God flicker in a commuter information screen above the highway.
You see him in a boy asleep on the grass under a monument to the Niños Heroes.
Life changes quickly and often that is consolation.
A woman nurses her baby at the tollbooth.
Beyond a guardrail, a colt rolls in the dirt.
A man steps out of cornfields; his shadow grazes the road.
Dissatisfaction, writes André Tridon, breeds either neurosis or creation.

Towards a Poetics of the Dow

Every day has a number attached to it. Great additions, subtractions. This is not just an aesthetic problem (see Ashbery). There is a "natural impulse toward the boundedness of closure." The bell rings, trading stops. But the world is "unfinished" (Hejinian). Both the rivers and their banks are moving. The poem remains incomplete. The trading day long over.

I do not believe if I follow the Dow I will find nirvana, but I often check the numbers, sit for meditation.

Even when we think we are at the end, there are decimals.

***

When the Buddha touched his finger to the ground at the moment of enlightenment, all the leaves fell from the Bodhi tree. It is February 10, 10:04 in the morning, the Dow falls to 12194. The present poetic strives toward total awareness, incessant recording.

Ravenous as a black walnut tree roots sucking at the sewer line, the Dow touches everything: the taste of our water, color of our sky, torque of our engines. It is February 10, 10:15 in the morning, the Dow at 12203 is rising. The poet—like the trash tree—uses all of it.

A poem moves as does the Dow influenced by a variety of factors and events: mergers, oil spills, revolutions, suffering. Sometimes what does not move tells the story. I like poems that go to prisons and coal mining towns. I like poems that act as archive or a view to Elizabeth Street (Schuyler) I admire circuitry and cosmology. I write with a power industry dictionary on the bookshelf behind my desk, a copy of the King James, a guide to Texas trees.

Poems should evidence some degree of control, but poets should be a little volatile. The poem is a high-risk investment, a long-term commitment. Like a big dirty city, it should make you feel

a little uncomfortable.

It is February 10, 1:11 in the afternoon, the Dow falls to 12197. The poet wants to remind the Dow that the bird has something to teach it about falling and song.

***

The theoretical physicist says, "I've always wanted to find the rules that governed everything."
The theoretical physicist says, "Deep laws emerge."
I have a friend who asks about "truth" in poetry. Whenever he does, I want to send him a valentine on musty pink paper. He lives in a Mid-Century modern house with Mid-Century modern furniture carefully culled from vintage stores and eBay. He owns an old mahogany stereo cabinet, jacked up so you can listen to an iPod through it. That's the kind of truth in which I am interested.

Plus the silence, plus the static.

Charles Olson writes, "no event/is not penetrated, in intersection or collision with, an eternal/event."

To which I offer this corollary: no event is not penetrated, in intersection or collision with the stock market.

I wish more poets would write about money.

***

The New York Stock Exchange began when brokers met under a buttonwood tree in 1792, the year that Blake wrote "Song of Liberty," the year Shelley was born. Charles Dow created the Dow Jones Industrial Average, representing the dollar average of 12 stocks from leading American industries, on May 26, 1896, six days after the U.S. Supreme Court introduced the "separate but equal" doctrine.

Now corporations have the same rights as people. Why can't poems? I nominate Robert Duncan's "Poem Beginning with a Line from Pindar" for president, Frank O'Hara's "Having a Coke with You" for chairman of the Senate's foreign relations committee, Gwendolyn Brooks' "In Montgomery" for attorney general – although the House will not approve it.

Brenda Hillman explains, "Shelley wants you to visit Congress when he writes/*a violet in the crucible* & when he notes/ *imagination is enlarged by a sympathy*."

Bernadette Mayer asks us "to show and possess everything we know because having it all at once is performing a magical service for survival by the use of the mind like memory."

Blake reminds us, "For everything that lives is Holy!"

***

And there is this: When you make the poem, you can hear the swish of dollars washing down the sewer line, second by second, you can hear the stock ticker ticking away.

Meditation

In the PartyStore/PierOne/Target/Kohl's parking lot,
find a desert willow among the shopping carts,

walk around it sunwise repeating:

I am the avant-garde, I am the avant-garde, I am the avant-garde

repeating:

DIY, DIY, DIY

Imagine a chart of median family incomes
as big as the parking lot—
use it to determine where to abandon your car.

I default, I default, I default

Your mind is a blood blister rising on your thumb, a ladybug. Vescica sanguinolenta

Among these shopping carts, you fortress,
among the plastic bags you affirm:
Lo! the light from the desert trees
does not speak in numbers, costs us nothing.
Here, as in a butterfly garden, everyone crawls before flight.

The Market is a Parasite That Looks Like a Nest

The Market scowls
crosses the street against traffic, settles, hovers
over a spread-sheet with his administrative assistant
as if it were an infant, sleeps in another bed / infidelity
after 3 ½ years of marriage,
can only sleep on half the bed
after 43 years of marriage, sees a coffin

in a shop window, grows nostalgic
for shop windows on crowded city streets
where men made picture frames, repaired
television sets, piled tools in doorways, nursed
machines to roast and grind coffee,
operated a printing press. The Market wants to apprentice,
cannot apprentice, looks like a nest in a tree. The Market
is a parasite that looks like a nest in a tree, howls
through the ventilation system, hairless, blind, a newborn
calf sleeping on your chest, the curdling Market
whose milk has come in.

The Market wonders where the soul goes,
decides that God must be a cripple to make the rest of us
feel whole, remembers a trip to Mexico
when he was just out of college.
O the beggars in clown paint! O the girl he never wrote!

Jacaranda, jacaranda, jacaranda

Cheap purple leaves dirtying the sidewalks.

A street named for revolution.
A street named for insurgents.
A street named for reform.

Nights when church bells rose to Aztec temples.

Like the soul?

At the hostel, she told him
a body must train to hold the light of the spirit.
They fucked listening to the Rolling Stones, burning candles.
God, the Market loved Mexico and the Rolling Stones.

Then the Market had kids and it was all profit
margin and technostructure

roller-blades for a few years,
mostly he all but forgot his legs – aging –
it must be okay to be nothing
but sight after a while
all this over here, that over there
the packing slip, the manifes-
toes, arches, heels, calves
like his doctor told him, relax each muscle
against all this shimmer:
grass sequined with difference,
butterflies trembling like addicts,
in a cornfield the violet is weed.

- What does pink and yellow make?
The Market's youngest daughter asks him.*
- Orange, he says.
- What does chocolate and cookies make?
- Your favorite treat.
- What do all those numbers make, Daddy?
The Market looks up from the W*all Street Journal.*
- The ones in your hands.
The Market sighs.
Why does anyone have to make anything?
* Can you **imagine** *smell* the Market picking up ~~his~~ *your* daughter ~~from school~~
in its teeth dragging *parts of* her *bod*y across a ~~playground~~ *landscape* touch-
ing everything ~~he~~ *it* touches as if it were a screen? See how reflective the glass,
how *he* is an *it* is a *we*.

The Market always feels so heavy
by the sea, weighted by a thousand
sacks of coins impossible to sort, to let
go without hemorrhage, to lighten
would be to dissolve not like an ocean
against a horizon but to sink
from continent to silt / to slam
down / taking walls and foundations
root systems, swing sets, whole cul-de-sacs

the Market worries he is nothing
but a pile of stones when he feels so much
inside of him slipping in and out of place
and is somehow expected to speak
from one throat.

Eight three three nine eight three three nine.
Eight three three nine eight three
       three nine eight.
Three three nine eight three three
Nine eight three three nine eight three
three nine, three nine, three nine
eight three three nine eight three three nine eight
three three nine eight three three nine eight three three
—nine eight three three nine eight three three nine eight three
three nine eight.

The Lesson of the Nest

The Market as Composition

On February 10, 10:04 in the morning, the Dow falls to 12194. Who swims? Who rafts or islands? Rivers rise like the Southern Pacific Railroad Company. Characters ticker between us; characters leaf. Both the river and its banks are moving

past a grove of southern trees. Mimosa, magnolia, osage orange. Our indexing makes trails through a forest of mind. Hot linked, jumpy. On the day William Carlos Williams died the Dow closed up 667. Branches

scrawl across a winter white sky. Black branch, yellow leaf. Sequined with difference. At the moment of enlightenment, when the Buddha touched his finger to the ground, all the leaves fell off the Bodhi tree. Religion

has the touch of a bird through grass. Wood duck, gadwall, northern pintail. On the day Robert Creeley died the Dow closed up 10540. The Dow closed down 1130 on the day Prince released *Purple Rain*.

You call a yellow leaf gold to stop a child's crying. Golden rain tree, rusty back haw, sycamore, elm. A penmanship branches across sky, stiff as dialect, hard as the 14th amendment.

An eddy in a river makes a small cup of world. Hooded merganser, cooper's hawk, northern harrier. Write your headnote in the sky, like the court reporter, J.C. Bancroft Davis who wrote, *obiter dictum,* corporations have the same rights as individuals. It is sad

to be among people who don't read, who fear art because they think it mocks them. The river is nothing but river. Or your mother. Or the nation. Merck,

Microsoft, Pfizer. Draw water, carry firewood, bear this instant. In the prolonged present, you hear dollars tick. Leaves static. Leaves distract. On the day Robert Rauschenberg died the Dow closed up 12828. Water rushes over stones with a touch as light as a court stenographer. Winter branches scribble

obiter dictum. Nothing changes from generation to generation except the thing seen. Rusty backhaw, golden rain tree, 3M, Alcoa, AT&T. Hot linked and jumpy as the sunset over a gas station

and that makes composition, makes an index, makes a footpath out of yellow leaves.

Ivan Schiavone

from Preliminaries to The Description of a Hunt
Translated by Dominic Siracusa & Gianluca Rizzo

to Nanni Balestrini, in memoriam

value went from vase to vase — for another history is possible
if we want it — he took a cup of cold water and tossed wheat flower on it —

the birds in silhouette against the dying sun — after stirring the mix
with a sprig of mint — from the center to the circle and yes from the circle to
the center

— know that the vase — he drank it and left —
what time is it? Five. Five in the morning or in the evening?

*

reflections of placentas and blind eyes in organic lights
intrauterine animal metamorphoses absorbed by crackles
interferences of halos at the brief passing of the dead
the field of the future seduced by fertility — egg white light is the moon tonight
and it's stasis the sphere from weekend to weekday
an ashen fury
                    a sight in seclusion
moonless the walls imposed as a posture — vanished and the skyscrapers loom
                                                        shortened by fog
rapacious traces of remote apexes remain
lights untied by derived verticals
            jagged lines of enormous piers

*

crooked claw inflicted on the bare arm
drawn to hunt by instinct
                    to your high call by intent
forced by compulsion and art to an exact predation — what is it in beauty
that urges us to possess it? — from thin arms the bloodless flesh
detached hovers in symmetrical flight
a crow and the petals nadir and zenith

— teenagers in school uniforms, white shirts and black skirts
on bike or on foot scattered in groups against the rural landscape of Vietnam

*

from Asia that offers milk to she bears
the rent rose sleeved in a vase
budded without wilting turned into writing
emblem of man exposed to winter
— a journey is but its own tale — reduced from divine to body
                                          to the measure of the beast
forced to venereal habitations
to changing furies and quick runs along genealogies

— for the city limits of Cantò precede the city limits of Cantò
the city of Cantò wound up occupying the entirety of the dry land

*

meek and foreign appeared to me
                            a doe
golden antlers bright in the uncertain hour of summer dusk
spotted with freckles white the coat
brown the lashes
black the pupils — clinging to the banks with dread
                                  the construction echo of an iterated suburb
silenced in the end

                        in part
by the river shaking off at the large bend
                        the Hudson snowed in
train cars running on the levy — a girl squatting in the reeds urinates
surprised by a few approaching boats
                        unaware of a snake

The Tally of Days
Translated by Alessandro Giammei

what is it that in us   that makes us   that broke?
what is it (the words
what is it that breaks words?
                        they halted on the threshold
and did not come in
                        why on the threshold?
                        why don't you come in, why are
                        you sitting on the doorstep?
when the cripple passed by
but even before the cripple passed
were the words (even before the cripple passed
                        were the words broken?
        yeah, the words were
                        even before
                even now
                        and in between
                the soror mystica came with Phoenician sandals and voice
(you listener can you tell if the agnition was true?
                        with the skull's skin pulled away at the mandible
                was singing
a word, not even a word
                was said
                        that was a single word
not even a word she was singing for herself
                        not even a word
                was heard
                through the hollow echo of millennia

not even a word was heard that wasn't
    Cassandra, beautiful Cassandra, enthralled by her voice and lost to love
    Cassandra whom the word veils
        whom the word denies your sense and the others' conceals
    Cassandra whom the word makes blind
    dulls
all that exists
    when the cripple passed by
        for ages no one heard
            the sound of the rebec
that the word denies sense
        for ages no one heard
            the soror mystica
    came with the white dress and a hat on her head
        among men that are not and take steps all around
        on the naked stairs shout
            the absence and a seagull
        then more and their sound
                it's ages since anybody's heard
        the rebec playing
    the soror mystica who gnaws
the sealed flesh of the stomach
    (you listener can you tell if the agnition revealed by the stomach was true?
        if love was in her
            (and he ignores it
        if there was
            between them
                a word
        that was not a single word
            if there was
            (beyond the river
    dressed in white
        she followed step by step
            if there was between them a word
    or a bridge
or a word that was a bridge
        to cross

                              beyond the river
we
          who are nothing
          but the tally of days
                    between you are born and you are dead
we
          who are not
          who don't know
the real name of our desiring
                              that may save
                                        us
                              (beyond the river she
                    on the other side he
followed step by step
without a word between them or a bridge to cross
                                        behind Sunday
that the word makes blind
                              she hypothetical
whom the word conceals
                              the eidetic word does not
                                        (pronounced aloic without knowing its meaning
you did not come at the hour
                              you gave a word to the wind
                                             which may have been a word
                                             that no one heard
                              behind Sunday
                    Monday
is tallied in the tally of wasted days
                                        that bite without extinguishing existence
without sound of voice
                              that comes at the expected hour
without being what is it
                    in us
that broke?
                    man
thing among things that break
                              thing that breaks, by now

    beyond the river she
                                 and you know the flora of expired objects
                                          inept at any sense at all
                                                    wedged in our inhabiting
            you know the flora of objects
                              flourished artificial
                                      along the riverfront distracts
                                              her vision
                                the word, you know
                                object among objects
                                      inept at any sense at all
                                      in the nostalgia of self-deception
                              the reality of necessity
                in the nostalgia of the encounter
                the other's weft
and you know by now we who don't (when from the bushes flew the bird
                                            he turned around
and saw the world
        (and did not see the bird's beak
                                going away with the functional god
        saw the world
            opening
for each of its particles
                in myriads of other worlds
(and did not see her
                when he turned around
        he saw the man
                hatching in (and did not see her
who veils, denies, conceals
who makes blind
        the wonder of multiplicity
he saw her when he turned around (you listener remember there was not a single word between them
                                                            or a bridge
                                                               to cross

beyond the river you listener
                can you tell

                          you listener can you tell?
you listener can you tell
                    what in us broke?
what is it that in us   that makes us   that broke? (you listener
remember you became a stranger to your mother's house
                                        and another residence
                         since then
                    you haven't had
when the cripple passed by
                    between a table
          a bed
                    and a crapper
and a myriad of other places
                         this labored dragging down through time
with no destiny and no verb
                         when the fury of the cripple reached its peak
look at the humans
               fish mouths heaped in a silent scream
look at them desperate to close
                         the fragments of a dialogue to be preserved
(ears that are blind to the blessing that sustains (when the cripple was disfigured
                    the primordial words
that've strolled along human mouths since the dawn of history
                                        and tongue
                                             and teeth closed
               on the fragments of a dialogue to be preserved
(frantically they interlaced hands
                              the telephone's frayed cables
                                   when the cripple (the
tarot lies
the XVII arcanum? (no spousal veil will ever come
                              that dares response
                    face spent in poses
                              no voice will ever come
                                   arriving at the expected hour

                        the soror mystica who gnaws
                                    followed step by step
he
        in a dark night
                outcast
                        body abandoned to the rain
she in a bed
        to the delight of
                        (encounters extinguished before they even began
water begins to fall ill
            she, the word, gone mad
turned on herself
        a suicide naming the inferno to forget her wound
                                    the infirm to desire herself
(when the screen woman passed by
                                    out of savage delight
        left the woman and her appearance
                skinned from (being late she felt the scorn
time
        with its phantom limb
                caressed her
(and is not maimed and is not crippled
                the word
                the oracle
(fragments of a dialogue to
            when you say the wonder is gone
        that no one heard
behind Sunday
                Monday
is tallied in the tally of wasted days
        waiting
            beyond the river
he
beyond the river she (you listener remember there was no bridge between them
                                    or a word to cross
                                                to us
who are not, who know not

                            us
            who don't know what is it that makes us
                what is it that in us   that makes us   that broke
                                                                she
                                            the word
                                        gone mad
                        beyond the river
                                                        you talk to yourself
and you don't listen
                                                    utter sounds in language
you don't understand
(she squeaked excuses to the endocrine mother within her
                                                    while she masturbated
                                        he
                            beyond the river
                                                        beyond the river she
(you listener remember she can't tell if the agnition was true
                                    if love was in her
                                she still ignores
            if it was (you listener can you tell why she doesn't speak up and ask
                                a word
                                that dares an answer
                                a word
                                that comes at the expected hour
                                a word
                                not even a word
                                        she sang for herself
as long as
        words fell between them
as long as
        the forbidden
                        singing of the world's happening endured
as long as
        one sang
                the happening of thought in worlds
                                        that are shadows of the world
                    blindness

Postulates & Apostasies
Translated by Dominic Siracusa & Gianluca Rizzo

everything tangled and bound with everything else, from the machine's lust for inertia
to the rotations along the ellipticals, moved and rapt by a single law
the infinitesimal and the infinite, animated by a pulse, a breath
the howling manifested in the call of a beast, in the language that traces
a perimeter in which our psyche builds, screen against reality, the world
feeble lantern for scrawny light against the vast vaults of the night
*
the first writing, the track left in the snow, the sand, the mud
the forgetful surface of the waters, the alternating cadence of the gaits
out of necessity or instinct, the first rhythm under the exact number of the solstice
the black from the combustion of bones, the red from oxide and rust
through dejections the image of the world is rewritten at every season and latitude
faiths and apostasies as trimmings on the grin of an ape already armed for space
*
the word channels an absence, the eco and the ghost of what was once present
reduced to distance for us, extinguished in grief, sacrificed to language
it channels a denial, the forbidden pleasure of naming the essence
appeased by an onanism focused on the game of reconfigurations
in the mirage of totality, it channels its being reflected, when grabbed,
disappears or unravels at the intercourse in which we drown prowling
*
all we can do is retreat into imagination and dwell therein
for the contemplation of all that is closest to us would annihilate us
all we know of reality is the links and margins of our language
where truths entities and events exclusively happen, and the world
the absolute availability, is a footprint on which man while naming treads
as a stranger in his own home from which language does not hide but steals

Mariano Bàino (Translated by Sandro-Angelo de Thomasis)

Four Little Objects to Befit a Request for a Note on Poetics, Drawing Upon the Present of the Past

1. From a "Private" Letter to Francesco Muzzioli (October, 2000) about *Fax Giallo* [*Yellow Fax*]

Dear Francesco,
 I don't know whether what follows can be said to be a declaration of poetics. In fact, I fear it is not. Simply put, it is about some information taken from a letter found among the pages of *Yellow Fax* (1993; 2001), in which I was trying to provide a friend a few days after the book's release some help to orient themselves in the text. To the kind addressee, I was promising that I would try not to take into account the clear sensation that I was feeling, consistent with the feeling I hold of being the least adept person to provide them adequate coordinates (it's incredible how that feeling has known how to remain so vivid).
 I was writing that *Yellow Fax* was, for me, a form of interrogation on the world's distortions and disconnections (emblematized, at a certain point in the text, through the theme of bad weather, on which I will return later). I was saying this in 1993. But I would not swear on my certainty, already then, of the presence of a sense of the mundane fidgeting about. In any case, I was calling the attention of the stupendous reader to the macaronic French ("fronsay mozzarellà"), whose impertinence occupies the last page of *Yellow Fax*: "magàr non è toute une boutanade il dir que il gran / problem è plus la relation col mond que le mystère du mond" [Translated by Rizzo, 2015]. Further ahead:

> The idea of the fax continuously irrupting into the stream of consciousness (but often it is difficult for the reader to distinguish between the 'information' and, so to say, internal production) answers the necessity to allude to violent pressure exerted on the contemporary subject by technology and *multitudes of imaginary* that interfere with the I; they disconcert it, they undermine its attempts to constitute itself as center.

In connection to this set of problems, the I of back then informs me to have tried to accept the challenge that the post-modern condition seems to throw at those who write, compelling them to the communicative modalities of the *pastiche*. In the text, the theme of rain and deluge (the bad weather mentioned at the beginning) is expressed in the form of the *pastiche* using either a 'primary text' (*The Rain in the Pinewood* by D'Annunzio) or a 'secondary text,' which is its parody (*It Rains* by Montale). The attempt is to bring elements of criticality and unpredictability inside the *pastiche*, expressive form *proper* to the post-modern era (admitting that it be so, but such is the hypothesis by Jameson, whom I welcome together with others in Gruppo '93).

The rest of the letter also talks about a *game* (but a game to which is entrusted the chance of critique) as a search for new connections between the consciousness of the poet and the very mobile drifts that traverse said consciousness:

I think of the term *game*'s acceptance in mechanics: "In a mobile mechanic coupling, residual space between the two surfaces. Or, rather, movement allowed by such space" (Zingarelli). *Yellow Fax*, perhaps, wants to constitute itself as a space that avoids the blockage and paralysis between two surfaces, from where one is constituted by the unstable and ambiguous rifts of contemporary reality, the other by the vigilance and level of reactivity or capacity to react by the subject.

In sum, the *me* of back then confides to the friend the hope that "something novel be there, in *Yellow Fax*." As for certainties, there is that of "witnessing, already now, a technological passing of the baton that can reveal itself to be crucial, with the passage from the hardcopy and Gutenberg to the multimedia universe, which has—for the humanists who, perhaps, we still are—something disquieting, and that nonetheless we do not have the right to call barbaric."

In *Yellow Fax*, the theme of the virtual is also referenced, albeit with a tinge of irony: "up up with a new mind a new deck a new emptiness a new microsoft / behind the ear inside the white noise inside gravitational wells / thevoiceofgod...". Brought back to political and cultural "discoordinates" that are quite distressing and as though caused by some compass gone mad: "sound system in a wind south of marx east of hitler north of / blade runner west of kitsch..." [Translated by Rizzo, 2015].

Rummaging through the trunk of unwritten memories, dear Francesco, I find an image made by Barilli during one of the meetings of "Ricercare" at Reggio Emilia's Valli theatre, that more or less used to invoke, for *Yellow Fax*, the thumping of luggage one on top of the other on a conveyor belt, like at times in airports. And I also find the satisfied look of a student—always in Reggio—after my answer to their question on what is there of the Baroque in *Yellow Fax*. I told them, more or less, that in the twenty *laisses* of my text, there is some Baroque in so much as it flows into Expressionism: the will of art and the tension of the new.

Ciao, hugs,

Mariano.

2. Excerpt from an Interview from the 24th of April 2015 about my Dialect Poetry[1]

Ônne' e terra [*Earth Waves*] (1994) proposes a strongly literary use of dialect in a theorization of the "comic" since it exalts the richness of linguistic possibilities. How important is the dialectal component in your linguistic experimentation?

I would say that it is very important. The dialectal component has something to do with a return of the repressed: historical and anthropological. Nevertheless, the contact with shards of a dialect (a losing "tongue," a minority, victim of Italian and other more "globalizing" tongues) never held the meaning of a nostalgic endeavor, a reflux of language toward irrecuperable matrixlike depths, emaciated communities. Poetry cannot waste time re-echoing questions that no longer correlate with reality. The world, to say it like Diderot, begins and ends without a break ("Le monde commence et finit sans cesse" *Le rêve de d'Alembert*, 1769). The "dialectal field" has attracted me as a phenomenon of ongoing transformation and metamorphosis, a space of friction where the dissolution of old identities and traditional communities is the point from which to move. The use of dialect is somewhat present in all my writings, mixed with Italian, French, and Spanish. With *Earth Waves*, I wanted to write about Naples, to give life to poetry that is not "local" but of that "place." In a questionnaire sent to me by the journal *Diverse Lingue* (Year X, no. 14, 1995), I said:

> The necessity of an expression entirely dialectal continued to seem to me the sole guarantee to cut across, in their specificity, my places of existence; how-

---

[1] AN: See Caffeorchidea.It/Lultimo-Poeta-Del-Novecento-Intervista-Con-Mariano-Baino/

ever, it was complicated by the multilingual ingredients of my already ongoing work. My 'dialectal' research consists of having accepted the *flânerie* in those spaces, carrying with them the distractions relative to the possibility of constructing a style that is 'other' to what exists; the need to equip, with codices and diverse tongues, a non-irenic linguistic instrument; the cultural mediations necessary to not conceal today's Babel of languages and not grant to dialect special statuses of poetic value. But it also consists of having accepted to dialogue with the *genius loci* of Naples, letting its language, Neapolitan, be, I would say, the factor assembling the other compositional factors. The meaning of this *flânerie dialogique*, of this cutting across the labyrinth-city through the network of its language, can perhaps be considered […] the constitutive nucleus with which, in the collection *Earth Waves*, I chose dialect.

As for the comic, a carnivalesque thinking acts upon the text. This is not only because dice games, greasy poles, and joker kings are evoked but also because what is proper to the carnivalesque is eccentricity and the continuous mobility of form. The dialogic and the comic obviously bring to mind Bakhtin, whose rereading was for me and my companions bent on the attempt of lowering polyphony, the interdiscursivity—thought of by the Russian theorist as exclusive to the genre of the novel—in the traditional monody of poetry. As a carnivalized literary text, *Earth Waves* proposed itself as an allegorical turning upside down, the desecrating "uncrowning" of the fixity of a mask: that of Naples and its "Neapolitanness." The comic also peers out in the continuous changes of rhythm and intonation, almost surprised in the face of linguistic possibilities. It seemed to me that it was preferred by Neapolitan's capacity to revive, in a particular *linguistic multiverse*, diverse historical epochs.

3. Annotations on the Form of the Sonnet

A sonnet whose lexicon is an organism deprived of phonic luxury, left as though fasting from connotations, dissolved by discursivity, aimed at purging itself of the word as rhyme. Or, on the contrary, a meter of verbal redundancy and heat of the Baroque grandeur of rhymes. An alternation, a combination, of these two modes?

The sonnet as a tensile structure. The complexity and lightness of a thing not stably anchored to the ground. The tension, plasmability of the tents of nomads. The "so complicated and portable" object, as it becomes in the definition of the sonnet by Sainte-Beuve ["cet instrument si compliqué à-la-fois et si portatif," *Des soirées littéraires ou les poètes entre eux*, 1831].

4. Letter to Andrea Cortellessa that Found Itself in *Terra della prosa. Narratori italiani degli Anni Zero*, the Anthology Curated by Him (429–430).

Dear Andrea,

For some time now, as you know, I have been in Southern Argentina in a type of voluntary exile. While I am writing to you, I do not know if your anthology is already in print and if there is still time for the note on poetics that you had asked of me. For which, with all the speed that I am capable of, and, in a disorderly manner:

I let myself be guided by the experiences I make. However, I fail to resolve them into concepts, and for this purpose, I use narration. What does not transform itself into something clear and obvious remains to me, because of my constitution, foreign. Certainly, narration has not always been, for me, the novel. My personal tradition is born out of the crossing of prose and poetry, which has interested all of the Novecento and generated conversations about an "unstoppable dynamism" that mobilizes genres. In sum, already in the days of the journal *Baldus*, I experimented with "rhythmic quasi-prose, de-structured, ritornello sequences and even shadows of characters. (Martignoni)

It is only that today, inadequateness is not only for the novel and its alleged predatory and "representational" nature, its continuous structure. The cultural Disneyland or the videogame in which we find ourselves for some time now makes it such that prose that searches for a little bit of narrative stability, just like prose all about perspectives, ellipses, temporal jumps, just like, obviously, poetry, are inevitably and equally typographical and mass media culture. "Graecum est, non legitur" ("It's Greek, [hence] not readable") would jokingly tell Pizzuto about his writings. Studying the stagnant properties of genres today, or even how to overcome them, means studying fossils. In any case, I continue to experiment, and my novels are presumed also to be the heirs of the anti-novel. Carmelo Bene said: "Two computers meet and deprogram one another." Beautiful. Only that, after having deprogrammed one another, what do they do? They remain dead in entropy and deprogrammed, or do they seek to reprogram themselves? A whole other discourse, I would say, is the "good health" of the supermarket aisle "novel." But, if I am where I am, in Patagonia, it is also to flee from *editors* and certain types of *fiction*. Poetry, novels, or more "scalene" forms of writing are all together my pleasure and pain of narrating. Maybe even an anomalous narrating, perhaps.

In the end, I would say—and perhaps we can discuss this calmly some other time—that, in Italy, the holding as distinct certain stylistic phenomena of the genre of the novel, which often contained them, went a little overboard.
In my work of stylistic-linguistic and narrative tension, I would like plots to coexist, more or less concluded may they be...

Hugs, M. B.

Ivan Schiavone (Translated by Sandro-Angelo de Thomasis)

Poet-re-mix[1]

1. Landscape

> As in every landscape, the I in this part of the text is collective.
> — Heiner Müller, *Despoiled Shore Medea-material Landscape with Argonauts*, n.p.

Electric fences, beyond which animals appear, and, further away, an old village with two bell-towers: one Baroque, the other Romanesque, a tunnel out of which cars exit at irregular intervals, publicity billboards along the road, beside apiaries in modern, colored cases monitored by complex digital equipment, the forest, the steep and rocky slopes of the mountains, a hunter's hut, an hydroelectric power station further down, Tibetan flags, dandelions and columbines, on piles of snow on the side of the trail footprints of hoofed mammals, canines, I wouldn't be able to tell whether wild or domesticated. In this landscape, like in almost all domesticated environments that we experience, elements from heterogeneous contexts, diverse spaces and times, from multiple types of human activities, in turn, informed by various lifestyles and practices, hybridize themselves. This post-identitarian landscape, a manifested syncretism, is the space I feel necessary to restore and have restored at a linguistic level, but even more so stylistically and metrically, through poetry, at least the one I have felt the necessity to write, read, and spell out. Hence, *landscape*, a term I use to

---

[1] AN: The current text derives from a montage of notes, theoretical texts, manifestos, interviews, and accompanying texts to groups of poetry, series, or volumes appearing in different forms. A thank you to Nanni Balestrini, Gabriele Belletti, Sara Davidovics, Francesco Forte, Vincenzo Frungillo, Milli Graffi, Lorenzo Mari, Davide Paone, Laura Pugno, Gianluca Rizzo, Federico Scaramuccia, Italo Testa—poet friends, consumers, interviewers, editors, co-writers and/or patrons of journals—without whom this text would be impossible—and the originals containing its fragments—and sound quite different. A particular thank you to Sandro-Angelo de Thomasis and Iuri Moscardi for their kind hospitality in New York and the accommodating request for this contribution.

define a textual typology, which I have often had recourse to, and a process based on sedimentation and compaction of disparate components that emulates the formation of the post-identitarian landscape as much as the capacity proper to each landscape to evoke emotional states through an empathetic and, hypothetically, unmediated pathway. Therefore, construction out of centrifugal fragments whose harmonization can make a nebula of meaning emerge, not a unitarian and pacified image but rather a set of elements carrying deformed traces of identity and historicity that give life to a discourse that can be instinctively sensed but not made explicit. A non-teleological, complex textual space that implicates an active reader who constantly deconstructs and reconstructs textual mechanisms to gain access to numerous unstable, undecidable, and vibratory semantic configurations.

2. Figural

"Painting has neither a model to represent nor a story to narrate. It thus has two possible ways of escaping the figurative: toward pure form, through abstraction; or toward the purely figural, through extraction or isolation. If the painter keeps to the Figure, if he or she opts for the second path, it will be to oppose the 'figural' to the figurative."
— Gilles Deleuze, *Francis Bacon: The Logic of Sensation* (2, translated by Smith).

Travel as a metaphor for sedentism, the home, our home: language, one of the first virtual realities implemented by humans. The domestication of language is the foundational act of the real. The distance from this source-moment is the historicity of our being in the world in this epoch where the end of identities facilitates the play of culture in the construction of hybrid imaginaries and the opening of new symbolic spaces. A space to map out with the awareness that the mapping out itself modifies what is mapped out, reinvents it, realizing the *figural* through landscape and alterity. Alterity: the occurrence of a you in which language shades and confuses itself, becoming experience and remembering, remembrance of the ways we interact with the other, with the beyond, creolization of an existence exposed to the varied fortunes of errancy. Non-narrative constellations that give life to landscapes, allegorical landscapes, yes, but of a hollowed-out allegoricality, in which the univocal interpretive contract between reader and author is interrupted, the singular figure and the constellations in which it is inserted are subject to an unstable and virtually infinite polysemic potential. An entrenched allegoresis flows out in a fugue of interpretations that imposes an inexhaustible hermeneutic labor, missing that shared background that would allow for a streamlined interpretation of the figures at play. A mapping out of the collective unconscious, those psychic spaces where the effects of abandoned poetics, remote traditions, by historical or geographical distances, resurfacing by excavation or fate, lived not as univocal local identities but as the summation of multiple practices and cultures living side-by-side simultaneously, an explosion of visions of the world and forms; the space where symbolic answers to determined historical tensions are developed, in dialectic with what is most disciplinary in the poetic act: metrics, rhetoric, and semantics, all that apparatus of techniques and procedures that make possible the opening of a work to a horizon of meaning that is common, communicable, and shareable. An emerging space of the fallow, due to the intense formal activity that makes out of a chaotic magmaticity, individual or collective, an opening toward the other, establishing a community of meaning. Making ourselves hounds on the trails of a phantasmal blunder, the residue of the passage from alterity to haecceity ["thisness"], so that that process, which does not seek exposition but expounds a direction, gives a sense of the limits that can be crossed within the constraints of the now.

3. Mannerism and Complexity

"An idea in art is always a model, for it reconstructs an image of reality. Consequently, an artistic idea is inconceivable outside a structure. The dualism of form and content must be replaced by the concept of 'idea' as something realized in a corresponding structure and non-existent outside that structure. An altered structure will convey a different idea to the spectator or reader. It follows that poems do not have 'formal elements' in the usual sense of the word. The artistic text is an intricately constructed thought. All its elements are meaningful elements."
— Jurij M. Lotman, *The Structure of the Artistic Text*, 1971 (Translated by Lenhoff and Vroon).

Any verbalization of given facts is an invention of given facts, with all the problems that come with it, just like the perception of an occurrence is an invention of an occurrence. Innovations in content, meter, and rhetoric are the product of determined historical contingencies—*obviously, external conditions really exist* for *us who are on the receiving end of the properties of time*. In literature, there are moments of invention and moments of functionalization of acquired novelties; this dialectic between avant-garde and mannerism is attributable to the historical climate and only in part the intelligence or will of individual authors. The inherent risk in searching for the novel at all costs is a reduction of literature to reproducing the identical. This type of "novelty" represents for the reader, especially one with an academic background, a peaceful territory in which, exchanging with false consciousness the same old for the new, that interpretive tension proper to works that are truly "other" with respect to a determined panorama of acquired meaning, is not imposed, works that are disruptive because of the necessary effort of reconstruction required by its beneficiaries, an effort that cannot be diminished by having recourse to established interpretive strategies. Therefore, not innovation as in a search for new forms but rather as a new deployment of stylistic instruments given to describe a world in rapid and violent transformation, a perspective closer to mannerism, understood here in Hocke's terms—than the Novecento avant-gardist renaissance.[2] The collective elaboration, over millennia, of linguistic techniques aiming at carrying higher-level information to the letter of the text remains the point of reference for a writing that cannot be but, by its very status, a public event, a doing-for-others, before even considering the efficiency and possible destinies of the singular linguistic product. Meter, rhetoric, and syntax remain the techniques for the creation of a horizon of meaning shared between writer and public in so much as they are founded on a "grammar" of the literary text that ought to be a common heritage to one who writes and reads and that ought to allow understanding or hypothesizing the reasoning behind a series of technical and stylistic decisions, interpreting them, verifying them. Poetry as an instrument of knowledge projected onto every single element of meaning to carry into the world usable and habitable images by an intransigent reader, who seeks in the work, goes on interrogating, challenging the acquiescence that while taking over, dulls and numbs. Construction of a text as a work of high-level formal engineering that asks of the reader an interpretive effort along all the directives of the linguistic act, a complex product, signifying a beyond, sometimes even against, the more directly accessible and manifest meaning; once more, *a mode of forming as a commitment onto reality.* Poetry as a vehicle of thought, a poetry aware of its own artificiality in contrast to any inexistent and impractical naturalness; a poetry founded on a tradition lived dialectically, in which the relation between now and then tells us the identities of living communities; a poetry that would have the audacity to speak this

---

[2] EN: Gustav René Hocke (1908–1985) was a journalist and art historian who employed *Geistgeschichte* in his philological and art historical studies of Mannerism. He had studied in Bonn under E. R. Curtius, under whom he wrote his dissertation in 1934. In 1957, he published *Die Welt als Labyrinth* and expounded his theory of the continual resurfacing of Manneristic tendencies in European art.

world, whether it be tragic, ecstatic or joyful; a poetry that is actual and does not fear being itself political, and is so not simply by habit, partiality, and party-interests; a psychoactive poetry, understood as coitus, psychosis, narcotic, passion; a poetry that supports itself on undetermined allegories from the play of infinite refraction of the figural sense in the friction between the cultures of the world; a poetry of archetypes, synchronies; a poetry based on montage, the sedimentation of heterogenous material, process, construction, the semantic precipitate, metrical awareness, technique; a hybrid poetry hybridized starting from the arts, but that does not justify by means of said hybridization its own misery; a disinhibited poetry that does not conform itself to the paradigms of the times, has the courage to name good and evil, construct its own alternative genealogies, refer itself to the sacred rejected by this secularized society and the mechanics of this misunderstood reality; a synthetic poetry, fertilized by technique in an envisioning of the future free of crude nostalgias and that attempts the most violent form of primitivism, calling into cause the ongoing process of total artificialization; a poetry as a trace of the transiting of energies, forces, and intensities; a poetry as secularization of rites, last form of sacrality that is conceded in these times, won over from religion by technique and science; a poetry as mystery, as excess, as myth in which the space of shadows overflows beyond clarity; a poetry open to dialogue and that rejects sterile partisanship in name of the coexistence of alterity in a complex project of testimony. Poetry as lying by paroxysm and consubstantiality with the process of falsification inherent in language; therefore, poetry as truth. A poetry that prefers to be rather than represent.

4. Italian, A Creole Language

> "The defense of language is indispensable because it allows us to defend and oppose ourselves to the standardization that can, for example, come from the universalization of the Anglo-American. I say that if this standardization ever becomes the norm worldwide, it will not only threaten French, Italian, or Creole languages but, first and foremost, English."
> — Édouard Glissant, *Introduction à une poétique du divers*, 1996 (Translated by de Thomasis).

After being posed for the last time in Italy during the Nineties, the question of language seems to be an outdated question stemming from an acritical and diffuse acceptance of the language of media, when not directly projected as the *standard* of the cultural industry, characterized chiefly by its lexical poverty, parataxis, calque or loan words from English. Poetic language tends to put the focus, sometimes regrettably, on the actual state of the linguistic illness Italian is experiencing. A language that is holistically impracticable because of the sectorization of lives and experiences, that describes well the linguistic compulsion, experiential and existential, which characterizes our lives: the state of language in a country that is slowly becoming a colony. The reduction of experience, discourses, and forms of life, deriving from the flattening out of existences on a post-communitarian urban model, highly medialized, marked by society's shift to the service sector, implies the selection, reduction, and standardization of linguistic capacities, a linguistic model torn between idiolect and cultural prop. I do not believe poetry could have any other duty besides *maintaining language* in such a context. And yet, this is no small thing, keeping the linguistic mechanism fluid and functional in a moment of strong impoverishment in the usage capacities of the word and its semantic possibilities, which are multiple and organizable according to various levels. In linguistic projection, just as in the selection of meter or rhetoric, I tend to prefer a composite language—Baroque and artificial simultaneously—that takes into account history's verticality and does not flatten itself on actual use (decidedly, it is no longer the time of Pound and Eliot's invitation to remake ourselves based on spoken language, since the total flattening has made the choice entirely conformist and incapable of carrying interpretations of the real that are shareable). A bustle of tongues, languages, techniques, and visions define the unstable identities of the environment in which we live: an accumulation of narratives and visions of the world, practices and traditions thrown together, confusing with each other with an aroma of incipient apocalypses or technological palingeneses, and, in the background, imminent collapse of ecosystems, pandemics, scenarios of permanent war. Against this backdrop, lives stand out, our precarious and obstinate biographies, the little narratives of a quotidian deprived of experience, sublimated into feeling, historicity made corporal.

5. Poleis [Cities]

> The new culture (of the world) is not new. It was a cultivation of viruses. Immobility and satisfaction were everywhere. It was an overflow of commonplaces on the benefits of life, and this life was now a nest of monsters. I did not see any dove come from the horizon as a sign that the flood was over.
> — Anna Maria Ortese, *Il porto di Toledo*, 1975 (Translated by de Thomasis).

We know all too well that any truth whatsoever is nothing other than the instrument with which a culture equips itself with the foundation of normative and disciplinary identity; starting from the post-colonial phase of the Novecento, it gradually becomes more apparent how *culture* and *identity* are nothing other than conceptual categories through which, Europe first and the United States after, have succeeded in justifying their own project of cultural imperialism parallel to, and, perhaps, more devastatingly so than its military, political, and economic forms. Nevertheless, it is impossible not to resort to different *truths* in the construction and management of our lives; among this infinite series of acts of faith that prop up our existence, there is poetry. Leaving aside poetry's absolute social marginality as the necessity of defining one's own status in the actual context, the responsibility of this medium is to be rethought, in fact, in light of its invisibility within the existing cultural system. The poet's public and political function, which had characterized the Novecento, has been depleted, and passing the baton to narrators, directors, and visual artists, representatives of aesthetic fields wherein investment and distribution are more important, the poet, having healed their narcissistic wound, turns to an examination of reality through the construction of images of the world that are pertinent, sole true responsibility implicit to art, when it succeeds in freeing itself from the constraints of the jacked and serial production imposed by the market. In this, it appears there is a certain good fortune of the poetic medium, in this distancing made necessary by mercantile constraints, in this possibility of having to submit only to one's own internal logic, one's own moral and formal law. Thus, the poet's liberty increases their responsibility since the choice of materials and forms they work upon is imputable only to them. It would be important for the poet to keep that in mind, just as important as being aware that the instrument used, i.e., language, social instrument *par excellence*, imposes awareness and intentionality in its use. The imaginary in which we find ourselves living is split: on one side, colonized by late-stage capitalism that, through the rituals of information, fashion, consumerism, and publicity, submerges us in a presentification wherein the new is nothing other than the constant repetition of the identical; on the other, the disorganized residues of archaic traces sifted through the deconstruction that happened in the last century, hybridized in the entropy brought about by general migration. If we carry the critique to its extreme, one understands how our scientific and functional reality has nothing but a linguistic essence. Beyond this alphabetical veneer, the world persists in its absolute unknowability, in the sacrality of a mystery that cannot even be scratched and for which we are no longer equipped, via rites, myths, or ideologies, to assign it a name and a cult. On this lies the necessity of *ethoi* and mores, unfounded but unavoidable for the design of one's own historical industriousness, of the domestication of the real, confirmed by way of habits but always more corroded by the absolute lack of belonging that determines the collapse of community ties and their derivative collective imaginaries. The central crux is what can be done with literature in a moment that is not novel, even if amplified very much by current affairs, wherein the alternative appears to be between civil war and extinction, where the definite collapse of any *grand narrative* has revealed the fictional nature of any intellectual construct, including the scientific one, in which a myriad of techniques, used militarily by a capital that has definitively declared war to humans, would appear to have definitely annihilated the possibility of elaborating collective ideologies and practices as a non-contemplative and active answer to the incoming apocalypse.

Tommaso Ottonieri (Translated by Sandro-Angelo de Thomasis)

intermezzo[1]

I suppose I began writing texts earnestly when I started to look at water in its concreteness. I used to pass countless magnetic minutes trying to gather in me (*comprehend*, in its etymological sense)[2] the sense of ebb and flow, the form of currents more so than waves, the (impossible) image of fluidity, the vertiginousness of that unattainable type of vision. In this way, I was born (into writing). From this matter, (my) voice has encountered its kind of wave, its flux.

Afterward, I imagine to have begun sensibly cutting verses, more or less when I discovered the process of photography and took to framing images, so that the form of language, cut, *découpée*, must have appeared to me, I suppose, inscribed among framework disciplines, *inside* and *outside* of the (linguistic) reality to inhabit, within an infinite array of crystals—*optics*, therefore, that nevertheless ought to be pushed and forced in order to *see*. Writing (verses, not only) as a type of image: in the form of expression, within the Gestalt of the page (and of sound), even before the form of the content in the logic of what is signified (through displacements/condensations that push meaning to drift and solidify itself metamorphically into images, let's say, of poetry).

From here, the scribal feeling, in/scribing, almost a definition of boundaries, plastically setting up a volumetry, as a clipping of the continuum but within the feeling itself of said continuum, the uncertain edification of bulwarks within which linguistic matter pours itself out but in a state that is still undetermined or of relative magmaticity: to convert itself in the regime of

---

[1] EN: This text has previously appeared in *Eutropia: revue italo-francaise / Rivista franco-italiana*. vol. 3: L'immagine, 2003, in the section "Intermezzi" dedicated to the question: "Qu'est-ce qu'une image?" ["What is an image?"]; later appearing in Tommaso Ottonieri's *Coro da l'acqua, per voce sola*. Edizioni d'if, 2003.

[2] EN: "to comprehend, perceive" (to seize or take in the mind), from *com* "with, together," + *prehendere* "to catch hold of, seize."

the beyond-visible—indistinct/unrecognizable precisely in its state of most blinding visibility—that belongs for me to an image, when it is an image.

So, *what is an image* then? Vortex in fixity. Flux in the immutable. Within what is evident, the invisible, its sinopite. A recess within the fullness of what is given to us as manifest. A centrifuge from which the fluid of sight sets into its last, slippery sign. A spiral in which everything that there is, pushed within the confines of its borders, a framed night, now continuously sticks out (now that we truly 'see it'). The trace of an internal fire, nestled at a depth that we cannot reach: a trace that here, always elsewhere, uncancelled, lies buried, as though alluding to that unheard of combustion in which we—poured outside of its borders—ceaselessly find and invent (its) origins.

Massimo Bacigalupo

"The Body's Beauty Lives": U.S. Poetry in Italy Today

American poetry has always been widely anthologized and influential in Italy, especially after World War Two, when Carlo Izzo, Roberto Sanesi, and others published several ample anthologies. The postwar generation, especially the Beat poets, was presented in 1964 in Fernanda Pivano's pathbreaking anthology *Poesia degli ultimi americani*. Meanwhile, scholars and poets prepared editions of mainstream postwar figures like Lowell, Berryman, and Bishop and (as in the case of Lowell and his translator Rolando Anzilotti) established long-standing friendships and collaborations, bringing them into Italy not only through their work but also as visitors. Likewise, Pivano and her husband, Ettore Sottsass, a prominent designer, were friendly and generous with Ginsberg, Corso, and others. And Ferlinghetti became one of the most continuously published American poets over the decades. In 2004, I even translated the first three books of his projected long poem *Americus*. Others attempted translations of more forbidding figures, like Charles Olson and even Louis Zukofsky. Ezra Pound's long-suffering daughter, Mary de Rachewiltz, loved and translated Robinson Jeffers and E. E. Cummings, her father's friends and contemporaries, but also translated Denise Levertov in 1968, and James Laughlin, publisher, writer, and another associate of her father, in 1970. Thus, the curious Italian reader had an unprecedented wealth of material to explore American poetry.

In comparison, publications of Italian 20th century and especially postwar poets in the U.S. are but a handful and often produced mainly for an academic audience. I am thinking of a few books by Andrea Zanzotto, who is a difficult read even in Italian and must be a hard nut to crack for an American, and some of whose writings have been translated with great care.[1] However,

---

[1] AN: See, for example, Zanzotto, Andrea. *Peasants Wake for Fellini's 'Casanova' and Other Poems*. Edited and translated by John P. Welle and Ruth Feldman. University of Illinois Press, 1997.

while it is possible to find in Italy recent publications of Charles Simic, Jorie Graham, Anne Carson, Louise Glück, and even the complete poems of Mark Strand, it would be more difficult to find the works of their Italian contemporaries. Patrizia Cavalli, Antonella Anedda, and Valerio Magrelli have been translated; however, the latter two in England. The audience for Italian poetry abroad is small. This is typical of the genre, which never translates well and is difficult to appreciate beyond national borders. So much is implicit about culture in the compact world of a poem—and much of its strength lies in language and inevitably can only be represented tentatively in translation, except for a stroke of genius—a rare thing anywhere and anytime. So, the undeniable popularity of several American poets abroad and especially in Italy, must be rated as a unique phenomenon of cultural history, probably associated with the curiosity for and attraction to all things American in the aftermath of the war, but also because clearly these works answered a need and elicited a shock of recognition in post-war and baby-boom Italian readers.

Interestingly, in 2004, the principal Italian newspaper, *Corriere della Sera* of Milan, offered its readers a series of hardback volumes of individual poets from all languages. Out of the thirty-two poets selected worldwide, no less than seven were American—over 7% of all poetry ever written! This has a lot to do with editors' choices, publication rights, and availability of translations but is nevertheless indicative. It is also instructive to see which American poets were regarded as sufficiently popular to figure on national newsstands. (The books were sold with the daily paper and were available for a week.) The chosen seven are Whitman, Dickinson, Masters, Pound, Eliot, Plath, and Ginsberg. (There was also Auden's *For the Time Being*, arguably an American book.) Thus, these are American writers whom literate Italian readers were expected to be familiar with and hopefully buy (for "€5,90 + the price of the newspaper"—not much for a well-bound hardback!). There is no Stevens or Frost, who, despite their massive importance and book-length translations (at least for Stevens), have yet to enter the general perception of Italian readers. But the others would all be recognized as familiar names, though perhaps Plath only by a certain audience and Ginsberg today by baby-boomers who grew up on Kerouac's *On the Road*.

The popularity or familiarity of Masters and Pound are peculiar Italian phenomena. Pound spent most of his life in Italy, wrote in quasi-Italian, and was endlessly discussed in the press because of his Rome Radio talks and subsequent detention in an insane asylum in Washington, D.C. Therefore, in Italy, he looms large—he is notorious and newsworthy—probably more so than any other 20th century poet. And, in recent years, he has even played a political role with the establishment of a right-wing organization called CasaPound, which claims his political and economic writings ("With usura hath no man a house of good stone" *Canto* XLV) as an inspiration.

As such, Pound has been appropriated by neo-Fascists but has also been highly regarded by some intellectuals of the Left (the arch-enemies Sanguineti and Pasolini among them). Masters has always been dear to liberals and radicals for denouncing hypocrisy, exploitation, and graft in his Midwest village. Unlike Pound and others, Masters is still enormously popular, also because of an album by the popular singer Fabrizio De André, and *Spoon River Anthology*, first translated by Pivano under the supervision of Cesare Pavese in 1943, has been continuously retranslated and adapted for the stage. One recent complete translation was offered and annotated by Luigi Ballerini in 2016. Also, among the 20th-century *Corriere della Sera* choices, Ginsberg, Ferlinghetti, Eliot, and Pound have been retranslated over the years, but nothing like the *Spoon River Anthology*, in which publishers are always happy to invest. No practicing poet probably takes Masters as a major figure, but perhaps this can also be said of Ginsberg and Plath. Yet, Masters alone has been able to speak to a large and undifferentiated Italian audience, not Beat-oriented or gender-oriented as is the case with Ginsberg and Path—specialized audiences anyhow.

An altogether different matter is the influence of these and other American writers on practicing Italian poets. Here, clearly, T. S. Eliot stands out since all the Italian literati were reading, translating, and learning from him in the second half of the 20th century, though only one authorized (and not faultless) translation was available and endlessly reprinted by the critic, poet, and translator Roberto Sanesi, who had a philosophical approach, and had a good ear; hence his translations became canonical. Though the most authoritative Italian scholar of English, the masterly Mario Praz, had presented his translation of *The Waste Land* as *La terra desolata-Frammento di un agone-Marcia trionfale* in 1949, and premier poet Eugenio Montale had memorably rendered *Song of Simeon* (1929), *La figlia che piange* (1933), and *Animula* (1947). Both Montale and Sanesi are poets who responded to Eliot in their own work, as did other major figures like Mario Luzi and Vittorio Sereni. It would be difficult to find a major or minor poet who was not attracted to and, to some extent, influenced by Eliot, either by his abstractions and ironies or by his fragmentation and multilingualism.

In the 1950s and 1960s, it was the surrealist and fragmentary Eliot of the 1920s who appealed to the Novissimi, among them Edoardo Sanguineti and Elio Pagliarani, whose narrative poem *La ragazza Carla* portrays the wasteland of postwar Italy by way of the life of a typist. Sanguineti liked the inclusiveness and wit of Eliot and, perhaps even more, Pound. Though a rigid Marxist in belief, he was able to review *The Pisan Cantos* in translation, omitting all references to their explicit political content. Sanguineti also used Pound's usura cantos in his libretto for Luciano Berio's musical work *Laborinthus II*. He read Pound as an opposer of financial and usurious exploitation and liked to place him next to Bertolt Brecht among writers who spoke to present economic conditions.[2] Also, Luigi Ballerini, in a recent poem, tells us, "I agree with Pound when he writes that if a state / claims that it lacks money to build roads / this is tantamount to saying that it can't build them for lack / of kilometers" (2021 17).[3] Poets respond to the provocations of fellow poets.

As mentioned above, Pasolini had no sympathy for the internationalism and Joycean experimentation of the 1960s avant-garde. However, he was enchanted by Pound's return to origins, the simple community of vegetation rituals—what post-war Italy had lost or forsaken in Pasolini's eyes. Pound haunted him to the end, and he used the late Chinese cantos (by which he was much impressed) on the soundtrack of *Salò o le 120 giornate di Sodoma*, a true horror movie about the final days of the Fascist puppet republic in Northern Italy, in which Pound was also a player, as *The Pisan Cantos* remind us. In fact, if today certain scholars of Modernism have some knowledge of the obscure events of 1943–1945 in Italy, this is because Pound was so closely involved in the death-throes of Italian Fascism and even wrote two entire cantos in his peculiar Italian as rallying call for the last stand of Mussolini and his followers. Pound was a poet who was not content with being a witness. He wanted—such was his naiveté—to make history. In Italy, this unique attitude parallels Gabriele D'Annunzio's career, the "aesthete in arms." It has also made Pound a unique if disquieting and often repellent presence in the peaceable panorama of 20th century U.S. poetry. He will probably continue to be studied, questioned, and talked about, if not widely read. This is also the case in Italy,

---

[2] AN: See Bacigalupo, Massimo. "Sanguineti fra Pound ed Eliot." *Ezra Pound: un mondo di poesia*. Ares, 2022, pp. 313–323.

[3] AN: See Luigi Ballerini's "Omaggio a Ezra Pound" in *Divieto di sosta*. Nino Aragno, 2021, p. 17.

though notable poets of today, like Antonella Anedda and Bianca Tarozzi, have also responded to Pound-the-poet, leaving aside the endless discussion of his politics and bigotry.

Which American poets are important reference points for today's younger Italian poets? Maria Grazia Calandrone has written sensitively on George Oppen[4] and conducted interviews for the Third Program of Italian Radio with Mary Jo Bang, Charles Bernstein, and others. Luigi Ballerini, Marco Giovenale, Milli Graffi, and others have translated an ample selection of Bernstein's poems.[5] Kathleen Fraser and Rachel Blau Du Plessis, also associated with the L=A=N=G=U=A=G=E"group, have likewise found Italian listeners. Du Plessis's translator, Renata Morresi, writes her own poetry in response to the formal radicalism of her American peer. Vincenzo Ostuni, born in Rome in 1970, is the author of an experimental work in progress, *Faldone*, of which twenty sections were published in 2012.[6] Its discursive and fragmentary style recalls Sanguineti and the neo-avant-garde of the 1960s. At the same time, the project of a long reflective autobiographical work in sections harks back inevitably to *The Cantos*. Also, Luigi Ballerini has written Poundian verse narratives, such as *Cefalonia* (2005), and courted abstraction in his earlier work. His commentary on life in *Divieto di sosta* (2021) has become more essayistic and even jocose. He also has been faithful to Ezra in his fashion.

In the spring of 2020, at the height of the pandemic, Maria Grazia Calandrone conducted a series of interviews for Rai Radio 3 with twenty-two younger Italian poets, *Da poeta a poeta*. She first sensitively read and commented on a poem by the interviewee, and then she asked them to speak of a poet that she regarded as an essential point of reference. I may have missed some of the interviews, but the only American poets I recall being mentioned as an essential inspiration were Dickinson—and Stevens. So, Stevens's arrival and possible pre-eminence are probably the latest developments in the Italian reception of American poetry. Actually, Italian is the language of the first book of Stevens to appear abroad, *Mattino domenicale ed altre poesie* (1953), edited and translated by the Harvard comparatist Renato Poggioli. It gave Stevens great pleasure to see his poems in a finely produced Italian edition published

---

[4] AN: In Pascoli, Giovanni. *Il fanciullo. Un altro mondo, lo stesso mondo*. Edited by Maria Grazia Calandrone. Aragno, 2019.

[5] AN: See Bernstein, Charles. *Echo/Eco*. Edited by Carla Buranello. Edizioni del Verri, 2022.

[6] EN: See Ostuni 2022a, 2022b, 2019a, 2019b, 2018, 2014, and 2004.

by Einaudi with (I will add) Poggioli's magisterial preface (and quotations in English from Stevens's letters to Poggioli in the endnotes). Later editors and translators of Stevens, like me, could not compete with Poggioli's expertise nor benefit from his direct access to the master, yet they made up by offering more work by Stevens and attempting commentary until the publication in Mondadori's premier series "I Meridiani" of the complete poetry, *Tutte le poesie* (2015), a volume of 1325 pages. As a curiosity, let me mention that, in the Meridiani series, the other American poets present are Whitman, Dickinson, Pound, and Plath; Eliot and Ginsberg could easily have made it were they not appropriated by publishers other than Mondadori. So, we go back to the list of the seven essential American poets of the 2004 *Corriere della Sera* series. Yet there is Stevens, who counts chiefly for poets and savvy readers of verse.

When *Tutte le poesie* appeared in 2015, a reviewer in a popular weekly commented that Stevens's absolute quiet and concentration were the answer one needed to the pressure in our unsettled times. Little did he imagine that the outlook would shortly become even more bleak. One could return to *The Waste Land* for apocalypse and surrender or to Stevens for abstraction: "In the oblivion of cards / One exists among pure principles" (*Solitaire under the Oaks*). Stevens has been with us for a long time. *Sunday Morning* of 1915 is about as remote from us in time as Wordsworth's *The Excursion* was to Stevens, yet the young poet of 2020 senses a direct connection, if not with the set piece of *Sunday Morning*, then with *No Ideas about the Thing but the Thing Itself*—that is, the later Stevens. Even Pound's Objectivist followers, Zukofsky and Rakosi, couldn't get Stevens out of their systems.

If Stevens appears to count more than other American classics for today's Italian poets, it should be possible to find signs of this in recent publications. *The Wallace Stevens Journal* has a section of poems that respond to Stevens and, over the years, has published a poem (written in English) by Mary de Rachewiltz, Pound's daughter, *And Juda Becomes New Haven* (1998), which I understand to be a reflection on Harold Bloom and his affair with a younger scholar. In the Fall of 2009, the journal also published the translation of a poem by Carlo Vita, a journalist, artist, and friend of Umberto Eco, called *An Old Man*, a take on Stevens's *An Old Man Asleep*.[7] Elena Salibra, a poet scholar

---

[7] AN: See Vita, Carlo. "An Old Man." *The Wallace Stevens Journal*, 33, 2, 2009, p. 260. The 25th anniversary issue also offered a translation in Romagna dialect of "The Snow Man" by a

from Pisa, also included a poem called *Leggendo Stevens* in her last volume, *Nordiche* (2014), a personal rewriting of *Questions Are Remarks*: "In the weed of summer comes the green sprout why" (1954, 462) becomes very simply "calpestavamo la gramigna estiva" (2019, 299).[8] *Questions Are Remarks* was originally published in 1949 in Marguerite Caetani's *Botteghe Oscure*, a journal featuring Williams, Lowell, and other American poets.

Incidentally, with the re-emergence of Stevens, William Carlos Williams is also due for a comeback. A new ample selection of his poems recently appeared, *A un discepolo solitario* (Bompiani, 2023). But Williams is important to Italian poetry chiefly because Vittorio Sereni and Cristina Campo translated him during his last years for the same Einaudi series in which Stevens's *Mattino domenicale* appeared, and Campo, an intriguing visionary poet, published with Scheiwiller her own minute fastidious selection *Il fiore è il nostro segno*.[9] As for Elena Salibra and Stevens, when I was working on the translations for the Meridiano complete poems, I often sounded her on the versions I was composing, and she responded helpfully. This correspondence is available online. Translation is always impervious. So far as my work on Stevens is concerned, I am most satisfied with my first venture in the field of the Hartford poet-executive, *Il mondo come meditazione* (1986). It was my second book of poetry in translation, the first being Pound's *Homage to Sextus Propertius* (1984). In fact, Salibra's *Leggendo Stevens* derived from our debate on how to translate "weed." In the Meridiano I find "Fra l'erbaccia estiva viene questo verde germoglio perché..." Elena perhaps rightly wanted *gramigna*. However, note Stevens's audacity in speaking of "this green sprout why." Later, he writes of his grandson questioning his mother on the sun...

A curious variation on Stevens was produced by Roberto Giannoni, a unique poet in the Genoese dialect. He composed narrative poems about characters, historical and invented. He planned a large work that would tell the history of the 20th century from the vantage point of Genoa, an ancient Mediterranean port that has been one of Europe's industrial and commercial hubs.

---

prominent writer: Tonino Guerra, "L'òm ad naiva," *The Wallace Stevens Journal*, 25, 2, 2001, p. 278.

[8] AN: See Salibra, Elena. *Dalla parte dei vivi. Poesie 2004–2014*. Manni, 2019, p. 299. Cf. "Questions Are Remarks," *The Collected Poems of Wallace Stevens*. Knopf, 1954, p. 462; see also *Tutte le poesie*, 802.

[9] AN: See Williams, William Carlos. *Il fiore è l nostro segno*. Translated by Cristina Campo. Scheiwiller, 1958; *Poesie*. Translated by Cristina Campo and Vittorio Sereni. Einaudi, 1960.

Giannoni's culturally savvy poems often present mythical figures in modern dress. He has been included in another volume of Mondadori's Meridiani series, an anthology of Italian dialect poetry.[10] Usually, his texts are accompanied by a translation in Italian and numerous historical and literary footnotes. Giannoni composed a poem, published posthumously, titled *Loom Bay, Connecticut*. It derives from Srevens's moving late poem *The World as Meditation*, which presents Penelope in the act of waiting and ideally reuniting with Odysseus. Giannoni imagines an American woman in Stevens's Connecticut awaiting the return of her seagoing husband. Nearly every line is a variant of a line of Stevens. The closing phrases, retranslated in English, run roughly as follows:

> To be prepared for his arrival,
> she combed her hair and meanwhile
> said some fragmented words, some crumbs. As if
> she was shelling them and laying them straight...
> They were like a man's breathing. Or just a name.[11]

Compare Stevens's close: "She would talk a little to herself as she combed her hair, / Repeating his name with its patient syllables, / Never forgetting him that was coming constantly so near" (1954 521). It is hard to beat Stevens, especially in a poem like this, which is among his most profound and touching. Yet, it is wonderful that his Penelope should travel from Hartford to Genoa in a local historical dialect and still speak of her timeless condition of expectations of fulfillment. Giannoni's is one of the most original readings of Stevens that I have met.

A much younger and better-known poet, Guido Mazzoni, proposes his own takes on Stevens (he calls them "covers") in his award-winning collection *La pura superficie* (2017)—surely a Stevensian title. The book offers a series of sketches in verse and prose of contemporary life, emphasizing brutality and disaffection (one text is a participant's account of the demonstrations at

---

[10] AN: See Brevini, Franco, editor. *La poesia in dialetto. Storia e testi dalle origini al Novecento.* Mondadori, 1999, III, pp. 3656–3686.

[11] AN: "P'ëse pronta / 'a stava a pettinâse e 'a dïva intanto / d'e fregogge, de paole rotte, comme s'a 'e stesse a destegâ, a mettile in fïa... / Ëan 'o respïo de 'n òmmo. O giûsto 'n nomme." The full poem is quoted in Bacigalupo, Massimo. *Angloliguria: da Byron a Hemingway.* Il Canneto, 2017, pp. 83–86.

the Genoa G8 summit of 2001). In today's wasteland, Mazzoni inserts seven poems titled *Stevens*, paraphrases or "covers" of as many Stevens poems.[12] The effect is arresting: the aplomb of the American contemplative contrasting with everyday horrors. Yet, they have detachment in common, a lack of illusion, not ideals but the thing. There may be a question of appropriation: can you scatter classic poems by a master poet among your own journal notes? Perhaps Mazzoni relies on the fact that Stevens is not yet a byword in Italy, so one can really read his "covers" as if they were new poems. In any case, this is a notable example of Stevens's arrival among Italian readers and writers in the second decade of the 21st century.

Clearly, Eliot and Pound have had a demonstrably greater influence than Stevens on 20th century Italian poetry—also because the poets that read them, like Montale, Luzi, Sereni, Zanzotto, Pagliarani, Sanguineti, Pasolini, and Giudici, have become Modernist classics. Major American writers influenced writers who left a significant mark and belonged to a period that produced much first-rate work. Today's connoisseurs read Stevens and their American contemporaries in search of new points of reference (as I mentioned, Carson, Glück, Graham, Strand, and others like Adrienne Rice enjoy a certain following and get their share of reviews in the press and online). Luigi Ballerini has done lots of spade work here, editing massive anthologies of late 20th century poets,[13] mostly avoiding mainstream writers like the ones mentioned above and included in Mark Strand's anthology *West of your cities: nuova antologia della poesia Americana* (2003). These are competing accounts of the situation of poetry, a kind of poetry war, and one must be thankful to Ballerini and his collaborators for gathering and reflecting on so much material. One is reminded of Jack Foley's massive labors on California poetry, gathered in two large-format volumes that provide a rich cultural history for those who will follow in the historian's and anthologist's footsteps.[14]

Encounters with poetry are individual and need time, reflection, and even the right moment in a lifetime. A journal that used to be devoted chiefly

---

[12] AN: See pp. 21, 29, 34, 41, 46, 53, and 77.

[13] AN: Ballerini, Luigi et al. (editors), *Nuova poesia americana. Los Angeles*. Mondadori, 2005; *Nuova poesia americana. San Francisco*. Mondadori, 2006; *Nuova poesia americana. New York*. Mondadori, 2009; *Nuova poesia americana. Chicago e le praterie*. Aragno, 2019.

[14] AN: See Foley, Jack. *Visions & Affiliations: A California Literary Time Line, Poets & Poetry*. 2 vols. Pantograph Press, 2011.

to Ezra Pound, *Paideuma*, is preparing an issue on "Poems We Live By." It will make for interesting reading since it will presumably tell us of such personal encounters and thus further our understanding of work that we haven't yet found the right time (or "psychological moment") to consider.

I discovered a personal encounter of this kind when I last visited my friend mentioned above, Carlo Vita. He was over ninety, and his wife had died half a century before. He had framed a black and white photograph of this remarkably attractive young woman. Under it, within the frame, he had copied Stevens's mysterious line, "The body dies, the body's beauty lives."[15] I stared since the line is a paradox, like a Japanese koan, yet the beauty in the photograph could be said to "live." An old man at death's door, a young dark-haired wife, her left index finger touching her cheek, and a line of poetry that states an impossible truth. Here is an example of what one seldom sees: poetry becoming a part of everyday life, journeying through countries and languages to speak to one's present condition. This, to me, proved the truth of Stevens's statement about the poet: "His role, in short, is to help people to live their lives."[16]

---

[15] AN: Stevens, "Peter Quince at the Clavier." *Collected Poems*, p. 92.

[16] AN: Stevens, "The Noble Rider and the Sound of Words." *The Necessary Angel*. Knopf, 1951, p. 29.

CONCERT – XANTABLACKZ
A Verbiage and Sounding Event for Current Communization, 2021–2022, composed and conducted by Diego Minciacchi

Diego Minciacchi directed a spectacle for those in attendance: *Xantablackz. A Verbiage and Sounding Event for Current Communization*. Readers can view the performance by scanning this QR code and following the texts and lyrics supplied in the pages of this volume.

The official author's audio mix of *Xantablackz* performance is available by scanning this other QR code.

conventional and electronic words, conventional and electronic sounds, violin, percussion, trumpet, actor narrators, word materials, and electronics; duration: about 60 minutes.

World premiere of *The Disappearing Pheasant*: New York University, Casa Italiana Zerilli-Marimò
St. Mark's Church in the Bowery, 131 E. 10th St., New York, NY 10003, U.S.
Sunday, November 13, 17:00–18:00.

Music interpreters:
    Lauren Cauley   (violin)
    Caitlin Cawley   (percussion)
    Nate (Nathan) Wooley (trumpet)

Actor narrators:
    Luigi Ballerini
    Cecilia Bello Minciacchi

Word materials by Antonella Anedda, Mariano Bàino, Maria Grazia Calandrone, Vincenzo Frungillo, Marco Giovenale, Laura Liberale, Tommaso Ottonieri, and Ivan Schiavone.

Words, in friendship, by David Rosenboom

Electronics: Sound system to reproduce, mix, and diffuse three independent two-channel sound tracks plus the three interpreters and the two actor narrators.

Notes

The texts, in sporadic cases, have undergone negligible variations and adaptations.

The texts were sometimes differently adapted for the two narrators, so the distinction *narrator one* and *narrator two* is kept. Words materials by poets are given in alphabetical order, not as in the score.

from **Antonella Anedda**

narrator one

In nessun luogo c'è bisogno di noi
tra un mese l'anno
avrà una cifra baltica, bianca
millenovecentonovantuno
dove il mille indietreggia
fino a secoli-steppe
e l'uno, cavo,
tintinna.

Nessuno ci ha chiamato
erano voci d'orto, fischi
per scacciare gli uccelli
la poca pioggia che cola
dai tubi della casa
deserta
come carta.
Ci sono solo i fiati
e il bacile appannato
e le noci che dicono
autunno moltiplicato sopra i tavoli
pietre su posti vuoti.

In nessun tempo c'è bisogno di noi
le notti verticali
e il viale dei tigli, la lepre
trasparente nel cespuglio

la schiena-ombra di chi allora sostava
ora soffiano stanchi
sulla tempia del secolo.

C'è un cibo serale, lampi
sulle foto scoscese
e noi beviamo tra le forchette brune
i volti stretti ai bicchieri
per la lenta paura che s'incide
sul gomito che alza una ghirlanda.

---

narrator two

In nessun luogo c'è bisogno di noi
tra un mese l'anno
avrà una cifra baltica, bianca
millenovecentonovantuno
dove il mille indietreggia
fino a secoli-steppe
e l'uno, cavo,
tintinna.

Nessuno ci ha chiamato
erano voci d'orto, fischi
per scacciare gli uccelli
la poca pioggia che cola
dai tubi della casa
deserta
come carta.
Ci sono solo i fiati
e il bacile appannato
e le noci che dicono
autunno moltiplicato sopra i tavoli
pietre su posti vuoti.

In nessun tempo c'è bisogno di noi
le notti verticali
e il viale dei tigli, la lepre
trasparente nel cespuglio
la schiena-ombra di chi allora sostava
ora soffiano stanchi
sulla tempia del secolo.

C'è un cibo serale, lampi
sulle foto scoscese
e noi beviamo tra le forchette brune
i volti stretti ai bicchieri
per la lenta paura che s'incide
sul gomito che alza una ghirlanda.

Nessun tempo ha bisogno di noi
nessuno dice
il numero dei colpi
l'esatta cifra dell'erba

from **Mariano Bàino**

narrator one

ma io è un altro lo sai e indosso una fronte solcata
cosa che vive d'accordo all'incirca con nulla
e di ostricacee orecchie da gatto viziato da donne
spremo per voi questo punto nerastro che preme da dentro
l'anima blanda [quel che non sono] da occhi caldi di pioggia una chimera

lì svalvola e il secolo breve credo di averlo scontato
con giusto naso denti a stringere attrito col mondo
cartòcciolo di eventi tutti contrari ai molti
e il calare dell'immenso negli occhi dei molti lo vedi
rosso di sole e ingrifarsi di ombre più grandi del mondo

i filosofi-banchieri la moderna reincarnazione
dei reggitori platonici nemmeno all'ora del the

sottoporrebbero scelte quelle loro mirabolanti
e sempre cruciali scelte per il pianeta in black-out
a maggioranze aleatorie di un parlamento o addirittura

a casuali sentenze zampillate da un week-end
plebiscitario un apporto la democrazia lo dà pure
la discussione o valore espressivo la virtù
tutta sua all'andamento più giusto di ogni repubblica
ma sarà questo il suo quaglio l'essenza un fluido talk-show?

---

narrator two

ma io è un altro lo sai e indosso una fronte solcata
cosa che vive d'accordo all'incirca con nulla
e di ostricacee orecchie da gatto viziato da donne
spremo per voi questo punto nerastro che preme da dentro
l'anima blanda [quel che non sono] da occhi caldi di pioggia una chimera

lì svalvola e il secolo breve credo di averlo scontato
con giusto naso denti a stringere attrito col mondo
cartòcciolo di eventi tutti contrari ai molti
e il calare dell'immenso negli occhi dei molti lo vedi
rosso di sole e ingrifarsi di ombre più grandi del mondo

è fra gli interni petali dove la rosa non è più
vana che si contemplano gli uniti e fermi insiemi
della poesia di frasca ma scorgi anche un libero gioco
quasi di uno scultore che approfondisce sempre
il naturale gioco dei volumi e che concepisce

la tradizione ecco e quanto è moderno
come le due metà di una medesima sfera
la sfera gira e quello che è di sotto passa
sopra o un vedere cose visibili anche dagli altri
ma nel momento esatto in cui gli altri non guardano

from **Maria Grazia Calandrone**

narrator one

Splende, la vita, splende come vita. A volte
splende quieta
come il tuo corpo abbandonato al sonno. A volte
sfolgora come il lampo del sorriso.
Ma la terra non splende, la cenere
non splende.

Davvero, Mamma, non sappiamo niente
e non siamo che corpo e non siamo
più in nessun luogo, dopo, probabilmente

e questo precipizio di parole
non è buono a rifare
neanche una molecola del tuo sorriso.

Era vivo, il tuo corpo, e lo guardavo
come si guarda la casa
distesa nella luce del tramonto e il colle
dove stiamo tornando.

Faticavo a raggiungerti, alla fine. Ma eri vita
accessibile, vita dovuta e vita che ho dovuto
lasciar andare. Addio, Mamma. Addio, professoressa.

Senza difese, torni
vita che splende.
Senza difese, splendi come vita.

Vita
abbandonata.
Vita
di tutti.
Vita che torna,

a tutti.

---

narrator two

«Le lingue non hanno confini, i confini sono solo politici» «Esiste una lingua invisibile alla quale attingiamo tutti» «Ogni scrittura è traduzione di un mondo» «Io attraverso le lingue che conosco in cerca della lingua universale».
Questa è la vera avanguardia, la vera
profezia per il futuro della specie.

Fekrì, hubùn, dashùri
sirèl, bhālabāsā, agàpi
uthàndo, ài, jeclahày
süyüü, obichàm, aròha
lyubòv', hkyithkyinnmayttàr
khairtài, cariàd, upéndo
amour, is bràe, snēhàṁ
maxabbàt, szerelém, rudo,
ādaràya, fitiavàna
liebe, evîn, miq'vàrs.

Continuate in settenari chiari
con questi suoni, nuovi come il mondo
che dicono da prati
e da foreste, igloo, capanne
e palafitte, grattacieli e canoe: io, questo niente
caduto nel sogno della materia, *avrò cura di te*
fino alla fine del mondo.

from **Vincenzo Frungillo**

narrator one

Ai lati del sole ci sono reperti
d'altri mondi, come satelliti, consigli,
indicazioni dai raggi scoperti
-"i silenzi dei padri ricadranno sui figli"-

profetizzavano i nonni paterni
durante i pomeriggi, i continui sbadigli,
quando un velo sulla pupilla
nasconde a tutti ciò che brilla.

Una puttana ha notato i suoi capelli bianchi
è stata la prima, standogli sopra,
gliel'ha detto con gli occhi stanchi
"qui nella tempia. Vuoi che li copra?"
Ha spinto più forte con i fianchi
evitando qualsiasi parola,
voleva renderlo muto,
un senza nome. Lui ha goduto.

Ha la memoria ampia quanto il dolore,
vive un guasto della rimozione,
tutto è visto con gli occhi del torpore
mentre versa acqua ai piedi della nazione.
Giura sul suo onore,
ripete che è la sua opinione,
dice di appartenere al corpo sociale,
anche se non ne sente i sintomi nella carne.

Con metafore da meccanico,
espone teorie profetiche,
parla di regole come porte antipanico,
perché le masse sono isteriche
manovrabili con il richiamo sadico
alla minaccia nucleare, il ricatto della psiche,
che spinge a scappare da se stessi
per porre il Partito a controllare gl'ingressi.

---

narrator two

Ha la memoria ampia quanto il dolore,
vive un guasto della rimozione,

tutto è visto con gli occhi del torpore
mentre versa acqua ai piedi della nazione.
Giura sul suo onore,
ripete che è la sua opinione,
dice di appartenere al corpo sociale,
anche se non ne sente i sintomi nella carne.

Con metafore da meccanico,
espone teorie profetiche,
parla di regole come porte antipanico,
perché le masse sono isteriche
manovrabili con il richiamo sadico
alla minaccia nucleare, il ricatto della psiche,
che spinge a scappare da se stessi
per porre il Partito a controllare gl'ingressi.

Quel vuoto l'ha catturato, tenuto lontano,
impegnato in troppe discussioni,
dove nessuno offre la pietà d'una mano,
ma solo il riverbero dei suoni
che emette un uomo insano.
Ripete che "la Storia è come i tuoni,
squarci improvvisi che illuminano i cieli
e poi il buio... dietro quei chiari veli."

from **Marco Giovenale**

narrator one

Per un periodo della mia vita sono stato barista. C'erano dei déjà vu. Ero molto veloce, non mi potevo soffermare, io guardavo. Quando il ritmo rallentava avevo i déjà vu, sapevo che li giudicavo fondati però li volevo ignorare.

Per un periodo della mia vita sono stato assente, non mi trovavano da nessuna parte, in realtà stavo bene, poi sono tornato. Li salutavo con una energia.

Per un periodo della mia vita sono stato cinese. Avevo precisi tratti somatici, come gli occidentali e tutti. I miei erano cinesi. Parlavo e scrivevo anche, in cinese. Solo amici italiani, però, avevo. Non capivano gli scherzi nemmeno quando erano muti, gli italiani sono un popolo riflessivo.

Per un periodo della mia vita sono stato accanto alla finestra a guardare fuori che tuttavia non c'era niente. Non c'è niente nemmeno nel caminetto quando è acceso, ma è lo stesso: si guarda, uno guarda dentro. Cambia che è un dentro invece di un fuori. Le cose cambiano e per un periodo della vita non si sa come, poi si sa. Dopo lo sai, ma non sai quando è dopo

si aspetta diverso ma è proprio lo stesso e la situazione non cambierebbe se fosse diverso

(proprio la vita sarebbe – stata – diversa). però attualmente poi la situazione non cambia,

è anche diverso perché poi uno pensa lo sbaglio il lavoro e le strutture del lavoro.

sarò diverso finché non sarò disponibile poi sarò uguale

ti insegnano che vuol dire molto, poi che vuol dire tutto

poi il tutto che vuol dire ti supera e resti indietro, ti ha superato

finché poi uno cresce allora tutto è diverso tutto cambia

sei stato già superato non può più essere diverso
invece no poi un anno due anni sei superato ancora quindi questo in gergo sportivo si dice doppiato uno viene doppiato è strano che si usi la stessa che ha in verità due significati perché doppiare vuol dire sia appunto superare due volte un atleta in corsa oppure passare due volte per lo stesso.

ma 3 terzo significato vuol dire anche sovrapporre la propria voce alla voce originale di un attore quindi prestare la propria voce a chi parla in un'altra

quindi se ti doppiano è vuole dire che prendono la tua voce non te la ridanno indietro questo succede quando si cresce e non è diverso però allora è diverso ma da parte di un'altra persona perché la diversità te la danno loro non la costruisci più tu non la fai più tu non è più tua e quindi non si vede che sei diverso sei come tutti gli altri sei stato superato e doppiato come tutti considerando questo alcuni smettono proprio tanto capiscono che non sono loro a parlare

questa è una cosa che si capisce tardi in realtà c'era anche prima o almeno così dicono o gli è stato detto a meno che non sia un errore di traduzione
di doppiaggio

---

narrator two

si aspetta diverso ma è proprio lo stesso e la situazione non cambierebbe se fosse diverso

(proprio la vita sarebbe – stata – diversa). però attualmente poi la situazione non cambia,

è anche diverso perché poi uno pensa lo sbaglio il lavoro e le strutture del lavoro.

sarò diverso finché non sarò disponibile poi sarò uguale

ti insegnano che vuol dire molto, poi che vuol dire tutto

poi il tutto che vuol dire ti supera e resti indietro, ti ha superato

finché poi uno cresce allora tutto è diverso tutto cambia

sei stato già superato non può più essere diverso
invece no poi un anno due anni sei superato ancora quindi questo in gergo sportivo si dice doppiato uno viene doppiato è strano che si usi la stessa che ha in verità due significati perché doppiare vuol dire sia appunto superare due volte un atleta in corsa oppure passare due volte per lo stesso.

ma 3 terzo significato vuol dire anche sovrapporre la propria voce alla voce originale di un attore quindi prestare la propria voce a chi parla in un'altra

quindi se ti doppiano è vuole dire che prendono la tua voce non te la ridanno indietro questo succede quando si cresce e non è diverso però allora è diverso ma da parte di un'altra persona perché la diversità te la danno loro non la costruisci più tu non la fai più tu non è più tua e quindi non si vede che sei diverso sei come tutti gli altri sei stato superato e doppiato come tutti considerando questo alcuni smettono proprio tanto capiscono che non sono loro a parlare

questa è una cosa che si capisce tardi in realtà c'era anche prima o almeno così dicono o gli è stato detto a meno che non sia un errore di traduzione
di doppiaggio

sono bravi, piantano gli alberi
fanno una o la cassetta di legno

c'è tutto un perimetro di legno (contenitore) che loro fanno a cassetta come barriera, una, o specie di recinto mettono dentro al recinto la terra (contenuto) poi mettono dentro che scavano quando

hanno scavato mettono dentro di qualcosa il come un prima dell'albero un come fosse un albero
c'è un albero

mettono dentro l'albero e ha/hanno piantato un albero i suoi il è esso è il:

il grande albero della democrazia esso è il grande albero della democrazia

questo albero (della) produce frutti molto buoni ma bisogna con grande attenzione

questo albero produce frutti molto ma bisogna con grande attenzione rispettare i semi anche i semi sono molto e grande attenzione

alcuni li assaggiano alcuni se
ne cibano quanti più alberi si piantano tanto più si
cresce

la democrazia c'è tutta una foresta iniziano a ò - - parlarsi al telefono non sono
più tanto però comunque in campagna più tardi

gli alberi e tutta la popolazione (a tutta) può essere felice perché tranne pochi
tutti quanti possono votare come sceglie la cosa migliore (essi scelgono, essa
sceglie)

spesso il motivo per cui le cose in una città procedono
pulitamente speditamente è perché in queste persone alberga una saggezza e
tutte le persone decidono secondo questa

le cose vanno limpidamente speditamente veloci va tutto sono i riti piantano
alberi anche non della democrazia piantano quanti altri alberi alcuni sono alberi

alcuni sono alberi parassiti come per esempio la robinia ha fama pessima racconta sia una pianta parassitante in effetti se ne trovano tristi che stupenda
cosa è piantare gli alberi piantare la democrazia con poco sforzo puoi avere i
si tratta di aspettare

from **Laura Liberale**

narrator one

la pelle dei morti non assorbe più

finiti gli interscambi
la flessibilità della barriera

quello che avviene sotto
avviene al chiuso ermetico
ti taglia fuori

il morto è già incassato nella pelle
prima che in zinco e legno

quello che avviene sotto chiamalo
l'inespugnabilità
del totalmente solo

il morto canta dodecasillabi
prendendoti in prestito la bocca

quando ti svegli continui a cadenzare
ma, chiaro, sono perse le parole

cominciavano con qualcosa come
infiora la frase la gola s'indora

e rimavano senza vergogna

fu perché non seppero più essere
un lascito vivente che evolsero
in marsupiali

si portavano appresso i morti
maleodoranti e inutili
i quali si consumavano
senza peraltro perdere peso

fu perché non seppero più mettere
in oblio le ossa dei morti
né tacerne per sempre i nomi
che arrancavano sotto quel carico

narrator two

alla signora S. hanno aperto gli occhi per mostrarceli
la signora S. l'hanno estratta dal frigo e ora trasuda brina
è un pezzo d'inverno che si prepara a cedere a colliquare
il globo oculare ha un colore ottuso che non riconosciamo
qualcosa che vorremmo affondare sotto il peso di due monete

alla signora S. hanno sigillato le labbra con il Pattex

i piedi li diresti di una bambola

pensare di chiamarla la "non più mano"
per la definitiva cessazione funzionale

ma finché alla signora S. stendiamo sulle unghie
lo smalto rosa a coprire il vecchio rosso smangiato
finché teniamo tra le nostre le sue dita artiche
finché persiste un qualche tipo di commercio fra vivi e morti
quella della signora S. continua indiscutibilmente a essere
una mano

al signor T. è un momento immaginare
di togliere il completo blu di Prussia
e i calzini bianchi da ospedale
calcargli un copricapo di conchiglie
e canini di cervo, colorargli
d'ocra rossa pianta dei piedi e mani
corredarlo di semplici strumenti
di guerra e di ordinaria sussistenza:
la scheggia di una selce
un bastone forato
lo schema della chemio

from **Tommaso Ottonieri**

narrator one

Così ogni capanna ogni guscio, nel gemito della foresta che l'avvolge, allacciato il cavo alla polla sottotraccia, capta la sua onda flebile la vibra per il ceruleo corso tutto dalle vene di fiamma. Così la scia, saettata fuori, di particole rotanti, e invisibile di bocca in bocca si promana, diverge per la luce azzurrata dei cristalli.

Così specchiato all'essere, così nell'intermittenza, delle ombre delle voci. Così un vortice, alto un vortice un cono di micropunti può tenermi acceso, mi allaccia adesso al riapparire allo svanire delle ciglia delle tue parole, dietro il liquido specchio degli schermi. Suono e miraggio, nel fondo di spelonca.

Giù del concavo foderato di richiami, accecate le icone vibrano dal dentro, lungo la curva delle pareti illuminate. A fiore della pelle, come cablato un minuscolo serpente, soffice striscia il metallo della tua voce, spezza qui i riverberi di quello che c'è da dirsi ancora. Fin che ci sarà segnale.

Fin che parola a scatti ci circonda. Fino nel morso, elettrico un barlume ancora di parola. Solo un nastro esile di terra è rimasto a compattarsi difuori, tutt'intorno all'impalcatura di fibre; slittante striscia e isola, ed è laccio. Questa corona di polveri che cinge; e tiene ancora dai precipizi qui stretti all'assedio, senza che noi avessimo saputo.

Fino a che ancora ci sarà segnale, e che sordo il diluvio finirà di spegnerci nei suoi lieviti di cenere, più invisibile una tempesta di sillabe soffierà di noi dalle pupille spalancate, e bruceremo balsami contro il fuoco delle estinzioni.

Narrator two

Abito una capanna di fibra, nel cuore della foresta che si arretra.

Non c'è vento intorno se non le correnti della cenere, che di lontano si sollevano dal cerchio delle lunghe combustioni. Un tappeto di braci, la pelle viva del bosco; lo sfrigolìo, che sottocute non smette di vibrare, più sordo. Dal lembo di pianeta che è questo, nuvole a sbuffo, circoli di fumo, sulle volte fondono a un cifrarsi breve dei segnali, spiaccicati nell'alto come uccelli di carbone.

Abitando la bolla il centro dell'assedio, la fibra a tratti che si accende per ricevere, replica l'inerzia e flette, degli esorcismi che ci tennero. Di lontano le lingue, della fibra, penetrano; più acuti, dietro le resistenze di rame, dalla mia conca foderata di arcani, sento a giro crepitare gli aliti dei contagi.

Così ogni capanna ogni guscio, nel gemito della foresta che l'avvolge, allacciato il cavo alla polla sottotraccia, capta la sua onda flebile la vibra per il ceruleo corso tutto dalle vene di fiamma. Così la scia, saettata fuori, di particole rotanti, e invisibile di bocca in bocca si promana, diverge per la luce azzurrata dei cristalli.

Così specchiato all'essere, così nell'intermittenza, delle ombre delle voci. Così un vortice, alto un vortice un cono di micropunti può tenermi acceso, mi allaccia adesso al riapparire allo svanire delle ciglia delle tue parole, dietro il liquido specchio degli schermi. Suono e miraggio, nel fondo di spelonca.

from **Ivan Schiavone**

narrator one

se confluisse il senso della presenza
       in lingua
che faccia argine al nulla — se s'irraggiasse luce copiosa
          non da luna
ma da feroce sole
che denudi le sole e altere strade a senso unico
        o se da luna
che basti ad una lingua — se sgorgasse una luce per rischiarare il nulla
in cui l'ente s'annulla
     immemore del sole intellettivo
luce che di sé impregni il senso per tracimare in lingua — se sostanziasse in luna
motrice e madre all'una
     e all'altra spinta al nulla
l'eco velata in lingua mutuata da quel sole di cui riflette il senso

— se esperissi la luce che occulta in te traluce —

se il tempo di una luna durasse almeno il senso
di cui adorniamo il nulla
scambiando per il sole
ciò ch'è soltanto lingua — se
     tramite un all-in guastassi il gioco alla luce
con eclissi di sole
   per interposta luna — se comprendessi in nulla
per un totale assenso
     la lingua, nostra luna e luce

— se anche il nulla potesse un sole e un senso

s'affacciano dagli scafandri le vittime di Pol Pot
come da bolle
        dietro gli oblò — l'enigma del potere impresso
sui volti del Bayon
        ferocia, scherno, alterità e sarcasmo
qui come in Europa e ovunque dietro lo sfarzo la mattanza

— un canadian sphynx passeggia tra i tatuaggi traverso la pelle dell'esercente
l'altro in bilico su un palco di corna
        resta sopito

narrator two

ora ogni creatura riposa nella propria essenza. nell'assenza di turbamento. ferma e in movimento al contempo. serena nella sua sera. serafica? irenica? astratta dal contesto. districata dal conflitto. distratta dall'assetto. estinta. la mezzanotte è il quadrante perfetto. figlio di donna sterile universo. chiara la visione del futuro. definita. esatta. come in un cielo d'inverno terso. per profondità e nitore provoca vertigine. intensa. cristallizza in attesa raggelata. ghiaccia. nell'angoscia. per le traiettorie di un'apocalisse. certa. la lingua. che intarsia la materia del mondo. poiché celata esposta. io vado a farmi suicidare. soccombendo pongo fine a ogni potere. nelle stanze da bagno ha già trovato la sua lama. ineluttabile la fine. nominata avanza. domani, da morta, abortirò tuo figlio. voi ricordate le mie parole confuse. inconfutabili. Oramai.

se confluisse il senso della presenza
        in lingua
che faccia argine al nulla — se s'irraggiasse luce copiosa
        non da luna
ma da feroce sole
che denudi le sole e altere strade a senso unico
        o se da luna
che basti ad una lingua — se sgorgasse una luce per rischiarare il nulla
in cui l'ente s'annulla
        immemore del sole intellettivo
luce che di sé impregni il senso per tracimare in lingua — se sostanziasse in luna
motrice e madre all'una

                    e all'altra spinta al nulla
l'eco velata in lingua mutuata da quel sole di cui riflette il senso

— se esperissi la luce che occulta in te traluce —

se il tempo di una luna durasse almeno il senso
di cui adorniamo il nulla
scambiando per il sole
ciò ch'è soltanto lingua — se
                    tramite un all-in guastassi il gioco alla luce
con eclissi di sole
            per interposta luna — se comprendessi in nulla
per un totale assenso
            la lingua, nostra luna e luce

— se anche il nulla potesse un sole e un senso

from **David Rosenboom**

narrator one

In a beginning, whether walking on branches of trees or standing in tall grasses, gestures may silently signal prey or foe, coordinate groups, and broadcast affection for coupling. Slowly, vocalizing and gesturing conjoin. Semantics, meaning in sound, is born.

In the vast alluvial plain of *West Papua*, a seemingly endless world of tides, mud and bog, the coming and going of water, fish, crocodiles, log boats carrying friends and foe, stimulate wild gesturing and physical pulsing so intense that both chaotic and ordered shouting and chanting naturally emanate from the body. In an *Asmat* beginning, *Fumeripits*, the first wood carver and cultural hero, danced alone on a beach, but when he became tired of being lonely, he carved figures from wood and placed them in a long house, a *jeu*. He was still lonely until he created a drum of wood and lizard-skin, and with the pulse of his playing the figurines came alive. Their elbows came unstuck from their knees—elbows to knees, the position at birth to which we return at death—, and they began to dance. *Fumeripits* now had dancing partners. Thus, music and dance had their common origin at coming alive.

First language follows a need to signal. Musical signals soon come from drums and trumpets, while flutes and ocarinas beckon voices from spirits. As individual and group identities become recognized and need to be protected, time-space correlations and projections in minds differentiate present moments and present beings, each with its own synthesized past, *now*, and future. Articulating one's *nows* for others demands sequential logic. The tool that emerges we call syntax.

Elbows to knees at birth, elbows to knees at death, but how do we describe the in-between and where the ancestors go? Twenty-foot-high *Asmat* bis poles carved from upside down mangrove trees with root members judiciously left protruding at the top help transport souls of the dead to the realm of ancestors, commemorate important individuals, and promise the avenging of fallen warriors.

Elbows to knees at birth, elbows to knees at death, but how do we describe the in-between and where the ancestors go? Twenty-foot-high *Asmat* bis poles carved from upside down mangrove trees with root members judiciously left protruding at the top help transport souls of the dead to the realm of ancestors, commemorate important individuals, and promise the avenging of fallen warriors.

What is a beginning? Languages offer the blessing and curse of enabling speculation, often in the service of belief systems becoming so strongly expressed that a word can both serve love and cause war. And as our symbolic species develops twice-removed signs, fragile images and inscriptions gain comparable power to generate both fear and wondrous epiphanies.

"But how did it all begin?" (Callasso). For the West, the wonders of the universe and the crimes of mythical prototypes give life and haunt existence. Languages enable both grasping and freedom, while music, dance, and art support cathartic exorcism, release, and give illuminating license to try out potential new universes. Languages evolve with extraordinary speed.

Examples abound in the rugged geography of Papua New Guinea, which may still hold a quarter of the world's still viable languages, kept apart by mountains. When impenetrable barriers separate people, languages instantly diverge, disaffiliating multiple cultures and systems of belief. In the wake of simple divisions, humans quickly find the origins of conflict. Perhaps our art may someday lead to enjoying all selves without abiding, with vigorous living and doing, and most of all honoring our natural being. Even before awareness of self arises, we gesture. Sound, dance, images of light, and languages follow.

---

narrator two

Consider

active endogenous synthesis → perception
recognition
apprehension
understanding,
↑
imagination as intermediary.

active co-creation → interactive
communication
follows (succession)
differentiation.

scooping up nows — brain life—memory—
consciousness of time—
coagulation of *now* traces—idiologs—
representations to a self of *nows* involves imagination—
pretext of time travel only an issue for consciousness that projects pasts.

Universe as tapestry of rhythmical knots.

Rhythmical knots engendering perceived substance.

Rhythmical knots becoming self-aware.

Rhythmical knots making experiences of palpable stuff.

Perhaps offenses to the intellect wrought by ideas of probability stem from intoxication with certitude and a doctrine of necessity, so viewed from relative inexperience with the implicate balance of whole-ism and limits—undeniably, stunningly practical, deterministic constructions, most dazzlingly, mathematics—in describing an introspective knowability about the nature of universes. "Don't know!" (Seung Sahn).

Beauty is like laughter, an emotional response to a great distillation of that which is phenomenally natural.

brain life—memory—
consciousness of time—
coagulation of now traces—idiologs—
representations to a self of *nows* involves imagination—
pretext of time travel only an issue for consciousness that projects pasts.

Is mind is!

No fear of crashing, no intention of landing.

Separating truth from provability.

During instants when the mind stops moving, unity emerges.

What is the dimensionality of time?

Model building and experimenting are essentially cognitive domains aided by proprioceptive inputs and outputs correlating semantic networks with supposed physical experience. Attaching labels to physical experience is half the battle of physical science. Finding evocative means to communicate and stimulate conceptions in minds that give form and substance to abstract models is primary.

Creative model building can be absolute. Indulging in the beauty of abstract models may lie at the core of advances in conceiving physical propositions. For it must be fundamental in the biological constitution of humans to examine the phenomenon of true beauty as what nature must really be like.

Looking for best matching among intelligences is part of co-creative communication—emerging, intrinsic similarities and differences.

Duration is a measure of difference.

To conceive life as mentally palpable on large time-space scales—to use the battery of the small scale, local individual to fuel a broad and vast consciousness without losing its distinguished nature. The smaller the dimensionality and time-space scales of the differentiated, the greater the energy-essential-tension packed into those delineated entities—as long as they are not empty—undefined.

Nicholas Benson

Afterword: Notes on The Reappearing Pheasant

The three-day gathering of poets and critics offered a much-needed opportunity to compare notes on the condition of poetry in the two countries, from a variety of perspectives. Joined in relief at having been freed of lockdown — the conference was originally scheduled for 2020 — and by recognition of the strength of shared resistance to multiple global plagues (I refer the reader to the critical essays presented) the mood was collegial, collaborative — and grateful to the critically galvanizing, inclusive sociability of Luigi Ballerini, without whom so many would not have a chance to meet, discuss their work, forge and deepen mutual understanding of the situation of poetry in Italy and the U.S.

As noted with some surprise and relief by Luigi Ballerini, in spite of differences in approaches to poetry, at this gathering there were no verbal fisticuffs, and more joined than divided the poet/critics of the two countries. Whereas, as Luigi explained, when the pheasant disappeared, a rift emerged between the American and Italian writers—the result of a misapprehension, a misplaced arrogation of critical superiority on one side or the other—thirty-one years later, in retrospect and with the reappearing pheasant, it had become clear that this divide was based on a misunderstanding, a misreading, a battle over primacy of commitment.

To this gathering, all had been invited, like those included in the encyclopedic critical and poetic anthology, *Those who from afar look like flies*, edited by Ballerini and Beppe Cavatorta, on an "ecumenical—but biased" basis. The three days were filled with a range of critical and compositional approaches by speakers who remain avid listeners in the field of poetry and poetics. "Perhaps the pheasant should reappear every five days," Luigi suggested toward the end of the conference. And everyone would have signed up for that immediately — as perhaps the excellent support crew feared! (Stefano Albertini, the director of the Casa Italiana Zerilli-Merimò, and his tireless staff choreographed a seamless three days in conjunction with the Istituto di Cultura Italiana.)

Although I was not present at the first conference, it was noticeable to me how many productive links there are between the two literatures, bridges constructed by those who have long worked in both languages, or to foster ties between the two literatures—Ballerini, Charles Bernstein, Massimo Bacigalupo, Marjorie Perloff, and many others. These were three days packed with thought provoking presentations and readings. The sense of repaired factionalism, of an alliance between forces that don't always agree, or even hear one another (and that's just within one country!) was particularly interesting to me as a translator—and as one currently working on the story of the early futurists, I found an echo in Francesco Cangiullo's observations regarding the alliance between the Florentine and Milanese factions that joined together for a time under the Futurist umbrella (as cane or cudgel). Sometimes opposition or incomprehension leads to a closer alliance. The same rifts that seemed irreparable in their time in the Italian *avanguardia*, in retrospect, may appear exaggerated, but also part and product of a cultural dynamism we might now envy.

Envy? one might ask. A palpable sense of belatedness attaches itself to the engagement of the poet/critic, more prone to self-critique than to direct action to effect change in the sociopolitical sphere. As a result, as Francesco Muzzioli suggests, some writing is really asking, "shouldn't we be doing something else?" Full circle to the poet Marco Giovenale's ironic commentary on intellectuals being here still, not quite extinct, still discoursing on...Pasolini. Giovenale's deadpan delivery of a perfectly-timed utterance conjured by the fine-dicitore (a no-longer extant figure of theater history, conjured in Giovenale's talk, a kind of comic-critic, with the talent for acid commentary of some late-night hosts) — and his contribution's generous disposition regarding the possibilities of writing ("loose writing" is his term to describe this openness to various non-linear and *asemic* forms of writing) — far from dividing one faction from another, cut through rhetoric to lay bare a common drama of ineffectuality, that we have run panting onto the station platform as the train vanishes, leaving an echo and a puff.

So what is one to do, how to write? Certainly the answers are many, and are in your hands. Franca D'Agostini's concluding words — that the logic of poetry is to preserve facts and truth at the margin of the abyss — may be the clearest way to link together the wide range of voices. It is a range of strategies, tones, mediums, a multiplicity that embraces contradiction (a 'paraconsistent logic,' to use D'Agostini's term, cited by Achille Varzi), that resists hierarchy and categorization. The legacy of the programmatic, factional tendencies of the past may be the shared work of saving the word from the maw of what Mark Fisher (cited by more than one speaker) termed 'capitalist realism.' Not in the service of a 'new evangelism' (as Marco Giovenale pointed out), but in reimagining ourselves instruments more sensitive to the current time. The concluding, encompassing metaphor (well-suited to the NYC setting) was heard in a poem by one of the last poets to read, Susan Briante: "the poet is like the trash tree…"

Stefano Albertini

Luigi Ballerini

Marjorie Perloff

Andrea Cortellessa

Antonella Anedda

Peter Gizzi

Marco Giovenale

Tommaso Ottonieri

Chris Mustazza

Fabrizio Bondi

Tom Huhn and Paul Bové

Franca Agostini

Achille Varzi

Cecilia Bello

Gianluca Rizzo

Charles Bernstein, Gianluca Rizzo, and Luigi Bonaffini

Charles Bernstein and Gianluca Rizzo

Mary Jo Bang

Maria Grazia Calandrone

Vincenzo Frungillo

Rosmarie Waldrop

Laura Liberale

Fabrizio Bondi, Marco Giovenale, and Daniele Poletti

Thomas Peterson

Fabrizio Bondi, Marco Giovenale, Daniele Poletti;
in the background, Francesco Muzzioli

Giorgio Patrizi

Ugo Perolino

Mariano Bàino

Anselm Berrigan

John Latta

Susan Briante

Ivan Schiavone

Massimo Bacigalupo

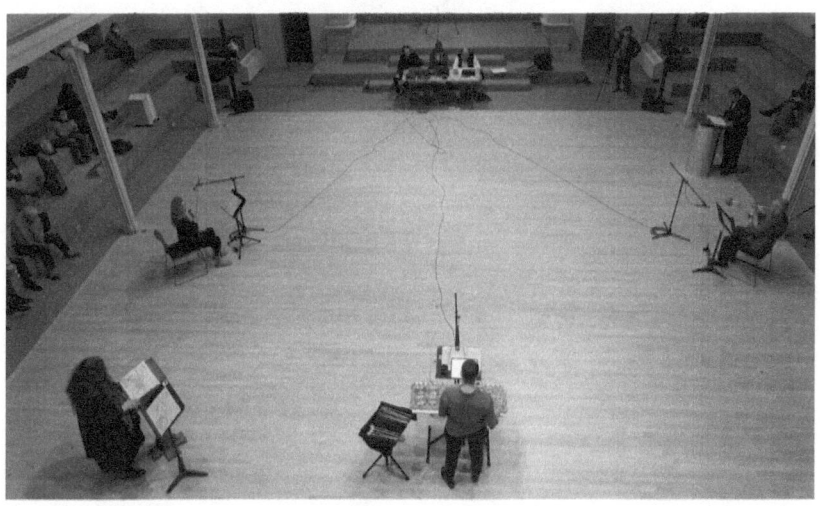

View of St. Mark's Church in the Bowery, set of the concert
"Xantablackz. A Verbiage and Sounding Event for Current Communization"
directed by Diego Minciacchi

Diego Minciacchi

Caitlin Cawley; Lauren Cauley; Cecilia Bello;
Diego Minciacchi; Luigi Ballerini; Nate Wooley

Luigi Ballerini

Sandro-Angelo de Thomasis and Iuri Moscardi

Nicholas Benson

Biographies

Massimo Bacigalupo is an experimental filmmaker, scholar, essayist, literary critic, and translator. Bacigalupo grew up in Rapallo, where his family's house was a center of cultural life attracting writers, poets and composers like Robert Lowell, Czeslaw Milosz, Ezra Pound, and Isaiah Berlin. His father, Giuseppe Bacigalupo, was Pound's doctor and his encounters with the famous American poet facilitated his literary exchange with many intellectuals. As a filmmaker, he was a founding member of the Cooperative of Independent Filmmakers in Rome and was influenced by the New American Cinema. His films have been screened by the Beaubourg Museum in Paris, the Tate Gallery in London, the Vienna Filmmuseum, the Cineteca Nazionale in Rome, Italy, and the Anthology Film Archives in New York. In his films, experimentation with a stream of consciousness approach gave rise to visual phantasmagoria, sometimes inspired by travels and encounters with other cultures. In addition to creating numerous films, Bacigalupo wrote pieces of film criticism on the underground cinema for magazines such as *Filmcritica*, *Bianco & Nero*, and the New York-based journal *Film Culture*. As a scholar, Bacigalupo earned a PhD from Columbia University writing a dissertation about the post-war Cantos of Ezra Pound. Then, he specialized in Ezra Pound, T. S. Eliot, Wallace Stevens, W. B. Yeats, Seamus Heaney, Herman Melville, Emily Dickinson, and other American, English and Irish writers, whom he has edited and translated. From 1990 to 2007, he was Professor of American Literature at the University of Genoa. In this city, Bacigalupo initiated the International Poetry Festival in the late 1970s. As a translator, he engaged in a series of studies on American and British authors: Ezra Pound, Marianne Moore, Wallace Stevens, William Butler Yeats, Emily Dickinson, and Herman Melville. In 1992, he was awarded the Monselice Prize for literary translations and, in 2001, received the Premio Nazionale di Traduzione (National Translation Award).

Mariano Bàino (b. 1953) is one of the founders of the journal *Baldus* and Gruppo '93. His poetry: *Camera iperbarica* [*Hyperbaric Chamber*], Tam Tam, 1983, with a preface by Matteo D'Ambrosio; *Fax giallo* [*Yellow Fax*], Il Laboratorio, 1993 (non-commercial edition with fifty numbered and signed copies), later published by Zona, in 2001, with a note by Gabriele Frasca (the text, with other poems, has been translated in the U.S.A.

by Gianluca Rizzo with the title *Yellow Fax and Other Poems*, Agincourt Press, 2019);); Ônne'*e terra* [*Earth Waves*], Pironti, 1994, with a postface by Clelia Martignoni, later, Zona, 2003, with a new postface by Clelia Martignoni; *Pinocchio (moviole)*, Manni, 2000, with an introduction by Francesco Leonetti; *Sparigli marsigliesi (passar d'imago in mago fra i tarocchi),* Il Laboratorio, 2002, with a note by Andrea Cortellessa, later published by Edizioni d'if, 2003; *Amarellimerick,* Oèdipus, 2003, preface by Remo Ceserani; *Prova d'inchiostro e altri sonetti*, Aragno, 2017, note by Andrea Cortellessa; *Ritratto immaginario di Hiccer,* Il Laboratorio, 2022 (non-commercial edition with seventy numbered and signed copies, with illustrations by 8ki and notes by Francesco Muzzioli and Gianluca Rizzo). His prose: *Le anatre di ghiaccio,* l'ancora del mediterraneo, 2004; *L'uomo avanzato,* Le Lettere, 2008, postface by Remo Ceserani, later published by Oèdipus, 2021, with an essay by Cecilia Bello Minciacchi; *Dal rumore bianco,* Ad est dell'equatore, 2012; *In (nessuna) Patagonia,* Ad est dell'equatore, 2014; *Il cielo per Roma,* Exorma, 2021.

Cecilia Bello Minciacchi (Rome, b. 1968), MA in Modern and Contemporary Italian Literature, and PhD in History of Women writings, is Associate Professor at the Department of European, American, and Intercultural Studies, La Sapienza University of Rome, where she directs the Archivio del Novecento and several research projects (The Paul Getty Foundation in Los Angeles Research Grant, 2003). She is a member of the Doctoral program in Italian Studies and of the Ungaretti Foundation. She published studies on Ungaretti, Marinetti, Cacciatore, Manganelli, Volponi, Sanguineti and Berio, Ungaretti and Nono, Balestrini, Porta, Niccolai, Malerba, Ballerini, Masino, Agnetti, Anedda, Carnaroli, Tadini, Malaparte, Mesa, Durante. She edited Emilio Villa's *Zodiaco* (with Aldo Tagliaferri, 2000); *Proverbi e Cantico. Traduzioni dalla Bibbia* (2004); and *L'opera poetica* (2014). She edited the anthology *Parola Plurale. Sessantaquattro poeti italiani fra due secoli* (2005, along with G. Alfano, A. Baldacci, A. Cortellessa, M. Manganelli, R. Scarpa, F. Zinelli, and P. Zublena). In 2006, she also edited Vittorio Reta's *Visas e altre poesie*, in 2007 an extensive anthology of futurist women writers *Spirale di dolcezza + serpe di fascino*, in 2009, Patrizia Vicinelli's *Non sempre ricordano*, and, in 2019, Vito Riviello's *Tutte le poesie*. She also published *Scrittrici della prima avanguardia. Concezione, caratteri e testimonianze del femminile nel futurismo* (Firenze, 2012) and *La distruzione da vicino. Forme e figure delle avanguardie del secondo Novecento* (Salerno, 2012). Since 2014 she is on the editorial staff of *Avanguardia* (since 2019 co-director) and *Semicerchio*. She collaborates with *Il Verri, L'Illuminista,* as well as *Alias*, the literary supplement of *Il Manifesto*. She is now working on a momographic volume devoted to Nanni Balestrini (Carocci Editions).

Nicholas Benson holds a PhD in Italian (New York University, 1999) and an MFA in Writing (Vermont College of Fine Arts, 2009). He has published translations in various journals of works by Antonia Pozzi, Angelo Lumelli, Gabriele Tinti, Paolo Lagazzi, and Beppe Salvia. He has also translated the following volumes: Attilio Bertolucci's *Winter Journey* (*Viaggio d'inverno*, 2005); Aldo Palazzeschi's *The Arsonist* (*L'incendiario,* 2013), for which he was awarded an NEA Translation Fellowship; and, with Elena Coda, Scipio Slataper's *My Karst and My City* (*Il mio Carso*, 2020), which was awarded the John Florio Prize by the Society of Translators (UK).

Charles Bernstein was born in 1950 in New York and graduated from Harvard College in 1972, after which he worked for many years as a freelance medical/healthcare writer. From 1989 to 2003, he taught at the State University of New York at Buffalo, where he was co-founder and Director of the Poetics Program and a SUNY Distinguished Professor. Then, from 2003 to 2019 he taught poetry and poetics, with an emphasis on modernist and contemporary art, aesthetics, and performance, in the English Department at the University of Pennsylvania (now Emeritus). He has published five collections of essays: *Attack of the Difficult Poems: A Poetics* (1992), *My Way: Speeches and Poems* (1999), *Content's Dream: Essays 1975-1984* (2001), *Essays and Inventions* (2011), *Pitch of Poetry* (2016). His books of poetry include *Republics of Reality: 1975-1995* (2000), *With Strings* (2001), *Girly Man* (2006), *All the Whiskey in Heaven: Selected Poems* (2010), *Recalculating* (2013), and *Near/Miss* (2018). His libretto *Shadowtime*, for composer Brian Ferneyhough, was published in 2005 and performed as part of the 2005 Lincoln Center Festival. Bernstein is the editor of several collections, including *The Politics of Poetic Form: Poetry and Public Policy* (1990), *Close Listening: Poetry and the Performed Word* (1999), *American Poetry after 1975* (2009), as well as the poetics magazine L=A=N=G=U=A=G=E, whose first issue was published in 1978. He is editor of the Electronic Poetry Center and co-director (with Al Filreis) of PennSound. He has collaborated with painters Susan Bee, Mimi Gross, Amy Sillman, Francie Shaw, and Richard Tuttle on several artist's books and projects. In 2001, he curated *Poetry Plastique* with Jay Sanders, a show of visual and sculptural poetry at the Marianne Boesky Gallery in New York. He has written libretti for Ben Yarmolinsky, Anne LeBarron, Dean Drummond, and Ferneyhough. He has been the recipient of fellowships from the Guggenheim Foundation, the New York Foundation for the Arts, and the National Endowment for the Arts, and of the Roy Harvey Pearce/Archive for New Poetry Prize of the University of California, San Diego. In 2006 he was elected a Fellow of the American Academy of Arts and Sciences. In 2015 he was awarded the Münster Prize for International Poetry and the Janus Pannnious Grand Prize for Poetry and in 2019 he received the Bollingen Prize for American Poetry from Yale University, the premiere American prize for lifetime achievement, on the occasion of the publication of *Near/Miss*.

Luigi Bonaffini is Professor Emeritus of Italian Language and Literature at Brooklyn College. He has translated many books from the Italian and various dialects: Dino Campana, Mario Luzi, Vittorio Sereni, Giose Rimanelli, Giuseppe Jovine, Achille Serrao, Eugenio Cirese, Albino Pierro, Cesare Ruffato, Antonio Spagnuolo, Luciano Troisio, Pier Paolo Pasolini, Attilio Bertolucci, and others. He has edited or co-edited five trilingual anthologies of Italian dialect poetry, including the two trilingual volumes *Dialect Poetry of Southern Italy* and *Dialect Poetry of Central and Northern Italy*. He has also co-edited the bilingual anthologies *A New Map, a bilingual anthology of migrant writers in Italy* with Mia Lecomte and *Poets of the Italian Diaspora* and *Poeti della diaspora italiana* with Joseph Perricone . He is the editor of *Journal of Italian Translation* www.jitonline.org. He has received several awards, including the Italian National Translation Award and the Translation Award from the Academy of American Poets.

Fabrizio Bondi teaches Letteratura italiana. Metodi, strumenti e risorse tradizionali e digitali (Italian Literature. Methods, Instruments, Traditional and Digital Resources) at Suor Orsola Benincasa University, in Naples. He graduated in Italian Literature from the University of Parma under the supervision of professor Marzio Pieri, one of the greatest scholars of Baroque Literature. His thesis was a commented edition of a strange Baroque meta-novel, with strong relationships with History of Medicine, History of Politics, Visual Arts, and Philosophy. He then developed other research interest in Mannerist and Baroque Emblems, History of Passions, exchange between words and images in the illustrated editions of epic poems (Ariosto, Tasso) in the Sixteenth and Seventeenth Century. He took his PhD at Scuola Normale Superiore di Pisa, working there for six years with the team of professor Lina Bolzoni on an ERC grant founded project, "Looking at Words trough Images: some Case Studies for a Visual History of Italian Literature". He published articles on contemporary Italian literature (Ottieri, Sanguineti, Frasca).

Paul A. Bové is Distinguished Professor of English at the University of Pittsburgh and the Editor of *boundary 2*, an international journal of literature and culture published by Duke University Press. He is the author of *Love's Shadow* (Harvard University Press, 2021), *Poetry Against Torture* (Hong Kong University Press, 2009), *Mastering Discourse* (Duke University Press, 1992), *Intellectuals in Power* (Columbia University Press, 1986), *Culture in the Bush Era* (Dartmouth College Press, 2013), and dozens of articles in reviewed journals. He has lectured in leading U.S. and foreign universities as well as most major national and international conferences in the literary fields and was elected a member of the International Association of University Professors in 2010. His current book project focuses on Henry Adams.

Maria Grazia Calandrone is a poet, playwright, journalist, and performance artist. She was born in Milan in 1964 and is based in Rome, where she is currently the director of cultural programming for RAI Radio 3. Calandrone also directs video programs for Corriere della Sera web TV and has also collaborated with the Italian TV channels Rai Letteratura, Rai Cultura, and Cult Book for other presentations concerning culture and literature. A proponent of literature for all, she leads poetry workshops in schools, prisons, and mental health units, and she volunteers with the Piccoli Maestri children's reading center. Her first book of poems, *Illustrazioni* (Illustrations, 1994), was awarded the Eugenio Montale Prize. Her other works include: *Pietra di paragone* (Touchstones, 1998, Nuove Scrittrici Prize); *La scimmia randagia* (The Stray Monkey, 2003, Pasolini Award); *Come per mezzo di una briglia ardente* (By Means of a Burning Bridle, 2005); *La macchina responsabile* (The Responsible Machine, 2007), *Sulla bocca di tutti* (On Everyone's Lips, 2010, Napoli Award); *Atto di vita nascente* (Act of Nascent Life, 2010); *La vita chiara* (The Clear Life, 2011); *Serie fossile* (Fossil Series, 2015, Marazza and Tassoni Awards, shortlisted for the Viareggio Prize); *Gli Scomparsi – Storie da Chi l'ha visto?* (*The Disappeared. Stories from* Chi l'ha visto?, 2016, Dessì Award); *Il bene morale* (The Moral Good, 2017; 2019, Europa and Trivio Award); and *Giardino della gioia* (Garden of Joy, 2019; 2020). Her poetry has been translated into over twenty languages including *Serie fossile* in Ireland (*Fossils*, 2018) and Spain (*Sèrie Fòssil*, 2019); and the Arabic anthology *Questo corpo, questa luce* (This Body, This Light, 2020). A series of her poems is also included in the anthology *Nuovi poeti italiani 6* (New Italian Poets, 6, 2012). Calandrone's prose works include the pseudo-novel *L'infinito mélo*, with an audio CD of her readings (The Infinite Apple Tree, 2011); *Per voce sola* (For Voice Alone, 2016), a collection of dramatic monologues, drawings, photos, and CD by the actress Sonia Bergamasco; the noir short story *La grande illusione* (The Grand Illusion, 2018); and the novel *Splendi come vita* (You Shine like Life, 2021, shortlisted for Strega and Campiello Prizes). In this book, she recollected the traumatic events surrounding her first years: born out of an adulterous relationship, both her parents committed suicide and she was adopted by Giacomo Calandrone, an Italian politician, and his wife Consolazione (Ione), with whom she had a difficult relationship while growing up. She has also written short stories published in the anthologies *Nell'occhio di chi guarda* (In the Eye of the Watcher, 2014), *Deaths in Venice* (2017), and *Princesa e altre regine* (Princesa and Other Queens, edited by Concita De Gregorio, 2018). Her literary criticism includes *Dalla sua bocca. Riscritture da undici appunti inediti di Alda Merini* (From Her Mouth. The Rewriting of Eleven Unpublished Notes by Alda Merini, 2013 with Michele Caccamo); *Un altro mondo, lo stesso mondo. Una riscrittura del* Fanciullino *di Giovanni Pascoli* (Another World, the Same World. A rewriting of Pascoli's *Fanciullino*, 2019, Bo-Descalzo Award); and she edited and introduced the Italian translation of Edgar Lee Masters' *Spoon River Anthology* published by Giunti in 2015 and 2019. Calandrone also edited Nella Nobili's *Ho camminato nel* *mondo con l'anima aperta* (I Walked in the World with my Soul Wide Open, 2018) and Dino Campana's *Preferisco il rumore del mare* (I Prefer the Sound of the Sea, 2019). She is the editor of the collection "I domani" (Tomorrows) for the publisher Aragno. A member of the editorial staff of the monthly *Poesia*, Caldanone also writes literary criticism for *il manifesto* and *Corriere della Sera Sette*. In 2017 she appeared in Donatella Baglivo's documentary *Il futuro in una poesia* (The Future in One Poem) and in Israeli filmmaker Omri Lior's *Poems With a View* project. Since 2008 she has been appearing in Italy and Europe in the video concerts *Senza bagaglio* (Without Baggage) and *Corpo reale* (Real body) along with the composer Stefano Savi Scarponi. In 2010 her text *My language is the rose* was chosen by the Malaysian composer Lee Chie Tsang as a finalist in the Unique Forms of Continuity in Space in Melbourne, Australia. Also, in 2010 she was chosen as a representative for Italian poetry in *Evropa jedna báseň*, a Czech documentary directed by Lucie Kralova. Her website is www.mariagraziacalandrone.it.

Andrea Cortellessa teaches contemporary Italian literature at the University of Roma Tre. He graduated from "La Sapienza" in 1992, with a thesis on Carlo Emilio Gadda's war diaries, and holds a PhD in Italian Studies, obtained in 1998 with a thesis on Tommaso Landolfi's diaries. His initial interests in the poetry of the early twentieth century (*Le notti chiare erano tutte un'alba. Antologia di poeti italiani nella Prima guerra mondiale*, Mondadori 1998; then, Bompiani 2018); *Ungaretti*, Einaudi 2000) turned to contemporary authors (the anthology *Parola plurale*, edited with other young literary critics, Sossella, 2005, and *La fisica del senso. Saggi e interventi su poeti italiani dal 1940 a oggi*, Fazi 2006), and later on narrative and travel literature in the new millennium (with the two anthologies *Le terra della prosa*, L'orma 2014 and *Con gli occhi aperti*, Exòrma 2016). He partnered with writers and critics such as Nanni Balestrini ("alfabeta2" from 2010 to 2019), Gianni Celati and Franco Cordelli, with directors Giancarlo Cauteruccio (staging Dino Campana's *Canti Orfici* and Dante's Comedy) and Luca Archibugi (2010 tv documentary *Senza scrittori*). He has edited works by an impressive number of twentieth-century Italian authors and artists, such as Amelia Rosselli, Nanni Balestrini, Giorgio Manganelli, Elio Pagliarani, Giovanni Raboni, Luigi Di Ruscio, Giulio Paolini, Claudio Parmiggiani, not to mention such classics as Francesco Petrarca and Giacomo Leopardi and their presence in Italian XXth century literature. On the occasion of the centenary of the Zanzotto's birth, he co-organized three major conferences ["Zanzotto, un secolo. Da Pieve di Soligo al mondo" (Pieve di Soligo, 8-10 October), "Zanzotto europeo, la sua poesia di movimento" (Paris and Berlin, École Normale Superieure and Italian Cultural Institutes, 25-30 November) and *"Un'Arcadia horror*. Roma per Andrea Zanzotto (Rome, 6-8 June 2022)], the exhibition "Un'evidenza fantascientifica" (Venice, 15 May-17 October), and published *Zanzotto. Il canto nella terra* (Bari-Roma: Laterza, 2021). Recently he has also turned to art criticism, co-editing a volume of Giorgio de Chirico's writings (*Scritti. 1910-1978. Romanzi,* *poesie, scritti teorici, critici, tecnici e interviste*, Milano: La nave di Teseo, 2023), a monograph on Piero Manzoni (*Monsieur Zero. 26 lettere su Manzoni, quello vero*, Roma-Trieste: Italo Svevo, 2018), and several articles on Lucio Fontana, Alberto Burri, Elisabetta Benassi, Roberto Cuoghi, Flavio Favelli, Giosetta Fioroni, Abel Herrero and Luigi Ontani. He is the scientific coordinator of *Portatori del tempo. Enciclopedia delle arti contemporanee* directed by Achille Bonito Oliva, whose first four volumes were published by Electa between 2010 and 2018. He is a frequent contibutor to Alias, the weekly supplement of il manifesto, Tuttolibri, the weekly supplement of La Stampa and Il Sole 24 ore-domenica, and with the online magazines Doppiozero and Le parole e le cose2. A member of the editorial board of il verri and a co-founder with Federico Ferrari and Riccardo Venturi of the online magazine Antinomie, Cortellessa continrutes regularly to the cultural programs of the Italian national public radio, for which in 2003, he conceived and produced the program Occasioni, a comparative arena of poets belonging to different generations featuring readings and archive interviews. From 2006 to 2018 he has served as a general editor of innovative poetry series published by "Le Lettere" and "L'orma editore." Currently, he directs Pietre d'angolo and, together with Maria Grazia Calandrone and Laura Pugno, i domani, two poetry series published by Aragno Editore.

Franca d'Agostini is an Italian philosopher. She has taught for many years Logic and Philosophy of Science at the University of Turin (Politecnico), currently teaches logic and argumentation theory at the University of Milan (Depatment of Political and Social Sciences). She has given courses, lectures, and invited talks in other Universities, in Italy and elsewhere. Her areas of specialization are: Philosophical Logic, Metaphysics, Meta-philosophy and History of XX Century Philosophy. Her main topics are truth, paradoxes, the analytic and continental divide. She is author of many articles in major journals in Italian, English, German, and of 18 books, some of which have been translated in various languages. Among her books, *Analitici e Continentali* (1997), *Logica del nichilismo* (2000), *Disavventure della verità* (2002), *The Last Fumes. Nihilism and the Nature of Philosophical Concepts* (2008), *Paradossi* (2009), *La verità al potere. Sei diritti aletici* (co-authored with Maurizio Ferrera, 2019).

Sandro-Angelo de Thomasis was born and raised in Montréal-Nord, Québec, and now lives in Manhattan, New York. He is an Assistant Professor of Liberal Arts and Modern Languages at the Juilliard School, where he teaches French and Italian language classes, academic English for English Language Learners, literature electives such as "Dante's *Inferno*" and "Dante's *Purgatorio*," and graduate translation courses. Sandro holds a B.A. in Western Society and Culture from Concordia University's Liberal Arts College, an M.A., M.Phil., and Ph.D. in Italian Language and Literature from Yale University. As a graduate student at Yale, he taught all levels of Italian, whether on campus, remotely, or in Siena, Tuscany, during summer sessions abroad. His doctoral dissertation investigated the hermeneutic method known as "vertical reading" in Dante Studies, shedding light on the modalities of texts and images in the Middle Ages. His research at Oxford University was funded by Yale's MacMillan International Dissertation Research Fellowship and supervised by Prof. Simon Gilson (2018–2019). Sandro is on the editorial board of the second volume of *Those Who from Afar Look Like Flies* (University of Toronto Press, forthcoming), a bilingual anthology of contemporary Italian poetry containing several of his translations and critical essays on Andrea Inglese, Lorenzo Durante, Antonio Riccardi, Riccardo Held, and Daniele Poletti. In addition, Sandro has published an essay on Durante's *Quarantore*, a rewriting of Mallarmé's *Tombeau pour Anatole*, in *Deconstructing the Model in 20th and 21st-Century Italian Experimental Writings* (Cambridge Scholars Publishing, 2019). Other publications appear in the *Journal of Italian Translation*, *Italica*, and *Annali d'italianistica*. Another notable forthcoming publication is his translation of selected writings of Piero Gobetti in *An Intellectual Against Fascism. The Selected Writings of Piero Gobetti* (The Lorenzo Da Ponte Library, University of Toronto Press), co-edited by Mimmo Cangiano (Università Ca' Foscari Venezia), Davide Dalmas (Università degli Studi di Torino), and Marta Vicari (Centro Studi Piero Gobetti).

Vincenzo Frungillo (Naples, b. 1973) is a poet, writer and essayist. He graduated and received a doctorate in philosophy from the Federico II University of Naples in 2001. Also in Naples he took part in the round tables on biopolitics wanted by Roberto Esposito together with Giorgio Agamben, Remo Bodei, Mario Vegetti and others. He has published in verses: *Fanciulli sulla via maestra* (Palomar, Bari, 2002, "Periferie Prize", awarded by Michele Sovente), *Ogni cinque bracciate. Poema in cinque canti* (Le Lettere, collana FuoriFormato a cura di Andrea Cortellessa, Firenze, 2009, as finalist in "Antonio Delfini" Prize), *Il cane di Pavlov. Resoconto di una perizia* (d'If edizioni, Napoli, 2013, winner of the "Russo-Mazzacurati" Prize and the "Premio di dramaturgia Fersen"), *Meccanica pesante* (Marcos Y Marcos, 2013, included in the XI Quaderno di poesia contemporanea by Franco Buffoni), *Le pause della serie evolutiva* (Oedipus, Salerno, 2016, selected for the "Elio Pagliarani National Prize"), *Prime scene di caccia e di morte* (Zacinto, Milano, 2021, winner of the "Città di Como International Award"). The work *Ogni cinque bracciate* has been adapted several times for staging: with the care of Milo De Angelis, for the voice of Viviana Nicodemo, at the Palazzina Liberty, Casa della Poesia, in Milan; with the director Claudio Di Palma, with the actresses Frabrizia Sacchi and Anna Ferzetti, for the Campania Teatro Festival, at the Capodimonte park in Naples; for the *Xantablackz* contemporary music concert by Diego Minciacchi, with the voice of Cecilia Bello Minciacchi and Luigi Ballerini, at St Mark's Church in-the-Bowery, New York. His poetic texts are present in various anthologies on contemporary poetry both in Italy and abroad. It is included in the volume *Reisen durch* *die junge Lyrik Europas* (2019, edited by Jan Wagner and Federico Italiano), a survey on young European poetry commissioned by the German Academy of Literature, and in *Those who from afar look like flies* (University of Toronto) bilingual anthology in two volumes of Italian poetry from the post-war period to today commissioned by Luigi Ballerini. His texts have been translated into German, American and Spanish. He is the author of the essays, *Il luogo delle forze. Lo spazio della poesia nel tempo della dispersione* (Carteggi-Letterari, Messina, 2017), *Il rischio e la perdita. Su identità e linguaggio in Martin Heidegger* (Mimesis, Milano, 2022). He participated in the meeting between poets and critics held in Milan in 2017 to discuss the new forms of contemporary poetry, a meeting that gave birth to the volume *Teoria e poesia* (Biblion, Milano, 2018). He has published the novel *Un nome in meno* (Ensemble, Roma, 2021) and the play *Spinalonga. Un drammaturgia sulla corruzione* (Zona contemporanea, Genova, 2016).

Marco Giovenale is a writer, poet, editor, and graphic artist, born in Rome in 1969 where he currently lives and works as a curator and translator. He is among the founders of gammm.org (2006) and Punto critico (2011, currently the blog www.puntocritico.wordpress.com). He collaborates with *l'immaginazione*, *alfabeta2*, and the website of the magazine *Segno*, and is the editor of *SCRIPTjr.nl* and *Sibila*. He edits the series Syn – scritture di ricerca for IkonaLiber, and, with M. Guatteri, M. Zaffarano e G. Marzaioli. he edited the Benway Series for Tielleci publisher. His most recent books of poetry are *Shelter* (2010), *Storia dei minuti* (The Story of Minutes, 2010), *In rebus* (Puzzles, 2012, including texts that won the 2009 Antonio Delfini prize), *Delvaux* (2013), *Maniera nera* (The Wrong Way, 2015), and *Strettoie* (Bottlenecks, 2017). His earlier works include: *Criterio dei vetri* (The Criterium of Glass, 2007), *La casa esposta* (The Showed House, 2007), *Soluzione della materia* (The Dissolution of the Material, 2009); and the prose of *Numeri primi* (Prime Numbers, 2006), *Quasi tutti* (Almost All, 2010), *Lie lie* (2010), *Numeri morali* (Moral Numbers, 2014), *Il paziente crede di essere* (The Patient Believes He Exists, 2016). His texts are anthologized in *Parola plurale* (Plural Word, 2005), *Nono quaderno di poesia contemporanea* (Nonth Notebook of Contemporary Poetry, 2007), *Poeti degli anni Zero* (Poets of the Years 2000s, 2011), and *Nuovi oggettivisti* (New Objectivists, 2013). He is included in the collective book *Prosa in prosa* (Prose in Prose, 2009, along with the other editors of GAMMM). Giovenale is also the author of texts in English: *a gunless tea* (2007), *CDK* (2009), *anachromisms* (2014), and *white while* (2014). Giovenale has produced many graphic works and examples of visual poetry and asemantic writing, online and in anthologies, chapbooks, and at various exhibitions, predominantly with publishing houses and venues outside Italy. In 2008, he curated a large collection of the work of Roberto Roversi for Sossella. His blog is available at http://slowforward.me. Many of his visual and asemantic works can be found at http://differx.tumblr.com.

Tom Huhn is the chair of the Art History and BFA Visual & Critical Studies Departments at the School of Visual Arts in New York City. He has been a visiting professor at Yale University and the University of Graz, Austria. Books include: *Imitation and Society: The Persistence of Mimesis in the Aesthetics of Burke, Hogarth, and Kant* (Penn State Press, 2004); *The Cambridge Companion to Adorno* (Cambridge University Press, 2004); *The Wake of Art: Criticism, Philosophy, and the Ends of Taste* (Routledge, 1998); and *The Semblance of Subjectivity: Essays in Adorno's Aesthetic Theory* (MIT Press, 1997). His writings have appeared in: *New German Critique, Art & Text, Oxford Art Journal, British Journal of Aesthetics, Art Criticism, Telos, Eighteenth-Century Studies, Journal of Aesthetics and Art Criticism, Oxford Encyclopedia of Aesthetics, Philosophy and Social Criticism, Art Book, Art in America*. Huhn has been a Getty Scholar and Fulbright Scholar. Huhn's curatorial works include: "Ornament and Landscape," at Apex Gallery; "Still Missing: Beauty Absent Social Life," at the Visual Arts Museum and Westport Arts Center; "Between Picture and Viewer: The Image in Contemporary Painting" at the Visual Arts Gallery, NYC.

John Latta spent early childhood in the Pigeon River Country of lower northern Michigan and went to high school in Ann Arbor. He attended Cornell University (1971–1976, A.B.) in Ithaca, New York and while there learned letterpress printing, bookbinding, and editing at Ithaca House—the small press founded by Baxter Hathaway—and edited *Chiaroscuro*, a poetry journal (six issues, 1976–1986). Latta lived in Paris 1973–74 and, again, 1979–80, thanks to an NEA Creative Writing fellowship. He worked at Ithaca House (and held the formerly poet-requisite "succession of stupid jobs," janitorial to editorial) during most of the 1980s. Latta attended the University of Virginia (1987–1989, M.F.A.) and SUNY at Albany (1991–1995, Ph.D.) He married Joanne Tangorra in 1991; a son, Giancarlo, was born in 1995. Since 1997 Latta has worked in Hatcher Graduate Library at the University of Michigan, in a variety of positions. Latta's first collection, *Rubbing Torsos*, was published by Ithaca House in 1979. A second collection, *Breeze*, won the Ernest Sandeen Prize in Poetry (selected by John Matthias) and was published in 2003 by the University of Notre Dame Press. In 2022 *Some Alphabets* was solicited by Luigi Ballerini and published by Agincourt Press. Between 2006 and 2014 Latta kept a lively blog called Isola di Rifiuti.

Diego Minciacchi is an Italian composer. He studied both Medicine and Music (piano and composition), obtaining a diploma in piano and a specialization in Neurology. These two different fields – Composition and Medicine – are his main fields of study and research. Since the 1990s, he took an interest in the possibility of translating scientific data, which he obtained through lab work, into music. He has composed many works for traditional (like *Costa Contigua* for two violas, two cellos, and bass, 1994) and electronic instruments (*Klavierstück n. 4: Vae Victis* for piano and electronics,

1997; *Quintum Desertum* for three pianos and electronics, 2000). Horatio Radulescu influenced his predilection for natural sounds and their microformal relationships, while Curtis Roads inspired the architecture of his works. Since his debut in 1977 (*Op. '76-'77* for piano and electronics), Minciacchi wrote more than 60 compositions for conventional solo instruments, small and large ensembles, analog and digital electronic music, music for conventional instruments and electronic sounds, live electronic music. He collaborated with: Magnus Andersson, Pierre-Yves Artaud, Maurizio Barbetti, Alan Brett, Jeffrey Burns, James Clapperton, Philippe Geiss, Roberto Fabbriciani, Fernando Grillo, Kaya Han, Nicolas Isherwood, Daniel Kientzy, Jean Luc Mas, Istvan Matuz, Federico Mondelci, Adrian Peacoch, Jan Pilch, Ortwin Sturmer, Barrie Webb. He recorded the music of his electronic works in Freiburg, Paris, Stockholm, and at the Massachusetts Institute of Technology. In more recent years, Minciacchi composed works based on Italian authors from the 20th century, such as Edoardo Cacciatore, Emilio Villa, Mariano Bàino, and Antonella Anedda. Recently he realized the project *Prompf*, a series of electronic music objects (videos by Pier Paolo Cipitelli and Ivan Schiavone) that is available on web at Nuovo Commento (https://www.youtube.com/@nuovocommento618/playlists). His music has been premiered at main contemporary music Festivals in Germany, Mexico, Paris, Venice, and Berlin. He teaches at the University of Florence.

Iuri Moscardi is Visiting Assistant Professor of Italian in the Department of Transnational Italian Studies at Bryn Mawr College. He received his PhD in Comparative Literature (Italian Specialization) from the Graduate Center, CUNY, in New York City. His dissertation analyzed some Digital Social Reading projects organized by Twitteratura that took place on Twitter and allowed readers to comment on canonical authors from Italian literature in an innovative way. For this study, he focused on Digital Humanities, the reader-response theory elaborated by Wolfgang Iser, and Italian Contemporary Literature. He graduated from University of Milan with a thesis on Cesare Pavese's role in the first Italian translation of E.L. Masters's *Spoon River Anthology*, which was awarded the Premio Pavese 2012, and received a Master in Italian from Indiana University (2016). He edited the volumes *Cesare Pavese Mythographer, Translator, Modernist* (2023) and the complete English translation of Pavese's journal, *Il mestiere di vivere* (University of Toronto Press, forthcoming). He also collaborated with professors Luigi Ballerini, Beppe Cavatorta, and Gianluca Rizzo in the publication of the poetry anthology *Those Who From Afar Look like Flies*. Among his articles: "Note di traduzione: Cesare Pavese e i libri del fondo Molina" (*Italica*, 2023), in which he analyzed new discoveries on Pavese's translation process anticipated at a symposium at NYU in September 2023; "Pavese senza collina. Assenza del mito e incompiutezza estetica" (*Ticontre. Teoria Testo Traduzione*, 2021); "Betwyll: Social reading per la didattica dell'italiano in Nord America" (*América Crítica*, 2020); "#TwSposi: un matrimonio che s'ha da fare" (*Revue des Études Italiennes*, 2018).

Chris Mustazza is Co-Director of the PennSound Archive and teaches in the English department at the University of Pennsylvania. His work centers on literary audio, modern poetry & poetics, sound studies, and digital methodologies. His manuscript *Speech Labs: Collecting Poets' Voices During the Early Period of Recorded Sound*, is the first history of the poetry audio archive, tracing attempts to record and collect poets' voices back to the invention of recorded sound.

Tommaso Ottonieri, pseudonym of Tommaso Pomilio, is an Italian writer, singer, and poet, the son of the writer and journalist Mario Pomilio. He was born in Avezzano, near L'Aquila in central Italy, in 1958, and he was raised in Naples. There he had the opportunity to meet writers, artists, and other intellectuals such as Luigi Compagnone, Michele Prisco, Domenico Rea, Giancarlo Mazzacurati, and Ivos Margoni, as well as the poets Michele Sovente and Gabriele Frasca. Ottonieri's first book, *Dalle memorie di un piccolo ipertrofico* (From the Memories of a Little Hypertrophic, 1980), was inspired by a text by the French poet Jules Laforgue, and was published with an introduction by the poet Edoardo Sanguineti, who was its editor at Feltrinelli. The book was also inspired by the so-called Movimento del '77, a series of social and political tumults connected to the rebellion of 1968. Subsequently, in 1984, Ottonieri published *Coniugativo* (a pun translatable as Conjugative), a collection of prose that describes the unique experience of the Movimento del '77. The second part of this book, entitled *Coro da l'acqua, per voce sola* (Chorus for the Water, For Voice Alone), was later published, with some edits, in 2003. In 1998, Ottonieri published his first collection of poems: *Elegia Sanremese* (Sanremo Elegy), a concept-book that rewrites, as covers, some of the most famous songs that won the Italian musical Festival di Sanremo. The book pays homage to the singer Luigi Tenco, who took his life during the 1967 edition of the festival to protest the music establishment. Along with the book, Ottonieri published an audio CD with the music version of the poems, sung by Ottonieri himself and with some bonus tracks by Nanni Balestrini, Vivian Lamarque, and Alda Merini. In 1997, Ottonieri published the novel *Crema Acida* (Acid Cream), which he intended as a critique of postmodernism in the form of a dystopia. The novel was inspired by the theoretical proposals of the avant-gardist Gruppo 93, which Ottonieri himself joined. Together with Renato Barilli and Giuseppe Caliceti, Ottonieri organized the final convention of the group, 63/93, which took place in Reggio Emilia. After the convention, Ottonieri began the new writing workshop Ricercare (Research). In 2000, Ottonieri published another collection of short compositions in prose, *L'album crèmisi* (The Crimson Album). In 2000, Bollati Boringhieri published *La plastica della lingua: stili in fuga lungo un'età postrema* (The Plasticity of the Language: Styles Escaping a Posthumous Age), in which Ottonieri critically analyzed the topics of end of millennium literature. In the same year, Ottonieri edited the collection *Bassa Fedeltà: l'arte nell'epoca della riproduzione tecnica totale* (Low Fidelity: Art in the Epoch of the Total Technical Reproduction) with contributions by Andrea Cortellessa and Aldo Nove, among many others. In 2002, Ottonieri collected all his poems (except those in *Elegia sanremese*) in *Contatto* (Contact). For this book, Ottonieri won (along with Giovanni Raboni and Umberto Fiori) the Napoli Prize for poetry in 2003. In 2007, after twenty years of work, Ottonieri published *Le strade che portano al Fùcino* (The Roads Leading to Fucino). The book is almost impossible to classify, being a patchwork of the multiple experimentations in languages and forms that have characterized Ottonieri's career. It is considered his most important work, and in 2008 *Il Verri* dedicated the majority of its issue *La politica degli autori* (The Politics of Authors) to it. Ottonieri's last book is *Geòdi* (Geodes, 2015), awarded with the Feronia-Città di Fiano Prize in 2016. Here, Ottonieri collected the poems written after 2002, among them the short poem in prose *Lapilli della Gravitazione* (Lapillus of the Gravitation), a meditation on the so-called Terra dei fuochi (Land of the Fires), an area around Naples where the camorristi mobsters burn toxic garbage.

Giorgio Patrizi has been a researcher and teacher at the Università di Roma "La Sapienza." From 2002 to 2017, he taught as a full professor of Italian literature at the Università del Molise, where he headed the Department of Social and Historical Human Sciences. He is presently visiting professor at the online Universitas Mercatorum of Rome. He was a member of the administrative council of the National Institute of Antique Drama of Siracusa. He is a member of the Foundation "Artes Renascentes" and the Foundation Nievo's scientific council. He has long been a collaborator with RAI's radio and television cultural programs. His scientific production encompasses studies on Humanism and the Renaissance, Ottocento and Novecento literature, literary theory and criticism, and interdisciplinary themes. With the publication of *Gadda* (Salerno Ed. 2014), Patrizi was awarded the Premio Flaiano for literature in 2015. In 2020, the publishing house Editore Serra di Pisa printed the first issue of the annual *Immagine e Parola* dedicated to the relationship between verbal and visual languages, of which Patrizi is the director. He has published numerous essays on various authors, between the Cinquecento, Ottocento, and Novecento. Among his titles are "Criticism and Gadda" (1977), "Roland Barthes and the Adventures of Semiology" (1979), "The World from Afar. Facts and Narrative in Verga's Novels" (1988), "Stefano Guazzo and *The Civil Conversazione*" (1995), "Prose Against the Novel. Antinovels and Metanarrative in the Novecento" (1997), "The Umorismo of Pirandello" (1998), "To Narrate the Image. The Tradition of Art Writers" (2000), "Prohibited Literature" (2007), "The Essay in the Novecento" (2009). He has co-edited the volume "Under the Roman Sky. Rome in World Poetry" (2015). He has written the introduction to *Pasolini after Pasolini* (2017).

Ugo Perolino is an associate professor in the Department of Modern Languages and Literatures at the Gabriele D'Annunzio University in Pescara, where he teaches modern and contemporary Italian literature. He studied Italian poetry of the 20th century, from the early avant-gardes to 1960s hybrid political writings. He wrote on Alfredo Giuliani (La poesia divisa. Dalla neoavanguardia alle figure immaginarie di Alfredo Giuliani, The Divided Poetry. From Neo-Avant-garde to the Imaginary Figures of Alfredo Giuliani, 1995; Un trattatello d'amore del Novecento. Per Alfredo Giuliani, A 20th century Love Treatise. For Alfredo Giuliani, 1997; "La nuda arte delle sillabe". Note sulla poesia di Alfredo Giuliani, The Naked Art of Syllables. Notes on Alfredo Giuliani's Poetry, 2019); Edoardo Cacciatore (La poesia pensiero di Edoardo Cacciatore, The Poetry-Thought of Edoardo Cacciatore, 2006); Nicola Chiaromonte (Lo sguardo chiaro dei Greci. Umanesimo e società di massa in Nicola Chiaromonte, The Clear Sight of the Greeks. Humanism and Mass Society in Nicola Chiaromonte, 2013; La prova del gesto. Nicola Chiaromonte tra André Malraux e Simone Weil, The Proof of the Gesture. Nicola Chiaromonte Between André Malraux and Simone Weil, 2014; Chiaromonte tra Malraux e Moravia, Chiaromonte Between Malraux and Moravia, 2016); Alfredo Oriani ("Una bocca quasi sanguinolenta". Tipizzazioni dell'immagine femminile nella narrativa di Oriani, "An Almost Bleeding Mouth." Standards of the Feminine Image in Oriani's Narrative, 2008; Oriani e la narrazione della nuova Italia, Oriani and the Narration of the New Italy, 2011). He is also the author of the collection of essays Il sacro e l'impuro. Letteratura e scienze umane da Boine a Pasolini (The Sacred and the Impure. Literature and Human Sciences from Boine to Pasolini, 2012). With Leonardo Casalino and Andrea Cedola, he edited the collective volume Il caso Moro: memorie e narrazioni (The Moro Case: Memories and Narrations, 2016). He is part of the scientific committee of the Moving Texts / Testi Mobili series (Peter Lang, Brussels). In 2021, he edited the collection of essays Il remo di Ulisse. Saggi della poesia e la poetica di Luigi Ballerini (Ulysses' Oar. Essays on Luigi Ballerini's Poetry and Poetics).

Thomas E. Peterson is Professor of Italian at the University of Georgia. His research focuses on the lyric and epic poetry of the Italian tradition, 20th century Italian poetry and narrative, and the philosophy of education. His most recent books include his edition and translation of Pier Paolo Pasolini, *The Divine Mimesis* (Contra Mundum, 2014); *Petrarch's* Fragmenta: *The Narrative and Theological Unity of* Rerum vulgarium fragmenta (U of Toronto P, 2016); *Modern Mannerism in Italian Poetry* (Quodlibet, 2017); *Epistemology and the Predicates of Education: Building Upon a Process Theory of Learning* (Routledge, 2019).

Marjorie Perloff is an American poetry scholar and critic. She was born Gabriele Mintz in 1931 to a secularized Jewish family in Vienna: after the annexation of Austria by Nazi Germany in 1938, her family emigrated first to Zürich, and then to the United States, settling in Riverdale, New York. After attending Oberlin College, she graduated magna cum laude and Phi Beta Kappa from Barnard College in 1953. She completed her graduate work at the Catholic University of America in Washington, D.C., earning an MA in 1956 and a PhD (with a dissertation on W.B. Yeats) in 1965. In 1953, she also married the cardiologist Joseph K. Perloff, Streisand/American Heart Association Professor of Medicine and Pediatrics Emeritus at U.C.L.A.. She taught at Catholic University from 1966 to 1971, then she became Professor of English at the University of Maryland, College Park (1971–1976) and Professor of English and Comparative Literature at the University of Southern California (1976–1986) and Stanford University (1986–1990). She then became Sadie Dernham Patek Professor of Humanities at Stanford (1990-2000; emerita from 2001). In 2008–09, she was the Weidenfeld Visiting Professor of European Comparative Literature in St Anne's College, Oxford. She is currently Florence Scott Professor of English Emerita at the University of Southern California. Perloff is considered one of the foremost critics of contemporary, modern, and avant-garde poetry and poetics: she has published books, articles, and essays on issues ranging from digital poetics to philosophy, and her work has been translated into many languages, including Portuguese, Spanish, Slovenian, German, and French. More specifically, her work focuses on the writing of experimental and avant-garde poets and the major currents of modernist and postmodernist activity in the arts, including the visual arts and literary theory. Her first three books focused on three individual poets: *Rhyme and Meaning in the Poetry of Yeats* (1970), *The Poetic Art of Robert Lowell* (1973), and *Poet Among Painters* (1977; 1997, on Frank O'Hara). She began to focus more directly on the avant-garde from 1981, when she published *The Poetics of Indeterminacy: Rimbaud to Cage* (1981). Her multifaceted interests in this field are witnessed by titles like *The Futurist Moment: Avant-Garde, Avant-Guerre, and the Language of Rupture* (1986; 1994), while she discussed her approach to digital poetics in *Radical Artifice: Writing Poetry in the Age of Media* (1992), *21st Century Modernism* (2002), and *Unoriginal Genius: Poetry by Other Means in the New Century* (2011). *Poetics in a New Key* (2014) is a collection of some of her most relevant interviews. Others of Perloff's books include studies on philosophy (*Wittgenstein's Ladder*, 1996); the poetics of sound and recording technologies (*The Sound of Poetry/The Poetry of Sound*, 2009, co-edited with Craig Dworkin); the cultural memoir (*The Vienna Paradox*, 2004). Perloff has contributed reviews to the *Times Literary Supplement*, *The Washington Post*, and all the major scholarly journals; she has lectured at major American, European, Asian, and Latin American universities and festivals. In her work, Perloff promoted poetics and authors not yet academically studied in the United States, such as Louis Zukofsky, Kenneth Goldsmith, and Brazilian poetry. Her work on contemporary and avant-garde poetry opened a dialogue to overcome the classical categories of experimental, mainstream, and spoken word. Her book *Differentials: Poetry, Poetics, Pedagogy* (2004) was awarded the Robert Penn Warren Prize in 2005 and Honorable Mention for the Robert Motherwell Prize of the Dedalus Foundation. She was also awarded fellowships from the Guggenheim Foundation, the National Endowment for the Humanities, and the Huntington Foundation. She was member of the Advisory Board of the Stanford Humanities Center and President of the Modern Language Association in 2006 and is a member of the American Academy of Arts and Sciences and the American Philosophical Society. She received an honorary degree from Bard College in 2008, and the Kelly Writers House at the University of Pennsylvania honored her with a special symposium.

Daniele Poletti (Viareggio b. 1975) founder and promoter of the cultural project [dia•-foria: www.diaforia.org, he deals with poetry, experimental writings and performances, analyzing and producing materials from the point of view of "complexity." Some active books, participations in magazines and blogs.

Gianluca Rizzo, literary critic, translator, and poet, teaches at Colby College (Waterville, ME), where he is the Paganucci Associate Professor of Italian Language and Literature. He is General Editor (with Luigi Ballerini) of the Lorenzo Da Ponte Italian Library, a book series published by the University of Toronto Press. His research focuses on modern and contemporary macaronic writing, contemporary poetry, theater, and aesthetics. He published numerous articles, essays, poems, and translations, both from English to Italian and vice-versa (on *OR, Journal of Italian Translation, Chicago Review, Italica, Forum Italicum, Il Verri, Autografo, Studi Novecenteschi,* etc.). Among the volumes he edited are: Elio Pagliarani, *Tutto il teatro* (Marsilio, 2013); Carlo Goldoni, *Five Comedies* (with Michael Hackett, University of Toronto Press, 2016); *On the Fringe of the Neo-Avant-Garde* (Agincourt Press, 2017); Mariano Bàino, *Yellow Fax and Other Poems* (Agincourt Press, 2019), The Complete Poems of Michelangelo. Tusiani's Classic Translation (University of Toronto Press, 2023). With Luigi Ballerini and Paul Vangelisti he also edited *Nuova Poesia Americana. Chicago e le praterie* (Aragno, 2019). His latest monograph is titled *Poetry on Stage: The Theatre of the Italian Neo-Avant-Garde* (University of Toronto Press, 2020). His most recent book of verse is *Obelisks* (with photographs by Gary Green, Danilo Montanari Editore, 2021).

Ivan Schiavone is an Italian poet. He was born in Rome in 1983 and he graduated in modern philology in 2008 from La Sapienza University in Rome with a thesis regarding the poetical work of Emilio Villa. Schiavone has published three books: *Enuegz* (2010); *Strutture* (Structures, 2011); and *Cassandra, un paesaggio* (Cassandra, a landscape, 2014). The title of his first book, *Enuegz*, refers to a specific genre of lyric poetry practiced by the Provençal troubadours (In Occitan, Enuegz means complaint, vexation). Together with the poet Sara Davidovics, in 2009 Schiavone founded the collection ex[t] ratione for the publisher Polimata. This experimental collection published many of the most interesting new voices of the poetry of research. In 2012, Schiavone was awarded the Minturnae Prize for young poets. In 2014 he was the curator of *Generazione y. Poe-*

sia italiana ultima (Y Generation. Last Italian Poetry), an event at the Maxxi Museum in Rome that gathered many of the most interesting young Italian poets. Schiavone is the director of the poetry festival Giardini d'Inverno (Winter Gardens). He also participates in many collective artistic projects involving video, performing art, theater, photography, and music.

Achille C. Varzi is the John Dewey Professor of Philosophy at Columbia University, New York, where he has been teaching since 1995. He has published widely on logic, metaphysics, and the philosophy of language and literature. His first book, *Holes and Other Superficialities* (with Roberto Casati), appeared with MIT Press in 1994. His most recent book, *Mereology* (with Aaron J. Cotnoir), was published by Oxford University Press in 2021. He is an editor of *The Journal of Philosophy,* a subject editor of The Stanford Encyclopedia of Philosophy, and an associate or advisory editor of several other journals and book series in philosophy. He also writes for the general public and contributes regularly to some Italian newspapers, and has been teaching for the Prison Education Program sponsored by Columbia University's Justice-in-Education Initiative.

Works Cited

Abeni, Damiano, and Mark Strand, editors. *West of your cities: nuova antologia della poesia americana*. Minimum Fax, 2003.
Adorno, Theodor W. "On Lyric Poetry and Society." *Notes to Literature*, vol. 1. Edited by Rolf Tiedemann and translated by Shierry Weber Nicholsen. Columbia UP, 1991, pp. 37–54.
Alighieri, Dante. *De vulgari eloquentia*. Edited by Giorgio Inglese. Rizzoli, 1998.
——. *De vulgari eloquentia*. Translated by Steven Botterill. Cambridge UP, 1996.
——. *Convivio*. Translated by Richard Lansing. Garland, 1990.
——. *Literature in the Vernacular*. Translated by Sally Purcell. Carcanet New Press, 1981.
Allen, Donald, editor. *The New American Poetry 1945–1960*. Grove Press, 1960.
Altano, Brian. "Translating Dialect Literature: The Paradigm of Carlo Emilio Gadda." *Babel* 34.3, 1988, pp. 152–156.
Anceschi, Luciano. *Le istituzioni della poesia*. Bompiani, 1968.
——. "Prefazione." *Linea lombarda: Sei poeti*. Magenta, 1952, pp. 5–25.
Andrews, Bruce and Charles Bernstein, editors. *The L=A=N=G=U=A=G=E Book*. Southern Illinois UP, 1984.
Anedda, Antonella. *Historiae*. Einaudi, 2018.
——. *Residenze invernali*. Stamperia Bulla, 1989; Crocetti, 1992.
Apollinaire, Guillaume. *Calligrammes. Poèmes de la paix et de la guerre*. Mercure de France, 1918.
Aristotle. *The Complete Works of Aristotle. The Revised Oxford Translation*. vol. 2. Edited by Jonathan Barnes. Translated by Ingram Bywater. Princeton UP, 1984.
Ashbery, John. *The Tennis Court Oath*. Wesleyan UP, 1962.
Augustine. *Augustine, De libero arbitrio*. n.d. 22 March 2023. http://www.logicmuseum.com/wiki/Authors/Augustine/De_libero_arbitrio/L3.
Bacigalupo, Massimo. "Sanguineti fra Pound ed Eliot." *Ezra Pound: un mondo di poesia*. Ares, 2022, pp. 313–323.
——. *Angloliguria: da Byron a Hemingway*. Il Canneto, 2017.
Bàino, Mariano. *Prova d'inchiostro e altri sonetti*. Nino Aragno Editore, 2017.

——. Ônne 'e terra. Pironti, 1994; Editrice Zona, 2003.
——. Fax Giallo. Il Laboratorio, 1993; Editrice Zona, 2001.
Baldus. "A proposito delle 'Tesi di Lecce.'" *Gruppo '93. La recente avventura del dibattito teorico-letterario in Italia*. Edited by Filippo Bettini and Francesco Muzzioli. Manni Editori, 1990, pp. 121–123.
Balestrini, Nanni. *Contromano*. Diaforia e Cinquemarzo, 2015.
——. *Caosmogonia*. Mondadori, 2010.
——. *Le ballate della Signorina Richmond*. Cooperativa Scrittori, 1977.
——. *Ma noi facciamone un'altra. Poesie 1964–1968*. Feltrinelli, 1968.
——. *Come si agisce*. Feltrinelli, 1963.
——. *Tape Mark I*. Almanacco letterario Bompiani, 1962.
Ballerini, Luigi. *Divieto di sosta*. Nino Aragno Editore, 2021.
——. *Cefalonia*. Arnoldo Mondadori Editore, 2005.
——. *Il terzo gode*. Marsilio Editore, 1994.
——. *eccetera. E*. Guanda Editore, 1972.
Ballerini, Luigi, editor. *Shearsmen of Sorts. Italian Poetry 1975–1993*. Italian Poetry Supplement. Center for Italian Studies, SUNY Stony Brook, 1992.
Ballerini, Luigi, and Paul Vangelisti, editors. *Nuova poesia americana. San Francisco*. Mondadori, 2006.
——. *Nuova poesia americana. Los Angeles*. Mondadori, 2005.
Ballerini, Luigi, Gianluca Rizzo, and Paul Vangelisti, editors. *Nuova poesia americana. Chicago e le praterie*. Aragno, 2019.
——. *Nuova poesia americana. New York*. Mondadori, 2009.
Ballerini, Luigi, and Beppe Cavatorta, editors. *Those Who from afar Look like Flies. An Anthology of Italian Poetry from Pasolini to the Present*. Tome 1, 1956–1975. University of Toronto Press, 2017. Tome 2, 1975–2015, forthcoming.
Ballerini, Luigi, Beppe Cavatorta, Elena Coda, and Paul Vangelisti, editors. *The Promised Land. Italian Poetry After 1975: A Bilingual Edition*. Sun & Moon Press, 1999.
Barilli, Renato and Angelo Guglielmi, editors. *Gruppo 63. Critica e Teoria*. Feltrinelli, 1976; Testo & Immagine, 2003.
Basile, Giambattista. *Il Pentamerone*. Translated by Benedetto Croce, Laterza, 1925.
——. *The Pentamerone of Giambattista Basile*. Translated by Norman Mosley Penzer, E.P. Dutton, 1932.
Battisti, Eugenio, editor. "Gli amici dissidenti: Il Gruppo 63 a Reggio Emilia," *Marcatré*, 11–12–13, 1965, pp. 36–52.
Baudelaire, Charles. *Correspondance*. Tome I. 1831–1860. Edited by Claude Pichois. Gallimard, 1973.
——. *The Conquest of Solitude: Selected Letters*. Translated by Rosemary Lloyd, Weidenfeld & Nicolson, 1986.

Baudrillard, Jean. *De la seduction*. Éditions Galilée, 1979.
Bell, Daniel. *The End of Ideology. On the Exhaustion of Political Ideas in the Fifties*. Free Press, 1960.
Bellezza, Dario. *Invettive e licenze*. Garzanti, 1971.
Belli, Giuseppe. *Sonnets of Giuseppe Belli*. Translated by Miller Williams, Louisiana State UP, 1981.
Bellintani, Umberto. *Forse un viso tra mille*. Vallecchi, 1953.
Bello Minciacchi, Cecilia. "Per uno schemino terminale. Gruppo '93, poetica di fine millennio." *Rivista di Studi Italiani*, XXXIX, n.1, 2021, pp. 5–60.
Bene, Carmelo. *Sono apparso alla Madonna*. 1983. Bompiani, 2005.
——. *Nostra Signora dei Turchi*. 1966. Bompiani, 2005.
Benjamin, Walter. *Baudelaire*. Edited by Giorgio Agamben, Barbara Chitussi, and Clemnes-Carl Härle, translated by Patrick Charbonneau, La Fabrique, 2013.
——. "The Task of the Translator. An Introduction to the Translation of Baudelaire's *Tableaux Parisiens*." Translated by Harry Zohn. *Illuminations*. Edited by Hannah Arendt, Schocken Books, 2007, pp. 69–82.
——. *One-Way Street. The Critic's Technique in Thirteen Theses*. Translated by Edmund Jephcott and Kingsley Shorter, NLB, 1979.
Berisso, Marco. *Annali*. Oèdipus, 2002.
Bernstein, Charles. *Echo/Eco*. Edited by Carla Buranello. Edizioni del Verri, 2022.
——. *Topsy-Turvy*. University of Chicago Press, 2021.
——. *Pitch of Poetry*. University of Chicago Press, 2016.
——. *99 Poets 1999: An International Poetics Symposium*. Duke UP, 1999.
Bernstein, Charles, editor. *Close Listening: Poetry and the Performed Word*. Oxford UP, 1998.
Bertolucci, Attilio. *Fuochi in Novembre*. Minardi, 1934.
——. *Sirio*. Minardi, 1929.
Betocchi, Carlo. *Realtà vince il sogno*. Il Frontespizio, 1932.
Bettini, Filippo. "Progetto, tendenza, allegoria." *Gruppo '93. La recente avventura del dibattito teorico-letterario in Italia*. Edited by Filippo Bettini and Francesco Muzzioli. Manni Editori, 1990, pp. 59–62.
Bettini, Filippo and Roberto di Marco, editors. *Terza Ondata: Il nuovo movimento della scrittura in Italia*. Synergon, 2013.
Bettini, Filippo and Francesco Muzzioli, editors. *Gruppo '93. La recente avventura del dibattito teorico letterario in Italia*. Manni, 1990.
Bigongiari, Piero. *La figlia di Babilonia*. Parenti, 1942.
Biguenet, John, and Rainer Schulte, editors. *Theories of Translation. An Anthology of Essays from Dryden to Derrida*. The University of Chicago Press, 1992.
Birkenstein, Cathy, and Gerald Graff. *"They Say/I Say."* W. W. Norton and Co., 2006.
Blanchot, Maurice. *L'Entretien infini*. Gallimard, 1969.

———. *La conversazione infinita*. Translated by Roberta Ferrara and preface by Giovanni Bottiroli, Einaudi, 2015.
Bloom, Harold. *The Anxiety of Influence. A Theory of Poetry*. Oxford UP, 1973.
Bodini, Vittorio. *Tutte le poesie*. Edited by Oreste Macrì. Besa, 2015.
———. *Metamor*. Scheiwiller, 1967.
———. *Dopo la luna*. Sciascia, 1956.
———. "Risposta a Macrì." *Esperienza poetica*, no. 3-4, 1954, pp. 74–80.
———. *La luna dei Borboni*. Besa, 1952.
Bolaño, Roberto. *2666*. Anagrama, 2004.
———. *Amuleto*. Anagrama, 1999.
———. *Los detectives salvajes*. Anagrama, 1998.
Bolzoni, Lina. *Il teatro della memoria. Studi su Giulio Camillo*. Liviana, 1984.
Bonaffini. Luigi. "Translating Dialect Literature." *World Literature Today*, 71, 2, 1997, pp. 279–288.
Bonaffini, Luigi, editor. *Dialect Poetry of Southern Italy. Texts and Criticism. A Trilingual Edition*. Legas, 1997.
Bonaffini, Luigi and Achille Serrao, editors. *Dialect Poetry of Northern and Central Italy. Texts and Criticism. A Trilingual Edition*. Legas, 2001.
Bonaffini, Luigi, Giambattista Faralli, and Sebastiano Martelli, editors. *Poesia dialettale del Molise. Testi e critica / Dialect Poetry from Molise Texts and Criticism*. Marinelli Editore, 1993.
Bonenfant, Paul. *Philippe le Bon, sa politique, son action*. De Boeck & Larcier, 1996.
Borges, Jorge Luis. "Kafka and his predecessors" (1951). *Other Inquisitions. 1937–1952*. Translated by Ruth L.C. Simms, University of Texas Press, 1975, pp. 106–108.
Bourdieu, Pierre. *Les règles de l'art: genèse et structure du champ littéraire*. Éditions du Seuil, 1992.
Bové, Paul A. "R.P. Blackmur and the Job of the Critic: Turning from the New Criticism." *Criticism*, vol. 25, no. 4, 1983, pp. 359–80. *JSTOR*, http://www.jstor.org/stable/23105101. Accessed 16 Jan. 2024.
Brevini, Franco, editor. *La poesia in dialetto. Storia e testi dalle origini al Novecento*. Mondadori, 1999.
———. *Le parole perdute. Dialetti e poesia nel nostro secolo*. Einaudi, 1990.
———. *Poeti dialettali del Novecento*. Einaudi, 1987.
Brinkman, Bartholomew. *Poetic Modernism in the Culture of Mass Print*. Johns Hopkins UP, 2016.
Byung-Chul, Han. *Im Schwarm. Ansichten des Digitalen*. MSB Matthes & Seitz Berlin, 2013.
———. *Nello sciame. Visioni del digitale*. Translated by Federica Buongiorno, Nottetempo, 2015.

Cagnone, Nanni. *What's Hecuba to Him, or He to Hecuba.* Translated by David Verzoni, Out of London Press, 1975.
Cagnone, Nanni, translator and editor. *Æschylus-Agamemnon.* Edizione Galleria Mazzoli, 2020.
Cagnone, Nanni, translator. *Agamemnon.* Editore La Finestra, 2010.
Calasso, Roberto. *La folie Baudelaire.* Adelphi, 2008.
Campana, Dino. *Canti orfici.* Tipografia F. Ravagli, 1914.
Canevacci, Massimo. *Sincretismi. Esplorazioni diasporiche sulle ibridazioni culturali.* Costa & Nolan, 2004.
Capponi, Orlando. *Il fiume tra i morti.* Roma, 1958.
——. *Addio ad Erato.* Leonardi, 1955.
——. *La trilogia.* Il Presente, 1954.
——. *La veglia.* Il canzoniere, 1952.
——. *La nave.* Il canzoniere, 1952.
Cardarelli, Vincenzo. *Prologhi.* Studio editoriale lombardo, 1916.
Caron, Marie-Thérèse. "17 février 1454: le Banquet du Vœu du Faisan, fête de cour et stratégies de pouvoir." *Revue du Nord,* tome 78, no. 315, Avril–Juin 1996, pp. 269–288.
Carrieri, Raffaele. *Il lamento del gabelliere.* Mondadori, 1946.
Cavallo, Franco and Mario Lunetta, editors. *Poesia italiana della contraddizione.* Newton Compton, 1989.
Chiara, Piero and Luciano Erba, editors. *Quarta generazione. La giovane poesia* (1945-1954). 1 ed. Magenta, 1954; Nuova Editrice Magenta, 2014.
Chiara, Piero. "Consenso per Bellintani." *Stagione,* IV, no. 14, 1957.
Cisneros, Odile. "From Isomorphism to Cannibalism: The Evolution of Haroldo de Campos's Translation Concepts." *Traduction, Terminologie, Rédaction,* 25, vol. 2, 2012, pp. 15–44.
Coleridge, Samuel Taylor. *Biographia Literaria; or, Biographical Sketches of My Literary Life and Opinions.* vol. 1, Rest Fenner, 1817.
——. *Biographia literaria, ovvero schizzi biografici della mia vita e opinioni letterarie.* Translated by Paola Colaiacomo, Editori Riuniti, 1991.
Colonna, Valentina, et al. "Voices of Italian Poets: Project for the phonetic study of Italian poetry reading, *Laboratorio Fonetica Sperimentale Arturo Genre* website, 2023. https://www.lfsag.unito.it/ricerca/VIP_index.html.
Comi, Girolamo. *Poesia (1918–1928).* Al tempo della fortuna, 1929.
Contini, Gianfranco. "Un'interpretazione di Dante." *Un'idea di Dante.* Einaudi, 1976, pp. 69–111.
——. "Una lettura di Michelangelo" (1937). *Esercizi di lettura sopra autori contemporanei con un'appendice su testi non contemporanei.* Einaudi, 1974, pp. 323–346.

Contini, Serena, editor. *Gli anni di "Quarta generazione." Esperienze vitali nella poesia*. With a preface by Giorgio Luzzi. Nuova Editrice Magenta, 2014.
Cordelli, Franco. *Il poeta postumo. Manie, pettegolezzi, rancori*. Lerici, 1978; Le Lettere, 2008.
——. *Proprietà perduta*. Guanda Editore, 1983.
Cordelli, Franco and Alfonso Berardinelli, editors. *Il pubblico della poesia*. Lerici, 1975.
Corso, Gregory. *Elegiac Feelings American*. New Directions Publishing, 1970.
Cortellesa, Andrea, editor. *Terra Della Prosa. Narratori Italiani Degli Anni Zero, 1999–2014*. L'orma Editore, 2014.
Cortellesa, Andrea. *La fisica del senso. Saggi e interventi su poeti italiani dal 1940 a oggi*. Fazi, 2006.
Corticelli, Mario. *aria (comunione)*. ikonaLíber, 2014.
De Angelis, Milo. *Somiglianze*. Guanda, 1976.
de Andrade, Oswald. "Cannibalist Manifesto." Translated by Leslie Bary. *Latin American Literary Review*, vol. 19, no. 38, 1991, pp. 38–47. *JSTOR*, http://www.jstor.org/stable/20119601. Accessed 31 May 2024.
——. "Manifesto Antropófago." *Revista de Antropófagia*, 1, 1, May 1928.
de Campos, Haroldo. "Anthropophagous Reason: Dialogue and Difference in Brazilian Culture." *Novas*. Edited by A. S. Bessa and Odile Cisneros. Northwestern UP, 2007, pp. 157–177.
——. "Translation as Creation and Criticism." Translated by Diana Gibson and Haroldo de Campos. *Novas*. Edited by A. S. Bessa and Odile Cisneros. Northwestern UP, 2007, pp. 312–326.
——. "Transluciferação Mefistofáustica." *Deus e o Diabo no Fausto de Goethe*. Editora Perspectiva, 1981, pp. 179–209.
de Castro, Edoardo Viveiros. *Cannibal Metaphisics. For a Post-Structural Anthropology*. Translated and edited by Peter Skafish, Univocal, 2014.
——. "Exchanging Perspectives: The Transformation of Objects into Subjects in Amerindian Ontologies." *Common Knowledge*, 10.3, 2004, pp. 463–484.
Deleuze, Gilles. *Francis Bacon: The Logic of Sensation*, 1981. Translated by Daniel W. Smith, Continuum, 2005.
De Libero, Libero. *Eclisse*. Edizioni della Cometa, 1940.
——. *Solstizio*. Edizioni di Novissima, 1934.
de Rachewiltz, Mary. "And Juda Becomes New Haven." *The Wallace Stevens Journal*. 22, 1, Spring 1998, p. 83.
Di Marco, Roberto. "Lo stato delle cose." *Terza ondata. Il Nuovo Movimento della Scrittura in Italia*. Edited by Filippo Bettini and Roberto Di Marco. ABEditore, 2016, pp. 13–37.
Dias, Jamille Pinheiro. "Creativity As Transformation in Amerindian Poetics: Toward

Literary Deterritorialization in Brazil." *Romance Notes*, vol. 57, no. 3, 2017, pp. 407–413. *JSTOR*, https://www.jstor.org/stable/90017649. Accessed 4 June 2024.

Donati, Alba. *Idillio con cagnolino*. Fazi, 2013.

Doolittle, Hilda (H. D.). *Ion. A play after Euripides*. Black Swan Books, 1986.

Du Val, John. "Translating the Dialect: Miller Williams' Romanesco." *Translation Review*, 32–33, 1990, pp. 27–31.

Dummett, Michael. *The Seas of Language*. Oxford UP, 1993.

Duncan, Robert. *The H. D. Book*. Edited and with an introduction by Michael Boughn and Victor Coleman. University of California Press, 2011.

Durante, Lorenzo, Tommaso Lisa, and Federico Scaramuccia. *Trilorgìa*. Editrice Zona, 2006.

Dworkin, Craig. *Against Expression: An Anthology of Conceptual Writing*. Northwestern UP, 2011.

Eco, Umberto. "Del modo di formare come impegno sulla realtà." *Opera aperta*. 1962. Bompiani, 1993, pp. 235–290.

——. *Opera aperta*. Bompiani, 1967.

——. *Sugli specchi e altri saggi*. Bompiani, 1985.

Eliot. T.S. "Reflections on Vers Libre." *The New Statesman*, March 3, 1917.

Ellis, Bret Easton. *American Psycho*. Vintage, 1991.

Erba, Luciano. *Linea K*. Guanda, 1951.

Euripides. *Ion*. Translated by Anne Pippin Burnett, Prentice-Hall, 1970.

Falqui, Enrico, editor. *La giovane poesia. Saggio e repertorio*. Carlo Colombo, 1956.

Ferroni, Giulio. *Gli ultimi poeti. Giovanni Giudici e Andrea Zanzotto*. Il Saggiatore, 2013.

——. *Alfredo Giuliani, l'escrescenza del significante, l'algebra semantica degli oggetti: dall'astrazione fenomenologica al collage, alla manipolazione libido-fecale della lingua tautofonica*. Edited by Gianni Granna. Marzorati, 1983.

——. "Giorgio Manganelli." *Novecento. I contemporanei*. Edited by Gianni Grana. vol. X, Marzorati, 1979, pp. 10057–10081.

——. "La poesia di Alfredo Giuliani o l'impossibilità dell'avanguardia." *La Rassegna della letteratura italiana*, 1, 1970, pp. 90–111.

Ficara, Elena. *The Form of Truth. Hegel's Philosophical Logic*. De Gruyter, 2021.

Frasca, Gabriele. "*Un poeta che torna e incrocia. Ilaria de Seta intervista Gabriele Frasca.*" *Insula europea*, 28 June 2018. https://www.insulaeuropea.eu/2018/06/28/un-poeta-che-torna-e-incrocia-ilaria-de-seta-intervista-gabriele-frasca/. Accessed May 31, 2024.

Fisher, Mark. "Time-Wars: Towards an Alternative for the Neo-Capitalist Era." *Gonzo Circus*, 2012. https://www.gonzocircus.com/exclusive-essay-time-warstowards-an-alternative-for-the-neo-capitalist-era/. Accessed June 26, 2024.

——. "The Privatisation of Stress: The Numerous Pathologies Generated by Neoliber-

alism Can Only Be Cured Within a Revivified Public Sphere." *Soundings*, no. 48, May 2011, pp. 123–133.
——. *Capitalist Realism: Is There No Alternative?* Zero Books, 2009.
Foley, Jack. *Visions & Affiliations: A California Literary Time Line, Poets & Poetry.* 2 vols. Pantograph Press, 2011.
Fortini, Franco. "Di Sereni (1966)." *Saggi italiani.* De Donato, 1974, pp. 158–186.
Frege, Gottlob. *Posthumous Writings.* Translated by P. Long and R. White, Blackwell, 1979.
——. "The Thought: A Logical Inquiry." 1918. *Mind*, 65, no. 259, 1956, pp. 289–311.
——. "Über Sinn und Bedeutung." *Zeitschrift für Philosophie und philosophische Kritik*, vol. 100, 1892, pp. 25–50.
Frixione, Marcello. *Naturama (1981–2019).* Oèdipus, 2021.
——. "Goedel, Blob e la merda d'artista." *Gruppo 93. Le tecniche attuali della poesia e della narrativa. Antologia di testi teorici e letterari.* Edited by Anna Grazia D'Oria, Piero Manni, 1993.
——. *Diottrie.* P. Manni, 1991.
——. "Sull'eredità dell'avanguardia." *Baldus*, no. 1, a. II, 1991, pp. 41–42.
——. "Il linguaggio è in ordine così come come è." *Gruppo '93. La recente avventura del dibattito teorico letterario in Italia.* Edited by Filippo Bettini and Francesco Muzzioli. Manni Editori, 1990, pp. 141–142.
——. "Poesia oggettiva." *l'immaginazione*, no. 58, October 1988.
Frungillo, Vincenzo. *Prime scene di caccia e di morte.* Zacinto Edizioni, 2021.
——. *Il luogo delle forze. Lo spazio della poesia nel tempo della dispersione.* Carteggi Letterari le Edizioni, 2017.
——. *Le pause della serie evolutiva.* Oèdipus, 2016.
——. "Autoantologie-1. Vincenzo Frungillo." *Nazione Indiana.* 22 February 2016, https://www.nazioneindiana.com/2016/02/22/micro-antologie-1-vincenzo-frungillo/. Accessed May 31, 2023.
——. *Il cane di Pavlov (Resoconto di una perizia).* Edizioni d'If, 2013.
——. *Ogni cinque bracciate. Poema in cinque canti.* Le Lettere, 2009.
Fukuyama, Francis. *The End of History and the Last Man.* Free Press, 1992.
Gadda, Carlo Emilio. *Quer Pasticciaccio brutto de Via Merulana.* Garzanti, 1957.
——. *That Awful Mess on the Via Merulana.* Translated by William Weaver, NYRB Classics, 2007.
García Lorca, Federico. *The Selected Poems of Federico García Lorca.* Edited by Federico García Lorca and Donald Allen. Translated by Roy Campbell, Edwin Honig, Rolfe Humphries, and Harriet de Onis, New Directions, 1961.
——. *Poet in New York.* Translated by Ben Belitt, Grove Press, 1955.
Gardini, Nicola. *Lacuna. Saggio sul non detto.* Einaudi, 2014.
Gatto, Alfonso. *Poesie.* Panorama, 1939.

Giannone, Antonio Lucio, editor. *Vittorio Bodini tra Sud ed Europa (1914–2014)*. Atti del Convegno Internazionale di Studi (Lecce, Bari, 3, 4, and 9 December 2014). Besa, 2017.

Giannone, Antonio Lucio. *Recognizioni novecentesche*. Edizioni Sinestesie, 2020.

Giovanardi, Stefano. "Introduzione." *Poeti italiani del secondo Novecento*. 2 voll. 1996. Edited by Maurizio Cucchi and Stefano Giovanardi. Mondadori, 2004, vol. I, pp. vii–xlii.

Giovenale, Marco. *Quasi tutti*. Miraggi Edizioni, 2018.

Giuliani, Alfredo. "Preface to the 2003 Edition." Translated by A. Bregman and Federica Santini. *I Novissimi. Poetry for the Sixties*. Edited by Luigi Ballerini and Federica Santini. Agincourt Press, 2017.

——. "Introduction to the First Edition (1961)." *I Novissimi. Poetry for the Sixties*. Edited by Luigi Ballerini and Federica Santini. Agincourt Press, 2017.

——. "Introduction to the Second Edition of *I Novissimi*" (1965). *I Novissimi. Poetry for the Sixties*. Translated by David Jacobson, Sun & Moon Press, 1995, pp. 41–57.

——. *Chi l'avrebbe detto*. Einaudi, 1973.

——. *Il cuore zoppo*. Magenta, 1955.

——. *I Novisssimi. Poetry for the Sixties*. Prose and notes translated by David Jacobson. Poetry translated by Luigi Ballerini, Bradley Dick, Michael Moore, Stephen Sartarelli, and Paul Vangelisti. Sun and Moon Press, 1995.

——. *I Novissimi, Poesie per gli anni '60*. Rusconi e Paolazzi, 1961; Einaudi, 1965.

Gizzi, Peter. *Some Values of Landscape and Weather*. Wesleyan UP, 2003.

Gleize, Jean-Marie. *Sorties*. Questions théoriques, 2009.

Glissant, Édouard. *Introduction à une poétique du divers*. Gallimard, 1996.

Gödel, Kurt. "Über formal unentscheidbare Sätze der Principia Mathematica und verwandter Systeme I." *Monatshefte für Mathematik und Physik*, vol. 38, 1931, pp. 173–198.

Grande, Adriano. *Nuvole sul greto*. Edizioni di Circoli, 1933.

——. *La tomba verde*. Fratelli Buratti Editori, 1929.

——. *Avventure*. Edizioni del Baretti, 1927.

Grazioli, Elio. *Infrasottile. L'arte contemporanea ai limiti*. Postmedia books, 2018.

Guerra, Tonino. "L'òm ad naiva." *The Wallace Stevens Journal*, 25, 2, 2001, p. 278.

Haller, Hermann. *The Hidden Italy. A Bilingual Edition of Italian Dialect Poetry*. Wayne State UP, 1986.

Han, Byung-Chul. *Nello sciame. Visioni del digitale*. Translated by Federica Buongiorno, Nottetempo, 2015.

Harrison, Thomas J., editor. *The Favorite Malice. Ontology and Reference in Contemporary Italian Poetry*. Out of London Press, 1983.

Hecht, Jennifer Michael. *The Wonder Paradox: Embracing the Weirdness of Existence and the Poetry of our Lives*. Farrar, Straus and Giroux, 2023.

Heidegger, Martin. *Sentieri interrotti*. Translated by Pietro Chiodi, La Nuova Italia, 1991.

——. "A Dialogue on Language." *On the Way to Language*. Translated by Peter D. Hertz, Harper & Row, 1971, pp. 1–56.

——. "Language in the Poem. A Discussion on Georg Trakl's Poetic Work." *On the Way to Language*. Translated by Peter D. Hertz, Harper & Row, 1971, pp. 159–198.

——. *Holzwege*. 1968. Klostermann, 1984.

——. *Unterwegs zur Sprache*. Guinther Neske, 1959.

Houellebecq, Michel. *Les particules élémentaires*. Flammarion, 1998.

——. *Extension du domaine de la lutte*. Éditions Maurice Nadeau, 1994.

Hofstadter, Douglas. *Le Ton beau de Marot*. Basic Book, 1997.

Inglese, Andrea. *Prati*. La camera verde, 2007.

Inglese, Andrea and Paolo Giovannetti, editors. *Teoria e poesia*. Biblion Edizioni, 2018.

Jahier, Piero. *Con me e con gli Alpini*. Libreria della Voce, 1919.

Jakobson, Roman. "Poetry of Grammar and Grammar of Poetry." *Lingua*, 21, 1968, pp. 597–609.

——. "On Linguistic Aspects of Translation." *On Translation*. Edited by Reuben Brower. Harvard UP, 1959, pp. 232–239.

Jandl, Ernst. *Reft and Light. Poems with Multiple Versions by American Poets*. Edited by Rosemarie Waldrop. Burning Deck Press, 2000.

——. *Der künstliche Baum*. Luchterhand, 1970.

Johnson, Randal. "Tupy or not Tupy: Cannibalism and Nationalism in Contemporary Brazilian Literature and Culture." *On Modern Latin American Fiction*. Edited by John King. Hill and Wang, 1987, pp. 41–59.

Jones, David. *An Introduction to The Rime of the Ancient Mariner*. Clover Hill, 1972.

Klein, Naomi. *Shock Doctrine. The Rise of Disaster Capitalism*. Knopf Canada, 2007.

La parola innamorata. I poeti nuovi, 1976–1978. Edited by Giancarlo Pontiggia and Enzo Di Mauro. Feltrinelli, 1978.

La Stella, Enrico. *L'amore Giovane*. Mondadori, 1956.

Lacan, Jacques. "The Mirror Phase as Formative of the Function of I." Translated by Jean Roussel, *New Left Review*, 51, Sept./Oct. 1968, pp. 63–77.

Lajolo, Davide, and Giuseppe Ungaretti, editors. *I poeti scelti*. Mondadori, 1949.

Lautréamont. *Les Chants de Maldoror et autres textes*. Edited by Jean-Luc Steinmetz. Le livre de Poche, 2001.

Leopardi, Giacomo. *Zibaldone*. Edited by Michael Caesar and Franco D'Intino. Translated by K. Baldwin, R. Dixon, D. Gibbons, A. Goldstein, G. Slowey, M. Thom, and P. Williams, Farrar, Straus and Giroux, 2013.

Littré, Émile. "« conférer », définition dans le dictionnaire Littré." *Dictionnaire de La Langue Française*, www.littre.org/definition/conf%C3%A9rence. Accessed 17 January, 2024.

Lisa, Tommaso. *Le Poetiche dell'oggetto da Luciano Anceschi ai Novissimi. Linee evolutive di un'istituzione della poesia del Novecento*. Firenze UP, 2007.
Lotman, Jurij M. "On the semiosphere." Translated by Wilma Clark. *Sign Systems Studies*. 33, 1, 2005, pp. 205–229.
—. *La semiosfera. L'asimmetria e il dialogo nelle strutture pensanti*. Translated by Simonetta Salvestroni, Marsilio, 1985.
—. *The Structure of the Artistic Text*. 1971. Translated by Gail Lenhoff and Ronald Vroon, University of Michigan Press, 1977.
Löwith, Karl. "Vom sinn der Geschichte." *Sämtliche Schriften*, vol. IX. 1961.
—. *Sul senso della storia*. Translated by Marco Bruni, Mimesis, 2017.
Lukács, György. *History and Class Consciousness: Studies in Marxist Dialectics*. 1968. Translated by Rodney Livingstone, The MIT Press, 1972.
Luzi, Mario. *Avvento notturno*. Rizzoli, 1940.
—. *La barca*. Guanda Editore, 1935.
Macrì, Oreste. "Le generazioni della poesia italiana del Novecento." *Paragone*, no. 42, June 1953, pp. 45–53.
Mallarmé, Stéphane. "Crise de vers." *Divagations*. Eugène Fasquelle, 1897, pp. 235–251.
Marcuse, Herbert. *L'uomo a una dimensione*. Translate, by Luciano Gallino and Tilde Giani Gallino, Einaudi, 1999.
—. *One-Dimensional Man: Studies in the Ideology of Advanced Industrial Society*. Beacon Press, 1964.
Marniti, Biagia. *Nero amore rosso amore*. Edizioni Fiumara, 1951.
Mazzoni, Guido. *La pura superficie*. Donzelli Editore, 2017.
Meli, Giovanni. *Don Chisciotti and Sanciu Panza*. Translated by Gaetano Cipolla, Canadian Society for Italian Studies, 1986.
Mengaldo, Vincenzo. "Iterazione e specularità in Sereni." *Gli strumenti umani*. Einaudi, 1987, pp. 89–116.
—. "Iterazione e specularità in Sereni." *Strumenti critici*, VI, no. 17. February 1972, pp. 19–48.
Montaigne, Michel de. *Michel de Montaigne, The Complete Essays*. Translated by M. A. Screech, Penguin Books, 2003.
—. *The Complete Essays of Montaigne*. Translated and edited by Donald M. Frame, Stanford UP, 1958.
Montale, Eugenio. *Collected Poems 1920–1954*. Translated and annotated by Jonathan Galassi, Farrar, Straus and Giroux, 2000.
—. *Sulla poesia*. Mondadori, 1997.
—. *L'opera in versi*. Edited by Rosanna Bettarini and Gianfranco Contini. Einaudi, 1980.
—. *Selected Poems*. New Directions, 1965.

———. *Ossi di seppia.* Piero Gobetti Editore, 1925.
Morra, Gerri. *Parole udite domani.* Schwarz, 1953.
———. *Solstizio d'estate.* Gastaldi, 1951.
Morrison, James C. "Why Spinoza Had No Aesthetics." *The Journal of Aesthetics and Art Criticism,* vol. 47, no. 4, 1989, pp. 359–65. *JSTOR,* https://doi.org/10.2307/431135. Accessed 16 Jan. 2024.
Müller, Heiner. *Despoiled Shore Medea-material Landscape with Argonauts.* 1981 Translated by Denis Redmond. 2002. https://mullersmedea.wordpress.com/wp-content/uploads/2011/12/despoiled.pdf. Accessed 16 June, 2024.
Musil, Robert. *Diaries, 1899–1941.* Translated by Philip Payne, Basic Books, 1998.
———. *The Man without Qualities.* vol. 1. Translated by Sophie Wilkins and Burton Pike, Knopf, 1995.
———. "Sketch of What the Writer Knows." *Robert Musil. Precision and Soul: Essays and Addresses.* Edited and translated by Burton Pike and David S. Luft, University of Chicago Press, 1990, pp. 61–65.
———. *Tagebücher.* Edited by Adolf Frisé, Rowohlt, 1983.
———. *Der Mann ohne Eigenschaften.* Erstes Buch. Rowohlt, 1930.
———. "Skizze der Erkenntnis des Dichters." *Summa,* vol. 4, 1918, pp. 164–168.
Mustazza, Chris. "Machine-Aided Close Listening: Prosthetic Synaesthesia and the 3D Phonotext." *Digital Humanities Quarterly* 12, no. 3 (2018). https://www.digitalhumanities.org/dhq/vol/12/3/000397/000397.html.
Muzzioli, Francesco. "Sviluppi e direzioni dello sperimentalismo letterario." *Gruppo '93: La recente avventura del dibattito teorico letterario in Italia.* Edited by Filippo Bettini and Francesco Muzzioli, Manni Editori, 1990, pp. 45–49.
Nietzsche, Friedrich Wilhelm. *The Birth of Tragedy and Other Writings.* 1872. Edited by Raymond Geuss and Ronald Speirs, and translated by Ronald Speirs, Cambridge UP, 1999.
Nòbrega, Thelma Mèdici, and John Milton. "The role of Haroldo and Augusto de Campos in bringing translation to the fore of literary activity in Brazil." *Agents of Translation.* Edited by John Milton and Paul Bandia, John Benjamins Publishing Company, 2009, pp. 257–279.
O'Hara, Frank. *Lunch Poems.* 1964. The Pocket Poets Series: Number 19. Expanded 50th Anniversary Edition, City Lights Books, 2014.
———. *The Collected Poems of Frank O'Hara.* 1971. University of California Press, 1995.
Olson, Charles. "Projective Verse." *Poetry New York,* no. 3, 1950.
Onofri, Arturo. *Orchestrine.* Libreria della Diana, 1917.
Ortega y Gasset, José. "The Misery and the Splendour of Translation." Translated by Martin Boyd. *diálogos. Intercultural Services.* https://dialogos.ca/2015/05/the-misery-and-the-splendour-of-translation/. Accessed May 3, 2023.
Ortese, Anna Maria. *Il porto di Toledo.* Rizzoli, 1975.

Ostuni, Vincenzo, editor. *I poeti degli anni Zero. Gli esordienti del primo decennio.* Ponte Sisto, 2015.
Ostuni, Vincenzo. *Faldone zero-cinquantanove, novantotto-novantanove. Poesie 1992–2014.* Aragno, 2022.
——. *Opportune premesse.* Zacinto Editori, 2022.
——. *Il libro di G.* Il Saggiatore, 2019.
——. *Deleuze, o dell'essere chiunque chiunque.* Tic, 2019.
——. *Faldone zero-trentasette. Estratti, II.* Oèdipus, 2018.
——. *Faldone zero-trentanove. Estratti 2007–2010, I.* Aragno, 2014.
——. *Faldone zero-venti. Poesie 1992–2006.* Ponte Sisto, 2012.
——. *Faldone zero-otto. Poesie 1992–2000.* Oèdipus, 2004.
Ottonieri, Tommaso. *Le strade che portano al Fùcino.* Le Lettere, 2007.
——. "Intermezzo." *Eutropia: revue italo-francaise / Rivista franco-italiana.* vol.3: L'immagine. Quodlibet, 2003.
——. *Coro da l'acqua, per voce sola.* Edizioni d'if, 2003.
Oulipo. *La littérature potentielle (Créations Re-créations Récréations).* Gallimard, 1973.
Padua, Adriano. *La presenza del vedere.* Polìmata, 2009.
Pagliarani, Elio. *La ballata di Rudi.* Marsilio, 1995.
——. *Rosso corpo corpo lingua oro pope-papa scienza. Doppio trittico di Nandi.* Cooperativa Scrittori, 1977.
——. *Lezione di fisica e Fecaloro.* Feltrinelli, 1968.
——. "Per una definizione di avanguardia." *Nuova Corrente*, 37, 1966.
——. "Intervento." *Gruppo 63. Il romanzo sperimentale. Palermo 1965.* Edited by Nanni Balestrini. Feltrinelli, 1966, pp. 104–115.
——. *Cronache e altre poesie.* Schwarz, 1954.
Parola Plurale. Sessantaquattro poeti italiani tra due secoli. Edited by G. Alfano, A. Baldacci, C. Bello Minciacchi, A. Cortellessa, M. Manganelli, R. Scarpa, F. Zinelli, and P. Zublena. Luca Sossella Editore, 2005.
Pascoli, Giovanni. *Il fanciullo. Un altro mondo, lo stesso mondo.* Edited by Maria Grazia Calandrone. Aragno, 2019.
Pask, Gordon. *Conversation Theory: Applications in Education and Epistemology.* Elsevier Scientific Publishing Company, 1976.
Pasolini, Pier Paolo. *Saggi sulla letteratura e sull'arte.* Vols. I–II. Edited by Walter Siti and Silvia De Laude. Mondadori, 1999.
——. *The Divine Mimesis.* Translated by Thomas E. Peterson, Double Dance Press, 1980.
——. *La Divina Mimesis.* Einaudi, 1975.
——. *Empirismo eretico.* Einaudi, 1972.
——. *Trasumanar e organizzar.* Garzanti, 1971.

——. *Passione e ideologia.* Garzanti, 1960.
——. "Libertà stilistica." *Officina*, 9–10, June 1957, pp. 341–346.
——. "Il neo-sperimentalismo." *Officina*, 5, February 1956, pp. 169–182.
Pavese, Cesare. *Lavorare stanca.* Edited by Alberto Carocci. Edizioni di Solaria, 1936.
Pavolini, Corrado. *Patria d'acque.* Vallecchi, 1933.
——. *Elixir di vita.* Edizioni di Solaria, 1929.
——. *Odor di terra.* Fratelli Ribet Editori, 1928.
——. *Poesie.* Accademia dell'enciclopedia editrice, 1923.
Paz, Octavio, et al. *Renga. A Chain of Poems.* Translation by Charles Tomlinson. Braziller, 1971.
Penna, Sandro. *Poesie.* Parenti, 1939.
Per una ipotesi di "scrittura materialistica." Edited by Filippo Bettini, Mirko Bevilacqua, Marcello Carlino, Aldo Mastropasqua, Francesco Muzzioli, and Giorgio Patrizi. Bastogi, 1981.
Peregalli, Alessandro. *L'altopiano.* Guanda, 1955.
Perniola, Mario. *Contro la comunicazione.* Einaudi, 2014.
Perolino, Ugo. *La ricerca poetica da 'Quarta generazione' a 'Officina.'* Carabba, 2022.
Picconi, Gian Luca. "La controverità delle madri: la ballata «à la manière de Villon» tra Sanguineti e Pasolini." *Between*, vol. VI, no. 12, November 2016. https://ojs.unica.it/index.php/between/issue/view/73. Accessed May 31, 2023.
Pierri, Michele. *Contemplazione e rivolta.* With a preface by Carlo Bo. Istituto d'Arte, 1950.
Pivano, Fernanda, editor. *Poesia degli ultimi americani.* Feltrinelli, 1964.
Poe, Edgar Allan. "Review of *The Betrothed Lovers.*" *The Southern Literary Messenger*, vol. 1, no. 9, May 1835.
Poggioli, Renato. "The Added Artificer." *On Translation.* Edited by Reuben Arthur Brower. Harvard UP, 1959, pp. 355–366.
Policastro, Gilda. *L'ultima poesia. Scritture anomale e mutazioni di genere dal secondo Novecento a oggi.* Mimesis, 2021.
Porta, Antonio. *Piercing the Page: Selected Poems 1958–1989.* Edited by Gian Maria Annovi. Translated by Anthony Baldry, Rosemary Liedl, Paolo Martini, Anthony Molino, Lawrence R. Smith, Paul Vangelisti, and Pasquale Verdicchio, Otis Books, Seismicity Editions, 2012.
——. *Tutte le poesie (1956–1989).* Edited by Nina Lorenzini. Garzanti, 2009.
——. *Invasioni: 1980–1983.* Mondadori, 1984.
——. *Quanto ho da dirvi. Poesie 1958–1975.* Feltrinelli, 1977.
——. "Il grado zero della poesia." *Marcatré*, 2, January 1964.
Porter, James I. "Lasus of Hermione, Pindar and the Riddle of S." *The Classical Quarterly*, vol. 57, no. 1, 2007, pp. 1–21. *JSTOR*, http://www.jstor.org/stable/4493468. Accessed 28 Jan. 2024.

Portesine, Chiara. *"Una specie di Biennale allargata." Il giuoco dell'ecfrasi nel secondo romanzo di Edoardo Sanguineti*. Fabrizio Serra Editore, 2021.

——. "'Una febbriciattola di lieve paranoia.' Varianti 'novissime' nella *Beltà*." *E l'avanguardia ha trovato, ha trovato? Andrea Zanzotto*. *Il Verri*, no. 77, October 2021, pp. 105–117.

Pound, Ezra. *Omaggio a Sesto Properzio. Homage to Sextus Propertius*. Edited and translated by Massimo Bacigalupo. S.Marco dei Giustiniani, 1984.

——. "How to Read." *Literary Essays of Ezra Pound*. New Directions, 1968.

——. *La terra desolata-Frammento di un agone-Marcia trionfale*. Translated by Mario Praz, Fussi Editore, 1949.

Priest, Graham. "To Be and Not to Be—That is the Answer. On Aristotle on the Law of Non-Contradiction." *History of Philosophy and Logical Analysis*, vol. 1, 1998, pp. 91–130.

Quaderni di Critica. "Per un'ipotesi di scrittura materialistica." *Gruppo '93: La recente avventura del dibattito teorico letterario in Italia*. Edited by Filippo Bettini and Francesco Muzzioli. Manni Editori, 1990, pp. 20–24.

Quasimodo, Salvatore. *Lirici greci*. Introduction by Gilberto Finzi with an essay by Luciano Anceschi. Mondadori, 1979.

——. *Ed è subito sera*. Mondadori, 1942.

——. *Oboe sommerso*. Edizioni di Circoli, 1932.

——. *Acque e terre*. Edizioni di Solaria, 1930.

Quasimodo, Salvatore, editor. *Poesia italiana del dopoguerra*. Schwarz, 1958.

Raboni, Giovanni. "La musa pedagogica di Pagliarani" (1963). *Poesia degli anni Sessanta*. Editori Riuniti, 1976, pp. 79–81.

Rebora, Clemente. *Canti anonimi*. Il Convegno Editoriale, 1922.

——. *Frammenti lirici*. Libreria della Voca, 1913.

Ricoeur, Paul. *Per un'utopia ecclesiale*. Edited by Paolo Furia, Claudio Paravati, and Alberto Romele. Claudiana, 2018.

——. *Plaidoyer pour l'utopie écclésiale*. Éditions Labor et Fides, 2016.

Rimanelli, Giose. *Moliseide: Songs and Ballads in the Molisan Dialect*. Translated by Luigi Bonaffini, Peter Lang Publishing, 1992.

Risset, Jacqueline. "Il rischio della scrittura, intervista di Filippo Bettini." *Rinascita*, 44, 1982, pp. 22–23.

Romanò, Angelo. *Discorso degli anni Cinquanta. Saggi*. Mondadori, 1965.

Ronconi, Federico, editor. *Nuova poesia troll*. Argolibri, 2022.

Rorty, Richard. *Consequences of Pragmatism*. University of Minnesota Press, 1982.

——. "Pragmatism, Relativism, and Irrationalism." *Proceedings and Addresses of the American Philosophical Association*, vol. 53, no. 6, 1980, pp. 717–38. *JSTOR*, https://doi.org/10.2307/3131427. Accessed 18 January, 2024.

——. *Philosophy and the Mirror of Nature*. Princeton UP, 1979.

Rosenberg, Harold. *The Tradition of the New*. Horizon Press, 1959.
Rosengrant, Judson. "Toads in the Garden: on Translating Vernacular Style in Eduard Limonov." *Translation Review*, 38–39, 1992, pp. 16–19.
Rosselli, Amelia. *Variazioni belliche*. Garzanti, 1964.
—. *Documento*. Garzanti, 1976.
Rothenberg, Jerome. *Writing Through. Translations and Variations*. Wesleyan UP, 2004.
Rothenberg, Jerome, and Pierre Joris, editors. *Poems for the Millennium*. Volume Two. University of California Press, 1998.
Roversi, Roberto. *Registrazione di eventi*. Rizzoli, 1964.
Russell, Bertrand. *Our Knowledge of the External World*. 1914. Routledge, 2009.
Saba, Umberto. *Canzoniere*. 1st ed. Libreria Antica e Moderna, 1921.
—. *Poesie*. With a preface by Silvio Benco. Casa editrice italiana, 1911.
Sade (Marquis de), Donatien Alphonse François. *Juliette*. Translated by Austryn Wainhouse, Grove Press, 1968.
—. *Juliette, ou les Prospérités du vice. La nouvelle Justine, ou les malheurs de la vertu, suivie de l'Histoire de Juliette, sa sœur.* Hollande, s.l., 1797, vol. VIII.
Sainte-Beuve, Charles-Augustin. *Des soirées littéraires ou les poètes entre eux*. Paris ou le Livre des Cent et un, 1831.
Salibra, Elena. *Dalla parte dei vivi. Poesie 2004–2014*. Manni, 2019.
—. *Nordiche*. Stampa 2009, 2014.
Sanguineti, Edoardo. "Poesia informale?" *I Novissimi. Poesie per gli anni 60*. 1965. Einaudi, 2003, pp. 169–173.
—. "«A me della poesia m'importa pochissimo». Incontro con Edoardo Sanguineti." Edited by Massimo Gezzi. *Atelier*, 32, December 2003, pp. 54–69.
—. *Il gatto lupesco. Poesie (1982–2001)*. Feltrinelli, 2002.
—. *Novissimum testamentum*. P. Manni, 1986.
—. *Alfabeto apocalittico*. Maestri di Giardino, 1984.
—. *Segnalibro. Poesie 1951–1981*. Feltrinelli, 1982.
—. Postkarten: Poesie 1972–1977. Feltrinelli, 1978.
—. *Catamerone: 1951–1971*. Feltrinelli, 1974.
—. "Introduzione." *Poesia italiana del Novecento*. Edited by Edoardo Sanguineti. Einaudi, 1969, pp. xii–xxxvii.
—. *Ideologia e linguaggio*. Feltrinelli, 1965.
—. *Triperuno*. Feltrinelli, 1964.
—. *Opus metricum*. Rusconi e Paolazzi, 1960.
—. *Laborintus*. Magenta, 1956.
—. "Review of *Quarta generazione*." *Lettere italiane*, vol. 6, no. 4, October-December 1954, pp. 414-418.
Sanguineti, Edoardo and Jean Burgos. *Per una critica dell'avanguardia poetica in Italia e in Francia*. Einaudi, 1995.

Sbarbaro, Camillo. *Poesie e prose*. Mondadori, 2022.
Scalise, Gregorio. *Opera-opera. Poesie scelte 1968–2017*. Sossella, 2007.
Scappetone, Jennifer, "Introducing *PennSound Italiana*," *Jacket2 Magazine*, June 13, 2005. https://jacket2.org/article/introducing-pennsound-italiana.
Schiavone, Ivan. *Tavole e stanze*. Oèdipus, 2019.
Schleiermacher, Friedrich. "On the Different Methods of Translating." Translated by Susan Bernofsky. *The Translation Studies Reader*. 2000. 4th edition. Edited by Lawrence Venuti. Routledge, 2021, pp. 51–71.
Scotellaro, Rocco. È fatto giorno *(1940–1953)*. Mondadori, 1954.
Seconda antologia di poeti nuovi (Premio "S. Babila" 1950–Inediti). Edited by Andrea Zanzotto and Gian Piero Bona. Edizioni della Meridiana, 1951.
Sereni, Vittorio. *Gli strumenti umani*. Einaudi, 1965.
——. *Diario d'Algeria*. Vallechi, 1947.
——. *Frontiera*. Corrente, 1941.
Sewell, David R. *Mark Twain's Languages: Discourse, Dialogue, and Linguistic Variety*. University of California Press, 1987.
Shakespeare, William. *William Shakespeare: The Complete Works*. Edited by Alfred Harbage. 3rd. Penguin Books, 1969.
Sinisgalli, Leonardo. *Vidi le Muse*. Mondadori, 1943.
——. *Campi elisi (1937–1939)*. Scheiwiller, 1939.
——. *18 poesie*. Scheiwiller, 1936.
Solmi, Sergio. *Fine di stagione*. Carabba, 1933.
Spagnoletti, Giacinto, editor. *Antologia della poesia italiana 1909–1949*. Guanda, 1950.
Spatola, Adriano. *Verso la poesia totale*. Paravia, 1978.
Spicer, Jack. *My Vocabulary Did This to Me. The Collected Poetry of Jack Spicer*. Edited by Peter Gizzi and Kevin Killian. Wesleyan UP, 2008.
Stein, Gertrude. *Composition as Explanation*. The Hogarth Press, 1926.
Steiner, George. *The Poetry of Thought*. New Directions, 2011.
——. *After Babel. Aspects of Language and Translation*. 1975. 3rd ed. Oxford UP, 1998.
Stevens, Wallace. *Tutte le poesie*. Edited by Massimo Bacigalupo. Mondadori, 2015.
——. *Il mondo come meditazione. Ultime poesie 1950–1955*. Edited and translated by Massimo Bacigalupo. Acquario-Guanda, 1986.
——. *Collected Poetry and Prose*. Edited by Frank Kermode and Joan Richardson. Library of America, 1997.
——. "Adagia." *Opus Posthumous*. Knopf, 1957, pp. 157–182.
——. *The Collected Poems of Wallace Stevens*. Knopf, 1954.
——. *Mattino domenicale ed altre poesie*. Edited and translated by Renato Poggioli. Einaudi, 1953.
——. *The Necessary Angel*. Knopf, 1951.

———. *Ideas of Order*. Alfred F. Knopf, 1936.

———. "Like Decorations in a Nigger Cemetery." *Poetry. A Magazine of Verse*, vol. 45, no. 5, February 1935, pp. 239–249.

Stewart, Susan. "Antonella Anedda. The Art of Poetry. No. 109." *Paris Review*, no. 234, Fall 2020.

Stillman, Linda Klieger. *Alfred Jarry*. Twayne Publisher, 1983.

Superstudio. *Opere (1966-1978)*. Edited by Gabriele Mastrigli. Quodlibet, 2016.

Szabari, Antonia. "'parler Seulement de Moy': The Disposition of the Subject in Montaigne's Essay 'De l'art de Conferer.'" *MLN*, vol. 116, no. 5, 2001, pp. 1001–1024. *JSTOR*, http://www.jstor.org/stable/3251793. Accessed 17 January, 2024.

Tambornino, John. "Philosophy as the Mirror of Liberalism: The Politics of Richard Rorty." *Polity*, vol. 30, no. 1, 1997, pp. 57–78. *JSTOR*, https://doi.org/10.2307/3235320. Accessed 17 January, 2024.

Terracini, Benvenuto. "Il problema della traduzione." *Conflitti di lingue e di cultura*. Introd. Maria Corti. Einaudi, 1996, pp. 37–108.

Terreni, Alessandro. *La scelta della voce. La svolta lirica di Antonio Porta*. Arcipelago Edizioni, 2015.

Testa, Enrico. *Dopo la lirica. Poeti italiani 1960–2000*. Einaudi, 2005.

Teti, Fabio. *Spazio di destot*. Diaforia, 2011.

The Portable Mark Twain. Edited by Bernard de Voto. The Viking Press, 1968.

Toulmin, Rachel Meoli. "Shakespeare ed Eliot nelle versioni di Eugenio Montale." *Belfagor*, vol. 26, no. 4, 1971, pp. 453–471. *JSTOR*, http://www.jstor.org/stable/26142424. Accessed 13 June, 2024.

Tschumi, Bernard. *Architettura e disgiunzione*. Translated by Giovanni Damiani, Pendragon, 2005.

Tuchman, Barbara W. *A Distant Mirror: The Calamitous 14th Century*. Alfred A. Knopf, 1978.

Tynianov, Yuri. *The Problem of Verse Language*. Edited and translated by M. Sosa and B. Harvey. Ardis, 1981.

Twain, Mark. *Le avventure di Huckleberry Finn*. Translated by Giovanni Baldi, Garzanti, 1992.

Ungaretti, Giuseppe. *Allegria di naufragi*. Vallecchi, 1919.

———. *Il porto sepolto*. Stabilimento tipografico friulano, 1916.

Valéry, Paul. *Poésie et Pensée abstraite. The Zaharoff Lecture*. Clarendon Press, 1939.

———. "Poetry and Abstract Thought." Translated by Charles Guenther, *The Kenyon Review*, vol. 16, 1954, pp. 208–233.

Varaldo, Giuseppe. *All'alba Shahrazad andrà ammazzata. Capolavori in sonetti monovocalici*. Vallardi, 1993.

Varzi, Achille. "Cut-offs and their neighbours." *Liars and Heaps*. Edited by J.C. Beall, Oxford UP, 2003, pp. 24–38.

Vigolo, Giorgio. *Canto fermo*. Formiggini, 1931.
——. *La città dell'anima*. Studio Editoriale Romano, 1923.
Vita, Carlo. "An Old Man." *The Wallace Stevens Journal*, 33, 2, 2009, p. 260.
Viviani, Cesare. *L'ostrabismo cara*. Feltrinelli, 1973.
Waelkens, Laurent. "De la jurisprudence de Reuchlin aux *Artes* d'Érasme." *Languages and Cross-Cultural Exchanges in Renaissance Italy*. Edited by Alessandra Petrocch and Joshua Brown, Brepols, pp. 411–426.
Webb, James L. "Pragmatism(s) Plural, Part II: From Classical Pragmatism to Neo-Pragmatism." *Journal of Economic Issues*, vol. 46, no. 1, 2012, pp. 45–74. *JSTOR*, http://www.jstor.org/stable/23264932. Accessed 17 January, 2024.
West, Cornel. *The American Evasion of Philosophy: A Genealogy of Pragmatism*. University of Wisconsin Press, 1989.
Williams, William Carlos. *A un discepolo solitario*. Bompiani, 2023.
——. *Poesie*. Translated by Cristina Campo and Vittorio Sereni, Einaudi, 1960.
——. *Il fiore è l nostro segno*. Translated by Cristina Campo, Scheiwiller, 1958.
Wittgenstein, Ludwig. *Philosophical Investigations*. Translated by G.E.M. Anscombe, Blackwell 1953. (ISBN 9780631103202) German-English Edition, translation by G. E. M. Anscombe.
Whitman, Walt. *Leaves of Grass*. 1st Edition. Andrew and James Rome, 1855.
Worsdworth, William. *Lyrical Ballads*. 3rd Edition. Biggs and Cotte, 1802.
Zanzotto, Andrea. *Andrea Zanzotto. Scritti sulla letteratura*. 2 Vols. Edited by Gian Mario Villalta, Mondadori, 2001.
——. *Le Poesie e Prose scelte*. Edited by Stefano Dal Bianco and Gian Mario Villalta. Mondadori, 1999.
——. *Peasants Wake for Fellini's 'Casanova' and Other Poems*. Edited and translated by John P. Welle and Ruth Feldman, University of Illinois Press, 1997.
——. *Aure e disincanti nel Novecento letterario*. Mondadori, 1994.
——. *Fantasie di avvicinamento. Le letture di un poeta*. Mondadori, 1991.
——. *Il galateo in bosco*. Mondadori, 1978.
——. *La beltà*. Mondadori, 1968.
——. "I 'Novissimi.'" *Comunità*, no. 99, May 1962, pp. 89–91.
——. *Dietro il paesaggio*. Mondadori, 1951.
Zilio, Giovanni Meo. "Come un poeta veneto traduce se stesso (Per una critica stilistica della traduzione)." *Quaderni veneti*, 14, December 1991, pp. 95–107.
Zukofsky, Louis. "A-12." *A*. New Directions, 1959.

Books published by Agincourt Press in the Opuntia Series

Angelo Lumelli, *Poems*, edited by Eugenio Gazzola, translated by Gianpiero W. Doebler (2024)

Giorgio Bassani, *The Collected Poems*, translated, with an introduction and notes by Roberta Antognini and Peter Robinson (2023)

Laura Liberale, *Thanato-Aesthetics*, translated by Murtha Baca and Federica Santini (2023)

John Latta, *Some Alphabets*, with an introduction by Mark Scroggins (2022)

Gianfranco Contini, *An Idea of Dante*, translated by Stephen Sartarelli (2021)

Giani Stuparich, *One Year of School and The Island*, translated by Charles Klopp and Melinda Nelson, with an introduction by Charles Klopp (2021)

Michela Dall'Aglio, *In the Beginning There Was Freedom: An Itinerary between Science, Philosophy, and Faith*, translated by Thomas Haskell Simpson (2020)

Mariano Bàino, *Yellow Fax and Other Poems* (2019)

Alfredo Giuliani (ed.), *I Novissimi: Poetry for the Sixties*, edited by Luigi Ballerini and Federica Santini (2017)

Gianluca Rizzo (ed.), *On the Fringe of the Neoavantgarde / Ai confine della neoavanguardia, Palermo 1963 – Los Angeles 2013* (2017)

Massimo Ciavolella and Gianluca Rizzo (ed.), *Savage Words: Invectives as a Literary Genre* (2016)

Massimo Ciavolella and Gianluca Rizzo (ed.), *Like Doves Summoned by Desire: Dante's New Life in 20th Century Literature and Cinema. Essays in memory of Amilcare Iannucci* (2012)

Adriano Spatola, The Porthole, translated by Beppe Cavatorta and Polly Geller (2011)

Maurizio Cucchi, *The Missing*, translated with an introduction by Gianpiero W. Doebler (2008)

Elio Pagliarani, *The Girl Carla and Other Poems* (2009)

Remo Bodei, *We, The Divided: Ethos, Politics, and Culture in Post-War Italy, 1943-2006* (2006)

Standard Shaefer, *Water & Power* (2005)

Robert Crosson, *The Day Sam Goldwyn Stepped off the Train* (2004)

Paul Vangelisti, *Embarrassment of Survival* (2001)

www.ingramcontent.com/pod-product-compliance
Lightning Source LLC
Chambersburg PA
CBHW030507080526
44586CB00011B/105